T0138635

FUZZY
LEARNING
AND
APPLICATIONS

The CRC Press

International Series on Computational Intelligence

Series Editor
L.C. Jain, Ph.D., M.E., B.E. (Hons), Fellow I.E. (Australia)

L.C. Jain, R.P. Johnson, Y. Takefuji, and L.A. Zadeh
Knowledge-Based Intelligent Techniques in Industry

L.C. Jain and C.W. de Silva
**Intelligent Adaptive Control: Industrial Applications in the
Applied Computational Intelligence Set**

L.C. Jain and N.M. Martin
**Fusion of Neural Networks, Fuzzy Systems, and Genetic Algorithms:
Industrial Applications**

H.-N. Teodorescu, A. Kandel, and L.C. Jain
Fuzzy and Neuro-Fuzzy Systems in Medicine

C.L. Karr and L.M. Freeman
Industrial Applications of Genetic Algorithms

L.C. Jain and B. Lazzerini
Knowledge-Based Intelligent Techniques in Character Recognition

L.C. Jain and V. Vemuri
Industrial Applications of Neural Networks

H.-N. Teodorescu, A. Kandel, and L.C. Jain
Soft Computing in Human-Related Sciences

B. Lazzerini, D. Dumitrescu, L.C. Jain, and A. Dumitrescu
Evolutionary Computing and Applications

B. Lazzerini, D. Dumitrescu, and L.C. Jain
Fuzzy Sets and Their Application to Clustering and Training

L.C. Jain, U. Halici, I. Hayashi, S.B. Lee, and S. Tsutsui
Intelligent Biometric Techniques in Fingerprint and Face Recognition

Z. Chen
Computational Intelligence for Decision Support

L.C. Jain
Evolution of Engineering and Information Systems and Their Applications

H.-N. Teodorescu and A. Kandel
Dynamic Fuzzy Systems and Chaos Applications

L. Medsker and L.C. Jain
Recurrent Neural Networks: Design and Applications

L.C. Jain and A.M. Fanelli
Recent Advances in Artificial Neural Networks: Design and Applications

M. Russo and L.C. Jain
Fuzzy Learning and Applications

J. Liu
Multiagent Robotic Systems

M. Kennedy, R. Rovatti, and G. Setti
Chaotic Electronics in Telecommunications

H.-N. Teodorescu and L.C. Jain
Intelligent Systems and Techniques in Rehabilitation Engineering

I. Baturone, A. Barriga, C. Jimenez-Fernandez, D. Lopez, and S. Sanchez-Solano
Microelectronics Design of Fuzzy Logic-Based Systems

T. Nishida
Dynamic Knowledge Interaction

C.L. Karr
Practical Applications of Computational Intelligence for Adaptive Control

FUZZY LEARNING AND APPLICATIONS

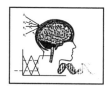

Marco Russo
Lakhmi C. Jain

CRC Press
Boca Raton   London   New York   Washington, D.C.

Library of Congress Cataloging-in-Publication Data

Fuzzy learning and applications / edited by Marco Russo and Lakhmi C. Jain.
    p. cm.--(CRC Press international series on computational intelligence)
Includes bibliographical references and index.
ISBN 0-8493-2269-3 (alk. paper)
    1. Computer science. 2. Programmable controllers. 3. Fuzzy systems. 4. Neurtal
networks (Computer science) I. Russo, Marco, 1967- II. Jain, L.C. III. Series.

QA76 .F895 2000
006.3′2—dc211   00-048560

Preface

The resurgence of interest in fuzzy logic over the past few decades has opened many new avenues in its applications. The most notable examples include autofocus cameras, automobile transmissions, air conditioners, aerospace, subway systems, robots, business, and medicine. Fuzzy logic leads to greater generality and better rapport with reality. It is driven by the need for methods of analysis and design which can come to grips with the pervasive imprecision of the real world and exploit the tolerance for imprecision to achieve tractability, robustness, and low cost solution. It also provides effective capability of processing uncertainties to model human thinking. Artificial neural networks and genetic algorithms can be fused with fuzzy logic to provide the learning abilities in machines.

This book presents a sample of research on fuzzy learning and their applications by notable researchers. It contains 11 chapters.

The first chapter, by Russo, is on evolutionary fuzzy learning. It uses the fusion of neural networks and genetic algorithms for fuzzy supervised learning. It is demonstrated that this approach is superior for tasks such as classification, function approximation, and time series prediction.

In chapter 2, Vidal-Verdú, Navas, Delgado-Restituto, and Rodríguez-Vázquez present a stored-programmable mixed-signal fuzzy controller chip with supervised learning capabilities. The proposed architecture consists of a programmable analog core which implement the active rule, a RAM memory for storing global rule set, and a selection circuitry for the identification of subregions.

The third chapter, by Botía, Barberá, and Skármeta, is on fuzzy modeling in a multi-agent framework for learning in autonomous systems. A number of learning techniques are proposed in the intelligent agents environment.

The fourth chapter, by Masulli and Sperduti, is on learning techniques for supervised fuzzy classifiers. A family of learning machines for supervised classification is developed using the neuro-fuzzy systems.

The fifth chapter, by Yeh and Chen, is on multistage fuzzy control. A general method to generate fuzzy rules for a multistage fuzzy controller from the performance index of the control system is presented. The simulation results using three-stage fuzzy inference showed that good performance is achieved using this approach.

The sixth chapter, by Lotfi, is on learning fuzzy systems. This chapter presents a review of techniques available for updating/learning the parameters of a fuzzy system.

In the seventh chapter, Tachibana, Furuhashi, Shimoda, Kawakami, and Fukunaga present an application of fuzzy modeling to the analysis of rowing boat speed. The fuzzy modeling is applied to reveal the relationships between the supplied power and the boat speed.

The eighth chapter, by Cavalieri and Russo, is on a novel fuzzy approach to Hopfield coefficients determination. It is shown that the proposed method features a search for the set of coefficients which guarantees valid solutions very close to the global minima of the energy function, or ones which guarantee robust solution.

The ninth chapter, by Fortuna, Muscato, Caponetto, and Xibilia is on fuzzy control of a CD player focusing system. The fuzzy controller is a classical Sugeno type Fuzzy-FD. A practical implementation on a real system using a fuzzy microcontroller validates the superiority of this approach.

The tenth chapter, by Ali, Ghafoor, and Lee, is on a neuro-fuzzy scheduler for a multimedia web server. The problem of multimedia synchronization in a web environment is considered. The results are validated and found satisfactory.

The last chapter, by Lęski and Henzel, is on a neuro-fuzzy system based on logical interpretation of if-then rules. The application of the proposed artificial neural network on standard pattern recognition problems is demonstrated.

We believe that this book will be of great value to researchers, scientists and engineers alike. The research students will receive an in-depth tutorial on the topics covered. The seasoned researcher will appreciate the applications and the gold mine of other possibilities for novel research topics.

We are grateful to the authors for their contributions. We also thank reviewers for their expertise and time, and CRC Press for their excellent editorial assistance.

M. Russo, Italy   L.C. Jain, Australia

CONTENTS

DEDICATION

This book is dedicated to my wife

Marco Russo

CREDITS

Figures 4.1, 4.2, 4.7, 4.8 and Tables 4.4 and 4.5 — From Alfonso, D., Masulli, F., and Sperduti, A., Competitive learning in a classifier based on an adaptive fuzzy system, in *Proc. Int. ICSC Symp. Ind. Intel. Automation and Soft Computing*, Anderson, P.G. and Warwick, K., Eds., Academic Press, Alberta, Canada, 1996. With permission.

Figure 4.3 — From Masulli, F., Bayesian classification by feedforward connectionist systems, in *Proc. Adv. Sch. Ital. Biomed. Phys. Assoc.*, Masulli, F., Morasso, P.G., and Schenone, A., Eds., World Scientific, Singapore, and Como, Italy, 1993, 145-162. With permission.

Figures 4.4 and 4.5 — From Giusti, N., Masulli, F., and Sperduti, A., Competitive and hybrid neuro-fuzzy models for supervised classification, in *Proc. IEEE Int. Conf. Neural Networks*, IEEE, Houston, 1997, 516-519. With permission.

Table 4.1 — From Masulli, F., Casalino, F., and Vannucci, F., Bayesian properties and performances of adaptive fuzzy systems in pattern recognition problems, in *Proc. Eur. Conf. Artificial Neural Networks ICANN*, Marinaro, M. and Morasso, P.G., Eds., Springer, Sorrento, Italy, 1994, 189-192. With permission.

Table 4.2 — From Casalino, F., Masulli, F., and Sperduti, A., Rule specialization and semantic phase transition in the adaptive fuzzy system, in *Proc. ICSC Int. Symp. Fuzzy Logic*, Steele, N.C., Eds., Academic Press, Millet Alberta, Canada and Zurich, Switzerland, 1995, B87-B92. With permission.

1

Evolutionary Fuzzy Learning

Marco Russo

M.Russo is with INFN Section of
Catania - ITALY and with the Dept.
of Physics, Univ. of Messina, Contrada
Papardo, Salita Sperone 31, 98166 ME
- ITALY. E-mails:
marco.russo@ai.unime.it,
marco.russo@ct.infn.it,
marco.russo@ieee.org

Evolutionary Fuzzy Learning

Abstract

This chapter presents the fusion of neural networks and genetic algorithms for fuzzy supervised learning. It is demonstrated that this approach is superior for tasks such as classification, function approximation, and time series prediction.

1.1   Introduction

Linguistic rules to describe systems are being used successfully in many application domains [1–7]. Fuzzy systems are very suitable to describe very complex systems where it is very difficult to give a mathematical description.

Until now, there has been no systematic procedure for the design of Fuzzy Logic (FL) systems. To overcome this problem some papers propose automatic methods to extract fuzzy rules using Neural Networks (NNs) [8,9], fuzzy clustering [10–12], genetic algorithms (GAs) [13–17], or GAs+NNs methods [18]. Some of these techniques generate fuzzy logic controllers [9, 13, 15, 16]. Other methods are used for fuzzy classification, fuzzy function approximation, or time series prediction.

This chapter presents a hybrid GAs+NNs approach (called GEFREX, which stands for GEnetic Fuzzy Rule EXtractor) for fuzzy supervised learning. It is able to deal with tasks such as classification, function approximation, and time series prediction. Its main characteristic is the low number of parameters needed in the description of the systems learnt.

The chapter is divided into two parts. In the former we have included in detail GEFREX and its capabilities. In the latter the distributed version of GEFREX is explained. This new software has been called PARGEFREX and shows very interesting properties in finding very difficult minima of the error function.

1.2   Fuzzy knowledge representation

The generic r-th fuzzy rule extracted by GEFREX has the following form:

$$\text{IF } \overbrace{\underbrace{(x_1 \text{ is } A_{1r})}_{Antecedent} \text{ AND ... AND } (x_I \text{ is } A_{Ir})}^{\text{Premise}}$$

$$\text{THEN } \overbrace{\underbrace{(y_1 \text{ is } Z_{1r})}_{Consequent} \text{ AND ... AND } (y_O \text{ is } Z_{Or})}^{\text{Conclusion}}$$

Each premise contains a maximum of I antecedents and each conclusion at most O consequents. I and O are respectively the number of inputs and outputs.

In the generic antecedent $(x_i \text{ is } A_{ir})$ there is the i-th crisp input x_i and the fuzzy set (FS) A_{ir} that is generally different from all the others (i.e., $A_{ir} \neq A_{i'r'}$ if $i \neq i'$ or $r \neq r'$). The Membership Function (MF) of a generic antecedent A_{ir} has a Gaussian shape, so:

$$\mu_{A_{ir}}(x_i) = e^{-\gamma_{ir}^2 (x_i - c_{ir})^2} \tag{1.1}$$

All the connectors in the premise are ANDs. The algebraic minimum is used for this operator. Therefore, the degree of truth θ_r of the r-th rule corresponds to the minimum among the degrees of truth of all the antecedents present in that rule.

In the conclusion there are no FSs but only singletons (z_{or}), i.e., Z_{or} are the FSs which always have a zero degree of membership except in z_{or} where the degree of membership is one. Two different versions of defuzzification method have been implemented. The first defuzzification method is:

$$y_o = \frac{\sum_{r=1}^{R} \theta_r z_{or}}{\sum_{r=1}^{R} \theta_r} \tag{1.2}$$

where R is the total number of rules. This method is a weighted mean (WM) [18] defuzzification and is similar to the Yager method [20]. If all θ_r are zero then all the outputs are zero. The second defuzzification method is simpler. It is the so-called weighted sum (WS) [21]:

$$y_o = \sum_{r=1}^{R} \theta_r z_{or} \tag{1.3}$$

In [18], experimentation revealed that, generally, if the derivatives of the problem to be learned are large then WM is more suitable; otherwise WS is preferable. Generally, WS works better as far as the approximation of functions is concerned, while WM is preferable in classification problems. Moreover, the WM generally has the advantage that the learnt knowledge base seems easier for a human to understand.

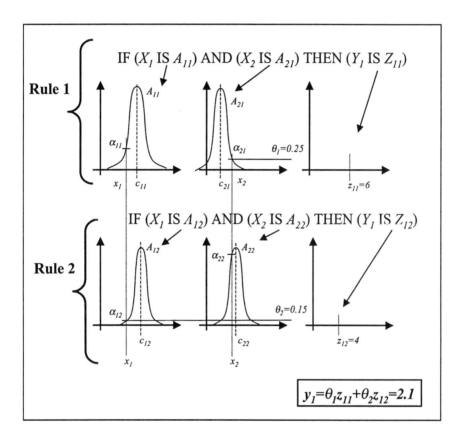

Figure 1.1   A fuzzy system made up of only two rules with the two inputs X_1 and X_2 and the output Y_1. The two crisp inputs x_1 and x_2 are used contemporarily in all rules to evaluate the degrees of truth of all antecedents (α_{ir}). Then the degree of truth θ_r of each rule is computed through a minimum operation. Finally, the output is obtained with a WS defuzzification.

Fig. 1.1 shows an example of calculation of a fuzzy inference made up of only two rules. This inference uses the WS and has only two inputs and one output.

1.3 GEFREX

1.3.1 General description

The algorithm proposed is a GA. The genetic population is placed on a rectangular grid. The core of the algorithm foresees a number of iterations, each of them consisting of the choice of two parents, the generation of only one offspring and its re-insertion in the population. The genetic coding of the fuzzy rules involves only the premises of the rules. It will be demonstrated that in the least squares sense the best consequents can be found in a robust manner with a SVD algorithm regardless of whether or not the WS or the WM defuzzification is used.

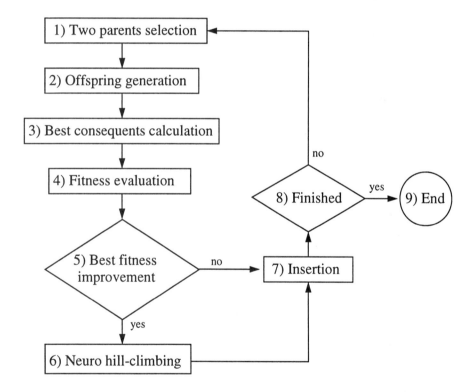

Figure 1.2 The GA used in GEFREX. Firstly, two parents are selected. Then, an offspring is generated. From the offspring the best consequents are computed. If the fitness improves the best value obtained so far, then the neuro hill climbing operator is used. Lastly, the individual is inserted in the population. The algorithm is repeated until the end criterion is met.

Fig. 1.2 summarizes the main steps of the proposed algorithm. After the choice of the two parents, an offspring is generated. Two customized crossover and mutation operators are used. A mixed coding is adopted. There is a real part that deals with all the parameters needed to code the MFs in the antecedents (the Gaussians in eq. (1.1)). Further, there is a binary part necessary to deal with the feature selection. In fact, the algorithm can identify significant inputs when requested by the user of GEFREX. After generating the offspring, the best consequents must be calculated. It is possible to show that there is a linear dependence among the degrees of truth of each rule of each learning pattern and the desired outputs. So the best output singletons are the solutions of a linear overdetermined system. It is well known [19] that the SVD is one of the most useful tools to resolve this kind of system. Through this step the consequent part of all the rules is found. Then the fitness function is calculated. The fitness function adopted, in conjunction with the proposed coding, permits good solutions to be found, simplifies these solutions, and eliminates unnecessary features. If the fitness of the new individual improves the best fitness found so far, the new individual is transformed into a neuro-fuzzy system. Then, the neuro-fuzzy system is trained. This neural-based genetic operator improves the performance of GEFREX with respect to learning speed and error. It is a nonstandard genetic hill climbing operator. The premises extracted from the neuro-fuzzy system are newly transformed into a genetic individual and it is reintroduced in the genetic population. If there is not a best fit improvement then the offspring is directly reinserted in the population. If some conditions are verified the genetic iterations end; otherwise another iteration starts.

The size of the genes involved for each fuzzy inference (individual) is proportional only to the number of inputs multiplied by the number of rules. This is a great step forward as compared to other genetic-fuzzy approaches where the genetic coding typically explodes with the number of inputs [14, 22–24]. However, there is an exception, in a previous work (see FuGeNeSys (fuzzy genetic neural system) [18]) that uses a similar coding method.

1.3.2   The evolution algorithm

To implement GEFREX an apomictic, continuous, and fine-grain evolution algorithm was used [25] (see Fig. 1.3). The characteristic of an apomictic population is that a complete mixing among individuals is forbidden. The continuous model establishes that selection and crossover are local in area and the isolation of demes, i.e., subpopulations, is a direct consequence of the distance between them. Thus, in an apomictic and continuous GA many generations are required before the whole genetic material can be mixed. This was done in order to avoid the phenomenon of premature convergence.

In practice, the individuals are assumed to be on a rectangular grid and

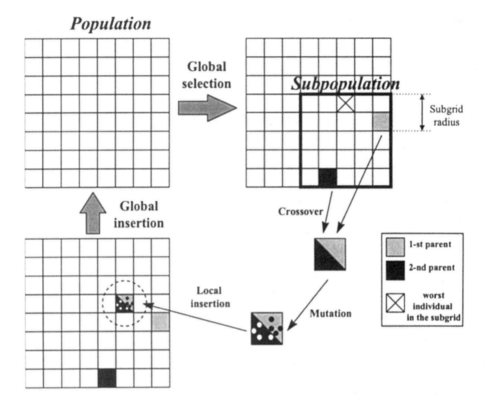

Figure 1.3 The evolution algorithm used. Each generation consists of the choice of a subpopulation. After, inside the subpopulation, two parents and the worst individual are selected. Only one offspring is generated and mutated. It replaces the worst individual.

are selected from a deme with a given radius. The selection is preservative, elitist, steady-state, and fitness proportional [25], as was the previous tool FuGeNeSys.

In fine-grain models there are two types of selections: global and local. In this case, global selection is fitness-proportional and identifies the center of the subpopulation deme. In GEFREX this radius is one, i.e., the subpopulation is a 3×3 subgrid. Local selection uses the same selection method but only in the subpopulation deme. Two parents generate a single offspring using the customized crossover and mutation operators described below. Whenever an individual is generated with a fitness value higher than the best one obtained so far a hill climbing operator is used too. The generated offspring replaces the individual in the subpopulation with the lowest fitness value.

In [18] there is a study that shows that the hill climbing algorithm based on a neuro-fuzzy system improves the convergence properties of the algorithm decidedly, i.e., if the hill climbing algorithm is not used the results are five to six times worse.

1.3.3   Genetic coding

Fig. 1.4 shows the genetic coding in detail. Each individual consists of two parts. The first part involves the Gaussians of all antecedents. The second part is dedicated to the enable bits. The number of inputs I depends on the application fields, whereas the number of rules R has to be specified by the user of GEFREX. In the same way as a multilayer perceptron, where the number of neurons implies the performance during the learning phase, too few hidden neurons imply high error whereas too many imply overfitting; the number of rules must be fixed taking into account the complexity of the problem to be learned by GEFREX.

Once these quantities are fixed, the coding size is given too. In fact, at maximum $R \times I$ antecedents (one for each rule and for each input) are required. Two parameters for each antecedent are required (the center and the width related parameters shown in formula (1.1)). So, the first part of the GEFREX coding requires $2 \times R \times I$ real values. Instead, the second part requires only I bits. These bits are used when the feature selection option is enabled during the learning phase of GEFREX. In a first approximation, these last I bits, in respect of the bits required to code the antecedents, can be ignored. Afterwards, the genetic coding in GEFREX requires a number of bits proportional to the quantity $R \times I$.

In the next sections of this chapter it will be demonstrated that the number of rules required is generally very small. That is, GEFREX needs fewer rules than previous works to reach the same learning error. Furthermore, GEFREX often reaches a lower error than previous work with a smaller number of rules. Besides, R is not tied to the number of inputs, but only to the complexity of the application itself.

The coding of the individuals is made as follows:

Binary genes: A string of I bits is associated to each individual. They represent the enabled inputs in the coded inference. More precisely if, for example, $I = 4$ and the string is $\{0, 1, 1, 0\}$, it means that in the fuzzy inference the first and the fourth inputs are not present. In this case GEFREX does not consider the information related to these inputs.

Real genes: Each individual in the population is made up of a set of $R \times I$ FSs too. They are respectively the I FSs of the premise of the first rule, the second I FSs of the second rule, ..., and the last I FSs of the premise of the last rule. As the MFs of the input FSs

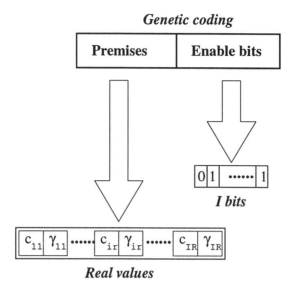

Figure 1.4 GEFREX genetic coding. The premises are coded with the real values corresponding to the center and gamma parameters of the input fuzzy sets ($R \times I$ couples of real values). Further, as many bits as the number of inputs (I) are inserted, to enable or disable one or more of the inputs.

(A_{ir}) are Gaussians; for each antecedent it is therefore necessary to store the real information concerning the center c and the width value γ. If the value of γ is equal to zero, it is assumed that in the rule in question the antecedent relating to the null γ is missing. The degree of membership α_{ir} of the ith antecedent of the rth rule corresponding to the ith crisp input x_i will be given by the $\mu_{A_{ir}}(x_i)$ shown in eq. (1.1).

1.3.4 Crossover

As GEFREX uses a mixed coding, two reproduction schemes are defined, one for the real and another for binary genes. For the offspring generation both real and binary genes come from only the two parents.

Binary genes: Once the two parents are defined the offspring is obtained in a stochastic manner. A multi-cut crossover is used. Each bit has a probability of 0.5 to be copied from one of the two parents.

Real genes: As widely used in literature, each offspring's real parameter is obtained from the two relative parents' parameters as a weighted mean. So if q_f and q_m are the two parents' parameters (a Gaussian width or center) the offspring's parameter q_s will be given by:

$$q_s = q_f a + q_m (1 - a) \qquad (1.4)$$

where a is a real value in [0,1]. The a value is randomly selected once for each offspring, i.e., the eq. (1.4) is applied with the same a to all the real parameters of the same offspring.

Mutation

Also in this case two different mutation operators are defined.

Binary genes: With a user-definable probability p_m regarding only these bits, each of them can be inverted. At the beginning all the binary values are set to 1. In this manner all inputs are enabled. If the user's GEFREX does not want to eliminate inputs the mutation probability p_m needs only to be set to zero. In case of feature detection p_m is 0.01.

Real genes: Both the center and the gamma are modified following the same procedure. Each of these parameters is changed in accordance to its value. In practice GEFREX adopts a multiplication mutation for which each parameter q_s is modified as:

$$q_s = q_s \left(1 - \frac{\delta}{2} + \text{rnd}(\delta) \right) \qquad (1.5)$$

where $\text{rnd}(x)$ is a random real number comprised in the interval $[0, x]$. The δ value is autonomously changed by GEFREX to sustain a minimum level of difference in the genetic population. Practically, the δ value is raised or lowered depending on the standard deviation σ of the fitness values, which has to reach a few percents of the average fitness. At each iteration, if σ exceeds some percents of the average fitness, δ is multiplied by 0.5. If it becomes too little it is multiplied by 1.1.

1.3.5   The error

The learning error formula is very important because the mathematical operations to calculate the best consequents derive directly from its definition. Further, a general formula, such as the one adopted in this chapter, permits the same learning tool to be applied in very different application fields. The error formula will be described in the following subsection. GEFREX uses supervised learning. Suppose there are P patterns each constituted by $I + O$ values. Therefore the generic pth pattern will be:

$$\underbrace{x'_{1p}, x'_{2p} \cdots, x'_{Ip}}_{\text{inputs}}, \underbrace{y'_{1p}, y'_{2p} \cdots, y'_{Op}}_{\text{desired outputs}}$$

Error formula The error E is calculated as:

$$E = \sqrt{\frac{1}{OP_{eq}} \sum_{o=1}^{O} \sum_{p=1}^{P} k_{op}^2 \left(y_{op} - y'_{op}\right)^2} \qquad (1.6)$$

where

- O is the number of outputs;
- P is the number of learning patterns;
- y_{op} and y'_{op} are respectively the calculated and desired oth outputs of the pth learning pattern;
- k_{op} are user definable coefficients;
- P_{eq} is generally equal to P, but it can assume other values.

Possible errors Using equation (1.6) it is possible to use different approaches to learning.

Root mean squared error: If $k_{op} = 1$ $\forall p, o$ and $P_{eq} = P$ we obtain the so-called root mean squared error (RMSE) [26].

Root mean squared normalized error: If Δ_o indicates the difference between the maximum and minimum values that the oth output can assume, if we put $k_{op} = \frac{1}{\Delta_o}$ $\forall p, o$ and $P_{eq} = P$, we obtain the root mean squared normalized error (RMSNE). It indicates how much each output differs on average from the desired value with regard to its range. This kind of error was adopted in the previously proposed fuzzy modeling method (see FuGeNeSys).

Root mean squared relative error: If $k_{op} = \frac{1}{y'_{op}}$ $\forall p, o$ and $P_{eq} = P$ we obtain the root mean squared relative error (RMSRE). It indicates the average relative error. This error measure was used in the field of High Energy Physics (HEP) [27].

Learning with compressed learning patterns: Many clustering techniques exist (see, for example, the K-means clustering algorithm and the self-organizing feature map [10] [28]). With the aid of these techniques a reduced set of significant samples (codewords) for the learning phase can be extracted.

The main drawback in using these reduced samples directly in the learning phase is the loss of the original statistic. For example, suppose that there are the 32 samples represented in Fig. 1.5 and any clustering method to search for three representative points is applied. These points will be placed approximately in the middle of the ellipsoids represented in Fig. 1.5. If a learning phase using only these points is executed, the information regarding the importance of each of these points is lost. In fact, the point representative of the greater ellipsoid should have a weight twice as great as the others. If there are a large number of learning patterns a clustering technique could be used. It would permit a decrease in the learning time. After obtaining the codewords it is possible to associate their weights w_p to each of them, i.e., the number of learning patterns closest to them. In this manner, the number of learning patterns is reduced and the statistic is not lost. Of course, the so-called quantization error (QE) is introduced. However, the QE can be lowered by increasing the number of codewords and consequently reducing the compression ratio.

With this technique and with the aid of formula (1.6) any of the previously described errors can be adopted. For example the RMSE can be calculated simply by putting $k_{op} = \sqrt{w_p}$ $\forall o, p$. Furthermore it is necessary that the $P_{eq} = \sum_{p=1}^{P} \omega_p$. Section 1.3.12 gives a significant example.

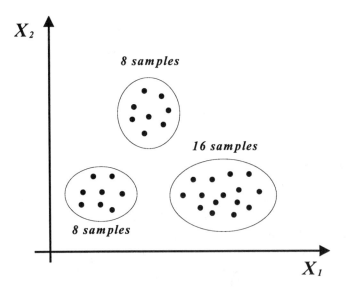

Figure 1.5 These 32 bi-dimensional samples characterize three different clusters. The error formula introduced permits the use, in the learning phase, of only the centroids of the clusters, with weights proportional to the number of samples belonging to each cluster, rather than all the samples.

Increasing the importance of some points: In a similar way as explained in the previous case it is possible to link a weight to some patterns to increase or decrease their weight in respect of the others.

Other considerations: Considering the generality of formula (1.6) it is possible to think of several other applications. For example, it is possible to give a weight to the outputs, too.

1.3.6 Output singletons

Now it will be shown that the information regarding the conclusion of all rules can be calculated using standard linear algebra. In the following the degree of truth of the rth rule deriving from the pth learning pattern will be denoted by the symbol θ_{rp}.

If we know all θ_{rp} in the case of WS or the normalized thetas $\overline{\theta}_{rp} = \frac{\theta_{rp}}{\sum_{r=1}^{R} \theta_{rp}}$ in the WM, it follows that the output is a linear combination of these values. Let us indicate with $\overline{\Theta}$ the matrix of P rows and R columns containing the thetas (in the WS case) or the normalized ones (in the WM case). Let us indicate with $\overline{Z}$ the matrix of R rows and O columns containing the output singletons z_{or} and with $\overline{Y}$ the matrix P rows and O columns containing the desired output values y'_{op} $\forall o, p$. The linear system must be solved:

$$\overline{\Theta}\,\overline{Z} = \overline{Y} \tag{1.7}$$

The system, which generally has many more equations than variables, can easily be solved in a robust manner with a SVD.

From linear algebra we know that the best solution of system (1.7), which minimizes the residual, is that obtainable with the aid of the pseudo-inverse of Moore-Penrose [19]. So system (1.7) can be rewritten:

$$\overline{T}\,\overline{Z} = \overline{Q} \tag{1.8}$$

where $\overline{T} = \overline{\Theta}^T \overline{\Theta}$ and $\overline{Q} = \overline{\Theta}^T \overline{Y}$. In this case the dimensions of the two matrices $\overline{T}$ and $\overline{Q}$ are respectively $R \times R$ and $R \times O$ that are generally much smaller than those of $\overline{\Theta}$ and $\overline{Y}$.

As eq. (1.6) is fully supported in GEFREX, some modifications are needed in the above matrix equations. Even if in eq. (1.6) only one k_{op} is different from the numerical value 1 we cannot use formulae (1.8). To simplify this it was imposed that $k_{op} = k_{1p}k_{2o}$ $\forall p, o$. If we define $\overline{K}_1$ and $\overline{K}_2$ the two diagonal matrices are built respectively with the values of the vectors k_{1p} and k_{2o} we must solve:

$$\overline{K}_1\,\overline{\Theta}\,\overline{Z}\,\overline{K}_2 = \overline{K}_1\,\overline{Y}\,\overline{K}_2 \tag{1.9}$$

If the matrix $\overline{K}_2$ is invertible the solution of this system, which minimizes the residual, coincides with the solution of the system:

$$\overline{T}' \, \overline{Z} = \overline{Q}' \tag{1.10}$$

where $\overline{T}' = \overline{\Theta}^T \, \overline{K}_1^T \overline{K}_1 \, \overline{\Theta}$ and $\overline{Q}' = \overline{\Theta}^T \, \overline{K}_1^T \, \overline{K}_1 \, \overline{Y}$.

1.3.7 Hill climbing operator

A hill climbing operator was introduced. It is only used whenever an individual is generated with a fitness value higher than the best one obtained so far.

Initially, the individual selected is transformed into a neuro-fuzzy system. That is, the equivalent neural network is built and all the trainable weights are initiated. Then, the system is trained. In this phase it is possible that some neurons can be deleted too. Finally, the trained system is retransformed into a genetic individual and introduced into the genetic grid in place of the starting individual selected. The neural network is trained with the gradient descending method.

GEFREX automatically adjusts the learning rate and proceeds until the error decreases. To give more detail, the learning rate starts from the value 0.5. If the error decreases, it is multiplied by 1.5, otherwise by 0.1. The iterations follow until the error reaches a local minimum.

Gradient descending formulas

For simplicity q_{ir} indicates one of the two coefficients $\{\gamma_{ir}, c_{ir}\}$. If $\theta_{rp} \neq \alpha_{ir}$ then $\frac{\partial E}{\partial q_{ir}} = 0$. Otherwise we obtain:

$$\frac{\partial E}{\partial q_{ir}} = \frac{1}{OP_{eq}E} \sum_{o=1}^{O} \sum_{p=1}^{P} \left(y_{op} - y'_{op}\right) k_{op}^2 \frac{\partial y_{op}}{\partial q_{ir}} \tag{1.11}$$

$$\frac{\partial y_{op}}{\partial q_{ir}} = \begin{cases} z_{or}\theta_{rp}\frac{\partial q'_{irp}}{\partial q_{ir}} & \text{if } WS \\ (z_{or} - y_{op})\overline{\theta}_{rp}\frac{\partial q'_{irp}}{\partial q_{ir}} & \text{if } WM \end{cases} \tag{1.12}$$

where $q'_{irp} = -\gamma_{ir}^2 \left(x_{ip} - c_{ir}\right)^2$.

$$\frac{\partial q'_{irp}}{\partial q_{ir}} = \begin{cases} -2\gamma_{ir}\left(x_{ip} - c_{ir}\right)^2 & \text{if } q_{ir} = \gamma_{ir} \\ +2\gamma_{ir}^2\left(x_{ip} - c_{ir}\right) & \text{if } q_{ir} = c_{ir} \end{cases} \tag{1.13}$$

In Fig. 1.6 there is an example with only two inputs, one output and two rules. When the WS is assumed (as shown in Fig. 1.6) the neuro-fuzzy system has four layers.

- The first is the input layer and it has a maximum of I neurons.

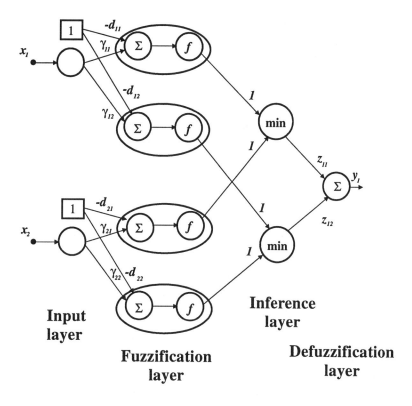

Figure 1.6 The architecture of the neuro-fuzzy system. The system has two-inputs, one output, and two rules. It is based on the WS.

- The second is the fuzzification layer. Here, the activation degrees α_{ir} of the antecedents are calculated. It is possible to distinguish the activation function $f = e^{-\text{net}_{ir}^2} = \alpha_{ir}$ where $\text{net}_{ir} = x_i \gamma_{ir} - d_{ir}$. Of course, $d_{ir} = c_{ir}\gamma_{ir}$. The weights that can be learned are γ_{ir} and d_{ir}. The total number of neurons is at maximum $R \times I$.

- After, there is the inference layer. It is necessary to calculate the degree of truth of the R rules. It has R neurons and weights fixed to one.

- Lastly, there is the linear output layer in which the WS defuzzification is calculated. The weights that can be learned are z_{or}. The neurons are O. Also in the neuro-fuzzy system the SVD is used to find the best output singletons.

1.3.8   The fitness function

The fitness function is a rational function in which some parameters can be varied directly by the GEFREX user. The fitness must be maximized. Two correction terms have been added. One forces the solution to search for simplified rules. In practice this factor privileges rules with few antecedents. The other factor allows the user to force the program to search for solutions that take the smallest possible number of features into account.

The analytical expression of the fitness function $\text{fit}(i)$ of the ith individual is given by:

$$\text{fit}(i) = \frac{K_{num}}{K_{den} + K_{err} \cdot e + K_{red} \cdot r + K_{red_2} \cdot r_2} \tag{1.14}$$

The coefficients K_{xxx} are the user defined numerical coefficients mentioned above.

Let us define the parameters that appear in equation (1.14).

- The parameter e represents percent learning error. This value corresponds to 100 times the learning error E described in section 1.3.5.

- The parameter r indicates the ratio between the number of antecedents used in all the rules and the total number $R \times I$. If the coefficient K_{red} is greater than zero, the fitness of a "simpler" fuzzy inference is greater. This option can be used whenever it is necessary to reduce, as far as possible, the complexity of the fuzzy inference learnt. It is also possible to use this feature to analyze the dependence of the fitness function on the features chosen. It may, in fact, happen that by forcing K_{red} to sufficiently high values some features are eliminated from the rules resulting from the learning phase. Care must be taken, however, not to let the $\frac{K_{err}}{K_{red}}$ ratio take excessively small values. When the ratio decreases, in fact, although increasingly simple rules are found, there is a collateral effect of an increase in the error e. So, when the user of GEFREX decides to obtain a simplified fuzzy system he/she must fix this ratio in the range $10 - 100$.

- The parameter r_2 is given by the percentage of inputs used in a fuzzy inference as compared to the total number. The considerations made for the parameter r hold again here, but this time they are restricted to the selection of features. The difference between the two parameters is that while the former simplifies the fuzzy rules by forcing the program to eliminate antecedents (and as an indirect consequence may lead to the elimination of some features), the latter is expressly meant to eliminate features. Consequently, it is more efficient in achieving this aim. Even in this case, when the user of GEFREX decides to make use of the feature selection option, he/she must fix the $\frac{K_{err}}{K_{red_2}}$ ratio in the range $10 - 100$.

1.3.9 GEFREX utilization

Choice of parameters

In GEFREX very few parameters must be set by the user. In fact, many of them are set autonomously.

The only parameters that must be set are the number of rules, the size of the population, the coefficients of the fitness function, and the termination criterion.

- **Number of rules.** In NNs the error is a function of the number of hidden units. The residual sum-of-squares decreases when the number of hidden units increases irrespective of the number of input variables [28]. The number of hidden units requested is a function of the complexity of the problem to learn.

  Up to now, the majority of tools presented in literature regarding fuzzy modeling, above all in the fuzzy control domain, require a number of rules that grows exponentially with the number of inputs. This is due to the universe of discourse partitioning. If, for example, we are working with a 10-input problem, the partitioning approach requires at minimum 2 fuzzy sets for any input and as a consequence 1024 rules are needed. Nowadays, another approach is becoming popular in the research field: Each premise of the rules uses fuzzy sets that are generally totally different from all the others. This approach is used in GEFREX and permits the limitation of the number of rules that is not tied to the number of inputs.

  Thus, R is correlated only to the complexity of the problem itself. We could associate R with the size of the hidden layer in NNs; both are tied only to the problem and not to the number of inputs.

  At the moment no study has been made with GEFREX regarding R. The choice of R depends only on the user. In all cases reported in the comparison section, R was chosen, taking into account what had already been done in literature.

- **Population size.** In [18], where a very similar evolution scheme is adopted for fuzzy learning, there is an accurate study regarding the relationships between the final error, the number of iterations and the size of the grid. This study shows that the error depends on the two other parameters. More precisely, when the size of the population increases the error decreases. The larger the population, the more iterations are required. So it is necessary to limit the size of the population to obtain a good result in a reasonable time.

Generally, when GEFREX is used in real problems [5], the population size is set below 100 individuals. In this paper, when not specified, this number is 25.

- **Coefficients of the fitness function.** In section 1.3.8 there is already an extensive explanation regarding the coefficients of the fitness function. So in this paragraph only some short guidelines regarding the choice of these coefficients are given.

  Generally, when no simplifications and no feature selection are required and the error cannot reach the 0 value, $K_{num}=100$, $K_{red}=K_{red_2}=K_{den}=0$ and $K_{err}=1$ are fixed. These values are used in the examples reported in the chapter when they are not specified. When the user wants to simplify the final fuzzy system he can give a value to K_{red} ranging from 0.1 to 0.01. Typically, 0.01 is a good choice. The same discourse is valid for K_{red_2} when GEFREX is also used for the feature selection.

- **Termination criterion.** Many termination criteria can be used to stop an iterative learning method. At the moment only two have been implemented in GEFREX: The maximum number of genetic iterations (number of offspring) and the final error to reach. Normally from 10000 to 100000 iterations are required for convergence. 10000 iterations are used in the examples reported in the chapter when they are not specified.

Evaluation of the number of consecutive runs to produce a significant error

Considering the stochastic nature of GEFREX it is necessary to understand when the result of a run can be considered as a significant result or only a fortunate or unfortunate trial.

With this aim, 60 learning phases were executed using the same problem. Figure 1.7 shows the 40 learning patterns used to teach a single-input single-output function. This function is quite complex because Gaussian type input MFs have been used.

There were three rules. The defuzzification was the WM.

To evaluate the results obtained the quantity ρ has been introduced. It is the ratio between the standard deviation and the average value of the final RMNSE obtained. Table 1.1 reports the value obtained in the column named Mean. The value obtained of 74.90% indicates that the result of only one run cannot be considered as a significant result at all.

Two or more runs were therefore considered. In the other 5 columns of Table 1.1 the results obtained each time taking the best results of 2, 3, 4, 5, and 6 consecutive runs are reported. In the last four columns the median values of 3, 4, 5, and 6 consecutive runs are present. The table shows that the best

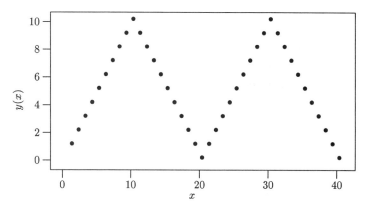

Figure 1.7 The 40 learning patterns used.

		Best value of					Median value of			
	Mean	2	3	4	5	6	3	4	5	6
ρ (%)	74.9	38.6	**9.6**	9.4	9.1	8.6	54.9	38.6	37.0	27.0

Table 1.1 Final error versus the number of runs considered. ρ represents the ratio between the standard deviation and the mean value. The result refers to 60 runs. The column Mean refers to the case when only one run is considered. In the other 5 columns is reported the average results when the best of 2, 3, 4, 5, 6 consecutive runs is chosen. The last columns refer to the case when the median value of 3, 4, 5 or 6 consecutive runs is considered.

method is to take the best result rather than the median result of consecutive runs.

For more runs, the more time is needed. For this reason the number of runs must be the smallest possible. Once again, the table indicates that the best trade-off between the ρ value and the total time is to execute three consecutive runs. We have a great decrease in the ρ value when we pass from two to three runs and only minor variations with more runs. With three runs ρ goes below 10%. In this case the average error is 3.88% and the standard deviation is 0.37%. Furthermore in 98% of cases the errors obtained in the 60 runs, each time taking three of them in consideration, are far from the mean error at maximum 1.2% times the standard deviation, i.e., about 12% of the average value.

This means that the best error of only three consecutive and independent runs is a quantity that can be safely used for evaluating GEFREX performance. From this point until the end of the chapter, when not differently specified, this kind of error is reported.

	Rule 1	Rule 2	Rule 3
c_{1r}	1.2569	0.29113	0.2736
γ_{1r}	2.1348	0.56270	2.2886
z_{1r}	2.8338	-1.4651	2.4026

Table 1.2   Narazaki and Ralescu's example rules

1.3.10   Comparisons

This section is devoted to the comparison of the performance of GEFREX with previous approaches that are able to extract fuzzy knowledge. The reader can find four distinct subsections. The first is devoted to four approximation problems and the second to two classification problems. The third deals with a complex time series prediction problem. The last shows the performance of GEFREX when the feature selection option is used.

Approximation problems

A number of approaches can be used for this kind of problem. These works are often based on neuro-fuzzy systems. But some papers show excellent behavior with genetic approaches as well.

Single input   In [29] and [21], function (1.15) is used to test the learning capacities of the method proposed.

$$y = 0.2 + 0.8(x + 0.7\sin(2\pi x)) \tag{1.15}$$

In both cases 21 points were taken as learning patterns and 101 uniformly distributed in the domain of the independent variable as testing patterns. The following formulae were taken as performance indexes for the learning and generalization capacity respectively:

$$J_1 = \frac{100}{21} \sum_{p=0}^{20} \frac{|y_p - y_p'|}{y_p'} \quad , \quad J_2 = \frac{100}{101} \sum_{p=0}^{100} \frac{|y_p - y_p'|}{y_p'} \tag{1.16}$$

where y_p is the output produced by the tool after the learning phase corresponding to x_i and y_p' is the desired value.

Table 1.2 shows the parameters regarding the three rules obtained with GEFREX. With only these three rules GEFREX obtained J_1=0.103% and J_2=0.090%. In all cases performance is better than those reported in [29] (J_2=3.19%), in [21] (J_2=0.987%) and in [18] (J_2=0.856%). Only nine parameters are required. The best result in literature is reported in [18] where 15 parameters were needed.

Two inputs **Case I:** In [11] Lotfi and Tsoi proposed an adaptive membership function scheme (AMFS) for fuzzy inference systems. To demonstrate the viability of the AMFS regarding the approximation of a nonlinear function they decided to use the equation:

$$y = \left(3e^{\frac{x_2}{10}} - 1\right) \tanh \frac{x_1}{10} + \frac{2}{30} \left(4 + e^{\frac{x_2}{10}}\right) \sin \left(\frac{\pi}{10}(x_1 + 4)\right) \qquad (1.17)$$

They obtained a fuzzy inference that contained 4 rules with two antecedents. They needed 3 parameters for each MF both for antecedent and consequent. So, in this example, the number of parameters was 36. They trained their neuro-fuzzy system and reached a not-very-well-explained error of 5%.

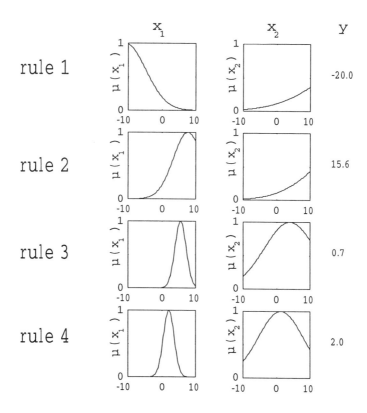

Figure 1.8   The four rules obtained for Lotfi and Tsoi's example.

A system with 121 equally spaced learning patterns and 10201 testing patterns was trained. There were four rules and only 20 parameters were required. GEFREX obtained a RMSNE of 0.846% and 0.983% respectively for learning

Author and reference	MSE
Delgado et al. [32]	0.231
Sugeno et al. [30]	0.01
Lin et al. [33]	0.005
Emami et al. [31]	0.004
GEFREX	**0.00078**

Table 1.3   Comparison results for Sugeno's nonlinear function approximation example

Rule	1	2	3	4	5	6	7	8
c_{1r}	4.76	1.49	0.77	-1.06		2.18	3.16	3.33
c_{2r}	2.24	1.07	1.51		-0.764	2.01	0.873	2.07
γ_{1r}	1.24	0.153	2.73	0.599		1.24	1.32	1.93
γ_{2r}	2.07	0.133	0.93		0.696	3.73	1.56	3.14
z_{1r}	0.477	1.73	1.57	11.2	12.9	0.188	-0.176	0.13

Table 1.4   The eight rules found by GEFREX for the Sugeno's benchmark

and testing patterns. The rules obtained are shown in Fig. 1.8. In the figure the four rules are shown in the rows. In the first two columns there are the input FSs in respect of the first and second inputs. In the last column there are the output singletons.

Case II: Now let us consider the nonlinear system presented by Sugeno et al. in [30] used widely in literature as a benchmark:

$$z = (1 + x_1^{-2} + x_2^{-1.5})^2, \quad 1 \leq x_1, x_2 \leq 5. \qquad (1.18)$$

The fuzzy system identification is based on 50 samples reported in [30]. The original samples were 4 inputs and one output with 2 dummy inputs.

GEFREX discarded the two dummy inputs. Table 1.3 shows results found in literature plus the error found by GEFREX. The last column of the table reports the mean square error. The fuzzy system trained by GEFREX, constituted by 8 fuzzy rules, shows an improvement of about five times in respect of the best result found in literature [31].

Next table, 1.4, shows all the parameters found by GEFREX. The number of significant parameters was 36. The best result in literature was in [33] and required 42 parameters.

   Five inputs and feature selection   This example deals with a chemical plant (see [30] for the original data). It has 70 data points and five input variables: monomer concentration, change in monomer concentration, monomer flow rate, and two temperatures. The same data was examined in [21]. Both decided that the two temperature measurements were not significant. In [30] six rules and in [21] seven rules were used. Only in [21] are there

	Rule 1	Rule 2	Rule 3	Rule 4	Rule 5
c_{2r}	-6.28E-2	1.55E-1	1.43E-2		
c_{3r}	2.49E+3		4.63E+3	4.95E+3	1.13E+04
c_{4r}	2.27E-1	-5.24E-1		-9.36E-2	
c_{5r}	-9.74E-2	7.12E-2	-6.46E-2		
γ_{2r}	3.27	5.24	9.66		
γ_{3r}	7.64E-4		8.21E-4	6.31E-4	1.63E-4
γ_{4r}	1.89	5.45		2.40	
γ_{5r}	3.31	2.83E+1	2.10		
z_{1r}	1.44E+3	9.03E+2	-2.24E+2	1.66E+3	1.10E+04

Table 1.5   Chemical plant rules

numerical results. They needed 70 parameters in total and their performance index was 0.002245.

A fuzzy inference with only four rules was trained, the parameters of which are shown in Table 1.5. As can be seen, GEFREX eliminated only the first input, that is the monomer concentration. What is more, it left only 31 parameters. With only these parameters GEFREX obtained a performance index of 0.001785.

Classification problems

Two inputs   In [18] the classification problem shown on the right at the top of Fig. 1.10 was used to demonstrate the performance of FuGeNeSys using WS and WM. Of course, the best results found were those in which WM was used. Figure 1.9 shows the best results obtained by FuGeNeSys.

GEFREX extracted a five-rule fuzzy system (with WM) starting from 20×20 equally-spaced samples. The surfaces obtained are shown in Fig. 1.10. The reconstructed surface is undoubtedly better than reported in Fig. 1.9. The RMSNE obtained was 0.614% and the five rules are shown in Fig. 1.10.

Iris Data   This is a four input-one output example. The best results in literature are reported in [34] and in [18], where all the 150 learning patterns are learned correctly with respectively 13 and 5 rules.

The integer numbers one, two and three were respectively associated to the three classes iris setosa, virginica and versicolor. GEFREX successfully extracted a fuzzy system with only 5 rules using WM defuzzification that correctly classifies all the 150 patterns. In Fig. 1.11 the five rules are shown. The inputs are in the order sepal length (SL) in cm (in the range [4.3,7.9]), sepal width (SW) in cm (in the range [2.0,4.4]), petal length (PL) in cm (in the range [1.0,6.9]), and petal width (PW) in cm (in the range [0.1,2.5]). Naturally, the output is in the range [0,2]. If the output is below 0.5 the class is iris setosa. If it is comprised in [0.5,1.5] the class is iris virginica, otherwise it is

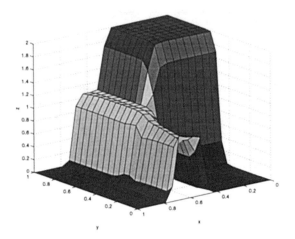

Figure 1.9   The results obtained with FuGeNeSys (testing patterns) in a classification example.

the remaining class. This result is equal to that obtained with FuGeNeSys. Five rules probably represent the minimum number necessary to classify these patterns when we attempt to resolve this problem with this kind of MF and inferential method.

Time series prediction

The aim of this subsection is to show the performance of GEFREX in a complex application field. A fuzzy predictor applied to the Mackey-Glass chaotic time series was developed.

From a mathematical point of view [35] predicting the future of time series consists in finding a mapping f_{pr}:

$$\hat{x}(t + T) = f_{pr}(x(t), x(t - \Delta), \cdots, x(t - (k - 1)\Delta)) \qquad (1.19)$$

where Δ is the lag time and k is an embedding dimension. Equation (1.19) means that an estimate $\hat{x}$ at the time ahead of T can be obtained from f_{pr} starting from the knowledge of n samples of the time series.

The chaotic Mackey-Glass time series is generated from the following equation:

$$\frac{dx(t)}{dt} = \frac{0.2x(t - \tau)}{1 + x^{10}(t - \tau)} - 0.1x(t) \qquad (1.20)$$

To make comparisons $k=4$ and $\Delta=T=6$ were chosen. The data points were generated with the initial condition $x(0)=1.2$ and $\tau=17$. The 1000 pat-

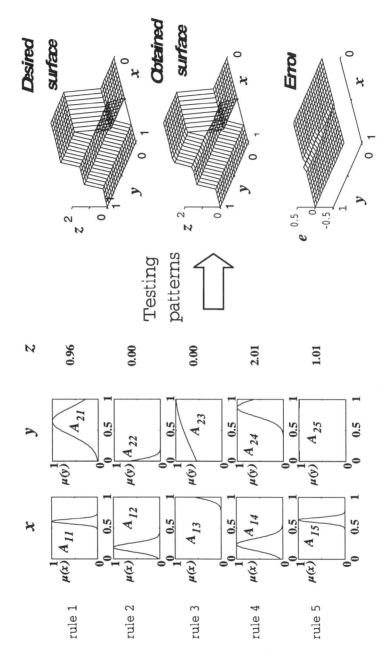

Figure 1.10 The fuzzy classifier system trained by GEFREX and the results obtained.

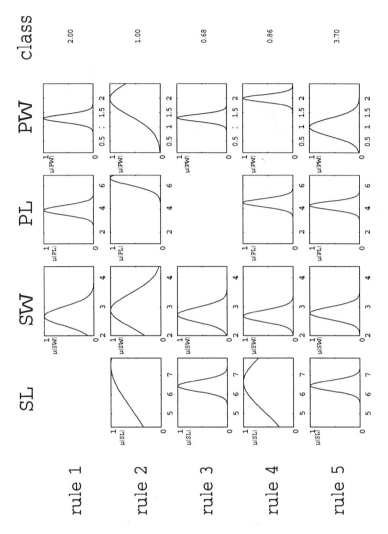

Figure 1.11   The five rules obtained by GEFREX for the iris classification example.

terns used in the training and in the testing phase have the following format
$[x(t-24);x(t-18);x(t-12);x(t-6);x(t);]$ from the generated data with t in
[124,1123]. The first 500 patterns were used in the learning phase, whereas
the last 500 in the testing one.

Fig. 1.12 reports the results obtained with GEFREX. These results refer to
a fuzzy system made of only 20 rules when WM defuzzification is used. The
parameters related to GEFREX training were 50000 iterations (about 1 hour
on a 300MHz Pentium-II) and 100 individuals. In subfigure (1) the desired

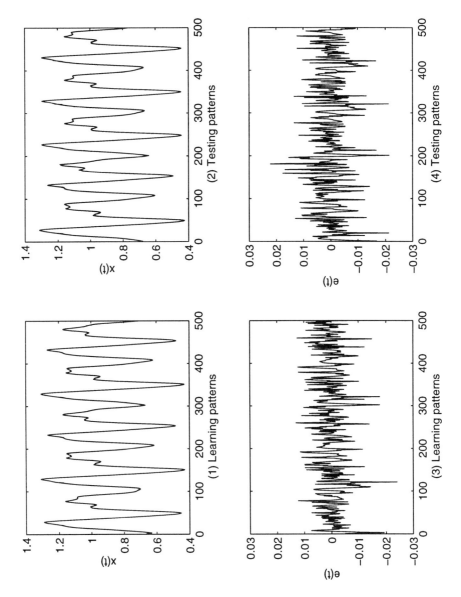

Figure 1.12 Mackey-Glass results: (1) Output desired and obtained (learning), (2) Output desired and obtained (testing), (3) Residual error (learning) RMSE=0.0054, (4) Residual error (testing) RMSE=0.0061.

and the obtained outputs are reported. This subfigure refers to the learning

Learning algorithm	RMSE
Kim & Kim	0.026
Wang (product operator)	0.091
Min operator	0.090
ANFIS	0.007
Auto Regressive Model	0.19
Cascade Correlation NN	0.06
Back. Prop. NN	0.02
6th-order Polynomial	0.04
Linear Predictive Model	0.55
GEFREX	**0.0061**

Table 1.6   Comparison results

patterns. As the reader can see there is no visible difference; so in subfigure (3) the difference between the two outputs is reported. The same thing happens in subfigure (2) and (4) for the testing patterns.

Table 1.6 shows the comparison results of the prediction performance among various predictors. The previous results were taken from [35]. The performance of the very compact fuzzy system obtained by GEFREX is better than all previous works. The best result reported in literature derives from AN-FIS, which requires $2^I = 32$ rules. So GEFREX improved both the prediction capability and the compactness of the fuzzy system.

Feature detection

In [18] the performances of FuGeNeSys, in respect of the task regarding feature detection, were shown. The function chosen was:

$$z = x^2 + y^2 \tag{1.21}$$

Each of the 50 patterns had 8 inputs ($x_i : 1 \leq i \leq 8$) and one output (z). Two of the inputs correspond to the independent variables x and y, both randomly and uniformly generated in the interval $[0, 100]$. Three inputs are linear combinations of x and y. The other 3 were generated quite randomly. More precisely:

$$\begin{cases} x_1 &= & x \\ x_2 &= & y \\ x_3 &= & \text{random} \\ x_4 &= & \text{random} \\ x_5 &= & \text{random} \\ x_6 &= & 2x \\ x_7 &= & 3y \\ x_8 &= & x + 2y \end{cases} \tag{1.22}$$

Rules	Error	Features
2	6.16%	1 and 8
3	3.76%	6 and 7
4	2.63%	2 and 6

Table 1.7 FuGeNeSys behavior as a function of the number of rules regarding the feature detection example

	Rule 1	**Rule 2**
c_{2r}	1.5035E+02	
c_{6r}	1.7221E+02	2.5188E+02
γ_{2r}	1.3888E-02	
γ_{6r}	4.6054E-03	8.3643E-03
z_{1r}	1.6443E+04	1.1645E+04

Table 1.8 Feature detection: The two rules trained

Table 1.7 shows the results (RMSNE) of three different runs using WS taken from literature. GEFREX was used for the same problem. The RMSNE reached with only two rules was of 1.085% and of course only two significant features were selected. Table 1.8 shows the eight parameters of the trained rules.

1.3.11 Computational complexity evaluation

In this section an experimental study regarding the computational complexity of GEFREX in comparison with previous work is reported.

The previous section showed that GEFREX achieves better results than previous works. Now it will be shown that GEFREX is able to reach a pre-fixed learning error in a shorter time than any other similar work. Furthermore, the improvement achievable with GEFREX increases with the number R of rules, i.e., the greater the R value, the greater the improvement.

As explained before, GEFREX uses the SVD extensively. This operation is particularly onerous with regard to the CPU resource. More precisely, in GEFREX a SVD of a square matrix $R \times R$ is calculated for each iteration. Using the big oh notation [36] we can say that this SVD decomposition has a complexity $O(R^3)$ [19]. Although the C++ objects regarding the matrices have been completely rewritten and in spite of the fact that these objects were designed taking into account, above all, the final speed of all matrix operations (no matter what the memory allocation), the limitation of the polynomial complexity of the SVD remains. So it could seem that GEFREX requires a lot of computer resources in comparison with previous works, particularly when the number R of rules increases.

To perform an accurate comparison, GEFREX was compared with FuGe-
NeSys, the other genetic rule generator that seems the most similar in literature [18] as regards to learning method and application domains. As both
tools are based on a genetic approach, it is very important to execute several
runs in the same hypothesis to have significant information. Each reported
value in the following graphs corresponds to the average of 10 different runs.

As a case-study the same example used for the testing of FuGeNeSys was
considered. It is the approximation of the single-input single-output function
[29]:

$$y = 0.2 + 0.8(x + 0.7\sin(2\pi x))\qquad(1.23)$$

The 21 learning patterns were taken to be uniformly distributed in [0,1]. As
there are only 21 learning patterns, the behavior of the tools was studied only
up to 9 rules. As Fig. 1.14 shows GEFREX reaches a negligible error with
$R=9$. For this reason the use of more rules has no sense.

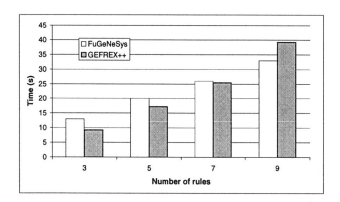

Figure 1.13   Time required by FuGeNeSys and GEFREX to reach 10000 genetic iterations during the learning phase of eq. (1.23.)

The first case analyzed regards the time needed to reach the same number of
genetic iterations, i.e., 10000. Fig. 1.13 shows the results obtained, which indicates that the requirements of the CPU results grow faster for GEFREX than
for FuGeNeSys. This figure shows the quality of the GEFREX software, too.
In fact, up to 7 rules, GEFREX is faster than FuGeNeSys, even if it requires
a SVD computation for each iteration and it is written in C++ (FuGeNeSys
was written in C).

In the following Fig. 1.14 the obtained final errors (RMNSE) are reported.

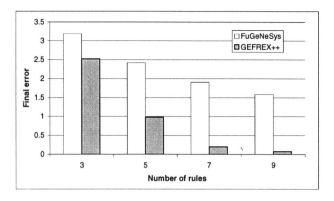

Figure 1.14 Final RMNSE obtained by FuGeNeSys and GEFREX after 10000 genetic iterations to learn the eq. (1.23).

On average, GEFREX finds lower errors. Moreover, when R increases, the difference becomes more significant.

However, to compare both tools well the evaluation of the time required by both tools to reach the same error is necessary. With this aim, the time required by GEFREX to reach the error that FuGeNeSys reaches, once the number R has been fixed, was estimated. More precisely, the error that FuGe-NeSys reaches in 10000 genetic iterations with R ranging from 3 to 9 (see Fig. 1.14) was considered and the mean time required by GEFREX to obtain the same error was calculated. In Fig. 1.15 these mean times and the one related to FuGeNeSys are reported.

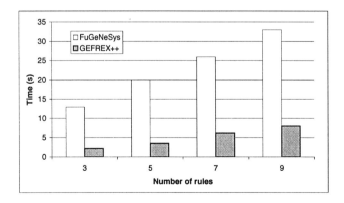

Figure 1.15 Time needed by FuGeNeSys and GEFREX to reach the same final error.

x_1	x_2	y	ω_p	x_1	x_2	y	ω_p
-7.3	-1.3	-1.9	3	-4.0	-1.0	-1.7	2
9.0	4.0	3.2	2	10.0	-1.0	1.4	2
-8.0	10.0	-7.5	3	-9.0	-10.0	-0.4	2
2.0	6.0	3.8	3	5.0	-4.0	1.1	2
-9.0	6.0	-4.8	2	-1.0	-6.0	-0.0	2
5.0	4.0	3.5	2	9.0	-6.0	0.4	2
-5.3	5.3	-4.2	3	-6.0	-5.0	-1.0	2
0.0	5.0	0.4	2	1.0	-9.0	0.4	4
-10.0	-1.0	-2.0	2	5.0	6.0	4.5	2
9.0	2.0	2.4	2	9.0	-4.0	0.8	2
-3.3	9.3	-5.8	3	-9.0	-7.0	-0.8	4
0.0	9.0	0.4	2	2.0	-4.0	1.1	3
-10.0	3.0	-3.4	2	-2.0	-9.0	0.0	2
2.0	1.0	2.1	2	9.0	-9.0	-0.0	4
-2.0	7.0	-3.6	2	-5.0	-9.0	-0.3	4
9.0	8.0	5.4	2	5.0	-9.0	0.3	4
-6.0	0.0	-2.2	1	-2.0	-1.0	-1.1	2
9.0	6.0	4.2	2	8.0	-1.0	1.5	2
-8.0	8.0	-6.0	3	5.0	8.0	5.7	2
9.0	10.0	6.8	2	5.0	-2.0	1.5	2
-8.0	3.0	-3.4	2	-0.7	-3.3	0.0	3
5.0	1.0	2.4	4	5.0	-6.0	0.7	2
-2.7	3.3	-2.5	3	-4.0	-5.0	-0.8	2
4.0	10.0	6.7	3	-5.0	2.0	-2.7	2
-9.0	-4.0	-1.3	2	0.0	1.0	0.3	2

Table 1.9   The compressed learning samples and their weights

Fig. 1.15 shows that GEFREX is more efficient than FuGeNeSys. Furthermore, the efficiency of GEFREX, in contrast with FuGeNeSys, grows with R.

1.3.12   A learning example with compressed learning patterns

This brief section shows that GEFREX is able to learn with compressed learning patterns. This capability is a direct consequence of the introduction of the coefficients k_{op} into the error formula (1.6) and of the re-adjustment of equation (1.8). This equation has been changed in equation (1.9) to take into account these coefficients.

The first example shown in Section 1.3.10 was used as a case-study. The 121 learning patterns were taken, and with the K-means clustering algorithm [28] a codebook of 50 codewords was extracted. The RMSNE found was 3.706%.

	Rule 1	Rule 2	Rule 3	Rule 4
c_{1r}	-7.79	3.263	9.051	5.355
c_{2r}	12.12	10.93	10.26	3.946
γ_{1r}	0.159	0.280	0.383	0.013
γ_{2r}	0.196	0.086	0.093	0.116
z_{1r}	-6.79	8.842	7.653	-2.95

Table 1.10 The four rules obtained without weights

	Rule 1	Rule 2	Rule 3	Rule 4
c_{1r}	2.627	-3.81	10.194	-7.36
c_{2r}	-1.01	-1.45	25.044	16.77
γ_{1r}	0.348	0.088	0.1306	0.170
γ_{2r}	0.134	0.128	0.0557	0.086
z_{1r}	1.564	-1.12	13.945	-10.14

Table 1.11 The four rules obtained using the weights

This value was calculated on the basis of all the three components, the two inputs and the output. The first three columns of Table 1.9 show the 50 codewords obtained. After the codebook extraction, the weight of each codeword was calculated, that is, how many learning patterns were nearest to each codeword. These values are shown in the last column of Table 1.9.

Afterwards two different learning phases were executed. In both, the testing patterns were the same as used in Section 1.3.10. In the first learning phase a fuzzy system with four rules was trained. The learning patterns were the codewords without the weights. A RMSNE of 2.079% and 3.203% for the learning patterns and the testing patterns respectively was obtained. The rules are shown in Table 1.10. In the second learning phase another fuzzy system with four rules was trained too. This time, the learning patterns were the codewords with the weights. A RMSNE of 0.355% and 1.715% for the learning and the testing patterns respectively was obtained. The first error value was obtained taking into account the weights, while the second without any weight. The rules are shown in Table 1.11.

This example clearly shows how GEFREX is able to generalize a few samples if they are considered with the correct weights.

1.4 PARGEFREX

This section describes PARGEFREX, a distributed approach to genetic-neuro-fuzzy learning. The performance of the serial version is hugely enhanced with the simple parallelization scheme described here. Once a learning dataset is fixed, there is a very high super linear speedup in the average time needed to reach a prefixed learning error, i.e., if the number of personal computers increases n times, the mean learning time becomes less than $1/n$ times.

1.4.1   A brief review of GEFREX

We briefly summarize some concepts regarding GEFREX already discussed in more detail previously.

In GEFREX, the learning phase is divided into two parts: initialization and iteration. In the initialization phase the population is randomly generated and evaluated. The learning dataset is examined during this phase. For each input the range of possible values is determined. The Membership Functions (MFs) are randomly arranged within these ranges. The iteration part consists of a number of iterations where, each time, a new fuzzy system is generated using customized genetic operators, evaluated and placed at the place of the worst individual. These iterations end when the termination criterion is met. Both in the initialization and iteration phase, when there is the improvement of the best individual found so far, a specialized neuro operator is called. This operator is very time-consuming and consists in the transformation of the fuzzy individual into a neuro-fuzzy system. After, this system is trained. Finally, it is re-transformed into a genetic individual and replaces the original fuzzy individual. As at the beginning, when there is the random generation of the population, the neuro operator is often invoked. After, it is used much less. In the following we will distinguish between the two parts above described calling them respectively neuro phase and genetic phase.

Figure 1.7 shows 40 learning patterns of a single-input single-output system. The function to be learned is complex enough, as Gaussian MFs were used, if low learning errors must be reached. For example, roughly 10 seconds are required on a computer based on a Pentium II 350 MHz to reach a RMNSE=3.4% with five rules. Figure 1.16 shows the learnt curve. The corresponding RMNSE is 3.22%. To learn, GEFREX was used fixing a population of 400 individuals, Gaussian fuzzy sets, 5 rules and the weighted mean as the defuzzification method.

In the following, in all simulations the same type of MFs, number of individuals, defuzzification method and number of rules were fixed.

1.4.2   The commodity supercomputer used

Figure 1.17 shows the commodity supercomputer implemented at the University of Messina. We named it MULTISOFT machine. At the moment there are 32 PEs. There are both PEs based on a mono Celeron 366 MHz (c366) and PEs with a mono Pentium II 233 MHz (p233). In particular there are 25 c366 and 7 p233. Each PE has one local HD (from 4.3 to 6.4 GBytes), a fast-ethernet card, and 32 MBytes of RAM. For some reasons one p233 and

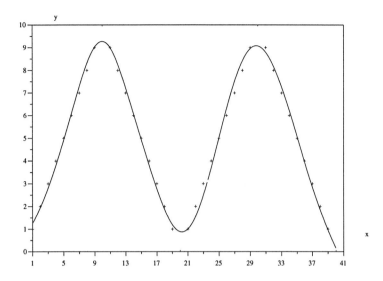

Figure 1.16   The 40 learning patterns and the learnt function with a RMNSE=3.22%.

three c366 have not been available in this experiment. There are two servers, too: one with two Pentium II 300MHz processors and one with one Pentium II 350 MHz processor. The servers have two ethernet cards: one to connect to the university LAN and another to the local fast-ethernet LAN. There is one 12 ports switch and four 12 ports hubs.

The OS is LINUX. The PEs remote boot from one server and see a network file system (NFS) shared by the server other than the local HD, too. The operating system files are resident on the local HD. An automatic procedure is executed every time it is required to update the OS or install new softwares on the MULTISOFT machine. This procedure is executed on the server and changes all local HDs contents.

The message passing communication paradigm has been used. The Parallel Virtual Machine (PVM) served to this purpose.

1.4.3   PARGEFREX description

Starting from the encuraging and preliminary results obtained in the previous work [37] we realized a parallel version of GEFREX well suited for the MULTISOFT machine.

Figure 1.18 shows the policy adopted in PARGEFREX realization. There is a master process that spawns a number of slaves. Then, every slave starts to

Figure 1.17   The MULTISOFT machine.

work and exchanges data with the other slaves. At the end the master collects results from slaves and kills them.

Effectively, there are not two different softwares, one for the slaves and another for the master. There is only one software that detects if it has been spawned from another copy of itself or not. If not, it acts as master; otherwise it is a slave. When the master starts it reads a configuration file which indicates how many PEs must be used. Further, for each PE this file specifies how many slaves must be run.

After the reading of the configuration file the master spawns all slaves, sends them initialization information and waits for results from slaves. After slaves run and their initialization phase ends, they start to exchange information among themselves excluding the master process. The data exchanged is the best individual found so far from the slave which is sent to another slave. They send their best individual at random times, but the average sending time is user definable. The receiving slave is randomly chosen too. The individual received replaces the worst one in the local population.

Several stopping criteria have been implemented. They are:

CI: The number of iterations. When all slaves reach a pre-fixed number of iterations they send their best individual to the master. The master collects these individuals, retains the best one, kills all the

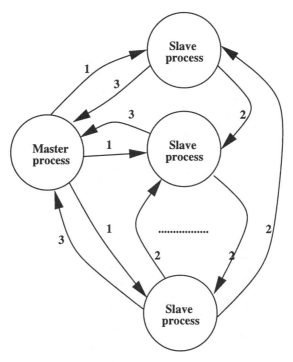

Figure 1.18 PARGEFREX scheme. 1) Spawning of slaves; 2) Data exchange among slaves; 3) Results collection by the slave.

slaves and ends.

CT: Simulation time. When all slaves run for a pre-fixed amount of time they send their best result to the master. Then the master behaves as described above.

CE: Final error. The first slave that reaches a pre-fixed error sends its best individual to the master. The master kills the other slaves and ends.

Figure 1.19 shows the real behavior of PARGEFREX. The graph was obtained with the XPVM software tool[1]. There is the master that is launched on the 7th p233 (p233h07 in the figure), and three slaves respectively launched on the 1st, 2nd and 3rd p233 of the MULTISOFT machine (p233h01, p233h02 and p233h03 in the figure). The run lasts for about 4s. The stopping criteria

---

[1]Available at http://www.epm.ornl.gov/pvm/pvm_home.html

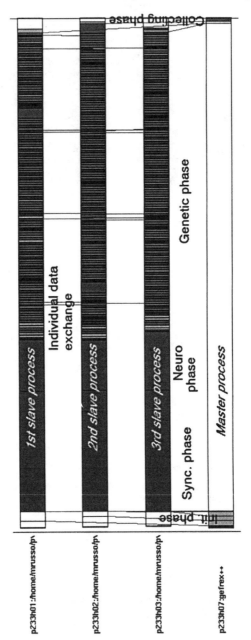

Figure 1.19   PARGEFREX simulation when 3 PEs are used.

was CT when the simulation time was fixed to 3s.

First, there is the initialization phase where the slaves are spawned and initial information is sent to them. After there is a synchronization phase. This phase is optional and has been implemented only for speedup evaluation. In this phase slaves and master synchronize their clocks, so they can start simultaneously. The beginning time is sent from the master to the slaves in the previous phase. This solution has been adopted, because when many PEs are involved in the simulation it is practically impossible to use the network to send a message that indicates the starting time to all PES contemporarily. In fact, in the PVM there is not the real broadcast function, but only a simulated one. When a broadcast message is sent there are as many equal messages sent as the number of receivers. So, when there are several PEs the start message arrives at the first addressee slave a long time before the last one. Obviously neither the implemented synchronizing method does guarantee that all slaves start exactly at the same moment, but the maximum difference in starting times is much less in respect of using the PVM broadcast.

Then the slaves start to work. At each iteration they see if a message has been delivered from another slave. Further, at random times they sent their best individual to other random slaves. In this simulation the average sending time was fixed to 1s. Two particular phases are characterized in the graph, the neuro and genetic ones. The slave starts to work in the neuro phase. In this phase it generates its population of 400 individuals. This phase lasts about 0.4s and it is forbidden to send anything to other slaves. After, the genetic phase starts. It lasts 2.6s. Finally, there is the collecting phase where the master receives all the best individuals found by the slaves and after kills them. This simulation clarifies which is the simulation time specified in the termination condition: the neuro phase time plus the genetic one.

Figure 1.20 shows another simulation in which all available PEs were used. The whole run lasted about 6s. The average sending time was fixed to 0.1s. Also in this simulation there is a synchronization phase of 1s. The termination criterion was CI with 0.5s of simulation time. The figure shows that the initialization phase is greatly enlarged due to the larger number of PEs. The neuro phase lasts about 0.3s and the genetic one only 0.2. So, the slaves exchange information for only 40% of the simulation time.

1.4.4 Performance evaluation

This section is devoted to the evaluation of the PARGEFREX performance using the MULTISOFT machine.

First of all the relative computational power among PEs was evaluated. With this aim 100 learning phases were executed using a p233 and successively a c366. The stopping criterion was CI, where the number of iterations was fixed to 100000. On average the final errors were almost equal. Furthermore, always

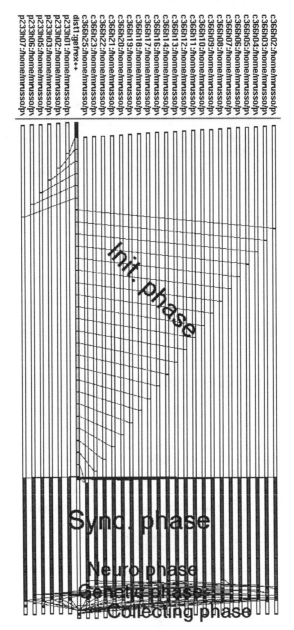

Figure 1.20 PARGEFREX simulation when all PEs are used.

on average, the learning time using a p233 was $r=1.57$ times the time needed
for a c366. This experimental number is very close to the ratio between the
two operating frequencies of the two different processors of the two classes of
PEs!

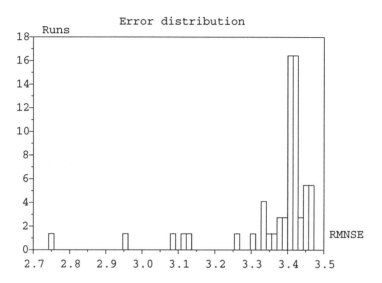

Figure 1.21   RMNSE error distribution when one p233 is used and the run lasts for 75s.

To evaluate the performance obtainable with GEFREX we need to introduce
two new quantities. Let us suppose we are using p p233 and c c366. A useful
piece of information is the equivalent computational power $P_{p,c}$ of these PEs,
that is, the sum of their relative performances. So, we have:

$$P_{p,c} = p + r \times c \qquad\qquad (1.24)$$

where r is the relative speed between one p233 and one c366 ($r=1.57$ in this
case).

A possible way of evaluating the speedup would be to fix a learning error
and to see how much time is required to reach this error when $P_{p,c}$ varies from
0 to 1. Unfortunately, this is impossible. In fact, PARGEFREX is mainly
a GA. Figure 1.21 shows the distribution of the final error when only one
p233 is used and the termination criterion is 75s of learning time. The Figure
shows the great spread in final error obtainable. If we used CE as termination
criterion we would have many problems, above all when fuzzy systems with

low learning errors are searched. In fact, the lower the error, the greater the number of simulations that do not converge in a reasonable time. In the case of Figure 1.21 if the termination condition CE were to reach an error of 3.0% only two runs among 50 would reach the error within 75s. If simulations lasted longer it would be possible that other runs reach the pre-fixed error. The author experienced that in these cases only very few simulations reach the error even if very long simulation times are allowed. This phenomenon, in conjunction with the great spread, would require an enormous number of simulations and too much time to obtain average values with an acceptable level of confidence.

To obtain significant results in a reasonable time the speedup was evaluated in an indirect manner. However, one month of intensive simulations were required to collect all the results reported in this chapter.

Rather than using CE as termination criterion and consequently not having control over the simulation time we choose to adopt CT. In this manner we can fix the learning time. The main idea for evaluating the speedup is to compare the simulation time when a fixed number of PEs are used (and an average error e is obtained) in respect of the time that would be required to reach e when a reference number of PEs are used. To do this, as regards the reference configuration, it is necessary to get the function $t(e)$ that links the learning time and the average error. This function can be obtained by a regression technique starting from a sufficient number of significant points. As will be shown after, for each point lots of runs are required. So, to minimize the time necessary to obtain the curve, all PEs have been used as the reference configuration. Any other reference configuration would require much more time to evaluate the speedup.

Figure 1.22 shows the function $t(e)$. The average migration time of individuals among slaves was fixed at 0.1s. When not specified this time has been used in the other simulations reported in this chapter. $t(e)$ was obtained as a cubic interpolation of eight significant points. These points were obtained ranging the simulation time in {0.3, 0.4, 0.5, 0.75, 1.0, 1.5, 2.0 4.0} seconds. Then for each of these times a set of simulations were executed. This set of simulations was ordered according to errors and the best 20% and the worst 20% were discarded. We must remember we are dealing with a GA. In this way we eliminate lucky simulations and simulations where premature convergence occurred. Further, we reduced the spread in the learning errors. With the remaining simulations the average error was calculated. As many simulations as needed to reach a confidence level of error under 0.01% were executed. However, at least 50 runs were executed. Table 1.13 reports the simulation times, the average error, and the number of runs. This table shows the great number of runs needed to reach the prefixed level of confidence.

Once the curve in Figure 1.22 was obtained it is possible to evaluate the speedup when the number of PEs range from one to all, i.e., when $P_{p,c}$ ranges

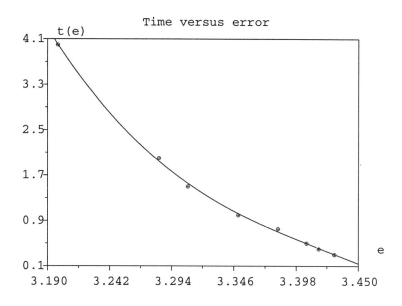

Figure 1.22 Time (in seconds) versus per cent RMNSE when 6 p233 and 22 c366 are used.

$t(s)$	e (RMNSE %)	Runs
0.3	3.43025	126
0.4	3.41711	92
0.5	3.40668	55
0.75	3.38288	83
1.0	3.34983	199
1.5	3.30783	360
2.0	3.28336	524
4.0	3.19867	758

Table 1.12 Average error and number of runs required versus simulation time when all PEs are used

from 1 to 40.54.

Let us run PARGEFREX using p p233 and c c366. Let us suppose the use of CT termination error with the simulation time fixed to $t'_{p,c}$. Let us indicate with $e_{p,c}$ the average per cent error (RMNSE) obtained in the same way as above: at least 50 runs and as many runs as needed to reach an average error with a confidence level of 0.01 once the best 20% and the worst 20% of runs are discarded. Let us introduce the quantity $S_{p,c}$ as follows:

p	c	$t'(s)$	e (RMNSE %)	Num. of runs
1	0	300	3.38522	51
1	0	150	3.38395	55
1	0	75	3.40597	50
6	0	50	3.33394	515
6	0	25	3.33306	646
6	0	12	3.37902	272
6	4	25	3.29377	848
6	4	12	3.30854	734
6	4	6	3.33523	548
6	8	16	3.25093	1104
6	8	8	3.27918	777
6	8	4	3.32113	473
6	12	12	3.22123	1016
6	12	6	3.26306	786
6	12	3	3.29831	615
6	17	9	3.18359	813
6	17	4	3.24619	713
6	17	2	3.30893	473

Table 1.13 Average error and number of runs required versus simulation time when the number of PEs varies

$$S_{p,c} = \frac{\frac{t(e_{p,c})}{t'_{p,c}}}{\frac{t(e_{1,0})}{t'_{1,0}}} \tag{1.25}$$

$S_{p,c}$ indicates indirectly the speedup. It represents the ratio between the time that would be needed to reach the error $e_{p,c}$ when all PEs would be used and the learning time $t'_{p,c}$ when only p p233 and c c366 are used. This ratio is normalized in respect of the case when only one p233 would be used.

To evaluate $S_{p,c}$ many runs were executed. For these runs it was decided to use in order: 1 p233, 6 p233, 6 p233 and 4 c366, 6 p233 and 8 p233, 6 p233 and 12 p233, 6 p233 and 17 c366. These choices imply $P_{p,c}$ in {1,6,12.28,18.56,24.84,32.69}. In all simulations the CT finishing criterion was used. In particular for 1 p233 three sets of runs were executed. In the first set all simulations lasted 300s, in the second 150s, and in the last 75s. For the other choice of PEs three sets of simulation were executed, too. Simulation times were fixed inversely proportional to $P_{p,c}$. The duration times were fixed respectively to about 300s/$P_{p,c}$, 150s/$P_{p,c}$, 75s/$P_{p,c}$. So three different $S_{p,c}$ curves were obtained. They are shown in Figure 1.23. The fourth curve represents the linear speedup.

The three sets of simulations were chosen after lots of runs to understand two distinct phenomena.

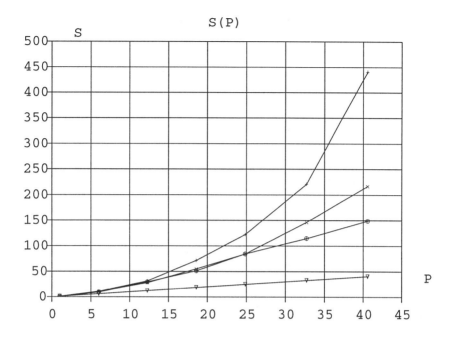

Figure 1.23   (+) Simulation time $\approx 300s/P_{p,c}$ ($\times$) $\approx 150s/P_{p,c}$ ($\oplus$) $\approx 75s/P_{p,c}$ (∇) Linear speedup

- The first one is related to the total power of our machine and the high $S_{p,c}$ values obtained. The shorter simulation using only one p233 must correspond to a significant point in the curve shown in Figure 1.22. Table 1.13 shows that with one p233 and 75s of learning time an error of about 3.41% is reached on average. This value corresponds (see Figure 1.22) to about 0.2-0.4s using all PEs. This value is at the limit. In fact, we remember that, as explained in describing Figures 1.19 and 1.20, when learning time than less of about 0.3-0.4s, the learning process is only in the neuro phase where the initial population is generated and no communication among PEs is allowed. So, to evaluate well the speed up achievable by the proposed implementation of PARGEFREX, simulations on a certain number of PEs must correspond to runs where the time required by all PEs to reach the same error is greater than 0.3-0.4s.

- The last consideration is related to the genetic convergence. Simulation cannot last too long because after a certain time the genetic-

t' (s)	e (RMNSE %)	Runs	$t(e)$ (s)
0.5	3.41779	88	0.41
1	3.39518	128	0.59
2	3.31133	318	1.50
4	3.23319	528	3.02

Table 1.14   Results obtained when all PEs are used and no exchange of data among slaves is permitted

> phase converges and no significant improvements are reachable in a
> reasonable time. Too long simulations with a number of PEs with
> a low $P_{p,c}$ would imply very high artificial speedups.

For these two reasons the simulations using one p233 were chosen to last 300s,
150 and 75s.

Figure 1.23 clearly states that the implementation of GEFREX gains significantly in performance when many PEs are used. Given that the network is always utilized less than 10% of its maximum possibility the results are surprising: PARGEFREX is particularly suited for commodity supercomputers rather than very expensive servers with few processors.

Figure 1.23 confirms our discussion regarding too long simulations. If one p233 is used and the simulations last for 300s the speedup is particularly high: almost 450! This phenomenon is due to the fact that after 100-200s all the simulations converge and do not succeed in improving significantly. If we evaluated the average error when the simulation time was greater we would have a huge speedup, because the error would be almost identical to that found in 300s. Simulations using a p233 that last for 75s and 150s are more suited to evaluating the speedup.

The reader can see that the speedup is always greater than one. This fact implies a clear concept: the use of several PEs rather than only one permits the finding, on average, of very low learning errors. It is very improbable to find the same error with only one PE even if many very long simulations are launched. In this sense we can say that PARGEFREX is more effective than GEFREX.

To understand how important inter-slave communication is, PARGEFREX was used avoiding any exchange of individuals. Table 1.14 shows the results obtained when all PEs are used and the CT criterion was chosen with the simulation times fixed respectively to 0.5, 1.2 and 4 seconds. The last column reports the time that would be needed in the case of a migration time of 0.1s. There is a clear advantage permitting migration. With the fastest simulation the advantage is less evident in comparison to other cases, but it needs to be underlined that in this case the simulation time is almost all constituted by the neuro-phase and the genetic phase, where migration is allowed, is very short.

PEs	t' (s)	Num. procs	Runs	Improvement
1 p233	75	5	88	+27%
1 p233	75	10	251	+83%
all	2	5	252	+85%
all	2	10	328	+117%

Table 1.15 Improvement as function of the number of processes per node and number of PEs

Further studies will investigate the optimal migration rate.

The last table 1.15 shows the behavior of PARGEFREX when more slaves are launched on the same PE. The first two rows show the results when PARGEFREX is launched using only one p233, but 5 and 10 slaves are spawned respectively. The last two refer to all PEs. The CE termination criterion was used. The simulation time is reported in column 3. The last column reports the percent improvement obtained in respect of the same simulation when only one slave is spawned per PE (see Table 1.13 to get mono-slave results). The results obtained show that more processes per PE imply greater performance. Moreover, this increase is more evident when the number of PEs used increases, too. Further studies will deal with this phenomenon.

1.5   References

[1] E.Shragowitz, J.Y.Lee, and Q.Kang, "Application of Fuzzy in Computer-Aided VLSI Design," *IEEE Transactions on Fuzzy Systems*, vol. 6, pp. 163–172, Feb. 1998.

[2] J.Yen and N.Pfluger, "A Fuzzy Logic Based Extension to Payton and Rosenblatt's Command Fusion Method for Mobile Robot Navigation," *IEEE Transactions on Systems, Man and Cybernetics*, vol. 25, pp. 971–978, June 1995.

[3] H.R.Boem and H.S.Cho, "A Sensor-Based Navigation for a Mobile Robot Using Fuzzy Logic and Reinforcement Learning," *IEEE Transactions on Systems, Man and Cybernetics*, vol. 25, pp. 464–477, Mar. 1995.

[4] K.Arakawa, "Fuzzy Rule-Based Signal Processing and Its Application to Image Restoration," *IEEE Journal on Selected Areas in Communications*, vol. 12, pp. 1495–1502, Dec. 1994.

[5] G.V.Russo, U.Becciani, C.Caligiore, L.Lo Nigro, D.Lo Presti, S.Panebianco, L.Pappalardo, C.Petta, N.Randazzo, S.Reito, and M.Russo, "Smart Readout of Silicon Drift Detectors using ON-LINE Fuzzy Logic," *Nuclear Instruments & Methods in Physics Research - Section A*, vol. 443, pp. 478–502, 2000.

[6] M.Russo, N.A.Santagati, and E.Lo Pinto, "Medicinal Chemistry and Fuzzy Logic," *Information Sciences*, vol. 105/1-4, pp. 299–314, May 1998.

[7] *Procceedings of the 21st International Conference on Industrial Electronics, Control and Instrumentation*, 1995.

[8] C.T.Lin and C.S.G.Lee, "Neural–Network–Based Fuzzy Logic Control and Decision System," *IEEE Transactions on Computers*, vol. 40, pp. 1320–1336, Dec. 1991.

[9] C.J.Lin and C.T.Lin, "Reinforcement Learning for an ART-Based Fuzzy Adaptive Learning Control Network," *IEEE Transactions on Neural Networks*, vol. 7, pp. 709–731, May 1996.

[10] M.Grabish and F.Dispot, "A Comparison of Some Methods of Fuzzy Classification on Real Data," in *Proc. 2nd Int. Conf. on Fuzzy Logic and Neural Networks (IIZUKA'92)*, (Iizuka, Japan), pp. 659–662, July 1992.

[11] A.Lotfi and A.C.Tsoi, "Learning Fuzzy Inference Systems Using an Adaptive Membership Function Scheme," *IEEE Transactions on Systems, Man and Cybernetics – Part A*, vol. 26, pp. 326–331, Apr. 1996.

[12] K.M.Lee, D.H.Kwak, and H.Lee-Kwang, "Fuzzy Inference Neural Network for Fuzzy Model Tuning," *IEEE Transactions on Systems, Man and Cybernetics – Part A*, vol. 26, pp. 637–645, Aug. 1996.

[13] C.L.Karr and E.J.Gentry, "Fuzzy Control of pH Using Genetic Algorithms ," *IEEE Transactions on Fuzzy Systems*, vol. 1, pp. 46–53, Feb.

1993.

[14] S.H.Park, Y.H.Kim, Y.K.Choi, H.C.Cho, and H.T.Jeon, "Self-Organization of Fuzzy Rule Base Using Genetic Algorithms," in *Proc. 5th IFSA Congress*, (Seoul, Korea), pp. 881–886, July 1993.

[15] A.Homaifar and E.McCormick, "Simultaneous Design of Membership Functions and Rule Sets for Fuzzy Controllers Using Genetic Algorithms," *IEEE Transactions on Fuzzy Systems*, vol. 3, pp. 129–139, May 1995.

[16] T.Hashiyama, T.Furuhashi, and Y.Uchikawa, "A Creative Design of Fuzzy Logic Controller Using a Genetic Algorithm," *Advances in Fuzzy Systems*, vol. 7, pp. 37–48, 1997.

[17] K.C.C.Chan, V.Lee, and H.Leung, "Generating Fuzzy Rules for Target Tracking Using a Steady-State Genetic Algorithm," *IEEE Transactions on Evolutionary Computation*, vol. 1, pp. 189–200, Sept. 1997.

[18] M.Russo, "FuGeNeSys: A Fuzzy Genetic Neural System for Fuzzy Modeling," *IEEE Transactions on Fuzzy Systems*, vol. 6, pp. 373–388, Aug. 1998.

[19] G.H.Golub and C.F.Van Loan, *Matrix Computations*. Baltimore and London: The Johns Hopkins Iniversity Press, 1996.

[20] M.Figueiredo, F.Gomides, A.Rocha, and R.Yager, "Comparison of Yager's Level Set Method for Fuzzy Logic Control with Mamdani and Larsen Methods," *IEEE Transactions on Fuzzy Systems*, vol. 1, no. 2, pp. 156–159, 1993.

[21] Y.Lin and G.A.Cunningham III, "A New Approach to Fuzzy-Neural System Modeling," *IEEE Transactions on Fuzzy Systems*, vol. 3, pp. 190–198, May 1995.

[22] M.A.Lee and H.Takagi, "Integrating Design Stages of Fuzzy Systems Using Genetic Algorithms," in *Proc. IEEE Int. Conf. on Fuzzy Systems 1993*, (San Francisco, California), pp. 612–617, 1993.

[23] H.Ishibuchi, K.Nozaky, and H.Tanaka, "Distributed Representation of Fuzzy Rules and Its Application to Pattern Classification," *Fuzzy Sets and Systems*, vol. 52, pp. 21–32, 1992.

[24] H.Ishibuchi, K.Nozaki, N.Yamamoto, and H.Tanaka, "Selecting Fuzzy If-Then Rules for Classification Problems Using Genetic Algorithms," *IEEE Transactions on Fuzzy Systems*, vol. 3, pp. 260–270, Aug. 1995.

[25] M.Russo, *Metodi Hardware e Software per Logiche di Tipo non Tradizionale*. PhD thesis, University of Catania, Catania, Italy, Feb. 1996. Ph.D. thesis in Italian.

[26] K.Liano, "Robust Error Measure for Supervised Neural Network Learning with Outliers," *IEEE Transactions on Neural Networks*, vol. 7, pp. 246–250, Jan. 1996.

[27] C.Petta, G.V.Russo, B.Batyunya, C.Caligiore, D.Lo Presti, S.Panebianco, N.Randazzo, S.Reito, M.Russo, and A.Zinchenko,

"Fuzzy Processing of ALICE Silicon Drift Detectors' Data," in *New Trends in Fuzzy Logic II, Proc. of the Second Italian Workshop on Fuzzy Logic*, (Bari, Italy), pp. 188–199, Mar. 1997.

[28] C.M.Bishop, *Neural Networks for Pattern Recognition*. Oxford: Clarendon Press, 1996.

[29] H.Narazaki and A.L.Ralescu, "An Improved Synthesis Method for Multilayered Neural Networks Using Qualitative Knowledge," *IEEE Transactions on Fuzzy Systems*, vol. 1, no. 2, pp. 125–137, 1993.

[30] M. Sugeno and T.Yasukawa, "A Fuzzy–Logic–Based Approach to Qualitative Modeling," *IEEE Transactions on Fuzzy Systems*, vol. 1, pp. 7–31, Feb. 1993.

[31] M.R.Emami, I.B.Türksen, and A.A.Goldberg, "Development of A Systematic Methodology of Fuzzy Logic Modeling," *IEEE Transactions on Fuzzy Systems*, vol. 6, pp. 346–361, Aug. 1998.

[32] M.Delgado, F.Gómez-Skarmeta, and F.Martín, "A Fuzzy Clustering-Based Rapid Prototyping for Fuzzy Rule-Based Modeling," *IEEE Transactions on Fuzzy Systems*, vol. 5, pp. 223–233, May 1997.

[33] Y.Lin, G.A.Cunningham III, and S.V.Coggeshall, "Using Fuzzy Partitions to Create Fuzzy Systems from Input-Output Data and Set the Initial Weights in a Fuzzy Neural Network," *IEEE Transactions on Fuzzy Systems*, vol. 5, pp. 614–621, Nov. 1997.

[34] R.A.Fisher, "The Use of Multiple Measurements in Toxonomic Problems," *Annals Eugenics*, vol. 7, pp. 179–188, 1936.

[35] D.Kim and C.Kim, "Forecasting Time Series with Genetic Fuzzy Predictor Ensemble," *IEEE Transactions on Fuzzy Systems*, vol. 5, pp. 523–535, Nov. 1997.

[36] S. Sartaj, *Data Structures, Algorithms and Applications in C++*. Computer Science, Singapore: McGraw-Hill, 1998.

[37] M.Russo, "Parallel Fuzzy Learning," in *Proc. of IWANN'99* (J.Mira and J.V.Sánchez-Andrés, eds.), vol. 1606 of *Lecture Notes in Computer Science*, (Barcelona, Spain), pp. 641–650, Springer, June 1999.

2

A Stored-Programmable Mixed-Signal Fuzzy Controller Chip with Supervised Learning Capabilities

Fernando Vidal-Verdú
Rafael Navas
Dto. de Electrónica,
Universidad de Málaga
Complejo Tecnológico, Campus de Teatinos, Málaga, SPAIN.
E-mail: vidal@ctima.uma.es

Manuel Delgado-Restituto
Angel Rodríguez-Vázquez
Instituto de Microelectrónica de Sevilla
Centro Nacional de Microelectrónica-C.S.I.C.
Edif. CICA-CNM, Avda. Reina Mercedes s/n, 41012-Sevilla, SPAIN.
E-mail: angel@imse.cnm.es

Abstract

Based on the concept of the active rule set, this chapter presents a multiplexed mixed-signal architecture for high-speed fuzzy controller chips. The proposed architecture consists of a programmable analog core which implements the active rule, a RAM memory which stores the parameters (global rule set) and a selection circuitry to identify the input subregion and retrieve the proper parameters from the memory. Thus, the global controller surface response is realized through dynamic programming and multiplexing of the analog core. This architecture can be programmed or trained by a set of input-output data pairs by means of a simple hardware-oriented learning rule which does not need to compute derivatives. The chapter presents also the circuit building blocks needed for implementation of the proposed architecture and illustrates the performance of the whole system through a chip realized in $0.7\mu m$ CMOS technology.

2.1. Introduction

Fuzzy controllers are used to map a multidimensional input signal $x = \{x_1, x_2, \ldots x_M\}^T$ onto a scalar output y, in accordance to a well-defined nonlinear relationship [1],

$$y = f(x) \tag{2.1}$$

In control applications the inputs are usually called facts, the output action, and the mapping law surface response. For instance, a fuzzy controller for a washing machine must univocally set the water level (action) as a nonlinear function (surface response) of the clothes' mass, the water impurity, and the time differential of impurity (facts) [2].

Fuzzy controllers employ the procedure of fuzzy logic inference[1] to construct the surface response. Some characteristic features of this procedure are [4][5]:

- The surface response, which is a global model predicting the system behavior for any input, is obtained as a composition of local functions, each one predicting this behavior only for inputs comprised in a limited region of the input space.
- These local functions represent insights in the system operation, and are described through inference rules of the type,

IF x_1 is A_{1k} AND x_2 is A_{2k} AND ... x_M is A_{Mk} THEN Consequent Action

where A_{ik} are called fuzzy labels, and the consequent action assigns values to y depending on the outcome of the combination of the antecedent clause statements.

- The validity of the statements "IF x_i is A_{ik}" is continuously graded from 0 to 1; the actual grade of each statement is calculated by evaluating a nonlinear membership function $s_{ik}(x_i)$ which is different from zero only inside a subinterval of the whole x_i interval.

Because the statements involved in the fuzzy rules are in natural language, for instance "if the temperature is low", this modeling technique is very well suited for capturing and emulating human expertise. On the other hand, the continuous grading guarantees generalization of the local pieces of knowledge and, hence, smooth surface responses. Finally, any change which affects only a limited region of the input space can be easily incorporated into the global model by just modifying the affected local functions – the transparency property [4].

There are many fuzzy controller applications where the inputs and the output are analog signals acquired from sensors and applied to actuators, respectively [1][2]. The hardware required for these applications can be implemented in two alternative ways [3]. One realizes the fuzzy processing in the digital domain by means of either general-purpose processors or dedicated ASICs [6]-[9]. Obviously, this approach must include A/D and D/A converters at the sensor/actuator interface circuitry. The other one realizes the fuzzy processing itself in the analog domain, thus precluding the use of data converters in the input-output signal path [12]-[17].

Generally speaking, analog fuzzy controllers feature larger operation speed and lower power consumption than their digital counterparts; they also occupy smaller silicon areas. As a counterpart, they have poorer programmability and reconfigurability, and obtain lower accuracy in the realization of the fuzzy operations. The problem of accuracy becomes especially relevant with the circuits employed for global computations [4][5], like the center of gravity computation, where errors are aggregated and may become prohibitively large except for low-dimension systems. This is especially true in control applications, where lattice partitions of the universe of discourse are common [5], and thus the course of dimensionality – exponential increase of the number of rules with input count – appears.

The mixed-signal architecture discussed in this chapter overcomes these drawbacks while keeping the advantages of analog implementations. This architecture, based on the concept of the active rule set [10], exploits the fact that in lattice partitions the output can be expressed as a function of a reduced set of parameterized rules (the active rule set) whose parameters are specific for each input space subregion, and hence dependent on the actual inputs applied. The proposed architecture consists of a programmable analog core which implements the active rule, a RAM memory which stores the parameters (global rule set) and a selection circuitry to identify the input subregion and retrieve the proper parameters from the memory. Thus, the global surface response is realized through dynamic programming and multiplexing of the analog core.

The resulting architecture can be programmed or trained by a set of input-output data pairs by means of a simple hardware-oriented learning rule which does not need to compute derivatives. This learning process can be carried out off-chip, with a software model or even with some dedicated hardware [11], or it can be easily implemented on-chip. In Section 2.5 we discuss this capability and show a learning example.

2.2. Architecture and Functional Description

2.2.1. Inference Procedure

The proposed architecture realizes the type of fuzzy inference where rule consequents are singletons,

$$\text{IF } (x_1 \text{ is } A_{1k}) \text{ AND } (x_2 \text{ is } A_{2k}) \text{ AND} \dots (x_M \text{ is } A_{Mk})$$
$$\text{THEN } y = y_k^* \qquad (1 \leq k \leq N) \tag{2.2}$$

This type of fuzzy inference reduces the silicon area and the power consumption and eases the incorporation of programmability. Besides, it has been shown that singleton fuzzy controllers are universal approximators, i.e., capable of approximating any surface response by properly choosing rules and singletons [4][5].

The membership functions $s_{ik}(x_i)$ are the elementary non-linearities from which the surface response is built. Fig.2.1(a) shows a typical membership function shape [5] – described by three parameters: width (2Δ), measured as

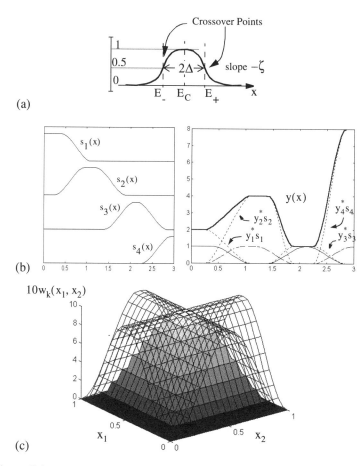

Figure 2.1: (a) One-dimensional membership function shape; (b) Illustrating function approximation through singleton fuzzy controllers; (c) Two-dimensional membership function.

the length of the interval defined by the crossover points; center (E_C), the central point of this interval; and slope (ζ), the absolute value of the function slope at the crossover points. For a complete controller description, the surface response formula has to be generated from these elementary non-linearities. Fig.2.1(b) illustrates the building procedure for a one-dimension, four-rule controller. Here, each rule involves only a fuzzy label, "IF x is A_k THEN y = y_k^*", whose validity is evaluated by using the corresponding membership function $s_k(x)$. If the actual input x is at the center of the interval I_k for the k-th membership function, then $s_k(x) = 1$ and the output is given by the value of the k-th singleton $y = y_k^*$. At any point different from the centers of the membership function intervals, the output does not coincide with any of the singletons but is interpolated by using the following formula,

$$y = y_1^*s_1^*(x) + y_2^*s_2^*(x) + y_3^*s_3^*(x) + y_4^*s_4^*(x) \tag{2.3}$$

where $s_k^* = s_k / \left[\displaystyle\sum_{k=1,4} s_k \right]$ − normalized to preclude that the output becomes larger than the largest singleton at any point. Thus, a global response curve is built from the local data represented by the singletons, as Fig.2.1(b) illustrates.

In the general multi-dimensional case, the surface response is interpolated from the singletons by using multi-dimensional membership functions $w_k(x)$,

$$y = f(x) = \sum_{k=1,N} y_k^* \frac{w_k(x)}{\displaystyle\sum_{k=1,N} w_k(x)} \tag{2.4}$$

where function $w_k(x)$ is evaluated by choosing the minimum among the values of the uni-dimensional membership functions $s_{ik}(x_i)$ associated to the k-th rule,

$$w_k(x) = \min\{s_{1k}(x_1), s_{2k}(x_2), ..., s_{Mk}(x_M)\} \tag{2.5}$$

Fig.2.1(c) illustrates the build-up procedure and final shape of a two-dimensional membership function.

2.2.2. Non-Multiplexed Architecture

Fig.2.2 shows a non-multiplexed architecture for realizing the fuzzy inference leading to (2.4) for a system with M inputs, L fuzzy labels per input and $N = L^M$ rules [12]. The architecture is composed of the interconnection of blocks of two different types, namely: label and rule. Each fuzzy label, say A_{ij} (the j-th fuzzy label of the i-th input), has an associated label block which eval-

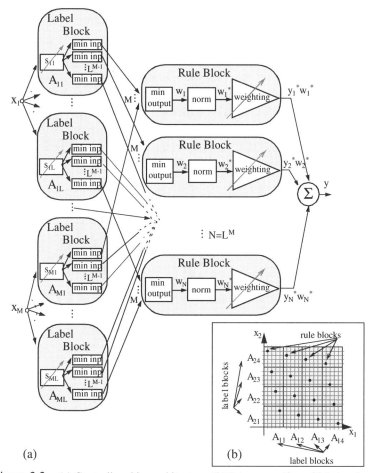

Figure 2.2:   (a) Controller chip architecture; (b) Interconnection of label and rule blocks in the 1μm CMOS prototype.

uates the corresponding membership function $s_{ij}(x_i)$ and generates L^{M-1} replicas of the result. These replicas are processed in the "min inp" sub-blocks of the label blocks as a first step towards the realization of the minimum. Each rule block combines M inputs coming from the label blocks first of all to realize the second step of the minimum operation; secondly, to evaluate the function $w_k^*(x)$; and, thirdly to multiply this function by its associated singleton in order to obtain $y_k^* w_k^*(x)$. The final aggregation leading to (2.4) is performed at the output node.

Fig.2.2(b) illustrates the interconnection of label and rule blocks for a system with two inputs and four fuzzy labels per input. Each box in the grid corresponds to a rule, has an associated singleton value, and is defined by two labels, one per input. Each label block is shared by four different rules. Because of this membership function sharing, the architecture of Fig.2.2(a) can only generate lattice partitions (see Fig.2.3(a)). Tree (Fig.2.3(b)) and scatter (Fig.2.3(c)) partitions [5] are not allowed.

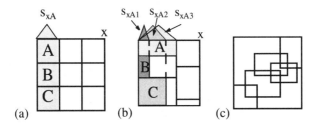

(a)   (b)   (c)

Figure 2.3: Examples of different types of input space partitions.

2.2.3. Multiplexed Architecture

Consider for illustration purposes the bi-dimensional lattice partition of Fig.2.4. It shows the universe of discourse split into interpolation intervals,

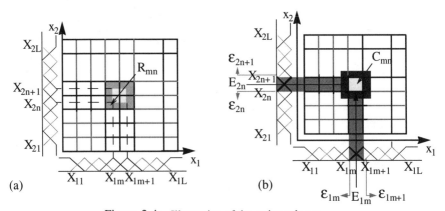

(a)   (b)

Figure 2.4: Illustration of the active rule set.

each having a different set of active rules. For instance, any input pair (x_1, x_2) in the light-shaded interval $C_{mn} = [(\varepsilon_{1m}, \varepsilon_{1m+1}) \times (\varepsilon_{2n}, \varepsilon_{2n+1})]$ maps onto an output determined by the rules in the dark-shaded interval (active rules) while all remaining rules have no influence on the output. Only the active rule membership functions and their associated singleton values (the output values defining the consequent action at the center of each rule interval) are needed for the interpolation procedure. In addition, the only membership function pieces needed are those which actually contribute to the system output. Thus, in the case illustrated in Fig.2.4, only the pieces drawn with thick lines and the singletons associated with the four active rule consequents, y_{mn}^*, $y_{m(n+1)}^*$, $y_{(m+1)n}^*$ and $y_{(m+1)(n+1)}^*$, are needed to generate the output in the interval C_{mn}.

Fig.2.5 shows the proposed architecture for a controller with M inputs, L labels per input (thus L^M rules), and P bits per singleton. It comprises the following blocks:

- A/D Converters: Their function is to encode the interpolation interval C_{mn} associated with the current input. These are M, one per input, with a resolution equal to the next superior integer $\log_2 L$, i.e., $\text{int}_s(\log_2 L)$.

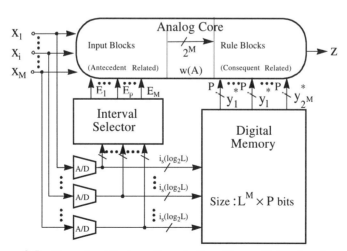

Figure 2.5:   General architecture of a controller with a multiplexed analog core.

Thus, this battery of converters provides a word of $M[\text{int}_s(\log_2 L)]$ bits which drive the interval selector block and the digital memory block.

- Interval Selector: This selects a set of voltage values $E_1...,E_p...E_M$ to drive the analog core and, thus, implements the active membership functions.
- Digital Memory: This selects the active singleton programming values $y_1^*..., y_1^*..., y_{2^M}^*$ which configure the rule block of the analog core consequents of the active rules. These are digital words of as many bits as are needed to encode the required set of singleton values.
- Analog Core: This performs the fuzzy computation having a set of programming inputs which are driven by the interval selector and the digital memory blocks. These inputs set up the analog core to work with the appropriate rule set, which means that the membership functions associated with the rule antecedents as well as the singleton values related to the consequents need to be specified.

Note that Fig.2.5 is valid and even more useful for an increasing number of inputs and labels. The number of outputs can also be increased with little effort because many blocks can be shared by the circuitry dedicated to generate each output. Specifically, each additional output involves one digital memory block, and 2^M rule blocks. For the controller described in this chapter, the parameters in Fig.2.5 take the value $M = 2$, $L = 8$ and $P = 4$.

2.3. Analog Core Implementation

The analog core follows the architecture of Fig.2.2 [12]. However, unlike the non-multiplexed case, where the $N = L^M$ rules must be physically implemented, the analog core of the multiplexed architecture contains only 2^M rule blocks, and two membership functions per input (both implemented in just one so-called input block). Below we first summarize the description of the circuit blocks when employed for the non-multiplexed case and then detail the modifications needed for the multiplexed architecture.

2.3.1. Non-Multiplexed Building Blocks

As shown in Fig.2.2, a modular non-multiplexed implementation of a lattice architecture can be carried out by connecting two high level building blocks: the label block and the rule block, associated respectively to antecedent related and consequent related tasks. In the following we describe an implementation of these building blocks.

Label Block

Each label block is driven by a component x_i of the input voltage vector first of all to obtain a membership function current $s_{ij}(x_i)$ and, secondly, to generate L^{M-1} replicas of voltage V_{Gij} which is a nonlinear function of this current − a preprocessing step for the realization of the minimum operator in the rule blocks. This section describes the membership function and minimum circuitry required.

A few alternative realizations of the pseudo-trapezoidal function shape of Fig.2.1(a) have been reported in literature [14][21]-[23]. One, shown in Fig.2.6(a), includes a linearized transconductor, to convert the input voltage into a current, and a current-mode nonlinear block to realize the pseudo-trapezoidal shape [20]; this latter block can be realized by using the techniques proposed in [14][21][22]. A drawback of this implementation is the extra area occupation and power consumption of the linearization circuitry. Also, because the transconductor cannot be linearized in the whole input range,

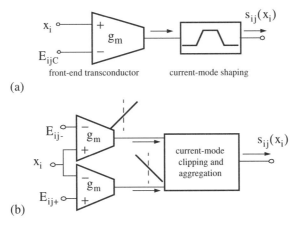

Figure 2.6: Concepts for the realization of a transconductance membership function by current shaping: (a) Global shaping in current-mode [20]; (b) Partial shaping in current-mode [23].

some of this range is wasted.

Fig.2.6(b) employs a slightly different strategy [23]. Here, two quasi-linear transconductance amplifiers first obtain monotone increasing and decreasing currents around the crossover points, and then, as a second step, these currents are first clipped and then aggregated in the current domain. This strategy shares the drawbacks associated with linearization. However, compared to Fig.2.6(a), it has the advantage that the centers and widths of the membership functions are controlled through voltages applied to high-input impedance nodes, which requires a simpler control circuitry and yields smaller loading errors in the application of the control signal.

The circuit in Fig.2.7 approximates the shape of Fig.2.1(a) by using the non-linear dc characteristics of a CMOS differential pair. This strategy is based on the work of Fattaruso and Meyer on CMOS function approximation [24], and

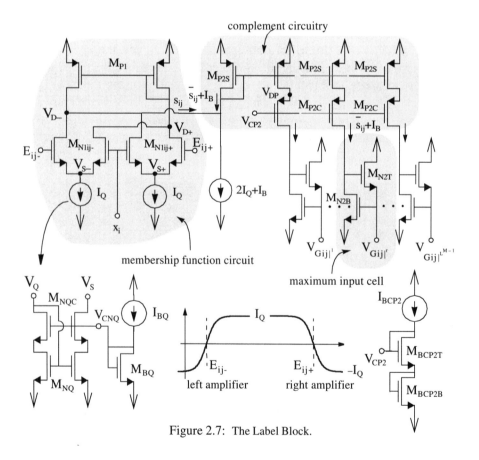

Figure 2.7: The Label Block.

was proposed for analog fuzzy design in [25]. Analysis of this circuit assuming equal differential pairs and using the square-law MOS transistor characteristics [26] yields:

$$
s_{ij} = \begin{cases} 0 & , \tilde{x}_{ij-} < -E_Q \\[2mm] \left(1 + \dfrac{\sqrt{2}}{E_Q}\right) I_Q \tilde{x}_{ij-} \sqrt{1 - \dfrac{\tilde{x}_{ij-}^2}{2E_Q^2}} & , -E_Q < \tilde{x}_{ij-} < E_Q \\[2mm] 2I_Q & , \text{otherwise} \\[2mm] \left(1 - \dfrac{\sqrt{2}}{E_Q}\right) I_Q \tilde{x}_{ij+} \sqrt{1 - \dfrac{\tilde{x}_{ij+}^2}{2E_Q^2}} & , -E_Q < \tilde{x}_{ij+} < E_Q \\[2mm] 0 & , \tilde{x}_{ij+} > E_Q \end{cases} \tag{2.6}
$$

where $\tilde{x}_{ij-} = (x_i - E_{ij-})$, $\tilde{x}_{ij+} = (x_i - E_{ij+})$ and $E_Q = \sqrt{I_Q / \beta_{N1}}$, β_{N1} is the large signal transconductance factor of the transistors in the differential pairs[1] and we assume that the membership function width is large enough to allow the output current to reach the unit logic value (I_Q) at the center.

This membership function circuit shares the advantages of Fig.2.6(b) regarding the control of the centers and widths by applying voltages to high input impedance terminals,

$$
2\Delta_{ij} = E_{ij+} - E_{ij-} \qquad\qquad 2E_{ijC} = E_{ij+} + E_{ij-} \tag{2.7}
$$

On the other hand, the slope at the crossover points ζ_{ij} is controlled by the large signal transconductance of the MOS transistor[2] ,

$$
\zeta_{ij} = \sqrt{2 I_Q \beta_{N1}} \tag{2.8}
$$

The main advantage of this membership function circuit is that it does not require any linearization circuitry – why linearize if the whole behavior is non-linear? Thus, it features a minimum area occupation and power consumption, and full usage of the transconductor input dynamic range. On the other hand, it has been shown that the shape in (2.6) can actually realize the universal

---

1. This equation shows the simplest case where the positive and negative input transistors are equal.
2. Using the bias current to control the slope is not convenient because the bias current sets the logical value "1".

approximation feature, even when parasitics (systematic as well as random) are taken into account [18].

With regard to the minimum operation, as mentioned in Section 2.2, it is realized in three steps: two in the label blocks and the other one in the rule block. However, for the sake of clarity, these three steps are described as a whole in this section. The minimum circuit has to select and propagate the minimum among a set of M input currents $s_{ik}(x_i)$. However, for convenience, we do not directly select the minimum among the input currents, but the maximum among their fuzzy complements

$$\overline{s_{ik}(x_i)} \equiv 2I_Q - s_{ik}(x_i) \tag{2.9}$$

where current level $2I_Q$ corresponds to the logic "1". This is based on De Morgan's law [38],

$$w_k(x) = \min\{ s_{1k}(x_1), s_{2k}(x_2), ..., s_{Mk}(x_M) \} =$$
$$= \overline{\max\{ \overline{s_{1k}(x_1)}, \overline{s_{2k}(x_2)}, ..., \overline{s_{Mk}(x_M)} \}} \tag{2.10}$$

and takes advantage of the greater simplicity of the current-mode maximum circuitry [27].

Fig.2.8(b) shows conceptual circuits for evaluating fuzzy complements by means of KCL, for positive (entering) and negative (leaving) currents. Regarding the maximum circuit itself, several alternatives appear which have to be evaluated bearing in mind the following major architectural features:

- Neither constraints nor penalties should be imposed on the number of inputs since it coincides with the number of controller inputs.
- The inter-block routing should be as small as possible for increased modularity.

These considerations lead us to discard realizations with $O(n^2)$ complexity [28]. Realizations based on sequential binary selection trees [29] are also discarded because, although they have $O(n)$ complexity, their implementation requires $\log_2(n)$ circuit layers, and causes the errors and delays to be accumulated proportionally to the number of inputs. The maximum circuit used in our chip (see Fig.2.8(a)) is based on the winner-take-all circuit by Lazzaro [30] and was proposed in [25]. Its steady-state circuit operation is simple: the bottom transistor driving the maximum current will force the common voltage V_G by means of its associated top transistor, while the remaining bottom transistors are driven into the ohmic region to comply with their input currents and, consequently, their associated top transistors are cut off. Thus, provided the output transistor works in the saturation region, its current coincides with the maximum one. When the maximum current is switched from one input terminal to another, a transient takes place where the difference between the new and the old maximum current is integrated in the latter terminal, thus driving this transistor into a conducting state and, eventually, changing the value of the common voltage V_G.

This circuit exhibits the architectural features mentioned above: a) it has $O(n)$ complexity; b) the different inputs share only the node V_G. This latter feature allows us to partition the circuit as Fig.2.8(a) shows, so that the rule block has only one input. Another current-mode maximum circuit also based on Lazzaro´s was proposed in [31] and used in [14]. It connects the output

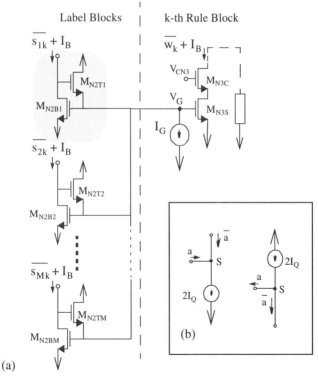

Figure 2.8: Circuitry for the minimum computation: (a) maximum circuit; (b) complement implementation.

transistor as a diode, removes the current source I_G, and connects the drains of the top transistors M_{N2Tk} to a common node which is the output node. Thus, the inputs share two nodes instead of one. Besides, the removal of the current I_G makes the resolution of this circuit dependent on the output current level and makes it specifically small for large currents [27]. Finally, because the output node load increases with the input count, the performance of this circuit is poorer than that shown in Fig.2.8(a), when the number of inputs increases.

Let us now describe the realization of the first two steps for the minimum in the label block of Fig.2.7. The first (complementation) is realized by KCL at the input node of the upper-right-hand current mirror in Fig.2.7. Its input current is $\overline{s_{ij}} + I_B$ where current I_B is added to preclude the transistors entering in the subthreshold, where the operation speed would become significantly degraded. Note, on the other hand, that this current mirror has with L^{M-1} output branches to generate the membership function output replicas $s_{ij}\big|^r$ for $1 \leq r \leq L^{M-1}$ for the different rules. The second step is also realized in the label block and consists of the generation of a set of intermediate voltages $V_{Gij|^r}$ as nonlinear functions of the currents $\overline{s_{ij}}\big|^r + I_B$. Each of these voltages is generated in the lower-right-hand shaded area of Fig.2.7 by a two transistor circuit (see also Fig.2.8(a); for proper operation of this two-transistor circuit, some extra circuitry must be added to discharge node V_G − provided by the current source I_G, included in the rule block).

The next step for the minimum operation is realized in the rule block (bear in mind, Fig.2.2(a), that this block has one input and one output). To that purpose, the set of voltages V_{Gik} for the M membership function values associated to the k-th rule are routed and tied together at the input node of the rule block (see the left-hand part of Fig.2.8(a)). Thus, a collective computation is performed at this common node so that the maximum among the set of voltages prevails. From this maximum voltage, the corresponding maximum current $\overline{s_{ik}(x_i)}\big|_{max} + I_B$ is generated by transistor M_{N3S} in Fig.2.8(a). According to (2.10) this corresponds to the fuzzy complement $w_k(x)$ of the multidimensional membership value shifted by I_B.

Rule Block

The k-th rule block is first intended to calculate the current w_k and, secondly, to generate an output current given by:

$$y_k = y_k^* \frac{w_k}{\sum_{k=1.N} w_k} \qquad (2.11)$$

These currents are then routed to a common node to implement (2.4) through KCL.

There are three main approaches for the analog implementation of (2.11) and/or (2.4): using an extension of Mead´s [32] follower-aggregation circuit with weighting capability [16][36]; using weighting-plus-division circuits [14][34] [35]; using normalization-plus-weighting circuits [25][23]. The first uses an elegant circuit concept (see Fig.2.9(a)) to implement a nonlinear version of (2.4) with a voltage output. However, because of the feedback, its transient response is not optimal; also, because a large signal current w_k is applied at the TA bias terminal, the linear operation range and the transient response are largely non-homogeneous over the university of discourse; finally, additional MDACs are required to incorporate digital programmability of the singletons. Fig.2.9(b) and (c) show the concepts of the other two approaches. Both permit transparent digital programmability of the singletons. However, different reasons lead us to use the normalization-plus-weighting approach. First, the weighting-plus-division approach requires replication of the input currents and the use of wide-range linear current-mode dividers, while the normalization can be realized through a collective computation circuit with only two transistors per input; the chosen approach results, hence, in simpler circuits. Secondly, because the transmission path for the numerator and the denominator of (2.4) are not the same in Fig.2.9(b), this approach is more sensitive to mismatching. Thirdly, the transient response of Fig.2.9(b) is largely dependent on the signal level. Fourthly, there is no simple way to compensate for the errors in the divider – the only way is using very accurate dividers.

Fig.2.10 shows the schematics of the rule block where four different operations are realized: first, the current $\overline{w_k} + I_B$ is generated as explained in Section 2.3.1; secondly, this current is complemented and shifted to obtain $w_{ks} = w_k + I_{OS}$; thirdly, a collective computation is carried out by all the rule blocks (they share global nodes A_{NOR} and B_{NOR}) to realize the normalization

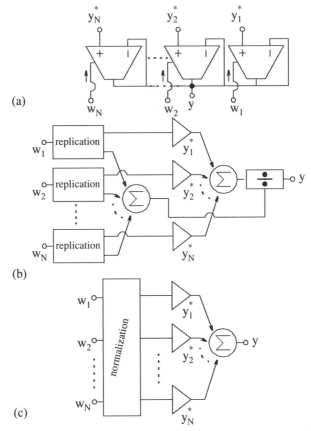

Figure 2.9: Singleton defuzzification strategies: (a) follower-aggregation; (b) weighting-plus-division; (c) normalization-plus-weighting.

operation; fourthly, the resulting current is weighted by a digitally-controlled current mirror to obtain the shifted version of the k-th rule output current.

Fig.2.11 shows the CMOS normalizer circuit used in the proposed chip, based on a translinear BJT circuit by Gilbert [33]. Unlike the normalizers used in [34][23], Fig.2.11 does not involve any global feedback loop and, hence, features much faster dynamic response. Note that Fig.2.11 can be split into N equal cells, one per each input-output pair, plus a common circuitry consisting of transistor M_{NA} and current source I_{SS}. Fig.2.10 exploits this modularity by incorporating one of these cells at each rule block.

Assuming that the transistors operate in strong inversion, where the BJT

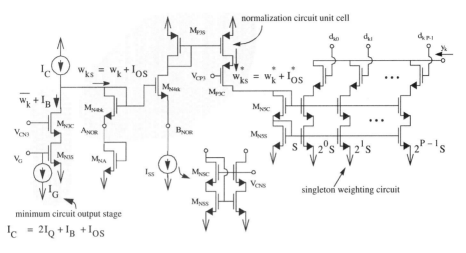

Figure 2.10: Rule Block.

translinear principle does not hold, the circuit is found to realize the following nonlinear transformation:

$$w_{ks}^* = \frac{\beta_{N4t}}{\beta_{N4b}} w_{ks} \left[1 + \frac{\eta(w_s)}{\sqrt{w_{ks}}} \right]^2 \qquad (2.12)$$

where function $\eta(w_s)$ is

$$\eta(w_s) = \frac{\sum\limits_k \sqrt{w_{ks}}}{N} \left(\sqrt{1 + \frac{NI_{SS}' - \sum\limits_k w_{ks}}{\sum\limits_k \sqrt{w_{ks}}^2}} - 1 \right) \qquad (2.13)$$

$$\left(I_{SS}' = \frac{\beta_{N4b}}{\beta_{N4t}} I_{SS} \right)$$

and

$$w_k^* = w_{ks}^* - I_{OS}^* \qquad I_{OS}^* = w_{ks}^*(I_{OS}) \qquad (2.14)$$

The offset current I_{OS} is added to improve the dynamic behavior. Note from Fig.2.10 that it is related to the bias currents in the rule antecedent by

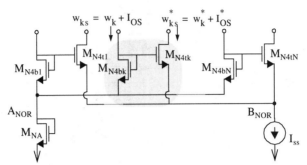

Figure 2.11: Normalization circuit schematics.

$I_{OS} = I_C - 2I_Q - I_B$. Thus, it can be introduced by just increasing current I_C without additional area cost, although it will be preserved in figures and equations to gain clarity.

The circuit in Fig.2.11 exhibits the following features: a) the sum of all output currents is constant and equal to I_{SS}; b) for each input, the input-output transformation is a soft monotonic one, i.e.i, the higher an input current, the higher the corresponding output current. Thus, the relative strengths of the different rule antecedents are preserved at the outputs – as required for defuzzification [1]-[5]. Hence, although this circuit does not realize the ideal normalization operation, it keeps the essential features needed for defuzzification; non-linearity is not problematic because the whole controller chip is highly nonlinear. Actually, system-level analysis shows that, despite this non-linearity, the normalization-plus-weighting defuzzification approach may feature smaller deviations from the linear interpolation than the ideal weighting-plus-division structure [27].

Fig.2.10 employs a digitally-controlled current-mirror (represented at the conceptual level in Fig.2.12(a)) in order to implement a programmable single-ton value y_k^*. As compared to analog-programmed current mirrors [37][45], the digital approach is preferred because it is more robust and accurate, compatible with standard memory circuits and directly controllable through conventional computers.

Regarding the mirror circuitry itself, and because the normalization circuit output stage does not impose major range limitations, a stacked (self-biased) cascode structure is used to minimize errors due to dc mismatching. On the

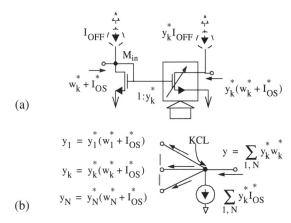

Figure 2.12: (a) Singleton weighting concept; (b) controller output node.

other hand, parallel-connected unit transistors are used to realize the binary weighting and, thus, reduce systematic errors caused by the lack of symmetry. The bias current depicted by the dashed lines in Fig.2.12(a) is added to reduce speed degradations due to the increase of parasitic capacitance for large singleton values.

After singleton weighting, the rule block outputs are wired up to the output node where a current $-\sum_{1, N} y_k^* I_{OS}^*$ is added to remove the offset, thus obtaining equation (2.4).

2.3.2. Modifications for the Multiplexed Architecture

The architecture of the analog core in Fig.2.5 is similar to that in Fig.2.2, but just 2^M rules are needed here, and only two membership functions per input. Building blocks are also quite similar to those described above, although we should point out some differences derived from the specific multiplexing strategy. First, as mentioned in Section 2.2.3., only the thick part of the membership functions in Fig.2.4(b) is needed in each interval. Hence, the membership function circuit must be able to generate two pieces with slopes of opposite signs. This is achieved in the simplest way by a differential pair, as Fig.2.13(a) depicts. Moreover, the differential pair provides two complementary curves, which can be exploited to save the explicit complement implementation if we perform the minimum by means of a maximum-plus-complement circuitry regarding De Morgan's law [38]. Fig.2.13(b) shows one high level building block that implements most of the circuitry associated to each input in the first layer of Fig.2.2. The proposed implementation has voltages as inputs, while

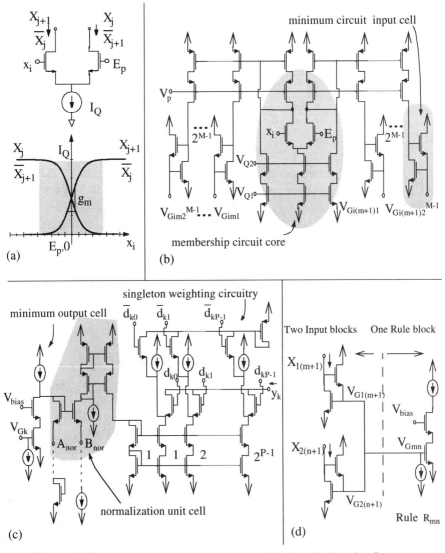

Figure 2.13: Analog Core Implementation; (a) Membership Function Generation, (b) Input Block, (c) Rule Block, and (d) Interface.

further processing is made in current mode. Current outputs of the differential pair are replicated to generate the 2^M outputs required to implement the 2^M rules that determine the output inside a specific interval. Such currents are converted into voltages by the minimum circuit input unit cell that is shaded in Fig.2.13(b). The 2^M voltage outputs of this block are attached to those provided by the remaining input blocks. As a result, 2^M rule antecedents are implemented. The voltage outputs of these antecedents feed 2^M rule blocks like those depicted in Fig.2.13(c). Circuitry in Fig.2.13(c) implements the blocks in the second layer of Fig.2.2. Fig.2.13(d) shows an example interface to build rule R_{mn} in Fig.2.4. In the example of Fig.2.4, we need two input blocks, which provide four voltage outputs each (note that the differential pair outputs are replicated to share the circuit and save area and power consumption). To build rule R_{mn}, outputs $V_{G1(m+1)}$ and $V_{G2(n+1)}$, corresponding to membership functions $X_{1(m+1)}$ and $X_{2(n+1)}$, are connected to the minimum output cell of the rule block associated to R_{mn}. Fig.2.13(d) is in fact a minimum circuit where the complement at input is saved because the complements are directly provided. Note that $X_{1(m+1)}$ and $X_{2(n+1)}$ are the complements of X_{1m} and X_{2n} respectively in the interpolation interval C_{mn} of Fig.2.4.

With respect to the high level block in Fig.2.13(c), it is very similar to the rule block described in Section 2.3.1., but two main differences are worthy of comment. The first refers to the design of the normalization circuit in Fig.2.11. Although the implementation for the new architecture has the same topology, the transistors are sized taking into account the multiplexing strategy. To understand this, see Fig.2.12(b) and note that an offset that depends on the singleton values associated to the rule set has to be removed at the output node. Since the core in Fig.2.5 is multiplexed, the singleton values set $y_1^* \ldots y_1^* \ldots y_{2^M}^*$ changes from one interpolation interval to the other; thus the offset also varies as a function of the input. It could be solved by properly programming the offset current source in Fig.2.12(b), as done with other circuitry in the analog core. However, a simpler solution is achieved by designing the normalization circuit in such a way that when an output of the normalization circuit is at maximum, the remaining ones are zero; thus there is no residual offset to be weighted by the output singleton-weighting mirror. This is accomplished by designing the circuit to work beyond its differential range associated to one input. If one input current in Fig.2.11 increases while the others are kept constant, the top transistor for the changing current will eventually drive all the current I_{SS}, and the other top transistors will be cut off. The differential input range obtained from this fact is:

$$0 \leq w_k \leq \beta_{N4b}\left(\sqrt{\frac{I_{OS}}{\beta_{N4b}}} + \sqrt{\frac{I_{ss}}{\beta_{N4t}}}\right)^2 - I_{OS} \tag{2.15}$$

where we have considered that the set of fuzzy rules is consistent [38], i.e., when an input is at maximum, the remaining ones are zero. The reader may possibly wonder why this methodology is not followed to design the rule block in the Section 2.3.1. The reason is to improve the dynamic response, by avoiding excessively small currents in the output branches. In the design of Fig.2.13(c), degradation of the dynamic response is prevented by introducing and removing a constant current offset at input and output branches respectively of the normalization and singleton-weighting circuits. This could be realized in the rule block, but with a higher circuit complexity.

The second main difference between Fig.2.10 and Fig.2.13(c) refers to the singleton circuitry, which is slightly different. Since such a cell is set up dynamically by the digital word $d_{k0}...d_{kP-1}$, the changes of this word generate transitories in the output current that look like quite large glitches. The main cause of such glitches is the current demanded by branches that do not contribute to the output current, whose transistors work in the ohmic region, when they are selected again to report some current to the output. A proposed solution keeps all transistors in saturation by providing an alternative current path through current switches driven by the complementary control signals $\bar{d}_{k0}...\bar{d}_{kP-1}$. A higher power consumption is, again, the price to pay for a better dynamic behavior. The global system output is obtained by aggregating the outputs of the rule blocks,

$$y = \sum_{k=1...2^L} y_k \tag{2.16}$$

which is realized just by attaching the rule block output nodes, because the rule block outputs are currents.

2.4. A/D Converters, Interval Selector and Digital Memory

2.4.1. A/D Converters

Many possible implementations of A/D converters have been reported and could be used for this block. However, since a resolution of $i_s(\log_2 L)$ bits is required and L (number of labels) is rarely higher than seven, a simple and fast flash converter like the one depicted in Fig.2.14(a) can be used. Although it is a common flash converter, some implementation details are worthy of comment here. First, the array of linear resistors generates twice the voltage levels needed for the A/D conversion. The "extra" voltage levels are used as programming values for the rule antecedent; thus they are a kind of analog read only memory. Note also that this array of resistors can be shared by all the converters (one per input) as long as the comparators have high impedance inputs. Secondly, these comparators are designed to have hysteresis, which is needed to filter the noise associated to the system inputs and to avoid an unstable out-

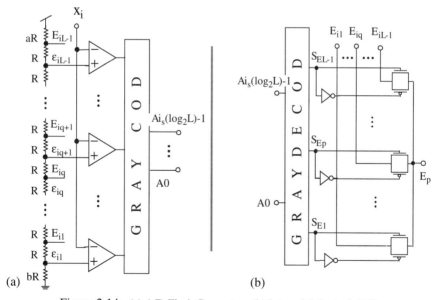

Figure 2.14: (a) A/D Flash Converter ; (b) Interval Selector k Cell.

put due to unstable programming inputs to the analog core. Finally, a Gray coder converts the thermometer scale into Gray code. Such an output code is used to minimize the transitions between logical values '0' and '1' in the interconnection lines, which avoids risks of spurious data due to the asynchronous operation and minimizes the noise injected in the remaining circuitry from these lines.

2.4.2. Interval Selector

The interval selector block is basically an analog bus whose analog data $E_1, ..., E_i, ... E_M$ are selected digitally from the set of reference voltages generated by the linear resistor array in Fig.2.14(a), $E_{i1}, ... E_{iL-1}$. Fig.2.14(b) shows one of the M cells (one per input) that constitute this block. A Gray decoder provides the control signals that drive the transmission gates from the digital word associated to a specific interpolation interval and supplied by the A/D converters.

2.4.3. Digital Memory

The digital word of $M \times i_s(\log_2 L)$ bits provided by the A/D converters and associated to each interval in the input space is used to address a digital memory. This memory must provide the singleton values needed to generate the output in each interval. Thus, the memory must provide a word of $2^M \times P$ bits, where P is the number of bits per singleton value and 2^M is the number of singleton values necessary to program the analog core. It is very important to note that the order of these singleton values inside the word must fulfill the programming requirements of the analog core. To explain this, let us show the simple case of Fig.2.15(a), where the words needed to program the analog core in two adjacent intervals share two singleton values (y_{mn}^* and $y_{m(n+1)}^*$), but these singleton values appear in a different order in these words. A possible strategy to implement the memory consists in storing one word for each interval with the singleton values associated to it in the proper location. However, this implies replicating each singleton value as many times as intervals are related to it, which is 2^M. A second strategy organizes the data properly and multiplexes the memory output bus to avoid redundancy, which is the strategy

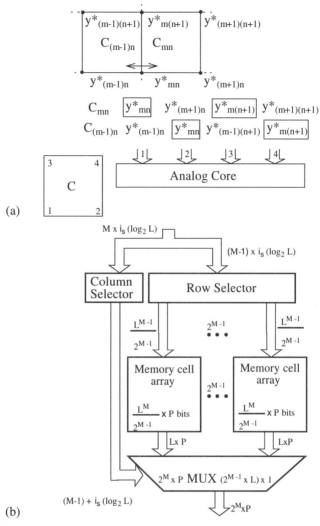

Figure 2.15: Digital Memory: (a) Analog Core Memory Interface; (b) Digital Memory architecture.

followed by the example controller of this chapter. The multiplexing is not carried out in time; the required data is put in the output bus in one step.

Fig.2.15(b) shows the proposed memory architecture that follows the latter approach. Singleton values are distributed into 2^{M-1} memory cell arrays of

$L^{M-1}/2^{M-1}$ rows and L columns. Every memory cell array stores pairs of singleton values which need to be addressed simultaneously. The row selector selects 2^{M-1} rows simultaneously, one for each memory cell array, to provide a set of $L \times 2^{M-1}$ singleton values. The column selector selects the correct singleton values from this set, and controls the multiplexor in order to place them in the right location to form the $2^M \times P$ output word, all in one step. To illustrate the data distribution and memory operation let us show the situation for a bi-dimensional case. Fig.2.16(a) shows four generic adjacent intervals $C_{mn}, C_{(m-1)n}, C_{(m-1)(n-1)}, C_{m(n-1)}$ with their associated singleton values. These values are distributed into two memory cell arrays as the top of Fig.2.16(b) shows. Memory cell array 1 contains the rows with odd n index, while memory cell array 2 contains the rows with even n index. Both arrays have L columns. Below these arrays in Fig.2.16(b) the result of a row selection is shown for the four intervals in Fig.2.16(a). All the singleton values needed to program the analog core (enclosed in squares in the figure) are in the resulting word. Finally, the column selector selects these singleton values and places them in the output bus. Note that each singleton value appears in the right location (see Fig.2.16(a)). Although somewhat tricky for internal accesses, the memory is configured as a conventional RAM for external accesses.

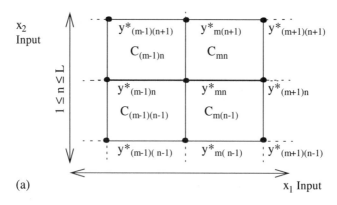

(a)

Figure 2.16: Caption on next page.

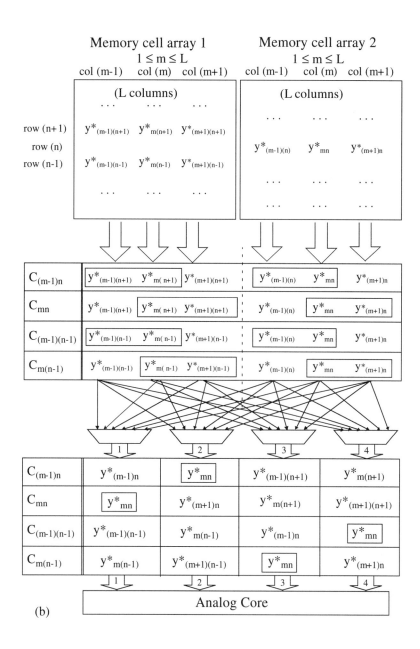

Figure 2.16: Memory operation example.

2.5. Learning Capability

The design strategy followed in the proposed chip is intended to provide a controller which is quite simple from the user's point of view. The resulting uniform lattice partition is common in control applications, thus the chip is easy to program. On the other hand, since the tunable parameter set does not include the location, width or slope of the membership functions, a higher number of rules is needed to approximate a surface with the same accuracy of a fully tunable controller. It is demonstrated that the approximation error depends on the smoothness of the target surface and the number of labels in a given interval [38]. In addition, a quantization error is caused by the limited number of bits of a singleton word (P in Fig.2.5). Provided that the controller can approximate the targeted surface with a sufficient precision, two possible approaches give the programming singleton set, the program approach and the learning approach, which are described in the following.

2.5.1. Program Approach

This approach is recommended when the function to be approximated $y = f(x)$ is well known in the whole input space, and when it is easy to obtain the input-output data pairs associated to the rule cores. The core of the i-th rule is the input region where $w_i^*(x) = 1$; thus, if we know the target output $y = y_d(x)$ for every rule core in the knowledge base, it is possible to derive the singleton values as

$$y_i^* = f(x) \qquad \text{for} \quad w_i^*(x) = 1 \quad \text{and} \quad i = 1, \ldots N \qquad (2.17)$$

where we assume that the target function does not change much inside the rule cores.

2.5.2. Learning Approach

When the function to be approximated is not well known, but it is a collection of input-output data pairs that are not necessarily distributed uniformly along the input space and do not include those pairs related to the rule cores, it is still possible to obtain the singleton values through learning procedures.

As mentioned above, the rule antecedent can be figured out as a multidimensional membership function. This circumstance allows us to recast the architecture in Fig.2.5 in a more general way, as Fig.2.17(a) depicts, where the membership functions are supposed normalized (Fig.2.17(b)). This point of view coincides with others in the artificial intelligent field, where we can find adequate learning rules. Specifically, the functional equivalence between the RBFN and the algorithm implemented in [4][39][40] has been demonstrated. Learning in these networks is realized in two steps [41]:

- Learning of the first layer (nonlinear)
- Learning of the output layer (linear)

Since the architecture in Fig.2.5 has a fixed partition of the input space (see Fig.2.4), there are no tunable parameters in the first layer, and the second layer is the only one which needs to be trained.

Suppose we have a set of K training input-output data pairs $\{x, y_d(x)\}$. If we introduce these pairs in (2.4), we get K equations and K unknown quantities which are the singleton values. For the controller in Fig.2.5, we can write it as:

$$Y_d = W^* Y^* \tag{2.18}$$

where Y_d is the column vector of dimension K which contains the K outputs provided in the training pairs, W^* is the $K \times N$ matrix which contains the outputs from the N multidimensional membership functions for every training pair, and Y^* is the column vector which contains the singleton values to determine $(y_1^*, \dots y_i^* \dots y_N^*)$. The best solution for (2.18) estimates the mimimum

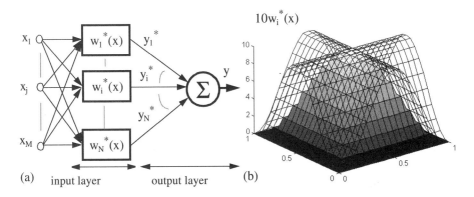

(a) input layer   output layer   (b)

Figure 2.17: (a) Two-layer architecture of a fuzzy controller; (b) normalized rule antecedent output.

least square error (LSE) $\left\| W^* Y^* - Y_d \right\|^2$ and is given by:

$$Y^* = (W^{*T} W^*)^{-1} W^{*T} Y_d \tag{2.19}$$

which can be computed in a recursive way [42][5].

The previous algorithm is a batch procedure, where the parameters (singletons) are updated from the whole training set. A simpler alternative is the incremental LMS rule, where the parameters are updated every time an input-output pair is presented [41],

$$y^*_{inew} = y^*_{iold} + \mu[y_d(x) - y(x)] w^*_i(x) \qquad i = 1, \dots N \tag{2.20}$$

where μ is a constant. It is interesting to note that (2.20) is also obtained from a gradient rule [43]. Note that the membership grade of input x to the fuzzy set whose singleton is being updated is taken into account by weighting the increment by $w^*_i(x)$. The closer the input is to the fuzzy set core, the larger the value of $w^*_i(x)$; thus the singleton is tuned depending on its influence on the output. Another way to consider such dependence consists in updating only the singleton whose associated rule antecedent is maximum, thus:

$$y^*_{inew} = y^*_{iold} + \mu(y_d(x) - y(x)) \tag{2.21}$$

where i is the index of the rule so that $w^*_i(x) = $ $= \max[w^*_1(x), w^*_2(x), \dots w^*_N(x)]$. This is certainly the outstar incremental rule, which is employed to train the Grossberg layer in the counterpropagation network. The latter is intended to be used for clustering purposes, but can also approximate functions [44]. The principle is just the same as in the general architecture in Fig.2.17, but in this network the sets in the first layer (Kohonen's layer) are crisp instead of fuzzy. The simplicity of the rule in (2.21) makes it a good candidate for silicon implementation; thus we have chosen it to demonstrate its viability.

The parameter μ in (2.21) determines the learning speed. Since we will have a minimum increment $\Delta y^*_{imin} = (y^*_{inew} - y^*_{iold})_{min}$ for the updated singleton value due to the limited resolution, this constant must be selected to fulfill:

$$\mu \geq \frac{\Delta \overset{*}{y}_{imin}}{\varepsilon_{ymin}} \tag{2.22}$$

where $\varepsilon_{ymin} = |y_d(x) - y(x)|_{min}$ is the minimum deviation of the output from the target which can be translated into an increment in the singleton value. In other words, beyond this minimum value the learning process stops and the parameters (singletons) are not updated anymore.

In order to illustrate how this simple learning procedure performs, we trained a controller (a software model) with a lattice partition of the input space, and six labels per input uniformly distributed along the input space. The input-output training samples were obtained from the function $y = 2 + \sin(\pi x_1)\sin(\pi x_2)$, up to 11×11 samples to cover the input interval $[0, 2] \times [0, 2]$. Then we trained the network with the outstar rule in (2.21), thus only the singleton values were updated from the initial value of 1 for all of them. The results are shown in Fig.2.18. Fig.2.18(a) shows the target function, which is built from the matrix sample data, while Fig.2.18(b) shows the output of the controller after 500 epochs (the whole sample set has been used 500 times to train the network). The final RMSE was 0.067 and the RMSE evolution is depicted in Fig.2.18(d) while the final error $y_d(x) - y(x)$ is shown in Fig.2.18(c). Furthermore, we later considered the limited resolution for the

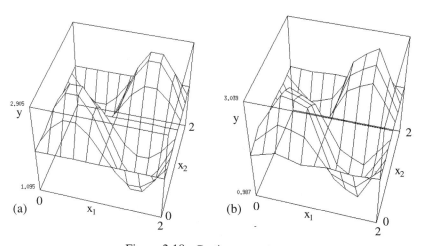

Figure 2.18: Caption on next page.

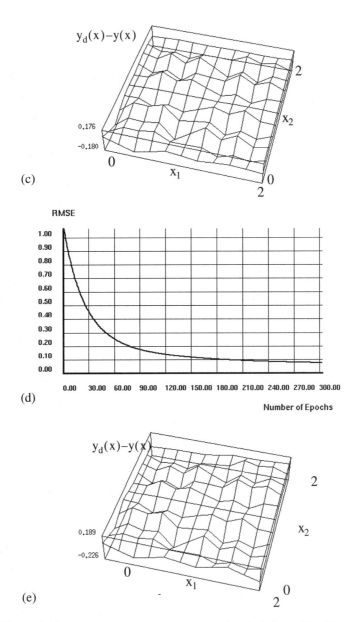

Figure 2.18: Learning example: (a) Target surface built from 11×11 samples; (b) learned surface with the outstar rule from a lattice partition and six labels per input ; (c) error surface; (d) RMSE curve; (e) error surface with truncated singletons (4 bits).

singleton values, hence we truncated the singleton values obtained to represent them with just four bits of resolution. The resulting RMSE was 0.078 and the error surface is that shown in Fig.2.18(e).

2.6. Results and Conclusions

An example 64-rule, 2-input, 4-bit singleton controller ($L = 8$, $M = 2$ and $P = 4$) has been designed in a CMOS 0.7μm technology to demonstrate the viability of the multiplexed architecture in Fig.2.5. Fig.2.19(a) shows a microphotograph of the chip, while Fig.2.19(b) shows the block diagram of a prototype board that has been designed for it. The latter comprises the circuitry needed to build the bias current sources, and the circuitry needed to interface to an 8255/8253 I/O Card for a PC. The PC interface provides read and write access to program the chip memory. It also provides write access to the D/A converters and read access to the A/D converter; thus the board works as a simplified data acquisition board. In addition, a TEKTRONIX TDS 520 digitizing oscilloscope is used to measure the dynamic response as well as to obtain sections of the dc control surface.

Fig.2.20 shows some experimental results obtained from this test environment. Fig.2.20(a) and Fig.2.20(b) depict the section of an example dc control surface and the transient response to a step input, respectively, both measured with the oscilloscope. The former illustrates the response (bottom) to a ramp in one input (top), while the other input remains constant, in a kind of Mexican-hat surface. The latter corresponds to a falling edge in one input which forces the output to change from its maximum to its minimum value, as well as to jump to a different interpolation interval, which means a dynamic programming of the analog core. The measured delay time is around 500ns. Since the oscilloscope is not able to sense currents, previous measurements are voltages in the output y_V (see Fig.2.19(b)). With regard to Fig.2.20(c) and Fig.2.20(d), they are built with data from the acquisition data board in Fig.2.19(b), where the current output of the chip is externally converted into a digital word and processed. These two examples illustrate the ability of the controller to interpolate nonlinear (Fig.2.20(c)) as well as linear functions (Fig.2.20(d)).

Measured chip power consumption was around 16mW, which is obtained by sensing the current from the supply voltage source. The controller was designed to take into account mismatching among transistors for a standard deviation (σ) associated to the output which equals an error of 3.3%, while the measured errors were around 10%. The latter corresponds to a worst case and

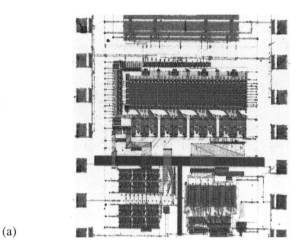

(a)

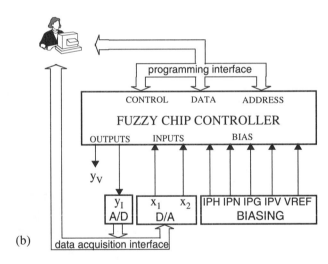

(b)

Figure 2.19: (a) Microphotography of the chip and (b) testing board block diagram.

still fits most control requirements [34].

It is illustrative to compare the speed, area and power of this mixed-signal controller with that of a purely analog one. While the circuit in [12] (designed in a 1μm technology) comprises 16rules with 470ns delay, 8.6mW power consumption and 1.6mm^2 area, the presented controller implements 64rules with almost the same delay, 16mW power and only 2.6mm^2 area. Since the power of this strategy grows with system complexity, let us make some simplifications to highlight such advantage over a fully analog implementation. Let us consider the area and power consumption of the interval selector and A/D converters, which are negligible when compared to that consumed by the analog core and the memory (note that just one array of resistors is needed in the system, no matter how many converters there are). In addition, let us suppose a similar interconnection area (which indeed must be much smaller in the proposed strategy). Since the digital memory has the same size in both implementations, the above assumptions allow us to make an estimation for the area and

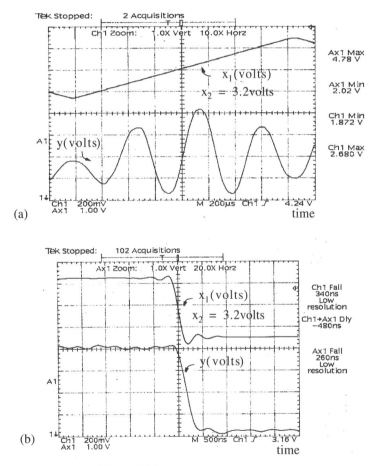

Figure 2.20: Caption on next page.

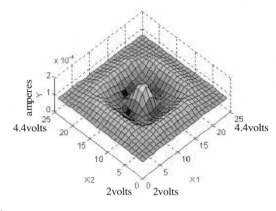

(c)

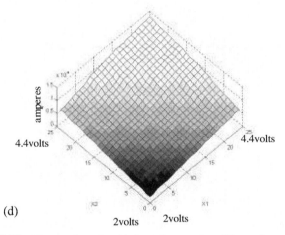

(d)

Figure 2.20:   Measured results: (a) dc surface section; (b) transient response;
(c) nonlinear surface and (d) linear surface.

power savings in the ratio between the total number of rules (L^M) which
should be implemented without multiplexing and the number of active rules
(2^M), which are those physically implemented in the proposal. Such a ratio is
$\alpha = (L/2)^M$ which is strongly dependent on the number of inputs and labels
per input, thus on system complexity. Hence, the higher the value of α, the

more suitable the proposed implementation is. Finally remember that only the implemented rules, i.e., the active rules, contribute to the error at output, which allows the system expansion for a given error bound with respect to a fully analog implementation.

2.7. Acknowledgement

This research has been partially supported by Spanish CICYT under contract TIC99-0826.

2.8. References

[1] J.M. Mendel, "Fuzzy Logic Systems for Engineering: A Tutorial". Proceedings of the IEEE, Vol. 83, pp. 345-377, March 1995.

[2] H. Takagi, "Applications of Neural Networks and Fuzzy Logic to Consumer Products". pp. 8-12 in Fuzzy Logic Technologies and Applications, New-York: IEEE Press 1994.

[3] Marco Russo, "Fuzzy Hardware Research From a Historical Point of View", Chapter 1 in FUZZY HARDWARE Architectures and Applications (edited by Abraham Kandel and Gideon Langholz), pp. 1-25, Kluwer Academic Publishers 1998.

[4] M. Brown and C. Harris, Neuro-Fuzzy Adaptive Modeling and Control. Englewood Cliffs: Prentice-Hall 1994.

[5] J.S.R. Jang and C.T. Sun, "Neuro-Fuzzy Modeling and Control". Proceedings of the IEEE, Vol. 83, pp. 378-406, March 1995.

[6] H. Watanabe, W. D. Dettloff, and K. E. Yount, "A VLSI Fuzzy Logic Controller with Reconfigurable, Cascadable Architecture". IEEE J. Solid-State Circuits, Vol. 25, pp. 376-382, 1990.

[7] K. Nakamura, N. Sakashita, Y. Nitta, K. Shimomura and T.Tokuda, "Fuzzy Inference and Fuzzy Inference Processor". IEEE Micro, Vol. 13, pp. 37-48, October 1993.

[8] H. Eichfeld, M. Klimke, M. Menke, J. Nolles and T. Künemund, "A General-Purpose Fuzzy Inference Processor", IEEE Micro, Vol. 15, pp. 12-17, June 1995.

[9] A. Costa, A. de Gloria, P. Faraboschi, A. Pagni and G. Rizzotto, "Hardware Solutions for Fuzzy Control". Proceedings of the IEEE, Vol. 83, pp. 422-434, March 1995.

[10] M. Masetti, E. Gandolfi, A. Gabrieli and F. Boschetti, "4 Input VLSI

Fuzzy Chip Design able to process an Input Data Set every 320ns". Proc. of the JCIS'95, Wrightsville Beach, North Carolina, USA, October 1995.

[11] Marco Russo, "Designing a Simple System to Greatly Accelerate the Learning Speed of a Large Class of Fuzzy Learning Methods", Chapter 10 in FUZZY HARDWARE Architectures and Applications (edited by Abraham Kandel and Gideon Langholz), pp. 207-229, Kluwer Academic Publishers 1998.

[12] A. Rodríguez-Vázquez, R. Navas, M. Delgado-Restituto and F. Vidal, "A Modular Programmable CMOS Analog Fuzzy Controller Chip". IEEE Trans. Circuits and Systems - II, Vol. 46, pp. 251-265, March 1999.

[13] J.W.Fattaruso, S.S. Mahant-Shetti, and J.B. Barton, "A Fuzzy Logic Inference Processor". IEEE Journal of Solid-State Circuits, Vol. 29, pp. 397-402, April 1994.

[14] J. L. Huertas, S. Sánchez-Solano, I. Baturone, and A. Barriga, "Integrated Circuit Implementation of Fuzzy Controllers". IEEE Journal of Solid-State Circuits, Vol. 31, pp. 1051-1058, July 1996.

[15] L. Lemaître, M. J. Patyra, and D. Mlynek, "Analysis and Design of CMOS Fuzzy Logic Controller in Current Mode". IEEE Journal of Solid-State Circuits, Vol. 29, pp. 317-322, March 1994.

[16] N.Manaresi, R. Rovatti, E. Franchi, R. Guerrieri, and G. Baccarani, "A Silicon Compiler of Analog Fuzzy Controllers: From Behavioral Specifications to Layout". IEEE Trans. on Fuzzy Systems, Vol. 4, pp. 418-428, November 1996.

[17] S. Guo, L. Peters, and H. Surmann, "Design and Application of an Analog Fuzzy Logic Controller". IEEE Trans. on Fuzzy Systems, Vol. 4, pp. 429-438, November 1996.

[18] F. Vidal-Verdú and A. Rodríguez-Vázquez, "Learning under Hardware Restrictions in CMOS Fuzzy Controllers able to Extract Rules from Examples". Proc of IFSA'95, pp. 189-192, Sao Paulo, Brazil, July 1995.

[19] A. Rodríguez-Vázquez, M. Delgado-Restituto and F. Vidal, "Synthesis and Design of Nonlinear Circuits", Chapter 32 in the The Circuits and Filters Handbook (edited by Wai-Kai Chen), pp. 935-972, CRC Press 1996.

[20] A. Rodríguez-Vazquez and M. Delgado-Restituto, "CMOS Design of Chaotic Oscillators using State Variables: A Monolithic Chua's Circuit". IEEE Transactions on Circuits and Systems-II, Vol. 40, pp. 596-613, October 1993.

[21] A. Rodríguez-Vázquez and M. Delgado-Restituto, "Generation of Chaotic Signals using Current-Mode Techniques". Journal of Intelligent and

Fuzzy Systems, Vol. 2, pp. 15-37, 1994.

[22] T. Kettner, C. Heite, and K. Schumacher, "Analog CMOS Realization of Fuzzy Logic Membership Functions". IEEE Journal of Solid-State Circuits, Vol. 28, pp. 857-861, July 1993.

[23] M. Sasaki, N. Ishikawa, F. Ueno and T. Inoue, "Current-Mode Analog Fuzzy Hardware with Voltage Input Interface and Normalization Locked Loop". IEICE Trans. Fundamentals, Vol. E75-A, pp. 650-654, June 1992.

[24] J.W. Fattaruso and R.G. Meyer, "MOS Analog Function Synthesis". IEEE Journal of Solid-State Circuits, Vol. 22, pp. 1059-1063. Dec. 1987.

[25] A. Rodríguez-Vázquez and F. Vidal, "Analog CMOS Design of Singleton Fuzzy Controllers". The Third International Conference on Industrial Fuzzy Control Intelligent Systems, December 1993.

[26] Y. Tsividis, Mixed Analog-Digital VLSI Devices and Technology. New-York: McGraw-Hill 1996.

[27] F. Vidal, Design of Mixed-Signal CMOS Neuro-Fuzzy Controllers. PhD Dissertation, University of Málaga, 1996.

[28] M. Sasaki, T. Inoue, Y. Shirai and F. Ueno, "Fuzzy Multiple-Input Maximum and Minimum Circuits in Current Mode and Their Analyses Using Bounded Difference Equations". IEEE Transactions on Computers, Vol. 39, pp. 768-774, June 1990.

[29] T. Yamakawa and T. Miki, "The Current Mode Fuzzy Logic Integrated Circuits Fabricated by the Standard CMOS Process". IEEE Transactions on Computers. Vol. C-35, pp. 161-167, February 1986.

[30] J. Lazzaro, R. Ryckebusch, M. A. Mahowald, and C. A. Mead, "Winner-take-all networks of O(n) complexity". Advances in Neural Information Processing Systems, (D. S. Touretzky, Ed.), Vol. 1, Los Altos, CA: Morgan Kaufmann, 1989.

[31] C. Y. Huang and B.D. Liu, "Current-Mode Multiple-Input Maximum Circuit for Fuzzy Logic Controllers". Electronics Letters, Vol. 30, pp. 1924-1925, 1994.

[32] C. Mead, Analog VLSI and Neural Systems Addison Wesley 1989.

[33] B. Gilbert, "Current-Mode Circuits from a Translinear View Point: A Tutorial". in Analogue IC Design: The Current-Mode Approach, C. Toumazou, F. J. Lidgey, and D. G. Haigh, (Eds.), London: Peter Peregrinus Ltd. 1990.

[34] T. Miki, H. Matsumoto, K. Ohto and T. Yamakawa, "Silicon Implementation for a Novel High-Speed Fuzzy Inference Engine: Mega-Flips Analog Fuzzy Processor". Journal of Intelligent and Fuzzy Systems, Vol. 1,

No. 1, pp. 27-42, 1993.

[35] V. Catania, A. Puliafito, M.Russo, and L. Vita, "A VLSI Fuzzy Inference Processor Based on a Discrete Analog Approach". IEEE Transactions on Fuzzy Systems, Vol. 2, No. 2, pp. 93-106, May 1994.

[36] K. Tsukano and T. Inoue, "Synthesis of Operational Transconductance Amplifier-Based Analog Fuzzy Functional Blocks and Its Application". IEEE Transactions on Fuzzy Systems, Vol. 3, pp. 61-68, February 1995.

[37] M. Sasaki and F. Ueno, "A VLSI Implementation of Fuzzy Logic Controller using Current Mode CMOS Circuits". The Third International Conference on Industrial Fuzzy Control Intelligent Systems, pp. 215-220, December 1993.

[38] Li-Xin Wang, A Course in Fuzzy Systems and Control Prentice-Hall 1997.

[39] J.S. R. Jang and C. T. Sun, "Functional Equivalence Between Radial Basis Function Networks and Fuzzy Inference Systems", IEEE Transactions on Neural Networks, Vol. 4, No. 1, pp. 156-159, January 1993.

[40] D. F. Specht, "A General Regression Neural Networks", IEEE Transactions on Neural Networks, Vol. 2, No. 6, November 1991.

[41] D. R. Hush and B. G. Horne, "Progress in Supervised Neural Networks", IEEE Signal Processing Magazine, pp. 8-39, January 1993.

[42] J. E. Perkins, I. M. Y. Mareels and J. B. Moore, "Functional Learning in Signal Processing Via Least Squares", International Journal of Adaptive Control and Signal Processing , Vol. 6, pp. 481-498, 1992.

[43] J. Nie and D. A. Linkens, "Learning Control Using Fuzzified Self-Organizing Radial Basis Function Network", IEEE Transactions on Fuzzy Systems, Vol. 1, No. 4, pp. 280-287, November 1993.

[44] J. M. Zurada, "Introduction to Artificial Neural Systems". West Publishing 1992.

[45] A. Rodríguez-Vázquez, S. Espejo, R. Domínguez-Castro and J.L. Huertas, "Current Mode Techniques for the Implementation of Continuous and Discrete-Time Cellular Neural Networks". IEEE Transactions on Circuits and Systems-II, Vol. 40, pp. 132-146, IEEE March 1993.

3

Fuzzy Modeling in a Multi-Agent Framework for Learning in Autonomous Systems

Juan A.Botía

Humberto Martínez
Barberá

Antonio F.Gómez
Skármeta
*Dep. Informática, Inteligencia
Artificial and Electrónica - Facultad de
Informática - Universidad de Murcia,
E-30001 Murcia, Spain*

Fuzzy Modeling in a Multi-Agent Framework for Learning in Autonomous Systems

Abstract

This chapter is on fuzzy modeling in a multi-agent framework for learning in autonomous systems. A number of learning techniques are proposed in intelligent agents environment.

3.1   Introduction

In recent years, fuzzy modeling, as a complement to the conventional modeling techniques, has become an active research topic and found successful applications in many areas. However, most fuzzy models are presently built based only on operator's experience and knowledge, but when a process is complex there may not be an expert available [60]. In this kind of situation the use of unsupervised learning techniques is of fundamental importance. The problem can be stated as follows. Given a set of data for which we presume some functional dependency, the question arises whether there is a suitable methodology to derive (fuzzy) rules from the data that characterize the unknown function as precisely as possible. Recently, several approaches have been proposed for automatically generating fuzzy if-then rules from numerical data without domain experts [38].

As we attempt to solve real-world problems, we realize that they are typically ill-defined systems, difficult to model and with large-scale solution spaces. In these cases precise models are impractical, too expensive, or non-existent. The relevant available information is usually in the form of empirical prior knowledge and input-output data representing instances of the system's behavior. Therefore, we need approximate reasoning systems capable of handling such imperfect information. The term **Soft Computing** describes the combination of different emerging computing disciplines, within which we have fuzzy logic, probabilistic reasoning, neural networks and genetic algorithms. In many situations the use of only one of these multiple possible approximate techniques is not practical. We need the collaboration between them and this is the approach taken by hybrid systems. Over the past few years we have seen an increasing number of hybrid algorithms, in which two or more soft computing technologies have been integrated to improve the overall algorithm performance [11].

Those hybrid systems are composed of several different and interchangeable techniques. The best combination of such techniques may vary from problem to problem. This leads us to the idea of a multiple loosely coupled co-processing distributed system. Each technique can be developed as a system component and encapsulated to offer a homogeneous interface in a distributed environment. Mechanisms apt for intelligent cooperation among these components (agents) should be supported to allow the design and implementation of cooperative distributed applications.

In this chapter we propose the use of intelligent agents which collaborate by means of a multiagent architecture, as a framework to investigate different learning techniques in a fuzzy modeling context. This approach involving agents, which embody the different problem solving methods, is a potentially useful strategy for enhancing the power of fuzzy modeling systems. Our objective is to show how this framework let us experiment with different techniques in order to select the combination that better approximated the system behavior.

3.2 Fuzzy Modeling and Agents

In recent times, several different techniques, which may be subsumed in the frame of Soft-computing, have appeared in the literature related with fuzzy modeling. Thus we find proposals that include fuzzy neural networks [58], and fuzzy subset theory combined with descent gradient techniques [62], or with clustering techniques [63, 62, 8], etc.... Recently combinations of those techniques have been used to try to solve different problems related with systems modeling [60, 55].

Fuzzy modeling is an approach used to form a fuzzy systems model. In fuzzy modeling, the most important problem is the identification method of a system. The identification of a fuzzy model using input-output data such as the ones we are concerned with consists of two aspects: structure identification and parameter identification [54]. Fuzzy modeling is based on the idea of finding a set of local input-output relations describing a process. So it is expected that the method of fuzzy modeling can express a nonlinear process better than an ordinary method. A fuzzy model consists of a number of fuzzy if-then rules. There are two parts in a fuzzy rule: the premise and the consequent part. These parts are formed by the combination of fuzzy sets defined in the different domains of the variables. Each input-output relation is described by a fuzzy rule. The fuzzy rules are formed by partitioning, in a fuzzy way, the input spaces and associating to each of them a consequent expression that could be a fuzzy set, a linear relation, or a singleton value. Therefore, the premise of a fuzzy rule indicates a fuzzy subspace of the input variables to which a relation with the output variables can be established.

The structure identification consists of the premise structure identification and the consequent structure identification. When we consider a MISO (Multiple Input, Single Output) system, the structure identification of a system has to find the input variables which affect the output from a collection of possible variables. Once the variables are identified the structure identification is concerned with the input-output relations identification. This is one of the most crucial problems in the fuzzy modeling, and it is concerned with the identification of an optimal number of fuzzy partitions of the input space, where the number of fuzzy subspace corresponds to that of the number of fuzzy rules. The parameter identification is concerned with the identification of the parameters of the membership functions of the fuzzy sets that are used in the fuzzy rules. In many cases some form of parameter identification is performed within the structure identification, and then a tuning parameter identification is separately performed after the structure identification [54].

In the context of fuzzy modeling, the use of clustering based techniques has had a great success. The objective of this clustering is to detect the behaviors present in the data obtained in a system under observation with no other additional information (to perform a process of fuzzy modeling through a set of fuzzy rules). Some different approximate and descriptive methods have been proposed in [18, 17, 42]. With the results described in those works, what we get is a rule set that is only a first approach to the problem of fuzzy modeling of the system we are studying. The next objective is to approach the problem of optimizing the rules generated using some of the proposed methods. To do so we propose the use of tuning techniques based in the modification of some of the parameters of the fuzzy rules obtained with the clustering techniques and give sense to the creation of hybrid systems applied to fuzzy system modeling.

It is clear that to obtain a good fuzzy model, it is not possible to apply the same kind of techniques to the different problems outlined in the fuzzy modeling process. The need of a combination of alternative and complementary techniques during the structure and parameter identification has shown the possibilities of the use of hybrid systems in fuzzy modeling, and particularly the use of intelligent agents as the component of this hybrid system.

To integrate intelligence there is no recent proposal broadly accepted; so we propose the creation of a MAS (Multi-Agent System) for learning in a fuzzy modeling environment, focusing all this technology with an objective: to develop a distributed software agent group that can collaborate asynchronously among themselves in the most autonomous and efficient possible way.

3.2.1 Distributed Artificial Intelligence(DAI)

DAI has been configured as a term to reference all systems that show some kind of collective behaviour of particular entities to reach a common and global goal. Those particular entities are the so-called agents. Following [46], we can say that there are three different approaches, corresponding to three different periods of research in AI(Artificial Intelligence), to look at DAI:

- Classic DAI, centered in the collective behaviour rather than in the individual one and understanding that the society formed by particular agents is more important than those individually considered;
- Autonomous DAI, focused in the individual study of agents, but taking into account that they are in a social world, and
- Commercial DAI, centered in the application of classic and autonomous DAI to practical problems of the real world.

Following the classical approach, research has been divided in the following two groups:

- **Distributed Problem Solving** (DPS) tries to solve particular problems using distributed modules(or nodes), and shared knowledge representing the problem.
- **Multi-agent Systems** (MAS) studies the coordination of the behaviours between intelligent and autonomous agents.

The main difference between the two groups is that DPSs are designed taking into account the particular problem from the beginning; so they are, in a sense, *ad hoc* solutions. Indeed, there is often a central coordinator and a preliminary established plan. However, MAS are very general mechanisms that present more autonomy in its particular members and the control is decentralized.

Nowadays, MAS have taken almost all attention among DAI researchers; so DPSs will not be mentioned anymore in this work. Instead, the study will be focused on MAS.

3.2.2 Tasks in MAS Development

The following typical tasks(or problems) have to be undertaken in the development of a MAS:

1. Formulation, description, decomposition and assignation of problems for a group of agents, in order to reach the desired results,

2. design of communication protocols to give the agents the capability to communicate and them to cooperate,

3. design of control mechanism to avoid the agents, make decisions or actions that are not compatible or suitable with the common goal

of the overall system,

4. to make the agents capable of representing and reasoning about actions and the state of other agents in the system,

5. how to detect and resolve conflicts between different points of view in the society of agents, and

6. the use of software engineering techniques to develop the MAS as the software system that it actually should be.

All points mentioned above are critical in the implementation process. However, the last point is very important in order to achieve a suitable software system.

In this engineering process, using an agent-oriented methodology is a necessary requirement, as building a MAS systems is not a trivial task. In section 3.2.3, issues related with agent-oriented methodologies are discussed. Moreover, in the implementation phase of this task, work can be started from scratch, building all necessary software needed to implement the designed agents, although this implies an enormous work to be done. Instead, a MAS platform, or toolkit, can be used for this task. This type of platform is composed of a set of software tools to help in the design and implementation of multi-agent systems. This point will be detailed in section 3.2.4.

3.2.3   An Agent-oriented Methodology

There are two main approaches in engineering methodologies to develop a MAS [35]. Each approach is determined by a particular main stream of influence on the basic concepts framework. The first group comes from extending object oriented methodologies and the second comes from the starting point of knowledge engineering techniques. The particular case in our work has been to use MAS-CommonKADS [35] as a methodology to develop MAS and MAST(Multi-agent Systems Tool) [30] as a software tool to build the whole system. This methodology extends CommonKads [49], that is a knowledge engineering methodology. MAS are, in a sense, knowledge based systems; so it seems natural to build a MAS methodology over it. Developing a system using MAS-CommonKADS is based on the description of the following models:

- Agent Model: describe the agents, in the terms of reasoning capabilities, skills, services, goals, etc.

- Task Model: describe the global task of the problem, its decomposition into subtasks and the correspondence between particular tasks and agents carrying out them.

- Expertise Model: this model focus on the knowledge based part of the problem. It follows the KADS approach that differentiate four types of knowledge: domain, task, inference and problem solving.

- Coordination Model: describe the interactions between agents, i.e., protocols and capabilities. There is a first stage of modeling protocols and a second one to test them in negotiation and self-organization situations.

- Organisation Model: describes the organisation in which the MAS is introduced and also the particular agents and their possible organisational structures.

- Communication Model: for describing the interaction between humans and the system.

- Design model: it is divided into three sub-designs, i.e., application design, architecture design and platform design.

There are a few more interesting methodologies extended from the same Knowledge engineering approach as CommonKADS. A concrete one will be mentioned here: *CoMoAS*. This methodology uses most of the models mentioned above, i.e., Agent, Expertise, Task, Cooperation and Design models. Models of expertise, in MAS-CommonKADS and CoMoMAS, are very similar, and the agent model includes the MAS-CommonKADS communication model and, in some way, its organization model is very similar to a new one in CoMoMAS: the System model.

3.2.4 MAST. The Multi-agent System Toolbox

Once the methodology is described, filling the gap between the design model and the final software product is needed. The concrete platform to be applied on the problem will be described.

Any multi-agent platform has, from the very beginning, a concrete agent model that the designer has to adopt if all features offered by the platform are made to be available. That is: the platform determines the concrete agent's basic capabilities. Hence, the agent model will be introduced first.

3.2.5 The MIX Agent model

In this section, the MIX agent reference model is introduced. MIX [23, 36, 43] is the reference architecture for all systems developed with MAST. This presents two basic models: the **agent model** and the **network model**.

The former sees an agent as a set of elements:

- Services: functionality offered to other agents.

- Goals: functions that an agent performs for self-interest(not as a result of a petition from another agent).

- Resources: information on external resources like services, libraries, ontologies, etc.

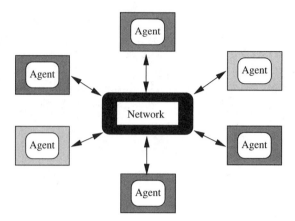

Figure 3.1   Mix Multiagent Model

- Internal Objects: data structures shared by all the processes that can be launched by the agent to carry out service requests or to achieve goals.
- Control: specification of how service requests are handled by the agent.

The network model defines two distinct agent types: network agents that offer network management services and application agents that offer their own services depending on their particular roles. The model is structured in three levels: interface, message and transport layer. The first one offers an API with both C++ and Java that supplies with communication facilities between agents by means of message passing. The second level services are offered to manage both addresses and the intentionality and body of the message. The transport level offers basic functionalities for sending and receiving messages over TCP/IP. The basic architecture is depicted in figure 3.1.

3.2.6   MAST: the Tool for Developing Multi-Agent Systems

MAST [30] is a toolbox for developing distributed processing information systems in an agent oriented fashion. It gives a mechanism to specify individual agents, with both offered and needed services and particular goals. It also incorporates agent group definition, tools for knowledge representation and exchange, and coordination mechanisms between agents.

Defining Agents with MAST

ADL(*Agent Definition Language*) [43, pg. 39-47] is a declarative language integrated into MAST for defining the externals of an agent. Internals of agents shall depend on each particular implementation. Two agents which

share the same ADL definition could be implemented differently and even
with different programming languages. ADL allows us to define agents in
a hierarchical way, using the well known concepts of class and inheritance.
Services offered, goals to achieve, resources needed, internal data structures
and possible policies to apply can be specified with ADL as well. Examples of
agent definitions using ADL can be seen in [43, pg. 73-80]. For the definition
of a concrete agent, the following elements must be declared:

1. Net address of the machine where the YP_agent is located.
2. Default language to be used for writting ontologies.
3. Default ontologies used, in the concrete application domain.
4. C++ libraries used for implementing services offered by the agent.
5. Agents can be organized in a class hierarchy with inheritance, so
   this structure must be specified.

3.2.7 Exchanging Information Objects with MAST

Once we have defined agents that make up the systems, we should be able
to exchange knowledge between them. CKRL(*Common Knowledge Representation Language*) [16] is the language used in MAST for declaring knowledge
objects to be sent, received and managed by agents. It has been developed by
the MLT Consortium under European ESPRIT PROJECT 2154.

3.3 A MAS Architecture for Fuzzy Modeling (MASAM)

In the following section, the MAS architecture for learning in the fuzzy modeling process is described. This architecture has been arranged to serve as
a generic meta-learning mechanism based on agents. Nowadays, this system
has been particularized to a GEneric data MINing System(GEMINIS) [14] in
order to learn what data mining techniques can be suitable for a given learning
task, learning requirements by the user and some data set features. What is
proposed here is the use of this architecture for fuzzy modeling(FM).

In the following, all agents taking some part in the system are presented.

- **User Agents**: they behave as front-ends of the system. Their tasks
  are clearly separated in two groups:

  - **User support tasks** to help the user to manage the avail-
    able modeling techniques, showing information about them,
    upgrading the system with new techniques, removing unsuit-
    able techniques, relocating resources and so on.

  – **Model management tasks** tutoring and providing documentation to the user along the modeling process interactively and complete configuration of the FM process.

• **Automatic Learning Agents(ALA)**: each one of these agents encapsulate one, and only one, learning algorithm. Problems related with encapsulation have been detailed in [13] and in [14]. These software agents are simple wrappers, for those algorithms, encapsulating and isolating their internals. These agents are the main element of the modeling process.

• **Directory Service Agents(DSA)**: number of different FM techniques and configurations for ALAs are potentially unlimited. Hence a mechanism for locating all available ALA must be incorporated into the system, for the shake of scalability. Here is where DSAs come to play. Each one of these agents are in charge of managing its own hierarchical list of available learning agents.

• **Meta-learning Agents(MLA)**: this agent development phase of our system will be in charge of deciding the most suitable configuration of ALAs for each FM session, if the user trusts MASAM for doing it. If the users do not trust MASAM, the FM planning will be obtained directly from the UA. In both cases this agent will make negotiation with the user about other possible configurations and their respective costs. The OMG Trading Service Specification [4] will be used as a base for the implementation of this service.

• **FM Process Control Agent(FMPCA)**: this agent controls the complete FM, once the right ALA, or ALAs planification, has been determined. It is in indirect interaction with the user, through the UA in order to accomplish the iterative nature of the FM process always interactively and with exhaustive information of what is happening (figure 3.3).

• **Logging Agent(LogA)**: logging agents are in charge of accounting and management of performed experiments in order to keep track of the process of FM. Information for accounting comes from:

  – The UA, providing with information about user requests,

  – The FMPCA, that gives information about the actual executed actions for modeling,

  – The ALAs, giving the real dimensions of realized task, depending on the experiment realised,

  – The local DSA, providing with information about interactions with available ALAs.

3.3.1   Agents Architecture

The agents architecture appears at figure 3.2. Two MASAM sites and a user environment appear in it. MASAM sites can be organized over DSAs databases of ALAs, depending on computing environments or even organizations inside different universities or such. To compound a user environment, it is planned that only a Web browser with a Java virtual machine will be needed to access the system. To give some idea of the front-end, different snapshots can be seen in figures 3.3, 3.4 and 3.5. They show a prototypical implementation, done in TCL/TK, of a client and a ALA acting like a wrapper for a backpropagation network [25]. In figure 3.3 the different learning related services that can be called can be seen. For example, in figure 3.4, and after calling `Configuration`, that interface appears in order to configurate the network topology. Once the topology is defined, and after calling `Learning`, the window appearing in figure 3.4 allows the user to configurate typical training parameters for a backpropagation algorithm.

3.3.2   Fuzzy Modeling in our MAS Architecture

Once we have defined the multiagent architecture we return our attention to the learning techniques our agents implement, and that constitute the ALA agents.

We will consider, without losing generality, a MISO system. We want to find a system that approaches the function $\phi: X^p \longrightarrow Y$ that models the system. We have a sample set of the behavior of the system in the space $(X^p \times Y)$, $\omega = ((x_{t1}, x_{t2}, \ldots, x_{tp}), y_t), t = 1, 2, K, n$, where $X_1, X_2, \ldots, X_p$ are the domains of the inputs and Y is the domain of the output. Suppose we have a collection of data that represent the behavior tendencies of the system. We want to obtain a characterization of such behavior using k fuzzy rules that will have this form:

$$R_h: If \ x \ is \ A_h \ then \ y \ is \ B_h, \ h = 1, \ldots, k \qquad (3.1)$$

where A_h and B_h are, respectively, the fuzzy sets in X^p and Y. Once all of those rules have been created (section 3.4 is dedicated to showing how they are created) an inference mechanism can be used for any new input, using approximate reasoning.

We have implemented in our MASAM architecture several different learning agents, using techniques like genetic algorithms, neural networks, fuzzy decision trees, and many others, although we will just describe the learning agents that are significant for the application domain in this chapter. In order to see other combinations see [20] [29].

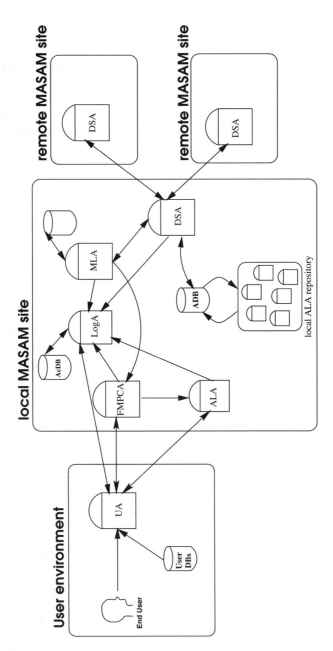

Figure 3.2   Agents Organization in MASAM

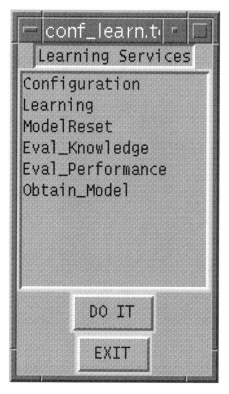

Figure 3.3 Graphic interface of an ALA in MASAM

Figure 3.4　Configuration of a 2-layer ANN inside an ALA

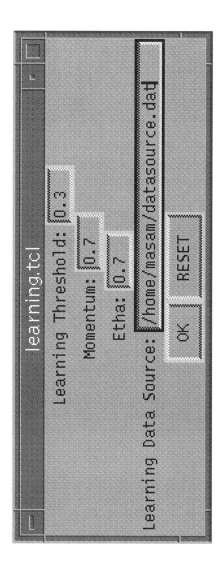

Figure 3.5 Arranging the learning process of a backpropagation newtwork inside an ALA

3.3.3   Fuzzy Clustering: a Central Component for Fuzzy Modeling

In the area of system identification the procedure of fuzzy clustering has been utilized in several modes. In [47] a standard form of the Fuzzy C-Means algorithm is exploited to construct linguistic labels treated as basic chunks of information, although then the construction of the fuzzy model is obtained using fuzzy relational equations; so this kind of technique can be considered the type of templated based models. Fuzzy clusters can also give rise to "local" regression models - this is in fact the essence of the idea introduced originally in [53] [56] and that has been used by others [54, 6, 5]. The overall model is then structured into a series of IF-THEN statements. The condition part of the statement might includes linguistic labels of the input variables, or directly fuzzy relations on the product space of the input variables, while the action part contains a linear (or generally nonlinear) numerical relationship between input and output variables. The clustering method applies to the formation of the condition part.

There are several advantages of the model development techniques based on fuzzy clustering:

- An automatic way of formation of fuzzy sets (fuzzy relations). The clustering techniques are unsupervised learning schemes and as such they do not require any initial knowledge about the structure in the data.

- We can treat all system variables uniformly and develop a fuzzy model in terms of the obtained clusters of data. By doing this the resulting model becomes structure-free and can be exploited from many different points of view. These methods exhibits reversibility, which means that any variable of the model can be accessed with the same level of flexibility.

Fuzzy Clustering in this way can be used in:

- obtaining the fuzzy sets in the product space X^p and in the output space Y - in this case if we have no information about a partition of the output space,

- obtaining the tendencies of the data in the product space of the behaviour $(X^p \times Y)$, so these tendencies can serve to assign a weight to the fuzzy rules that can be generated considering the different combinations of fuzzy sets detected in the input space X^p and the output space Y.

Once we have the possible rules with a weight assigned to them, it is possible to obtain first a description of the model considering the projection in each domain of discourse of the fuzzy sets that correspond to the fuzzy clusters found in the input product space, and if it is neccesary making a linguistic approximation if we want a qualitative model using a collection of predefined linguistic values. Using this approach we can reduce the solution search space, as we do not need to consider the amount of possible fuzzy rules as would be neccesary if we work with the collection of fuzzy sets defined in each domain of the input variables, although we can express in any case the model obtain using them. Moreover, as the model must be validate, by the expert, what is more important in the first step is to try to obtain a prototype model in a rapid way. So then this preliminary model can be tuned and pruned in as later step. It is important to note that, as we are obtaining an initial model, the methods we consider must be as simple as possible but with a good approximative capacity as well.

3.4 Clustering Agents

We present some of the different clustering agents that our multi-agent architecture can integrate. We have implemented in MASAM fuzzy clustering agents like the classical fuzzy C-Means algorithm [9], and several variants of it. Next we will explain two of these variants.

In any case we consider that we know, in some way, the existence of k clusters in the data. In this chapter we are not considering how the correct number of fuzzy cluster is obtained. In several papers the number of rules is decided by cluster validation using some of the validity measures present in the literature. We have made the use of preprocessing of the data by means of a Hierarchical Clustering over the data, where we can study and select the better partitions of the data [19]. Moreover these partitions then can serve as initialization of the fuzzy clustering algorithm, obtaining in this way a better performance of the algorithm.

We do not need to know any other information of the data structure (for example, linearity or non-linearity). We will use a clustering algorithm to find k centroids. An important aspect to stand out is that the clustering process is performed over the input and output product space. The objective of this process is, as is shown in several works [40, 41], to perform a better detection of the clusters that exists in the data. This is not only because the interactivity between input product spaces is taken into account but also the consequences of its interrelation with the output space. So the clustering will be performed over the $(X^p \times Y)$, that is, we will also take into account the output values of the examples. In this way, we will obtain k centroids C_h with this form $(c_{h_1}, c_{h_2}, \ldots, c_{h_p}, c_{h_{p+1}})$, $h = 1, 2, \ldots, k$, where $c_{h_1}, c_{h_2}, \ldots, c_{h_p}$ belong, respectively, to the domain $X_1, X_2, \ldots, X_p$ and $c_{h_{p+1}}$ belongs to the domain of Y.

3.4.1   Fuzzy LVQ

This method gets as input a set of pairs of input and output values. Our objective is to perform a data clustering, and be able to detect in this way the associated centroids to the different detectable clusterings. We have used a modified version of the classical Kohonen self-organizative algorithm as proposed in [58]. So in each loop it is not only the *winner* centroid or the closest to the learning sample that is modified, but a set of centroids of the vicinity. Vicinity will decrease when the number of iterations increases. The method works in this way. We first generate k random centroids inside the data space. Then, for each input sample x_t we measure the Euclidean distance between each center $c_i(t), i = 1, 2, \ldots, k$, and that input sample $x(t)$ and then select the closest *winner* center $c_c(t)$ according to $\| x(t) - c_c(t) \| = \min_i \{\| x(t) - c_i(t) \|\}$. The winner center $c_c(t)$ and some centers belonging to the set $N_c(t)$ are moved towards the input sample $x(t)$ according to

$$c_i(t+1) = \begin{cases} c_i(t) + g_c(t)[x(t) - c_i(t)] & \forall i \in N_c t \\ c_i(t) & \forall i \notin N_c(t) \end{cases} \qquad (3.2)$$

where $g_c(t)$ is a monotonously decreasing learning rate$(1 > g_c(t) \geq 0)$, and the centers set $N_c(t)$ is composed by the n-th closest centers to $c_c(t)$, the winner center. This number n decreases with each iteration down to zero. After it reaches zero only the winner center is modified. The parameters of this method are the starting n, and the number of iterations it needs to reach the zero value. The other parameters are the data set, the number of global iterations and the starting and ending learning rate $g_c(t)$.

3.4.2   Fuzzy Tabu Clustering

The tabu search is a heuristic that can be used to solve combinatorial optimization problems. It is different from the well known hill climbing local search techniques in the sense that it does not become trapped in local optimal solutions, i.e., the tabu search allows moves out of a current solution that makes the objective function worse in the hope that it eventually will achieve a better solution. In [21] we have presented a tabu search-based algorithm for fuzzy clustering. In this algorithm the objective function, the centroid and membership calculation are similar to that of the fuzzy C-Means algorithm [9], where the parameter m is the fuzziness of the clustering.

$$J = \sum_i^k \sum_j^n \| x_j - c_i \|^2 \mu_{c_i}^m (x_j) \qquad (3.3)$$

$$c_i = \frac{\sum\limits_{j=1}^{n} x_j \mu_{c_i}^m(x_j)}{\sum\limits_{j=1}^{n} \mu_{c_j}^m(x_j)}$$

$$\mu_{c_h}(x) = 1/ \left(\sum_{i=1}^{n} \| x - c_h \|^2 \, / \, \| x - c_i \|^2 \right)^{1/m-1}$$

To simplify the explanations we will name as *configuration* a tuple composed of a centroid's vector and the corresponding degrees of membership matrix, and it will be denoted as A_k. The following parameters are used:

- $MTLS$: maximum tabu list size,
- P: probability threshold,
- NTS: number of trial solutions,
- $ITMAX$: maximum number of iterations and
- TLL: tabu list length.

The algorithm can be described, by means of four simple steps, as follows:

- (s1) **Initialization.** Let A_0 be an arbitrary solution and J_0 be the corresponding objective function value computed using equation 3.3. Let $A_b = A_0$ and $J_b = J_0$. Select values for the following parameters: $MTLS$, P, NTS, and $ITMAX$. Let $k = 1$, let $TLL = 0$, and go to step s2.
- (s2) **Generation.** Using A_b generate NTS trial solutions $A_k^1, A_k^2, \ldots, A_k^{NTS}$, and evaluate their corresponding objective function values $J_k^1, J_k^2, \ldots, J_k^{NTS}$, and go to step s3.
- (s3) **Selection.** Order $J_k^1, J_k^2, \ldots, J_k^{NTS}$ in ascending order and denote them by $J_k^{[1]}, J_k^{[2]}, \ldots, J_k^{[NTS]}$. If $A_k^{[1]}$ is not tabu, or if it is tabu but $J_k^{[1]} < J_b$ then let $A_c = A_k^{[1]}$ and $J_c = J_k^{[1]}$, and go to step s4; otherwise let $A_c = A_k^{[L]}$ and $J_c = J_k^{[L]}$, where $J_k^{[L]}$ is the best objective function of $J_k[1], J_k^{[2]}, \ldots, J_k^{[NTS]}$ that is not tabu and go to step s4. If all $J_k[1], J_k^{[2]}, \ldots, J_k^{[NTS]}$ are tabu go to step s2.
- (s4) **Modification.** Insert A_c at the bottom of the tabu list and let $TLL = TLL + 1$(if $TLL = MTLS + 1$, delete the first element in the tabu list and let

$TLL = TLL - 1$). If $J_b > J_c$, let $A_b = A_0$ and $J_b = J_c$.
If $k > ITMAX$, stop (A_b is the best solution found and
J_b is the corresponding best objective function value);
otherwise, let $k = k + 1$ and go to step s2.

Different alternatives exist to generate the trial solutions, for example, to move the centroids over the space and then to calculate the new memberships matrix. For each centroid, if a random number is greater than P, the move is performed.

3.4.3   Rule Generation Agents

In order to approximate the function $\varphi : X^p \to Y$ that model the system, we assume the existence of a collection of data samples of the system behavior in the product space $(X^p \times Y)$, $\Omega = ((x_{t1}, x_{t2}, \ldots, x_{tp}), y_t)$ $t = 1, 2, \ldots, n$, where $X_1, X_2, \ldots, X_p$ are the domains of discourse of the inputs and Y is the domain of the ouput.

We consider that we have a collection of k_1 fuzzy sets in the input space X^p and a collection of k_2 fuzzy sets in the output space Y (collections obtained because we have done a fuzzy clustering in each of these domains, or because we have an a priori information about a fuzzy partition of these domains). In this way we have a collection of possible $k_1 * k_2$ fuzzy rules of the form:

$$R_h: \text{If } x \text{ is } A^i \text{ then } y \text{ is } B^j \ [w_{ij}]$$
$$i = 1, \ldots, k_1 \ j = 1, \ldots, k_2 \tag{3.4}$$

where $x = (x_1, \ldots, x_p)$ and A^i could be a fuzzy set obtained using a fuzzy clustering of X^p, or obtained as $A^i = \left(A_1^i * \ldots * A_p^i \right)$ with $*$ a T-norm.

In order to infer with the collection of fuzzy rules we have decided, because of its simplicity, to use as the approximate reasoning method the Mizumoto Simplified Method [45], where the fuzzy sets of the consequent are substituted by a singleton value, i.e., real numbers. As far as fuzzy control is concerned, it is well known that we can use fuzzy rules with singletons in the consequents without losing the performance of the control. This value can be obtained using the center of gravity defuzzification method over B_h:

$$v_h = \int B_h(y) y \partial y / \int B_h(y) \partial y$$

So we can rewrite(3.4) as:

$$R_h : \text{If } x \text{ is } A^i \text{ then } y \text{ is } v_j, h = 1, \ldots, k$$

where v_j is the singleton consequent associated to each fuzzy rule.

With the given I/O pairs (x_t, y_t), where $x_t \in X^p$, $y_t \in Y$, and $t = 1, 2, \ldots, n$, a fuzzy clustering is performed in the input-output product space $(X^p \times Y)$, which will group together I/O pairs that are geometrically close to each other in the joint universe of discourse. Such clustering can be achieved, for instance, by using a fuzzy clustering agent that implements the FCM (Fuzzy C Means)[9] or the Fuzzy Tabu Algorithm, and we obtain k fuzzy clusters in $(X^p \times Y)$ with centers or centroids denoted by

$$c_{XY}^h = (c_X^k, c_Y^k)$$

for $h = 1, ..., k$. The fuzzy relation corresponding to the hth cluster is such that:

$$\mu_{C_{XY}^h}(x_t, y_t) = \cfrac{1}{\left\{ \sum_{l=1}^{k} \cfrac{\left\| (x_t, y_t) - (c_X^h, c_Y^h) \right\|^2}{\left\| (x_t, y_t) - (c_X^l, c_Y^l) \right\|^2} \right\}^{1/(m-1)}}$$

where $m > 1$. Notice that $\mu_{C_{XY}^h}(x_t, y_t) = 1$ if $(x_t, y_t) = (c_X^h, c_Y^h)$ and that $0 \le \mu_{C_{XY}^h}(x_t, y_t) < 1$ otherwise.

Next using the information of each fuzzy cluster in $(X^p \times Y)$, we try to generate a possible weight to each fuzzy rule, aggregating the different sources of information in a unique matrix that represents the whole learning $W = \bigoplus_{h=1}^{k} W_h = F(W_1, W_2, ..., W_k)$.

$$w_{ij} = F_1(w_{ij}^1, w_{ij}^2, ..., w_{ij}^k) = \max_{h=1}^{k} w_{ij}^h \tag{3.5}$$

The key idea is to characterize this combination by a point in $(X^p \times Y)$ that aggregates the more coherent information about it. For example we can consider the weight:

$$w_{ij} = \max_{h=1}^{k} T\left(A_i\left(c_X^h\right), B_j\left(c_Y^h\right)\right)$$

being (c_X^h, c_Y^h) the components on X^p and Y of the centroids of the hth fuzzy cluster.

Despite a weight is assigned to each possible rule, to reduce the number of rules associated to any possible fuzzy sets in the input space is also interesting. This reduces the dimension of the weight matrices, i.e., the complexity of the system, as well as it improves the inference process. Once the matrix W is built, our proposal is to assign one or two output fuzzy sets to each input fuzzy sets A_i. For example, we can consider selecting only one fuzzy set of the output space B' associated to:

$$w_i' = \max_{j=1}^{s} w_{ij} \tag{3.6}$$

Normally the most common approach to the existence of different possible rules with the same antecedent is to just consider only one of these rules, the one with the greater weight, as indicated in expression(3.6).

Once we select from the collection of possible rules, for each antecedent the consequent corresponding to the fuzzy rule with the great weight w_{ij}, we need to generate finally fuzzy sets in each of the domains of the input variables. These fuzzy sets will be obtained by means of projecting the fuzzy clusters of the input space in each domain of the variables, then making the extensional hull of the fuzzy sets obtained, and finally we approximate them by trapezoidal fuzzy sets. As a consequence of this method we have a collection of $k_1 * k_2$ fuzzy rules:

R_h : If x_1 is A_{1h} and ... and x_p is A_{ph} then y is B_h, $h = 1, \ldots, k_1 * k_2$.

So, basically, each method has to:

1. Define the number of rules to be created.
2. Set the centers of the A_{jh} fuzzy numbers that constitute the antecedent of the rules.
3. Define the *membership degree* $\mu_{A_{jh}}(x_j)$ to be used.
4. Set the output value (v_j).

3.4.4   A Genetic Algorithm Based Method to Generate and/or Tune Fuzzy Rules

The fuzzy modeling normally is accomplished by a two step procedure. The first step is generation of a first approximation to the fuzzy model that describes the system. Implicit in this step is the determination of the necessary number of rules. The output of this step is a collection of rules which can be seen as rough estimates of the final rule base. The second step consists of a tuning of the initial rough rules to give us our final rule base.

Genetic Algorithms (GAs) have shown good results in obtaining fuzzy rule bases, although normally using different GAs in the generation and in the tuning process, or just using GAs only in one of these steps [33] [37]. We have defined an agent that implements a nonstandard GA to achieve either of the following tasks:

1. *Only tuning:* GA is used to tune a rule base with k rules (previously obtained by means of an expert or using the fuzzy clustering agent for rule generation). The final rule base will contain exactly k rules.
2. *Generating and tuning:* GA is used in this case to generate and to tune a rule base directly from data. It is also possible to incorporate an initial rule base with k rules as in the previous method, that "help" the search process. Final rule base will contain any number N of rules, with $1 \leq N \leq MAX$, where MAX is given by user.

Genetic Algorithms (GAs) [27] [44] are adaptive procedures of optimization and search that find solutions to problems by an evolutionary process inspired in the mechanisms of natural selection and genetics. Currently, these algorithms are being highly considered above all in those problems with complex solution spaces for those which we do not have good algorithms to solve them.

Next, we describe the main characteristics of the GA:

Representation

The number of rules is known and constant if the proposal is to tune a previous rule base with a fixed number k of rules, but it is unknown and variable ($N \in [1..MAX]$) if we want to achieve processing completely, i.e., "generating and tuning" task. Firstly, we show a possible representation of the solutions to generate and tune a rule base, and we will see how this representation can be used to tune a rule base introduced previously ("only tuning" task).

Populations in this GA are composed of individuals H_i, $i = 1, \ldots, popsize$, represented as follows:

$$Individual\ H_i :$$

$$\underbrace{R_1^i\ R_2^i\ \ldots\ R_{MAX}^i}_{Rule\ set}\ \underbrace{d_1^i\ d_2^i\ \ldots\ d_{MAX}^i}_{Control\ set}$$

where the rule $R_h^i = \{\tilde{A}_h^{i1} \tilde{A}_h^{i2} \ldots \tilde{A}_h^{ip} \tilde{B}_h^i\}$ ($1 \leq h \leq MAX$, $1 \leq i \leq popsize$) consists of fuzzy values for the p input variables and output variable, which are represented as:

$$\tilde{A}_h^{ij} = (a_{h1}^{ij}, a_{h2}^{ij}, a_{h3}^{ij}, a_{h4}^{ij}), \quad (1 \leq h \leq MAX,\ 1 \leq i \leq popsize,\ 1 \leq j \leq p)$$
$$\tilde{B}_h^i = (b_{h1}^i, b_{h2}^i, b_{h3}^i, b_{h4}^i), \quad (1 \leq h \leq MAX,\ 1 \leq i \leq popsize)$$

i.e., trapezoidal fuzzy numbers with $a_{hl}^{ij}, b_{hl}^i \in \mathbb{R}$, ($1 \leq h \leq MAX$, $1 \leq l \leq 4$, $1 \leq i \leq popsize$, $1 \leq j \leq p$). Values $d_h^i \in \{0, 1\}$ ($1 \leq h \leq MAX$, $1 \leq i \leq popsize$) indicate if rule h of the individual i is active in the solution ($1 =$ active, $0 =$ inactive). Thus, the number N of rules in the individual i is given by the number of values $d_h^i = 1$, $1 \leq h \leq MAX$.

Note that a control set is not necessary if we want to tune a previous rule base with a fixed number k of rules.

Initial Population

To create an initial population we take into account two criteria:

1. Explore available information (examples, rule bases, etc.).
2. Explore (randomly) solution space to obtain an appropriate diversity.

According to these criteria, we propose three different alternatives (F1, F2 and F3) to initialize the solutions, which will be applied with probabilities p_1, p_2 and p_3 respectively. F1 and F2 forms assume the existence of an initial rule base with k rules ($1 \leq k \leq MAX$).

(F1) All k rules of the initial rule base are introduced in random positions of the solution, and corresponding values in the control set are set to 1. Remainder rules ($MAX - k$) are obtained randomly according to the domains of input and output variables, and corresponding values in the control set are set to 0.
Example:

> *Initial rule base* ($k = 4$) :
> $R_1 \ R_2 \ R_3 \ R_4$
> *Initial solution* ($MAX = 7$) :
> $Rnd \ R_3 \ R_2 \ Rnd \ R_1 \ R_4 \ Rnd$ 0 1 1 0 1 1 0

where Rnd denote that a rule has been obtained randomly. Although other approaches can be used to obtain randomly fuzzy rules, we propose the following:
For each trapezoidal fuzzy number $\tilde{u} = (u_1, u_2, u_3, u_4)$ do

Step 1. $\Delta \leftarrow (b - a)/(m - 1)$;

Step 2. $u_1 \leftarrow$ random real number $\in [a - \Delta, b + \Delta]$;
   $u_2 \leftarrow$ random real number $\in [u_1, b + \Delta]$;
   $u_3 \leftarrow$ random real number $\in [u_2, b + \Delta]$;
   $u_4 \leftarrow$ random real number $\in [u_3, b + \Delta]$;

where $[a, b]$ is the domain of the variable, and m is the number of linguistics values associated with a variable (typically seven).

(F2) Each rule of the solution, with equal probability, either is selected from the initial rule base or is obtained randomly. All values in the control set are generated randomly.
Example:

> *Initial rule base* ($k = 4$) :
> $R_1 \ R_2 \ R_3 \ R_4$
> *Initial solution* ($MAX = 7$) :
> $R_2 \ Rnd \ Rnd \ R_4 \ Rnd \ R_1 \ Rnd$ 1 0 1 0 1 1 1

(F3) All MAX rules of the solution and all values in the control set are obtained randomly.
Example:

> *Initial solution* ($MAX = 7$) :
> $Rnd \ Rnd \ Rnd \ Rnd \ Rnd \ Rnd \ Rnd$ 0 1 0 1 1 0 1

Genetic Operators

Since solutions contain two different types of information (denoted as rule set and control set) it is necessary to use different genetic operators to achieve completely the recombination process. We have used the following genetic operators:

- **Rule set genetic operators**
  - *Simple crossover*
  - *Arithmetical crossover*
  - *Max-Min crossover*
  - *Simple mutation*
  - *Non-uniform mutation*

- **Control set genetic operators**
  - As control set is a bit string, simple binary crossover and mutation [27] are used in this case.

Parameters

The most significant parameters used by GA have been maximal generation number (T), population size (*popsize*), probabilities F1, F2 and F3 used in obtaining initial population (p_1, p_2 and p_3, respectively), probability of crossover (p_c) and probability of mutation (p_m). Note that to achieve the generating and tuning task when there is no initial rule base, it is necessary to set $p_1 = 0$, $p_2 = 0$ and $p_3 = 1$ in obtaining initial population. Note also that probabilities p_c and p_m correspond to the sums of the probabilities of all crossover and mutation operators respectively described above.

3.5 Robotics Application Example

3.5.1 Introduction

The operation of a mobile autonomous robot in an unstructured environment, as it occurs in the real world, needs to take into account many details. Mainly, the controller has to be able to operate under conditions of imprecision and uncertainty. For instance, the a priori knowledge of the environment, in general, is incomplete, uncertain, and approximate. Typically, the perceptual information acquired is also incomplete and affected by the noise. Moreover, the execution of a control command is not completely reliable due to the complexity and unpredictability of the real world dynamics. To cope with these difficulties, the controller should respond reactively to unpredicted events as soon as they are perceived.

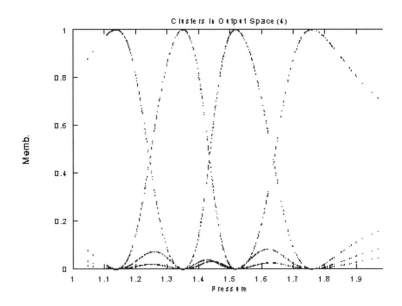

The use of cooperative intelligent agents, which implement the navigational control by means of fuzzy logic, is highly recommended due to the nature of the behavior an autonomous robot must follow. Autonomous robots literature contains many examples of approximations that look for decompositions of the global control function in smaller ones named behaviours [48]. Each behaviour is responsible for producing certain actions (typically sensing and control actions) in order to accomplish or hold a given objective, such as avoid obstacles. This interpretation fits into the notion of agent. Agents are autonomous entities capable of developing tasks either by themselves or by collaborating with other agents. If, in addition to that, we want our agents to be able to operate under imprecise and uncertain environments, fuzzy logic has been proven to be a valuable framework [10]. Moreover, intelligence is the degree of reasoning and acquired behaviour: the agent ability to accept objectives given by the user and to carry on such tasks. At least, there should be some kind of orders, maybe in rules form, with an inference motor or another kind of reasoning mechanism to actuate over them. Thus, it is feasible to apply fuzzy logic to manage imprecision and uncertainty [7, 1, 61]. Upper intelligence degrees include a user model or another form of knowledge and reasoning about what the user wants to do, and planning the way to reach that goal.

We will show how we put into practice these concepts by applying fuzzy logic in different aspects of a robot control application. As a test platform we have designed and built a custom autonomous mobile robot [50, 51], which is kinematically holonomic. The robot has a 40x40 cm square-shaped base and 55 cm of height. It has differential steering, with two wheels driven by D.C. motors and two smaller casters to provide stability in all ways. The total weight is roughly 15 Kg (batteries included). A 486DX2 based board is in charge of processing, while a MC68HC11 based board is in charge of sensors data acquisition and actuators control. The robot presents the following sensors and actuators:

- Two optical encoders mounted on the steering wheels.
- Four Polaroid 6500 ultrasonic range sonars working at the same frequency.
- A ring of switches mounted on bumpers to detect collisions.
- Three propioceptive sensors to measure batteries' levels.
- A LynxArm mechanical arm with 4 degrees of freedom.
- A 256 gray scale tones QuickCam camera.

In order for this simple robot to perform some relatively complex tasks, some tools and techniques are needed. In the following sections we will describe the techniques we use: the BG programming language, as the fundamental component of our architecture for autonomous mobile robots modeling, and its underlying blackboard based agent design. Next we will describe the different agents we have implemented and their decomposition in behaviours, and then how we apply learning techniques to the behaviour blending problem. Finally, we will present some results and conclusions.

3.5.2 The BG programming language

Several robot control languages have been proposed in the literature. Each one of them has its own pros and cons. As our main goal was to tackle the behaviour blending problem and the learning of the rules that drive the blending process, we chose COLBERT [39] as the working base. This makes extensive use of fuzzy rule bases both for the behaviours and the blender. As we wanted to try some different functionalities, we decided to define and implement a new high level programming language, named BG, which is based on the C language syntax and semantics and most of the COLBERT language features. It is based on the multi-agent paradigm, where each agent possesses a series of behaviours. Its intended use is robotics and control applications, mainly autonomous mobile robots. The examples in this chapter yield in the latter field, and it is supposed that a robot will execute them. In fact that robot is our custom one described in the previous section. The main goal of the language is to aid in the development cycle of robotics applications and in the behaviour modeling (as it is a robotics oriented high level language with built in fuzzy logic operations), as well as to expedite it (by using automated tuning systems). BG, in its current version, incorporates many traditional elements and control structures of classical imperative languages:

- Local and global variables.
- Expressions and assignments.
- Arithmetical, logical and relational operators.
- Conditionals.
- C-like functions.

Basically, BG supports two data types: real numbers and fuzzy sets with standard shapes (triangle, trapezoid, bell, and sigmoid). In addition to that, BG presents advanced nonstandard control structures like:

- Deterministic finite state machines.
- Fuzzy rule bases.
- Grid based calculations.
- Agents and behaviours definition and blending.

These elements are described in the following sections.

Finite state machines

The use of finite state machines allows the programmer to define tasks that need to be run sequentially, and the conditions to change from one task to an other. The BG language, as of its current implementation, does not have instructions for loops (while, for, or repeat-until), but these can be modeled using a finite state machine. The main reason for this lack of loops is to have under control the duration of each control loop (an error can not lock it). In the future, loops will be incorporated as in COLBERT [39], which, in fact, internally are finite state machines.

For instance, if we want the robot to move left or right (depending on sonar values) for a given amount of time, we can use the following (Listing 1) finite state machine definition, where NOTURN, TURNRIGHT, and TURNLEFT are the three possible states.

Fuzzy rule bases

One of the strengths of the BG language is the possibility of using fuzzy rule bases. These are intended for both control and behaviour blending (the latter will be discussed below). Two operators have been defined: a t-norm (the min) and a t-conorm (the max). The defuzzification is performed by means of the center of gravity method. Typically the rules will consist of an antecedent with some input variables and a consequent with some output variables (MIMO rules). There is a special kind of fuzzy rules, called background rules, that are useful to cover undefined input space. The way they work is by applying a fixed alpha-cut to the consequent part of the rule. For instance, if we want to maintain a given distance from the robot to a wall, it can be accomplished with the following code (Listing 2). Right is the input variable that measures the distance from the robot to the wall at the right. Turn is the output variable that controls if the robot should steer to the left (fuzzy sets TSL and TL), to the right (fuzzy set TSR) or none (fuzzy set TN).

Grid based calculations

The BG language provides a basic structure (*grid*) and methods to manage bidimensional spatial information. When a grid is initialized, the user provides three parameters: the number of square cells (N and M, for a $N \times M$ matrix) and the length in metres of the cell sides. The left-bottom cell is used as the origin of co-ordinates. Each cell has a value, ranging from 0 to 1, corresponding to the degree of certainty that the cell is an obstacle [26]. As the robot moves, the following data are processed:

- The current absolute location (x, y) of the robot.
- The current absolute location (x, y) of the goal place.
- The absolute location (x, y) of a possible obstacle.
- A relative sonar reading $(x, y, \theta, sonar\_measure)$ from the given absolute location.

Using a triangle scan-line algorithm, the values of the cells that are in each sensor cone are updated: the certainty of being a free cell is augmented inside the cone, and is reduced along the base of the cone. With these values an A^* algorithm searches for the shortest path to the goal from the current robot position. Then an absolute heading, which can be used for planning, is returned. A typical example of grid use is shown below (Listing 3). The robot has four sonar sensors (`sonar0, sonar1, sonar2, sonar3`), at different angles (`+40, +15, -15, -40 degrees`). For each control loop cycle, the current location and the current goal are updated. If the sonar measures are less than a given value (5 metres) the grid is updated with them. As a result, the variable *heading* is updated using the A^* output.

Agents and behaviours definition

The organizational units in the BG language are based in the agent notion [32]. We arrange these agents using a blackboard based architecture [31, 59] as the main paradigm for communication and control. Under this model, a series of agents (also known as knowledge bases) share the available information about the system and the environment. Each agent can read from the blackboard the information that is relevant for it, perform its own processing, and then write each possible result onto the blackboard. The proposed architecture has been designed according to the following principles:

```
float yutime,sleft,sright;

fsm start NOTURN
{//Initial state
  state NOTURN:
   {utime=0.0;
    sleft=sonar0+sonar1;
    sright=sonar2+sonar3;
    if (sleft<sright)
      shift TURNRIGHT;
    if (sleft>=sright)
      shift TURNLEFT;
   }
  //Turning to the left
  state TURNLEFT:
   {utime=utime+1.0;
    //Shift to initial state
    if (utime>5.0)
      shift NOTURN;
    turn=-10.0;
   }
  //Turning to the right
  state TURNRIGHT:
   {utime=utime+1.0;
    //Shift to initial state
    if (utime>5.0)
      shift NOTURN;
    turn=10.0;
   }
}
```

Listing 1. Example of a finite
state machine.

```
rules
{//Turn none
  background (0.1)      turn is TN;
  //Turn small right
  if (right is FAR)     turn is TSR;
  //Turn small left
  if (right is MEDIUM) turn is TSL;
  //Turn small left
  if (right is NEAR)    turn is TSL;
  //Turn left
  if (right is CLOSE)  turn is TL;
}
```

Listing 2. Example of a fuzzy rule base.

- Use of encapsulation mechanisms, isolation, and local control: each agent is a semiautonomous and independent entity.
- There are no assumptions about the knowledge each agent has or

the resolution method it implements.
- Flexible and dynamic organization.
- Adequacy of the architecture to the use of learning techniques.

A key idea is that each agent is decomposed in very simple behaviours. These access the blackboard by way of some input and output variables. As two different behaviours may modify the same variable a fusion method (called behaviour blending) is provided [48]. The advantage of this method is related to scalability and learning: while in a subsumption architecture [15] the management of agents depends on the behaviours they implement [51]; with the proposed architecture the management resides on the fusion method. A fuzzy rule base carries on this fusion, enabling/disabling the output of the different behaviours, both totally and partially [48, 3, 51]. This way, the system can be trained with only some simple behaviours, and then new behaviours can be added without modifying the previous ones: only the fusion rule base needs to be re-trained. When an agent is specified, the user may supply three kinds of blocks that are placed inside the agent's execution loop:

- A common block that is executed before any behaviour.
- Series of behaviours that are executed concurrently.
- A blender block that specifies how the outputs of the behaviours will be fused.

All these blocks must satisfy a constraint: the execution time of each one must be computer bound, so there must not be infinite loops. The language itself assures that this constraint holds for all the blocks, and it is a necessary requirement for getting basic real time support, although the language doesn't support fixed time scheduling. It is the user responsibility to make the appropriate tests to obtain a certain control cycle duration. For the blending process to work each behaviour defines what global output variables are to be fused. Thus they only modify local copies of those variables during the behaviour execution. The blender applies inference over fuzzy rules, defined using some input global variables as the antecedent and some behaviour names as the consequent. Last, the equation 3.8 is applied to each blended output variable.

$$\alpha_j = pri_j \cdot beh_j \qquad (3.7)$$

$$ov_i = \frac{\sum_j \alpha j \cdot lov_{ij}}{\sum_j \alpha_j} \qquad (3.8)$$

where:

- ov_i is the i-th global output variable,

- lov_{ij} is the local copy of the i-th output variable in the j-th behaviour
- pri_j is the priority of the j-th behaviour
- beh_j is the result of the fuzzy inference for the j-th behaviour

This way the fusion depends both on a fixed priority and a variable activation degree calculated using fuzzy inference. Each particular application will dictate which combination of priority and inference is the best (to use only priorities, to use only inference, or to combine both). Moreover, this novel approach for behaviour blending generalizes the concept of hierarchical fuzzy rules, because, in fact, this hierarchy may combine fuzzy rule base with other techniques (from both soft computing and classical imperative programming). In section 3.5.4 it is explained how learning techniques can be in conjunction with this blending mechanism. A simple agent definition is shown below (Listing 4). The agent has three behaviours: one which avoids obstacles (*avoid*), one which aligns to the left (*alignL*), and one which aligns to the right (*alignR*). The yblender block specifies how the output of these behaviours (*turn* and *speed*) will be fused.

3.5.3   Robot agents architecture

We wanted our robot to perform simple navigational tasks; so we decided that our final goal was to find some objects in our laboratory (with different rooms and corridors), both in known and unknown locations, then bring them back to a home position, neither colliding nor getting frozen in an infinite loop, of course. In addition to that, the robot will not have a model of the environment before it starts running. To accomplish this goal the robot must be able to perform certain tasks: navigation with obstacle avoidance, goal seeking, map building and localization, and some form of high level planning, etc. We have made a decomposition of such a system (robot and goal), extracting the most important elements [2], and defined a series of agents using the BG language and its implicit architecture. We have identified the following agents (3.6) that will be described in the next sections:

- Reactive Control. This is the agent that is in charge of the reactive navigation.
- Planning. This is the agent that is in charge of high level planning and global goal completion supervision.
- Localization. This is the agent that is in charge of building a more or less precise model of the environment, and then locating the robot on it.
- Vehicle Control. This is the agent that is in charge of low level elements control and signal filtering: sensors and actuators.

```
float a0,a1,a2,a3;

//Angle for sonar0
a0=alpha+(40.0*DTOR);
//Angle for sonar1
a1=alpha+(15.0*DTOR);
//Angle for sonar2
a2=alpha-(15.0*DTOR);
//Angle for sonar3
a3=alpha-(40.0*DTOR);

grid updates heading cells
40.0 by 30.0 side 0.1
{location (x, y);
 goal (goalx, goaly);

 if (sonar0<5.0)
   sonar(x,y,a0,sonar0);
 if (sonar1<5.0)
   sonar(x,y,a1,sonar1);
 if (sonar2<5.0)
   sonar(x,y,a2,sonar2);
 if (sonar3<5.0)
   sonar(x,y,a3,sonar3);
}
```

Listing 3. Example of a grid

```
agent basicControl
{blending left,right,front;

 common
 {/* Code goes here */}
 behaviour avoid priority 2.0
 {/* Code goes here */}
 behaviour alignL priority 0.5
 {/* Code goes here */}
 behaviour alignR priority 0.5
 {/* Code goes here */}

 blender
  {rules
    {background (0.1)
        avoid is LOW;
     background (0.1)
        alignR is LOW;
     background (0.1)
        alignL is LOW;

     if ((left is CLOSE)  ||
         (front is CLOSE) ||
         (right is CLOSE)
        )
        avoid is HIGH;

     if (left is MEDIUM)
        alignL is HIGH;
     if (right is MEDIUM)
        alignR is HIGH;
    }
  }
}
```

Listing 4. Example of agent and behaviours definition

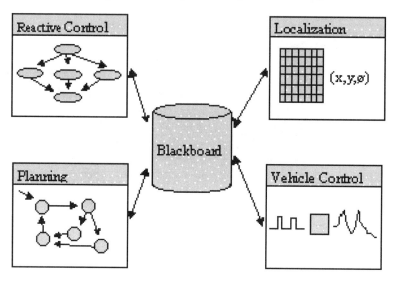

Figure 3.6   Agents Architecture Elements

Reactive control

This is the most important and crucial agent, which implements some basic reactive behaviours. These make extensive use of fuzzy logic in the form of fuzzy rule bases. These rules have been obtained both from previous experience [50, 51] (and even trial and error) and fuzzy modeling techniques (as described in section 3.2). A human user executes some control commands based on sensory data (i.e., wall-robot alignment, speed control, and so on). These are recorded and then passed to one or more fuzzy modeling agents. The latter will perform some cluster analysis and then produce the required fuzzy rules. Thus using the MAS architecture (see sections 3.3.2 and 3.4), these agents correspond to Rule Generation and Clustering ones. For the present application, we have identified and implemented the following reactive behaviours:

- *obstacle-avoider*: drives the robot in the opposite direction to the nearest obstacle (Listing 5).
- *align-right*: holds the robot at a given distance from the wall at its right (Listing 2).
- *align-left*: holds the robot at a given distance from the wall at its left (Listing 2).
- *move-to-goal*: drives the robot in the direction of the current goal.
- *move-backwards*: drives the robot backwards to the opposite direction to the nearest obstacle (Listing 1).

- *noise*: drives the robot in a random direction to escape from a hole.

The blending fuzzy rules (Listing 6) have been derived manually by trial and error. As an example, it is worth noting how we obtained the move-to-goal behaviour. We used a robot simulator and drove the robot performing a line following. This line was supposed to be the goal heading at each instant. The control and line heading data were passed on to a tabu search based fuzzy clustering agent (see 3.4.2). Then the result (fuzzy clusters) was used as the basis of the rule generation agent (see 3.4.3).

Vehicle control

This agent is composed of two kinds of behaviours: sensor related and actuator related ones. The first are in charge of processing and filtering the information provided by the sensors, and the second are in charge of sending the right signals to the actuators to perform the given control commands. In our system we have the following behaviours:

- Range sensors acquisition and filtering.
- Collision detection.
- Robot control vector (v, θ) execution.

The navigation of the robot depends completely on the range information. Ultrasounds [12] are characterized by producing an imprecise perception of the environment, due to well-known problems: crosstalking, noise, and low reliability over polished surfaces at incidence angles greater than 15 degrees. Due to this, a failure in the ultrasonic subsystem can condition the performance of the whole system. To avoid the special treatment of these situations by all dependent agents, some agents are designed to get the ultrasonic information, process it, and give a reliable result. This method reduces the complexity of the system and, moreover, increments the reliability of it. To accomplish this, a fuzzy filter [22] is applied to each of the ultrasonic sensors. Basically, it is composed of three parts: a state memory, a predictor block, and an inference block. The memory block will remember the last n readings of the sensor. The predictor block will estimate the next sensor value. The inference block will give an output fusing the input value and the estimated one, trying to discard the a priori bad readings.

The state memory is implemented as a finite array of values. The predictor block implements a simple Kalman filter: the average of the state memory values. The inference block is implemented by way of a fuzzy inference system. The whole fuzzy filtering block works in the following way:

- The predicted measure is calculated, based on the state memory by the predictor block.

- Then the difference between the measured value and the predicted one is passed on to the fuzzy inference system as the input variable.
- The output of the inference system is used to weight the fusion of the current reading and the predicted one, and this value is returned as the output of the filtering block.
- The state memory is updated with the output of the filtering block.

$$S' = \frac{\sum\limits_{i=0}^{n} S_i}{n} \qquad (3.9)$$

$$S'' = \alpha S_c + (1 - \alpha)S' \qquad (3.10)$$

$$diff = |S' - S_c| \qquad (3.11)$$

where

- S' is the average of the state memory,
- S'' is the output of the filtering block,
- S_c is the current sensor reading,
- $diff$ is the input of the inference block and
- α is the output of the inference block.

To execute platform control vectors (v, θ) it is needed to take into account the fact that the robot possesses differential steering. So, this vector must be converted to different speeds for the two motors. Each motor has an agent in charge of maintaining a constant velocity using encoder information as feedback. This is accomplished by a typical set of five SISO fuzzy rules. Both these rules and the rules of the fuzzy filter have been obtained using our MAS architecture.

Planning

Due to the simplicity of the tasks the robot is going to perform, the planning agent is quite simple. At present, it is a deterministic finite state automata, whose states are: looking for object, grasping object, going back to home location. These states have associated goal co-ordinates that will be received by the reactive control agent, which will activate the corresponding behaviours to accomplish that.

Localization

The localization agent is in charge of building a map of the environment and keeping track of the robot location. To implement the map, a behaviour uses the grid structure provided by the BG language. This grid is updated continuously with the different sonar readings. On the map, the robot is located using odometry (currently we assume it has no important errors). This agent should integrate both the map building and the odometry correction tasks [26].

3.5.4 Learning behaviour fusion

A key issue of behaviour-based control is how to efficiently coordinate conflicts and competition among different types of behaviour to achieve a good performance. Instead of just inhibiting and suppressing strategies according to assigned priorities, a fusion method is used [51]. A fuzzy rule base carries on this fusion, enabling/disabling the output of the different behaviours, both totally and partially [7, 3, 48]. The use of learning techniques [7, 10, 24, 34, 57] in the fusion rule base can result in robot navigation performance improvement. This way, the system can be trained with only some simple behaviours, and then new behaviours can be added without modifying the previous ones: only the fusion rule base needs to be re-trained.

Genetic Algorithms [28] are adaptive procedures of optimization and search that find solutions to problems, inspired by the mechanisms of natural evolution. They imitate, on an abstract level, biological principles such as a population based approach, the inheritance of information, the variation of information via crossover/mutation, and the selection of individuals based on fitness.

GAs start with an initial set (population) of alternative solutions (individuals) for the given problem, which are evaluated in terms of solution quality (fitness). Then, the operators of selection, replication and variation are applied to obtain new individuals (offspring) that constitute a new population. The interplay of selection, replication and variation of the fitness leads to solutions of increasing quality over the course of many iterations (generations). When finally a termination criterion is met, such as a maximum number of generations, the search process is terminated and the final solution is shown as output.

As our main concern is the learning of the fusion rule base, we apply GAs for the task [52]. The user selects an agent, which will serve as the base of the learning procedure. The key idea is to start with a predefined set of fuzzy rules for behaviour blending, and then to apply a learning method to them (rule tuning mode). This set can even be the empty set (rule discovery mode). In either case, the individuals of the GA are fuzzy rule bases, and the result of the GA is the proposed fusion fuzzy rule base.

Initial population and representation

If the algorithm is run in the rule discovery mode the initial population is set randomly. Otherwise, the initial population will consist of the user-defined rules and random modifications of them. The latter corresponds to a typical

```
behaviour avoid priority 2.0
{fusion turn,speed;
 float sleft,sright,diff;

 sleft=sonar0+(sonar1*0.7);
 sright=sonar2+(sonar3*0.7);
 diff=sleft-sright;
 diff=sgn(diff);

 rules
  {background (0.9)
     turn is TC;
   background (0.1)
     speed is SFULL;

   if ((diff is LT) &&
      !(right is CLOSE)
      )
     turn is TR, speed is SFULL;
   if ((diff is GT) &&
      !(left is CLOSE)
      )
     turn is TL, speed is SFULL;
   }

   if (front is NEAR)
     turn = turn * 2.0;
}
```

```
blender
{rules
  {background (0.1)
      backup is LOW;
   background (0.1)
     avoid is LOW;
   background (0.1)
     toGoal is HALFL;
   background (0.1)
     alignR is LOW;
   background (0.1)
     alignL is LOW;

   if (collision is TRUE)
     backup is HIGH,
     toGoal is LOW;
   if ((left is CLOSE) &&
       (front is CLOSE) &&
       (right is CLOSE))
     avoid is HIGH,
     toGoal is HALFL;
   if (left is CLOSE)
     alignL is HALFL;
   if (right is CLOSE)
     alignR is HALFL;
   if (left is MED)
     alignL is HALFH;
   if (right is MED)
     alignR is HALFH;
   if (left is FAR)
     alignL is HIGH;
   if (right is FAR)
     alignR is HIGH;
   if (front is MED)
     toGoal is HIGH;
   if (front is FAR)
     toGoal is HIGH;
} }
```

Listing 5.   Basic behaviour obstacle-avoider

Listing 6.   Initial fusion fuzzy rule base

set up, because it narrows the search space.

The representation of the individuals imposes some constraints to the rule bases: the fuzzy sets must be trapezoidal. This is not really a hard constraint because the conversion from triangular to trapezoidal is straightforward. We extract the fuzzy rule base from the blender of a fixed given agent. The user also specifies the different input variables that will be used in the rules. The output variables are the different behaviours of that agent. Each rule is coded, using real numbers, by concatenating the points that define the fuzzy sets of those input and output variables, plus two parameters: the first one indicates if the rule is a regular or a background rule, and the second indicates if the rule is active or not. The representation of the individual (Pittsburg coding) is the concatenation of all the different rules (both active or not). For this reason the user additionally establishes the maximum number of rules allowed.

Genetic operators and parameters

The user must set up a series of parameters [52] [28] that control how the algorithm proceeds, basically, which kind of genetic operator is going to be used, the probabilities of both mutation (P_m) and crossover (P_c), the maximum number of generations (*Geners*) and the population size (*Popul*).

We have implemented several [28] genetic operators:

- Nonuniform mutation,
- Classical crossover,
- Arithmetical crossover and
- MaxMin crossover.

Each time the algorithm needs to apply crossover or mutation, it randomly selects one of the previous methods. Additionally the user may specify different probabilities for the different operators. In our examples we have kept all the operators with the same probability.

Objective function

While the other topics are quite standard, the definition of the objective function is not straightforward. This function measures the goodness of each individual. As the individuals, in fact, affect the performance of the robot, the objective function must take into account how the robot executes a predefined task. For this task the user must define a simulation framework with the following properties:

- *Goal*: where the robot starts, where the robots ends, and what the robot has to do.
- *Map*: a corridor with walls and obstacles.
- *Iters*: number of simulation runs per individual.

To avoid infinite loops in the simulation some additional parameters are needed:

- *Timeout*: maximum allowable time for each run, measured in epochs.
- *Maxcolls*: maximum allowable number of collisions.

When running the simulation, the current individual is used as the fusion fuzzy rule base of a given agent. Then each simulation run returns four values:

- *Gotcha*: 0.0 if the goal is accomplished, 1.0 otherwise.
- *Epochs*: number of simulations steps performed.
- *Colls*: number of robot-wall collisions.
- *Way*: percentage of distance left from the starting location to the goal one.

Using the different parameters and values defined above, the fitness function is calculated using the following formulae:

$$Total = \sqrt{(start_x - goal_x)^2 + (start_y - goal_y)^2} \tag{3.12}$$

$$ToGoal = \sqrt{(robot_x - goal_x)^2 + (robot_y - goal_y)^2} \tag{3.13}$$

$$Way = \frac{Total \times 100}{ToGoal} \tag{3.14}$$

$$Fitness = \sum_{i}^{Iters} [(Timeout_i - Epochs_i) - 25Colls - Gotcha \times 100 - 5Way] \tag{3.15}$$

3.5.5   Experimental results

We have developed, using the JAVA language, an integrated development environment for the BG language. This way we have a multiplatform application named BGen (it is available at `http://ants.dif.um.es/ humberto/asy`). This implements an interpreter for the BG language, a simulator for our custom robot, some data visualization and recording tools, and the GA based learning tool. The BGen output includes a representation of the grid map that the robot (Figure 3.7) and the degree of activation of each behaviour (Figure 3.8) as a result of the fusion mechanism. Both are updated in each simulation step.

Parameter	Pc	Pm	Geners	Popul	Iters	Timeout	Maxcolls
Value	0.8	0.75	24	4	1	500	5

Table 3.1 Learning parameters

Using this software we have performed some tests to verify the validity of our theses. We will focus on the results of one of such tests. Basically, the goal is to navigate on a simple floor plant (Figure 3.9), starting from a given location (the left of the arena) and finishing in the opposite side (small circle on the right of the arena). The robot has no idea about the floor plant but for the coordinates of the finishing point. The agents, behaviours, and control rules are the ones showed in the previous sections. We have fed the learning tool with these agents and the following GA parameters (see Table 3.1).

Then we have obtained the following results. Initially, the robot neither achieves the goal nor collides. This is a good starting point for learning because the controller is pretty fair and intuitive (in fact designed on the fly just a while before the tests), and the learning time should not be very high. As shown below (Figure 3.10), the fitness function starts with negative values (goal not achieved) and ends up with high positive values (goal achieved in a small number of epochs, near the optimum). This can graphically be observed in the last two figures. The first controller makes a safe wander (Figure 3.11) and does not drive into the goal because there are walls near it. The best individual does drive into the goal (Figure 3.12) despite the fact of the surrounding walls, making tighter turns and minimizing the total distance travelled. Just for curiosity, the learning tool running on a PowerPC at 350 MHz took 15.2 hours to finish.

3.6 Conclusions and Future Work

In this chapter a multiagent system for fuzzy modeling based on learning agents that implement different intelligent techniques is described. This architecture lets the user analyse the combination of different techniques that can be applied to the identification of a model by means of the integration and collaboration of the agents that encapsulate the intelligent techniques. Due to the use of several learning techniques, the system will tend to use those techniques that produce better results for each particular task. Our fuzzy modeling schema could use different agents that implement:

- variable identification,
- fuzzy sets generation using clustering techniques,
- fuzzy rule systems generation,

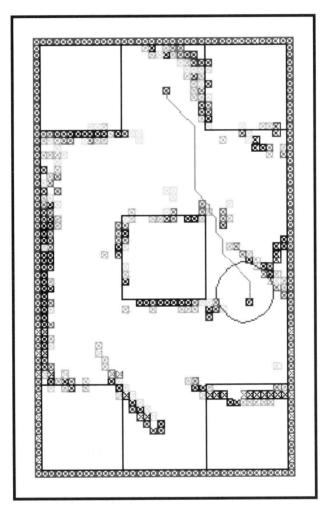

Figure 3.7   Robot's view of the world: grid map

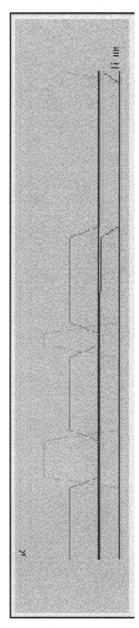

Figure 3.8 Behaviours fusion

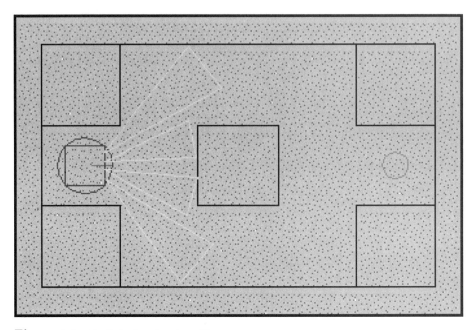

Figure 3.9   Goal start and end positions

- tuning of such rules using GAs,
- optimization of the models using gradient descend techniques like neural networks,
- use of the rule systems for inference.

By providing relatively small intelligent components that may be more easily integrated into more general software products, we can try to solve problems that could not be solved using a large and complex software system. The provision of facilities for the inclusion of multiple fuzzy modeling problem solving paradigms in a single software system has several advantages: different strategies may be applied to solve different aspects of a problem with the most appropriate approach being selected for each aspect.

As an application of the use of this flexible architecture of learning agents a hybrid fuzzy-genetic agent based system for autonomous robots in uncertain environments is described. These agents are composed of two components: first a collection of fuzzy controllers that implement the different behaviours-based schemes of the robot, and second, a fuzzy meta-controller that combines the different behaviours and where the weights associated to each behaviour are learned using a genetic algorithm. In this way this meta-controller coordinates conflicts and competition among multiple behaviour efficiently. We can

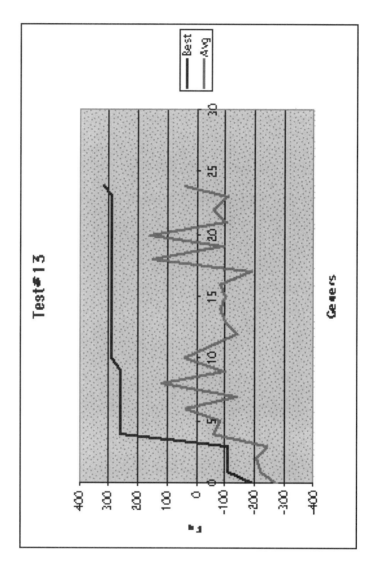

Figure 3.10   Fitness function vs Geners.

summarize our results as follows:

- The programming interfaces are simple and intuitive, thus speeding up the development phase of the system's life cycle.
- The system is quite reliable in terms of fault tolerance and protection against noise.
- The architecture permits the integration of several resolution methods, and the use of learning techniques in the fusion of behaviours output.

Finally, as we have indicated when we described the MASAM Architecture, one of the final objectives of our system is to develop an intelligent agent that learns about the learning process. Hence it can help the user in the decision about the combination of the learning algorithms to be used in the fuzzy modeling. This Meta-Learning Agent (MLA) is actually in an implementation phase, and we hope it could be included in our MAS system.

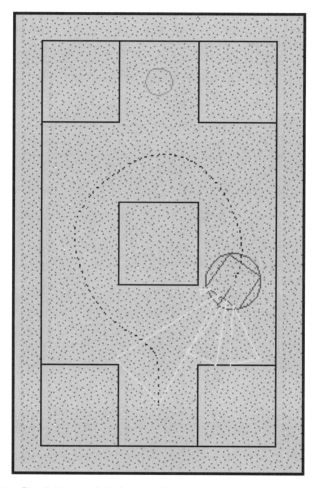

Figure 3.11 Simulation result before learning

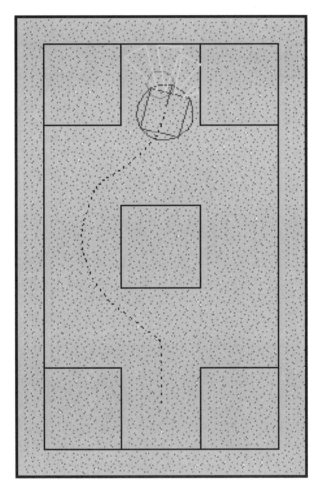

Figure 3.12   Simulation result after learning

3.7 References

[1] A. Saffiotti et al. Robust execution of robot plans using fuzzy logic. In Ralescu A., editor, *Fuzzy Logic in Artificial Intelligence: IJCAI'93 Workshop. Lectures Notes in Artificial Intelligence 847*, pages 24–37. Springer-Velag, 1994.

[2] D. G. Armstrong and C.D. Crane. A modular, scalable, architecture for intelligent, autonomous vehicles. In *3rd IFAC Symposium on Intelligent Autonomous Vehicles*, pages 62–66, Universidad Carlos III, Madrid, Spain, 1998.

[3] B.C. Arrúe, F. Cuesta, B. Braunstingl, and A. Ollero. Fuzzy behaviours combination to control a non holonomic mobile robot using virtual perception memory. In *Sixth IEEE Intl. Conf. on Fuzzy Systems (FuzzIEEE'97)*, pages 1239–1244, Barcelona, Spain, 1997.

[4] AT&T, DSTC, DIC, HP, ICL, Nortel Limited, and Novell. Trading Object Service. OMG RFP5 Submission. Technical report, OMG, 1996.

[5] R. Babuska and H. B. Verbruggen. Applied fuzzy modeling. In *Proceedings IFAC congress AIRTC*, Valencia, Spain, 1994.

[6] R. Babuska and H.B. Verbruggen. A new identification method for linguistic fuzzy models. Aachen, 1994.

[7] H.R. Beom and H.S. Cho. A sensor-based navigation for a mobile robot using fuzzy logic and reinforcement learning. *IEEE Trans. Syst. Man Cyber*, 25(3):464–477, 1995.

[8] H. R. Berenji and P. S. Khedkar. Clustering in product space for fuzzy inference. In *Proceedings of the IEEE Int. Conf. on Fuzzy Systems*, pages 1402–1407, 1993.

[9] J.C. Bezdek. *Pattern recognition with fuzzy objective function algorithms*. Plenum, New York, 1981.

[10] A. Bonarini and F. Basso. Learning to compose fuzzy behaviors for autonomous agents. *Intl. Journal of Approximate Reasoning*, (17):409–432, 1997.

[11] P. Bonissone. Soft computing: The convergence of emerging reasoning techniques. *Journal of Soft Computing*, 1(1), 1997.

[12] J. Borenstein, H.R. Everett, and L. Feng. *Navigating Mobile Robots: Systems and Techniques*. Wellesley, MA, 1996.

[13] Juan A. Botia, Juan R. Velasco, Mercedes Garijo, and Antonio F. G. Skarmeta. Intelligent agents for generic data mining. In F. J. Garijo and C. Lemaitre, editors, *Workshop on DAI and MAS*, 1998.

[14] Juan A. Botia, Juan R. Velasco, Mercedes Garijo, and Antonio F. G. Skarmeta. Geminis: a multi-agent system proposal for generic data mining. In F. J. Garijo and Vicente Botti, editors, *MAAMAW-99*, 1999.

[15] R.A. Brooks. A robust layered control system for a mobile robot. *IEEE J. Robotics and Automation*, (1):14–23, 1986.

[16] K. Causse, Marc Csernel, and Jörg-Uwe Kietz. Final specifications of the Common Knowledge Representaion Language of the MLToolbox. Document ITM 2.2, MLT Consortium, ESPRIT project 2154, March 1992.

[17] M. Delgado, A.F. Gómez-Skarmeta, and F. Martín. Generating fuzzy rules using clustering based approach. In *Proc. Third European Congress on Fuzzy and Intelligent Technologies and Soft Computing*, pages 810–814, Aachen, Germany, 1995.

[18] M. Delgado, A.F. Gómez-Skarmeta, and M.A. Vila. Hierarchical clustering to validate fuzzy clustering. In *Proc. of the IEEE Int. Conf. on Fuzzy Systems*, pages 1807–1812, 1995.

[19] M. Delgado, A.F. Gómez-Skarmeta and M.A. Vila. An unsupervised learning procedure to obtain a classification from a hierarchical clustering. In *Proc. Second European Congress on Fuzzy and Intelligent Technologies and Soft Computing*, pages 528–533, Aachen, Germany, 1994.

[20] M. Delgado, A. Gómez Skarmeta, J. Gómez Marin-Blázquez, and H. Martinez Barberá. Fuzzy hybrid techniques in modeling. In *Proc. 11th International Conference on Industrial and Engineering Applications of Artificial Intelligence and Expert Systems IEA-98-AIE. Lecture Notes on Artifical Intelligence*, number 1226, pages 180–189, 1998.

[21] M. Delgado, A. Gómez Skarmeta, and F. Martín. Some methods to model fuzzy systems for inference purposes. *Int. Journal of Approximate Reasoning*, (3-4):377–391, 1997.

[22] M. Delgado, A.F. Gómez Skarmeta, H. Martínez Barberá, and J. Gómez. Fuzzy range sensor filtering for reactive autonomous robots. In *Fifth Intl. Conference on Soft Computing and Information / Intelligent Systems (IIZUKA '98)*, Fukuoka, Japan, 1998.

[23] Tomás Domínguez. *Definición de un modelo concurrente orientado a objetos para sistemas multiagente*. PhD thesis, Dep. Ingeniería de Sistemas Telemáticos, E.T.S.I. Telecomunicación, Universidad Politécnica de Madrid, 1992.

[24] M. Dorigo and M. Colombetti. *Robot Shaping: an Experiment in Behavior Engineering*. The MIT Press, Cambridge, MA, 1998.

[25] Stephen I. Gallant. *Neural Network Learning and Expert System*. MIT Press, Cambridge, MA, 1993.

[26] J. Gásos and A. Martín. Mobile robot localization using fuzzy maps. In A. Ralescu and T. Martín, editors, *Lecture Notes in Artificial Intelligence*. Springer-Verlag, 1996.

[27] David E. Goldberg. *Genetic Algorithms in search, optimization & machine learning*. Addison-Wesley, Reading, MA, 1989.

[28] David E. Goldberg. *Genetic Algorithms in Search, Optimization &*

Machine Learning. Addison Wesley, 1989.

[29] A. Gómez-Skarmeta and F. Jiménez. Fuzzy modeling with hybrid systems. *Fuzzy Sets and Systems*, (2):199–208, 1999.

[30] José C. González, Juan R. Velasco, Carlos A. Iglesias, Jaime Alvarez, and Andrés Escobero. A multiagent architecture for symbolic-connectionist integration. Technical Report MIX/WP1/UPM/3.2, Dep. Ingeniería de Sistemas Telemáticos, E.T.S.I. Telecomunicación, Universidad Politécnica de Madrid, November 1995.

[31] B.A. Hayes-Roth. Blackboard for control. *Artificial Intelligence*, pages 251–324, 1985.

[32] J. Hendler. Making sense out of agents. *IEEE Intelligents Systems*, (2):32–37, 1999.

[33] F. Herrera, M. Lozano, and J.L. Verdegay. Tuning fuzzy logic controllers by genetic algorithms. *International Journal of Approximate Reasoning*, (12):299–315, 1995.

[34] F. Hoffmann and G. Pfister. Evolutionary learning of fuzzy control rule base for an autonomous vehicle. In *Proc. Sixth Int. Conf. Information Processing and Management of Uncertainty in Knowledge-Based Systems (IPMU'96)*, pages 1235–1240, Granada, Spain, 1996.

[35] Carlos A. Iglesias, Mercedes Garijo, and José Carlos Gonzalez. A Survey of Agent-Oriented Methodologies.

[36] Carlos A. Iglesias, José C. González, and Juan R. Velasco. MIX: A general purpose multiagent architecture. In M. Wooldridge, K. Fischer, P. Gmytrasiewicz, N.R. Jennings, J.P. Müller, and M. Tambe, editors, *Proceedings of the IJCAI'95 Workshop on Agent Theories, Architectures and Languages*, pages 216–224, Montreal, Canada, August 1995. International Joint Conference on Artificial Intelligence. (An extended version of this paper has appeared in *INTELLIGENT AGENTS II: Agent Theories, Architectures, and Languages*, Springer Verlag, 1996, pages 251–266.).

[37] H. Ishibuchi, K. Nozaki, N. Yamamoto, and H. Tanaka. Selecting fuzzy if-then rules for classification problems using genetic algorithms. *IEEE Trans on Fuzzy Systems*, (3):260–270, 1995.

[38] F. Klawonn and R. Kruse. Constructing a fuzzy controller from data. *Fuzzy Sets and Systems*, pages 177–193, 1997.

[39] K. Konolige. Colbert: a language for reactive control in saphira. In *German Conference on Artificial Intelligence*, Freiburg, 1997.

[40] A. Kroll. Identification of functional models using multidimensional reference fuzzy sets. *Fuzzy Sets and Systems*, pages 149–158, 1996.

[41] R. Langari and L. Wang. Fuzzy models, modular networks, and hybrid learning. *Fuzzy Sets and Systems*, pages 141–150, 1996.

[42] A. F. Gómez-Skarmeta M. Delgado and F. Martín. Using fuzzy clusters to model fuzzy systems in a descriptive approach. In *Proceedings*

of the Information Processing and Management of Uncertainty in
Knowledge-Based Systems. IPMU'96, Granada, Spain, 1996.

[43] Luis Magdalena. Analysis of hybrid models: Fuzzy logic/neural
nets. Technical Report MIX/WP2/UPM/1.2, Dep. Ingeniería de Sistemas Telemáticos, E.T.S.I. Telecomunicación, Universidad Politécnica
de Madrid, March 1995.

[44] Zbigniew Michalewicz. *Genetic Algorithms + Data Structures = Evolution Programs.* Springer-Verlag, 1992.

[45] M. Mizumoto. Method of fuzzy inference suitable for fuzzy control. *J. Soc. Instrument and Control Engrs,* (58):959–963, 1989.

[46] Hyacinth S. Nwana. Software Agents: An Overview. *Knowledge Engineering Review,* 1996.

[47] W. Pedrycz. An identificaction algorithm in fuzzy relational systems. *Fuzzy Sets and Systems,* (13):153–167, 1984.

[48] A. Saffiotti. Fuzzy logic in autonomous robotics: behavior coordination. pages 573–578, 1997.

[49] A. Th. Schreiber, J. M. Akkermans, A. A. Anjewierden, R. de Hoog,
N. R. Shadbolt, W. Van de Velde, and B. J. Wielinga. *Knowledge Engineering and Management. The CommonKADS Methodology. Version 1.1.* University of Amsterdam, 1999.

[50] A.F. Gómez Skarmeta and H. Martínez Barberá. Fuzzy logic based intelligent agents for reactive navigation in autonomous systems. In *Fifth International Conference on Fuzzy Theory and Technology,* pages 125–131, Raleigh, NC, 1997.

[51] A.F. Gómez Skarmeta, H. Martínez Barberá, and M. Sánchez Alonso.
A fuzzy agents architecture for autonomous mobile robots. In *International Fuzzy Systems World Congress (IFSA'99),* Taiwan, 1999.

[52] A.F. Gómez Skarmeta and F. Jiménez Barrionuevo. Generating and tuning fuzzy rules with hybrid systems. In *Sixth IEEE Intl. Conference on Fuzzy Systems (FuzzIEEE'97),* pages 247–252, Barcelona, Spain, 1997.

[53] M. Sugeno and K. Tanaka. Successive identification of a fuzzy model and its applications to prediction of a complex system. *Fuzzy Sets and Systems,* pages 315–334, 1991.

[54] M. Sugeno and T. Yasukawa. A fuzzy-logic-based approach to qualitative modeling. In *IEEE Trans. Fuzzy Systems,* number 1, pages 7–31, 1993.

[55] Ron Sun. *Integrating Rules and Connectionism for Robust Commonsense Reasoning.* John Wiley & Sons, New York, 1994.

[56] T. Takagi and M Sugeno. Fuzzy identification of systems and its applications to modeling and control. *IEEE Transactions on Systems, Man, and Cybernetics,* (1):116–132, 1985.

[57] E. Tunstel and M. Jamshidi. On genetic programming of fuzzy rule based systems for intelligent control. *Intl. Journal of Intelligent Automation*

and Soft Computing, (1), 1996.

[58] P. Vourimaa. Fuzzy self-organizing map. *Fuzzy Sets and Systems*, pages 223–231, 1994.

[59] S. Vranes and M. Stanojevic. Integrating multiple paradigms within the blackboard architecture. *IEEE Transactions on Software Engineering*, (3):244–262, 1995.

[60] L. Wang and R. Langari. Complex systems modeling via fuzzy logic. *IEEE Trans. on System Man and Cybernetics*, pages 100–106, 1996.

[61] L. Wang and R. Langari. Complex systems modeling via fuzzy logic. *IEEE Trans. on Systems, Man and Cybernetics*, (1):100–106, 1996.

[62] R.R. Yager and D.P. Filew. Generation of fuzzy rules by mountain clustering. tech. report mii-1318. Technical report, 1993.

[63] Y. Yoshinari, W. Pedrycz, and K. Hirota. Construction of fuzzy models through clustering techniques. *Fuzzy Sets and Systems*, (54):157–165, 1993.

4

Learning Techniques for Supervised Fuzzy Classifiers

Francesco Masulli

Istituto Nazionale per la Fisica della Materia, Via Dodecaneso 33, 16146 Genova, Italy, and DISI - Dipartimento di Informatica e Scienze dell'Informazione - Università di Genova, Via Dodecaneso 35, 16146 Genova, Italy, email: masulli@ge.INFM.it

Alessandro Sperduti

Dipartimento di Informatica, Università di Pisa, 56125 Pisa, Italy, e-mail: perso@di.unipi.it

Learning Techniques for
Supervised Fuzzy Classifiers

Abstract

In this chapter we present a family of learning machines for supervised classification, developed starting from neuro-fuzzy systems based on Fuzzy Basis Functions Networks (FBFNs). FBFNs hold universal function approximation capabilities, can learn their parameters from data, and are able to approximate the Bayes Optimal Classifier in supervised classification tasks. A gradient descent approach for learning is described and the classification capabilities of the trained system are compared with respect to Multi-Layer Perceptrons and Radial Basis Functions networks on a handwritten digit recognition task. Moreover, a simplified version of the model is described that is faster in learning. This simplified version cannot reach the same level of performance as the original model; however, an extended version of it, based on competitive learning, shows a significant increase in classification performance, still retaining a relatively short training time. Further improvement in performance can be obtained by using the k-Nearest-Neighbour Rule for input instances which cannot be classified with high confidence by the system. The increase in performance is paid with a slowdown in the response time. This slowdown, however, can be modulated through the use of *off-line* or *on-line* editing strategies for the k-NN Rule.

4.1 Introduction

The development of Fuzzy Logic Systems (FLSs) [16,19] requires the definition and tuning of the shapes and sizes of the membership functions. Neuro-fuzzy systems allow the automatic adjustment of these parameters on the basis of training data [12,13,28].

In this chapter, we present a FLS with *singleton* fuzzification, *max-product* composition, *product inference* and *height* defuzzification which can be described as a Fuzzy Basis Functions Network (FBFN) [15,28–30]. This system is demonstrated to possess universal approximation capabilities and is particularly suited to be trained on data by a gradient descent technique. Moreover, the system is able to approximate a Bayes Optimal Classifier, when trained using a suitable error function.

We show the details on how gradient descent can be applied to the FBF network and we compare, on a handwritten digit recognition task, its performances versus two other learning machines, namely Multi-Layer Perceptrons (MLPs), and Radial Basis Functions Networks (RBF). Moreover, we discuss a structural feature of the proposed model, i.e., the Semantic Phase Transition observed when passing from the training of a model with less rules than classification classes to a model with a number of rules which is equal to or greater than the number of classification classes.

The performance of the FBFNs are very interesting; however, very often, the resulting systems are very complex and may require long training times. Thus, it is of paramount importance to devise simple systems which are fast to train and still hold a very good generalization performance. For this reason, starting from the original formulation, it is possible to derive a simplified version of the model (SFBF), faster in training and still retaining much of the performance in classification of the original model. In fact, at the expenses of an increased training time, but still not so heavy as in the case of the original model, the SFBF model can be improved by introducing competition among rules belonging to the same class.

Finally, we show that performance can be further improved in a significant way by using the k-Nearest-Neighbour (k-NN) Rule [8] over input instances which cannot be classified with high confidence by the SFBF system. This time, the computational cost which must be paid for the increase in generalization is in terms of the average response time of the system. The tradeoff between the increase in performance and response time can be controlled by using both *off-line* or *on-line* editing strategies for the *k*-Nearest-Neighbour Rule.

4.2 The Fuzzy Basis Function Network

Fuzzy Logic Systems with *singleton* fuzzification, *max-product* composition, *product inference* and *height* defuzzification can be represented as [19]

$$y = f(\mathbf{x}) = \sum_{l=1}^{M} \overline{y}^{\,l} \phi_l(\mathbf{x}) \tag{4.1}$$

where $\overline{y}^{\,l}$ denote the center of gravity of the output fuzzy set, and $\phi_l(\mathbf{x})$ are called *fuzzy basis functions* and are given by

$$\phi_l(\mathbf{x}) = \frac{\prod_{i=1}^{p} \mu_{F_i^l}(x_i)}{\sum_{l=1}^{M} \prod_{i=1}^{p} \mu_{F_i^l}(x_i)} \tag{4.2}$$

where $l = 1, 2, ..., M$. We can refer to these FLS as *fuzzy basis expansions* or *networks of fuzzy basis functions* (FBF network)[1]. The relationships between fuzzy basis expansions and other basis functions have been extensively studied in [15].

It is worth noting that the FLS with universal function property studied by Mendel and Wang [28, 29], which is a singleton FLS using product inference, product implication, Gaussian membership and height defuzzification, can be rewritten as a FBF network expansion[2]. The universal function approximation property gives a strong mathematical ground when applying FLSs in critical applications, ranging from control, to time series prediction, to pattern recognition.

In this chapter we study a fuzzy logic system based on a Multi-Input-Multi-Output (MIMO) version of this FBF network. Specifically, if there are K units in the input layer, J fuzzy inference rules and I outputs, the rule activations can be expressed as:

$$r_j = \prod_k \mu_{jk}(x_k), \qquad (4.3)$$

where $\mu_{jk}(x_k)$ is the value of the membership function of the component x_k of the input vector for the jth rule and is defined as:

$$\mu_{jk}(x_k) = \exp\left(-\frac{(x_k - m_{jk})^2}{2\sigma_{jk}^2}\right), \qquad (4.4)$$

where m_{jk} and σ_{jk}^2 are the means and the variances of the Gaussian membership functions. The values of the output units are:

$$y_i = \frac{\sum_j r_j \bar{y}_{ij}}{\sum_j r_j} = \sum_j \bar{y}_{ij} \phi_j(\mathbf{x}) , \qquad (4.5)$$

where $\bar{y}_{ij}$ is the center of gravity of the output fuzzy membership function of the jth rule associated with the output y_i,[3] and

$$\phi_j = \frac{\prod_k \mu_{jk}(x_k)}{\sum_j \prod_k \mu_{jk}(x_k)} \qquad (4.6)$$

is the fuzzy basis function associated to rule j, and represents its normalized activation.

---

[1] In [19] fuzzy basis expansions for FLS with nonsingleton fuzzification are also introduced.
[2] Mouzouris and Mendel [21] do the same for a nonsingleton FLS that uses a range of t-norms, arbitrary membership functions and modified height defuzzification.
[3] Without loss of generality, we could assume that the fuzzy membership functions are singletons ($\bar{y}_{ij} \equiv s_{ij}$).

The FBF network can be regarded as a feedforward connectionist system with one hidden layer whose units correspond to the fuzzy rules. In Figure 4.1 a connectionist interpretation of the FBF network is shown. In the drawing, circles represent adaptive units, while squares stand for not-adaptive units, and free parameters are evidenced near the corresponding units.

The FBF network can be identified both by exploiting the linguistic knowledge available (*structure identification problem*) [16] and by using the information contained in a data set (*parameter estimation problem*) [16].

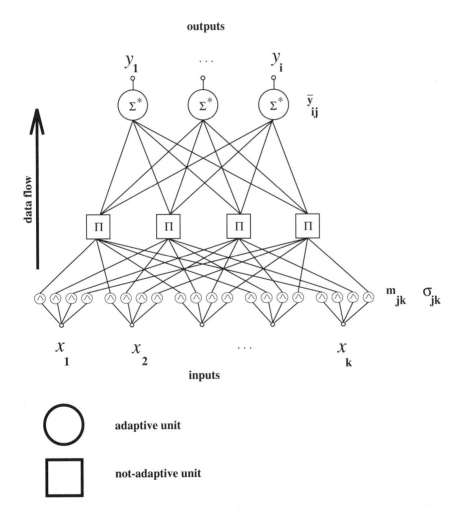

Figure 4.1 Connectionist interpretation of the FBF network.

4.3   Bayes Optimal Classifier Approximation

In the neural network literature, it has been demonstrated that a classifier based on an MLP can approximate the Bayes optimal discriminant function, for suitable choices of the cost function to be minimized during the training phase, and in the large training set limit [2, 11, 14, 20, 25].

In [18], we generalized this result and demonstrated, following Ruck et al. [25], that *a classifier based on a system holding the universal function approximation property can approximate the Bayes discriminant function*[4]. The demonstration we present here concerns the two-class case.

Let c_1 e c_2 be two classes of patterns. Let χ_i be the set of all possible patterns $\mathbf{x}$ belonging to class c_i; then $\chi = \chi_1 \cup \chi_2$ represents the set of all patterns. The training set consists of a subset of possible patterns belonging to the two classes. In general, it is a finite set $X = X_1 \cup X_2$, where $X_1 = \{\mathbf{x}_1, \mathbf{x}_2, ..., \mathbf{x}_{n_1}\} \subset \chi_1$, $X_2 = \{\mathbf{x}_{n_1+1}, ..., \mathbf{x}_{n_1+n_2}\} \subset \chi_2$, and $n_1 + n_2 = N$.

Let $\mathbf{w}$ be the set of adaptive parameters, $g(\mathbf{x})$ be the discriminant function of a Bayes dichotimizer

$$g(\mathbf{x}) = P(c_1 \mid \mathbf{x}) - P(c_2 \mid \mathbf{x}), \tag{4.7}$$

and $F(\mathbf{x}, \mathbf{w})$ be the system output.

Moreover, let us suppose that the system is trained in such a way that its response is $+1$ when $\mathbf{x}$ belongs to the class c_1, and -1 when $\mathbf{x}$ belongs to c_2:

$$F(\mathbf{x}, \mathbf{w}) = \begin{cases} +1 & \text{if } \mathbf{x} \in c_1 \\ -1 & \text{if } \mathbf{x} \in c_2 \end{cases}. \tag{4.8}$$

This is accomplished by minimizing (e.g., with the error backpropagation technique [26]) the *sample data error function*:

$$E_s(\mathbf{w}) = \sum_{\mathbf{x} \in X_1} [F(\mathbf{x}, \mathbf{w}) - 1]^2 + \sum_{\mathbf{x} \in X_2} [F(\mathbf{x}, \mathbf{w}) + 1]^2. \tag{4.9}$$

We shall demonstrate that in the large N limit, when $\mathbf{w}$ minimizes $E_s(\mathbf{w})$, then $\mathbf{w}$ minimizes also:

$$\epsilon^2(\mathbf{w}) = \int_\chi [F(\mathbf{x}, \mathbf{w}) - g(\mathbf{x})]^2 p(\mathbf{x}) dx, \tag{4.10}$$

i.e., $F(\mathbf{x}, \mathbf{w})$ approximates $g(\mathbf{x})$.

---

[4] As pointed out by Ruck et al. [25], this demonstration is not based on any assumption about the particular feedforward system used; only the system's capability for function approximation is assumed.

Let us define the *average error function* as the function

$$E_a(\mathbf{w}) = \lim_{N \to \infty} \frac{1}{N} E_s(\mathbf{w}) \tag{4.11}$$

where N is the total number of pattern vectors. $E_a(\mathbf{w})$ represents the error surface that is obtained when all possible vectors are used for the computation.

As assumed, in the large N limit, we can suppose that the function E_s is a reasonable approximation for E_a.

Let us rewrite the function E_a as follows:

$$E_a(\mathbf{w}) = \lim_{N \to \infty} \left[\frac{n_1}{N} * \frac{1}{n_1} \sum_{\mathbf{x} \in X_1} [F(\mathbf{x}, \mathbf{w}) - 1]^2 + \frac{n_2}{N} * \frac{1}{n_2} \sum_{\mathbf{x} \in X_2} [F(\mathbf{x}, \mathbf{w}) + 1]^2 \right] \tag{4.12}$$

where n_i is the number of vectors belonging to the class c_i, and $\frac{n_1}{N}$ and $\frac{n_2}{N}$ represent, in the large N limit, the a priori probabilities $P(c_1)$ and $P(c_2)$, respectively.

The quantities $\frac{1}{n_i} \sum_{\mathbf{x} \in X_i} [F(\mathbf{x}, \mathbf{w}) - 1]^2$ represent the average value of $[F(\mathbf{x}, \mathbf{w}) - 1]^2$, over the patterns, provided that $\mathbf{x} \in c_i$.

By exploiting the strong law of large number [23], we can rewrite Eq. 4.12 as

$$
\begin{aligned}
E_a(\mathbf{w}) &= P(c_1) \int_\chi [F(\mathbf{x}, \mathbf{w}) - 1]^2 p(\mathbf{x} \mid c_1) d\mathbf{x} + \\
&\quad + P(c_2) \int_\chi [F(\mathbf{x}, \mathbf{w}) + 1]^2 p(\mathbf{x} \mid c_2) d\mathbf{x} \\
&= \int_\chi [F^2(\mathbf{x}, \mathbf{w}) + 1][p(\mathbf{x} \mid c_1) P(c_1) + p(\mathbf{x} \mid c_2) P(c_2)] d\mathbf{x} + \\
&\quad - 2 \int_\chi F(\mathbf{x}, \mathbf{w})[p(\mathbf{x} \mid c_1) P(c_1) - p(\mathbf{x} \mid c_2) P(c_2)] d\mathbf{x}
\end{aligned}
\tag{4.13}
$$

The probability density function of the input vectors can be expressed as:

$$p(\mathbf{x}) = p(\mathbf{x} \mid c_1) P(c_1) + p(\mathbf{x} \mid c_2) P(c_2) \tag{4.14}$$

Moreover, by using the Bayes rule, we can write:

$$
\begin{aligned}
g(\mathbf{x})p(\mathbf{x}) &= [P(c_1 \mid \mathbf{x}) - P(c_2 \mid \mathbf{x})]p(\mathbf{x}) \\
&= P(c_1 \mid \mathbf{x})p(\mathbf{x}) - P(c_2 \mid \mathbf{x})p(\mathbf{x}) \\
&= p(\mathbf{x} \mid c_1)P(c_1) - p(\mathbf{x} \mid c_2)P(c_2)
\end{aligned}
\tag{4.15}
$$

Therefore:

$$
\begin{aligned}
E_a(\mathbf{w}) &= \int_\chi [F^2(\mathbf{x}, \mathbf{w}) + 1]p(\mathbf{x})d\mathbf{x} - 2\int_\chi F(\mathbf{x}, \mathbf{w})g(\mathbf{x})p(\mathbf{x}) \quad\quad (4.16)\\
&= \int_\chi [F^2(\mathbf{x}, \mathbf{w}) - 2F(\mathbf{x}, \mathbf{w})g(\mathbf{x})]p(\mathbf{x})d\mathbf{x} + \int_\chi p(\mathbf{x})d\mathbf{x}\\
&= \int_\chi [F(\mathbf{x}, \mathbf{w}) - g(\mathbf{x})]^2 p(\mathbf{x})d\mathbf{x} - \int_\chi g^2(\mathbf{x})p(\mathbf{x})d\mathbf{x} + \int_\chi p(\mathbf{x})d\mathbf{x}\\
&= \epsilon^2(\mathbf{w}) + \int_\chi [1 - g^2(\mathbf{x})]p(\mathbf{x})d\mathbf{x}
\end{aligned}
$$

The learning algorithm will minimize E_s with respect to $\mathbf{w}$. Then, as we assumed $E_s(\mathbf{w})$ to be a reasonable approximation for $E_a(\mathbf{w})$, the learning algorithm will minimize also E_a with respect to $\mathbf{w}$. Moreover, $\int_\chi [1 - g^2(\mathbf{x})]p(\mathbf{x})d\mathbf{x}$ is a quantity that does not depend on $\mathbf{w}$; hence the optimization algorithm minimizes $\epsilon^2(\mathbf{w})$, too, which was to be demonstrated.

For the multiclass problem, let us define the *mean square error* (MSE):

$$
MSE = \frac{\sum_{i,n}(y_i^n - t_i^n)^2}{N}, \quad\quad (4.17)
$$

where N is the size of the training set, $\mathbf{y}^n = (y_i^n)$ is the network output, and $\mathbf{t}^n = (t_i^n)$ is the n-th label of the associative pair of the training set. The components of $\mathbf{t}^n$ are defined as follows:

$$
t_i = \begin{cases} 1 & \text{if the pattern belongs to class } i, \\ 0 & \text{otherwise.} \end{cases} \quad\quad (4.18)
$$

In the large training set limit, one can demonstrate that, if the MSE is assumed as the cost function, then when $\mathbf{w}$ minimizes the MSE, the system outputs y_i approximate the Bayes optimal discriminant functions, i.e., the a posteriori class probabilities [25].

4.4   Learning in a FBFN Classifier

Exploiting the theory developed in the previous section for the multiclass problem, learning can be performed by minimizing the cost function shown in Eq. 4.17. This cost function can be minimized by many different techniques, among which are the gradient descent technique, clustering methods [30], Kalman filters [12], genetic algorithms [6], etc. In our experiments, the FBF network parameters (i.e., m_{jk}, σ_{jk} and $\overline{y}_{ij}$) were obtained by performing a gradient descent with respect to the MSE across the training set. The learning formulas are [13,30]:

$$
\Delta\overline{y}_{ij} = \eta_s[t_i - y_i]\phi_j \quad\quad (4.19)
$$

$$\Delta m_{jk} = \eta_m \phi_j \sum_i [t_i - y_i][\overline{y}_{ij} - y_i][x_k - m_{jk}]/\sigma_{jk}^2 \qquad (4.20)$$

$$\Delta \sigma_{jk} = \eta_\sigma \phi_j \sum_i [t_i - y_i][\overline{y}_{ij} - y_i][x_k - m_{jk}]^2/\sigma_{jk}^3 \qquad (4.21)$$

where

$$\phi_j = \frac{\prod_k \mu_{jk}(x_k)}{\sum_j \prod_k \mu_{jk}(x_k)} \qquad (4.22)$$

represents the normalized activation of rule j, and η_s, η_m, and η_σ are the learning rates for $\overline{y}_{ij}$, m_{jk}, and σ_{jk}, respectively. In our experiments, we adopted an adaptive learning-rate scheme, as proposed in [27], and we noticed a considerable speed-up of the training phase [3].

If a linguistic description of classes is available, in addition to the numerical training set, the FBF network permits the integration of these two types of information. On the contrary, if a linguistic description is not available, as is the case with our experiments, the structure identification must be achieved experimentally according to a performance-based criterion.

4.5 Data Base and Preprocessing

Rules	Parameters	(%L, %T)	epochs	(%L1, %T1)	Time (min)
24	3312	(97.55, 94.00)	30	(91.0, 88.0)	3.5
32	4416	(98.05, 95.00)	30	(89.0, 87.0)	4.0
48	6624	(98.65, 95.81)	30	(91.5, 88.5)	16.0
64	8832	(98.32, 96.02)	30	(93.5, 92.0)	23.0
128	17664	(98.97, 96.20)	30	(94.5, 93.5)	46.0

Table 4.1 FBF network performances. From left to right, the columns represent the number of rules mapped on the FBF network, the number of adaptive parameters, the percentages of learning success (%L) and of test success (%T) after the training phase, the number of epochs required by the training phase, the percentages of learning success (%L1) and of test success (%T1) at end of the first epoch, and the duration of each epoch (in min on a SUN 10/20).

All the experiments reported in the following sections were carried out on a SUN 10/50 workstation (except those in Table 4.1). We used a data set of 30000 samples extracted from the NIST-3 data base [9]. The NIST-3 data-base, distributed on a CD-ROM, contains 313389 handwritten characters coded as 128×128 binary-matrix images and labeled by the corresponding ASCII codes. We partitioned the data set in a training set, a test set and a validation set, each containing 10,000 associative pairs of segmented handwritten digits obtained from disjoint groups of writers. In order to improve the robustness

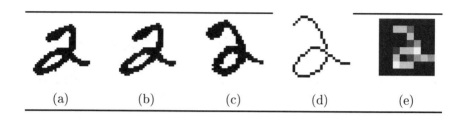

| (a) | (b) | (c) | (d) | (e) |

Figure 4.2 Preprocessing steps for a handwritten digit: Normalization (a), low-pass filtering (b), shear transform (c), skeletonization (d), local counting (e).

of the classifier to noise and distortion, some preprocessing operations were performed. Among these there are some which try to increase the invariance of the classifier to scaling, shear, and thickness transformations. The following preprocessing steps were applied:

1. Digit image extraction from the CD-ROM and normalization to a 32×32 binary matrix.
2. Low-pass filtering in order to remove some small spots and holes from the image.
3. Application of a shear transform to the digit image to straighten the axis joining the first upper-left point of the digit image to the last lower-right point.
4. Image skeletonization [23], in order to be invariant to the thickness of the strokes.
5. Finally, transformation of the digit representation into a 64-element vector, each vector element representing the number of black pixels contained in adjacent 4×4 squares (local counting).

An example of application of the preprocessing is shown in Figure 4.2.

4.6   Classification Performances

In [18] a comparison is made between the performances of three connectionist feed-forward classifiers, namely a MLP [26], a Resource Allocating Network (RAN) [24], and a FBF network. The Resource Allocating Network is a Radial Basis Function neural network characterized by the growth of its architecture during the training phase [24]. The structure of each of the three systems was made up by 64 input units, 48 hidden nodes, and 10 output units (one for each class to be recognized). As shown in Figure 4.3, the three nets exhibit similar generalization properties, as we expected from a theoretical standpoint.

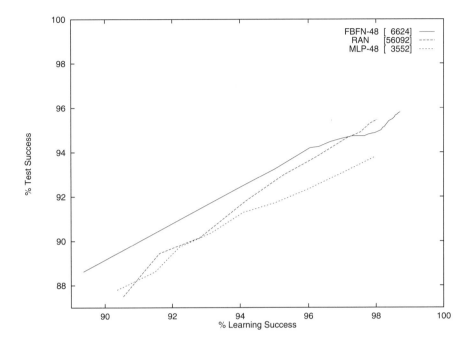

Figure 4.3 Comparison among the performances of the MLP, of the FBF network and of the RAN. The numbers within brackets refer to the parameters used by each of the three systems.

The MLP reaches a generalization value smaller than those of the other two learning machines. This may be due to the problem of *false positive*, as discussed by Lee [17]. The training phase of the FBF network is faster than that of the MLP. The RAN is the slowest one during the training phase; this depends on the growth of its architecture up to more than $50,000$ parameters (each of them to be optimized !). Moreover, it is worth noting that the RAN shows the highest derivative of the Test Success, as compared with the Training Success. This depends on the possibility of allocating new units dynamically during the learning phase that characterizes this learning machine.

Table 4.1 gives the results of experiments on FBF networks with a different number of rules. FBFNs show very good performances; for instance, in the case of an FBF network with 128 rules, a single epoch of 46 min is enough to obtain a percentage of test success equal to 93.5%.

Training set		FBF_1	FBF_2	FBF_3	FBF_4	FBF_5
Class	Examples	%	%	%	%	%
0	1052	100	100	100	100	100
1	1134	100	100	100	1.234	1.410
2	966	100	100	100	100	100
3	1059	100	100	100	100	100
4	967	100	3.177	1.964	2.378	3.309
5	842	100	100	100	100	100
6	948	100	100	100	100	4.00
7	1052	100	100	100	100	100
8	978	0.0	1.87	5.725	6.032	6.748
9	1002	100	100	2.295	2.694	2.694
Training set		FBF_6	FBF_7	FBF_8	FBF_9	FBF_{10}
Class	Examples	%	%	%	%	%
0	1052	1.615	1.711	1.711	1.711	1.806
1	1134	1.410	1.410	1.499	1.499	1.587
2	966	100.	4.968	5.590	6.004	6.107
3	1059	100	100	100	3.966	4.438
4	967	3.826	3.826	3.826	3.826	3.826
5	842	100	100	100	100	11.63
6	948	4.00	4.113	4.113	4.113	4.535
7	1052	100	100	2.471	2.471	2.471
8	978	6.952	7.668	7.873	8.077	8.691
9	1002	2.894	3.093	3.393	3.493	3.592

Table 4.2   Training set error rates on 10,000 patterns by ten different FBF networks, ranging from 1 to 10 rules.

4.7   FBFN Structure Identification and Semantic Phase Transition

In [4], ten different FBF networks have been trained on the training set described in Section 4.5. The FBF networks differ in the number of rules, ranging from 1 up to 10. In Table 4.2, for each class of digit the numbers of patterns in the training set and the percentage of patterns not correctly recognized by each FBF network at the end of the training phase are shown. It is worth noting a close relationship between the number of rules in the FBF network and the number of classes which are recognized by the FBF network: $10 - \beta$ classes are not recognized at all for FBF network with β rules, while the other classes are well recognized. On the contrary, in the case of FBF_{10} (or of FBF networks with more than 10 rules) the error rate is uniformly distributed along all the classes. This behavior of the FBF network, that we call *semantic phase transition*, has been confirmed by further series of simulations, and is not common in other feedforward connectionist systems. The semantic phase transition phenomenon gives a lower bound to the FBF network structure: the FBF network must contain a number of rules at least equal to the number of classes to be discriminated. The *semantic phase transition* observed for the FBF network can be explained by the *specialization* of each rule in a specific class. Even though it is hard to fully understand how a single rule of the system works, it is very easy to deduce the functional problem solved by each rule. Moreover, we have observed that the set of rules in a system with more than 10 rules can always be partitioned into 10 different subsets, each responsible for the classification of the examples of a specific class. Thus, even if the FBF network is organized as a supervised feedforward network, its behavior is closer to the one of a *competitive model* showing a strong specialization of the fuzzy rules. A pruning technique was proposed by Casalino et al. [5], in order to automatically remove less relevant fuzzy rules from an oversized system.

4.8   The Simplified FBF Network and Its Extension

For pattern recognition applications, from this FBF network a *Simplified FBF network* (SFBF network) can be obtained by assuming, in accordance with *rule specialization* [1]:

$$\overline{y}_{ij} \equiv \delta_{ij} = \begin{cases} 1 & \text{if rule } j \text{ is} \\ & \text{associated to class } i, \\ 0 & \text{otherwise.} \end{cases} \tag{4.23}$$

This assumption leads to both a system with as many units as classes and a strong simplification of the learning formulas, which become:

$$\Delta m_{jk} = \eta_m \phi_j \Upsilon_{ij} [x_k - m_{jk}] / \sigma_{jk}^2 \tag{4.24}$$

$$\Delta \sigma_{jk} = \eta_\sigma \phi_j \Upsilon_{ij} [x_k - m_{jk}]^2 / \sigma_{jk}^3 \tag{4.25}$$

with

$$\Upsilon_{ij} = \begin{cases} (y_i - 1)^2 & \text{if } j = i \\ y_i^2 - y_i & \text{if } j \neq i \end{cases} \tag{4.26}$$

It is worth noting that, from Eq. 4.23 and the form of the defuzzifier, $y \in (0, 1)$ follows, and consequently

$$\Upsilon_{ij} = \begin{cases} \geq 0 & \text{if } j = i \\ \leq 0 & \text{if } j \neq i \end{cases} \tag{4.27}$$

holds.

Therefore, the learning rules of the SFBF network are competitive. During training, the means of the Gaussian membership functions of each rule move towards the patterns of the class associated to that rule, and escape from patterns belonging to other classes. At the same time, sigmas of Gaussian membership functions of each rule grow in order to increase the value of the membership function μ for patterns of the class associated to that rule, or shrink in order to reduce the value of the Gaussian membership function for patterns belonging to other classes. An interesting property of these new learning formulas is that they reduce by one order of magnitude the time of training.

MODEL	%S-Validation	Epochs	Epoch Duration (sec)
NR	92.89	−	−
FBF_{48}	94.09	13	1925
FBF_{12}	92.26	36	307
FBF_{10}	92.23	55	180
SFBF	91.36	10	30
$ESFBF_{20}$	93.80	250	49

Table 4.3   Comparison among the NR, the FBF network (with 48, 12, and 10 rules), the SFBF network, and the ESFBF with 20 rules (two for each class). %S-Validation is the success rate on the validation set.

One problem with the SFBF model is that, since it must have as many units as classification classes, it cannot be used for complex classification tasks. This constraint can be removed by introducing a new level of competition among units. The new defined network, called Extended Simplified FBF system (ESFBF), possesses n_j units associated to each class j, for a total of $J = \sum_{j=1}^{I} n_j$ units. During learning the output of each unit is computed and the best unit for each class is selected, i.e., for each class j the unit $i_j^* \in Idx_j = \{1, \ldots, n_j\}$ such that $i_j^* = arg \max_{i \in Idx_j}\{\phi_i\}$ is selected. In that way the number of selected units is equal to the number of classes and the learning rules of the SFBF network can be applied. Thus, at each learning step, only the selected rules have the weights changed. During the operational phase, the input pattern is classified by the class label associated with the unit having maximum activity.

4.9   Performance of the SFBF and ESFBF networks

For comparison purposes, in Table 4.3 we have reported the performance of Nearest-Neighbor Rule (NR) [8], FBF networks with different number of units, SFBF network and EFBF with 20 rules on the validation set. In Figure 4.4 we have reported the performance of the k-Nearest-Neighbour for different values

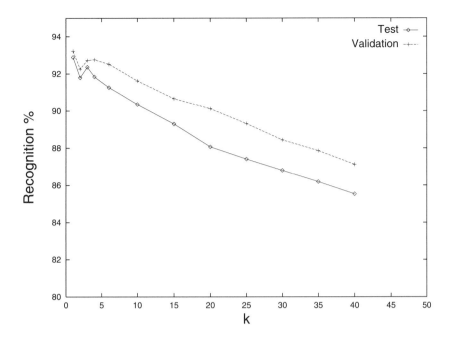

Figure 4.4 Performance of the k-Nearest-Neighbour on the test and validation sets using as reference data base the training set.

of k. Due to noise in the data, the best performance was obtained for $k = 1$. The training of the networks was stopped using the test set (early stopping).

We remark that the FBF_{48} network got a better performance with respect to NR. Moreover, the average recognition time per pattern of the NR was .733 sec, while for the FBF_{48} network it was .004 sec. In addition, it can be observed that the generalization performances of the FBF_{10} network and the SFBF network were similar, while the SFBF network resulted to be faster in learning, in accordance with the lower complexity of the learning rules.

Finally, a significant improvement was obtained by the ESFBF with 20 rules (2 for each class). The training and test curves for this network are reported in Figure 4.5. It must be noted that the performance of this network was very close to the performance of the FBF network with 48 units, thus showing that the ESFBF networks, besides being much faster in training (i.e., it is comparable with a FBF with 10 rules), can reach generalization performances which are comparable to the ones obtained by more complex models.

In Figure 4.6, we have reported an histogram representing how many times a winning rule performs a correct classification after training. This histogram

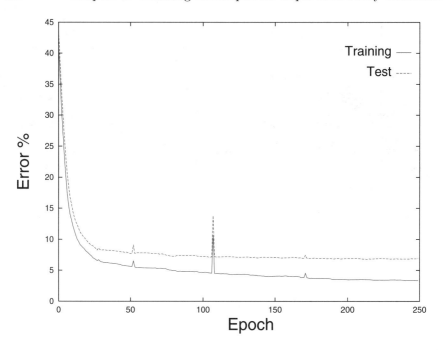

Figure 4.5   Training and test curves for a ESFBF with 20 units (2 units for each class).

is useful to understand whether, and to which extent, rules associated with the same class are used. From the histogram we deduce that all rules are used, even if in several cases there is one rule which is much more "active" than the other, which means that more patterns are covered by it.

4.10   Hybrid Network

An alternative way for recovering the loss in generalization exhibited by the SFBF network consists in resorting to a hybrid pattern recognition scheme (HS) based on a hierarchy made up by an SFBF network with rejection, followed by a Nearest-Neighbor Rule classifier working on the patterns rejected by the SFBF network (see Figure 4.7). This approach is discussed here for the SFBF; however, it can be directly applied to the ESFBF network as well, and experimental results, discussed elsewhere [10], confirm the improvement in performance for this case.

After the training of the SFBF network, a rejection rule is implemented, consisting in a *rejection threshold* on the level of the higher output. If no output of the SFBF network is greater than the threshold, the pattern is rejected

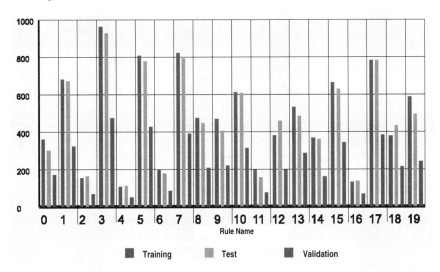

Figure 4.6 ESFBF system with 20 rules: histogram representing how many times a winning rule performs a correct classification. The rules are identified by numbers from 0 to 19: rules 0 and 1 are associated to class "0", rules 2 and 3 are associated to class "1", and so on. From the histogram it is clear that all the rules participate to the competition. The validation data refer to half of the validation set (i.e., 5000 patterns).

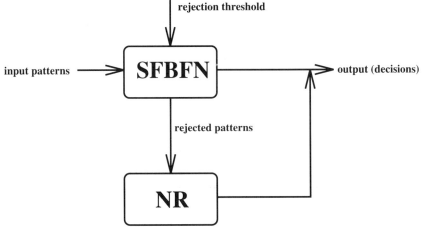

Figure 4.7 Hybrid Pattern Recognition Scheme combining the SFBF network and the NR.

from the SFBF network and the Nearest-Neighbour Rule classifier is applied
to it. By using the recognition threshold, the SFBF network classifies very
quickly most of the patterns with small classification error, while a minority
of patterns are forwarded to the NR for classification. For rejected patterns,
the recognition speed depends mainly on the dimension of the space of search
used by the NR.

In order to speed-up the recognition time of the NR classifier, we studied some optimizations of the hybrid scheme, consisting in editing strategies
able to reduce the dimensions of the data base to be used by the NR. The
first optimization consisted in an *off-line editing strategy* to be used at the
completion of the learning of the SFBF network. This method consists in a
condensation of the training set, obtained by filtering the original training set
by the SFBF network itself, with the application of the rejection threshold
to the classification algorithm. By using this strategy, for each value of the
rejection threshold on the SFBF network output, one obtains a *condensed data
base* (CDB) containing only the patterns close to the decision surfaces that are
the most important for classification. In Figure 4.8, for the SFBF network,
the rejection rate of patterns of the training set, versus the error rate on the
accepted (classified) patterns, is plotted. Near each experimental point, the
value of the corresponding rejection threshold applied to the SFBF network,
is reported. This information is used for the selection of the most suitable
threshold to be used within the hybrid scheme.

As shown in Table 4.4, the value of the rejection threshold (Rej-Thresh)
affects the overall performance of the hybrid scheme. In this table CDB-Dim
stands for the dimension of the resulting Condensed Data base, %E-Train is
the error rate on the accepted patterns of the training set, %S-Valid is the
success rate on the validation set, and Rec-Time is the average recognition
time for the input pattern.

Rej-Thresh	CDB-Dimen	%E-Train	%S-Valid	Rec-Time (sec)
.98	4549	.89	93.62	.0750
.95	3019	1.49	93.45	.0324
.70	713	3.95	92.43	.0020

Table 4.4 Hybrid Pattern Recognition Scheme: Performance with different rejection
thresholds (see text).

From Table 4.4, one could infer that improvements of the recognition times
with the hybrid scheme can be obtained to the detriment of the generalization
rate, or vice versa. However, at classification time one can use an efficient
on-line editing strategy, by considering for the Nearest-Neighbour Rule (NR)

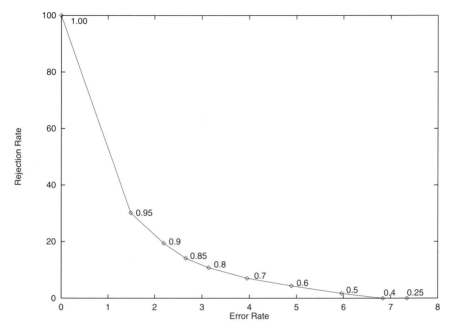

Figure 4.8   Effect of the rejections threshold (reported near each experimental point) on the training set.

only patterns belonging to classes that get the first L higher rates by the SFBF network.

In Table 4.5 for each value of L ($L \in [2, 10]$), the success rate on the validation set (%S-Valid) is shown. The rejection threshold for each experiment is set to .95. These experimental data point out that there is no significant dependence of the success rate on L. As a consequence a choice of $L = 2$ leads to good generalization performance and the higher recognition speed (about 5 times faster than for L=10, with our preliminary results).

In order to obtain a further speed-up in the search for the closest points by the NR, a parallel hardware can be developed, and/or the usage of optimized data structures, such as bumptrees [22], or randomized algorithms [7], can be experimented.

4.11   Conclusions

The universal function approximation results are a key property for many connectionist systems, such as MLP, RBF and FLS. Moreover the choice of a suitable cost function for parameter identification permits facing efficiently

L	2	3	4	5	6	7	8	9	10
%S-Valid	93.46	93.53	93.68	93.58	93.64	93.66	93.61	93.60	93.45

Table 4.5 Hybrid Pattern Recognition Scheme: Performance with on-line edited condensed data base (see text).

pattern recognition problems.

In this framework, efficient supervised non-parametric fuzzy classifiers can be easily obtained, as shown in this chapter. The peculiarity of a classifier based on FLS, such as the FBF network studied here, consists in the fact that, if a linguistic description of classes is available in addition to a numerical training set, it can exploit both kinds of information for the pattern recognition task.

Moreover, we have shown that, according to the computational resources at hand and according to the target classification performance, it is possible to define a range of models, all derived from the original formulation of the FBF network, covering a large spectrum of controlling values involving training time, performance, and response time.

4.12   Acknowledgments

This work was supported by grants from CNR, INFM, and MURST. We thank Nicola Giusti for implementing the competitive and hybrid algorithms.

4.13   References

[1] D. Alfonso, F. Masulli, and A. Sperduti. Competitive learning in a classifier based on an adaptive fuzzy system. In P.G. Anderson and K. Warwick, editors, *Proceedings of the International ICSC Symposium on Industrial Intelligent Automation (IIA'96) and Soft Computing (SOCO'96), Reading, England*, pages C2–C8, Millet, Alberta, Canada, 1996. ICSC.

[2] E. Barnard, F. Kanaya, and S. Miyake. Comments on 'Bayes statistical behavior and valid generalization of pattern classifying neural networks' (with reply). *IEEE Transactions on Neural Networks*, 3:1026–7, 1992.

[3] F. Casalino. Fuzzy systems for handwriting recognition. Laurea Thesis in Computer Science, University of Genoa, Genova - Italy, 1993. In Italian.

[4] F. Casalino, F. Masulli, and A. Sperduti. Rule specialization in networks of fuzzy basis functions. *Intelligent Automation and Soft Computing*, 4:73–82, 1998.

[5] F. Casalino, F. Masulli, A. Sperduti, and F. Vannucci. Semantic phase transition in a classifier based on an adaptive fuzzy system. In *Proceedings of the Third IEEE International Conference on Fuzzy Systems, IEEE-FUZZ94*, volume 2, pages 808–812, Orlando, FL, USA, 1994. IEEE.

[6] R. Caviglia. Soft-computing methods for time series forecasting. Laurea Thesis in Computer Science, University of Genoa, Genova - Italy, 1994. In Italian.

[7] K. L. Clarkson. A randomized algorithm for the closest-point queries. *SIAM Journal on Computing*, pages 830–847, 1988.

[8] R.O. Duda and P.E. Hart. *Pattern Classification and Scene Analysis*. Wiley, New York, 1973.

[9] M.D. Garris and R.A. Wilkinson. *NIST Special Database3 Handwritten Segmented Characters*. National Institute of Standard and Technology, Gaithersburg, MD, USA, 1992.

[10] N. Giusti, F. Masulli, and A. Sperduti. Competitive and hybrid neuro-fuzzy models for supervised classification. In *Proceedings of 1997 IEEE International Conference on Neural Networks, INNC'97*, pages 516–519, Houston, USA, 1997. IEEE.

[11] J. Hampshire and B. Pearlmutter. Equivalence proofs for multi-layer perceptron classifiers and the Bayesian discriminant function. In D.S. Touretzky, G. Hinton, and T. Sejnowski, editors, *Connectionist Models: Proceedings of the 1990 Summer school*, pages 13–19, Denver, 1990. Morgan Kaufmann, San Mateo.

[12] J.S.R. Jang. ANFIS: Adaptive-network-based fuzzy inference system. *IEEE Trans. on Systems, Man, and Cybernetics*, 23:655–684, 1993.

[13] C.C. Jou. Comparing learning performance of neural networks and fuzzy

systems. In *IEEE International Conference on Fuzzy Systems*, pages 1028–1033, San Francisco, 1993. IEEE, New York, NY.

[14] F. Kanaya and S. Miyake. Bayes statistical behavior and valid generalization of pattern classifying neural networks. *IEEE Transactions on Neural Networks*, 2:471–475, 1991.

[15] H.M. Kim and J.M. Mendel. Fuzzy basis functions: Comparisons with other basis functions. *IEEE Trans. on Fuzzy Systems*, 3:158–168, 1995.

[16] C.C. Lee. Fuzzy logic in control systems: fuzzy logic controller. I. *IEEE Transactions on Systems, Man and Cybernetics*, 20:404–418, 1990.

[17] Y. Lee. Handwritten digit recognition using k nearest-neighbor, radial-basis function, and backpropagation neural networks. *Neural Computation*, 3:440–449, 1991.

[18] F. Masulli. Bayesian classification by feedforward connectionist systems. In F. Masulli, P. G. Morasso, and A. Schenone, editors, *Neural Networks in Biomedicine - Proceedings of the Advanced School of the Italian Biomedical Physics Association - Como (Italy) 1993*, pages 145–162, Singapore, 1994. World Scientific. *(invited)*.

[19] J.M. Mendel. Fuzzy logic systems for engineering: A tutorial. *Proceedings of the IEEE*, 83:345–377, 1995.

[20] S. Miyake and F. Kanaya. A neural network approach to a Bayesian statistical decision problem. *IEEE Transactions on Neural Networks*, 2:538–540, 1991.

[21] G.C. Mouzouris and J.M. Mendel. Non-singleton fuzzy logic systems. In *Proc. 1994 IEEE Conf. on Fuzzy Systems*, Orlando 1994, 1989. IEEE, New York.

[22] S. M. Omohundro. Bumptrees for efficient function, constraint, and classification learning. In R.P. Lippmann, J.E. Moody, and D. S. Touretzky, editors, *Advances in Neural Information Processing Systems 3*, pages 693–900. San Mateo, CA: Morgan Kaufmann, 1991.

[23] Theo Pavlidis. *Algorithms for Graphics and Image Processing*. Springer-Verlag, 1982.

[24] J. Platt. A resource-allocating network for function interpolation. *Neural Computation*, 3:213–225, 1991.

[25] D.W. Ruck, S.K. Rogers, M. Kabrisky, M.E. Oxley, and B.W. Suther. The multilayer perceptron as an approximation to a Bayes optimal discriminant function. *IEEE Transactions on Neural Networks*, 1:296–298, 1990.

[26] D.E. Rumelhart, G.E. Hinton, and R.J. Williams. Learning internal representations by error propagation. In D.E. Rumelhart and J.L. Mc-Clelland, editors, *Parallel Distributed Processing*, volume 1, chapter 8, pages 318–362. MIT Press, Cambridge, 1986.

[27] T.P. Vogl, J.K. Mangis, A.K. Rigler, W.T. Zink, and D.L. Alkon. Accelerating the convergence of the back-propagation method. *Biological*

Cybernetics, 59:257–263, 1988.

[28] L. Wang and J.M. Mendel. Fuzzy basis functions, universal approximation, and orthogonal least-squares learning. *IEEE Trans. on Neural Networks*, 5:807–14, 1992.

[29] L. Wang and J.M. Mendel. Generating fuzzy rules by learning from examples. *IEEE Trans. on Systems, Man, and Cybernetics*, 22:1414–1427, 1992.

[30] L. X. Wang. *Adaptive Fuzzy Systems and Control*. Prentice-Hall, Englewood Cliffs, New Jersey, 1994.

5

Multistage Fuzzy Control

Zong-Mu Yeh
Email: zongmu@cc.ntnu.edu.tw, FAX: (02)2392944

Hung-Pin Chen
Department of Industrial Education,
National Taiwan Normal University,
Taipei, Taiwan, 10610, R.O.C.

0-8493-2269-3/00/$0.00+$.50
© 2001 by CRC Press LLC

Multistage Fuzzy Control

Abstract

This chapter is related to the design of a multistage fuzzy control system. A general method to generate fuzzy rules for a multistage fuzzy controller from the performance index of the control system is presented. The simulation results using three-stage fuzzy inference showed that the good performance is achieved using this approach.

5.1 Introduction

The recent success of fuzzy logic has encouraged its use in complex applications that have large amounts of rules and require real-time responses [1]. The typical fuzzy logic models contain various inputs and outputs and can be divided into three types: single-input and single-output (SISO), multiple-input and single-output (MISO), and multiple-input and multiple-output (MIMO) shown in Fig. 5.1. As application systems become more complicated, they would contain more complex knowledge which may be expressed in more complex ways, and they involve a large number of fuzzy rules that will increase quickly with the growing numbers of inputs, outputs and membership functions. For example, in a system of N input variables and single output variable with M fuzzy values for each variables, the total number of complete fuzzy rules is M^N. The completeness of fuzzy rules means that at any point in the input space there is at least one rule that will be fired. This large size of fuzzy rules would need great efforts to develop them and the inference computation time will be lengthy. Consequently, the typical single-stage fuzzy inference may not be suitable for human intelligent activities.

To reduce the complexity of the fuzzy systems, they are often performed via decentralized into a number of small fuzzy subsystem or divided into multistage inference system to solve complex problems. Since the decentralized control approach is reliable and practical in view of the implementation, it is the most popular approach which attempts to design control schemes where each subsystem is controlled independently based on local information. For example, a three-link robot may be treated as three subsystems and each subsystem is controlled independently. However, some complex systems are difficult to divide into subsystems; thus some of the complex systems are suitable to be controlled by hierarchical controllers (multistage).

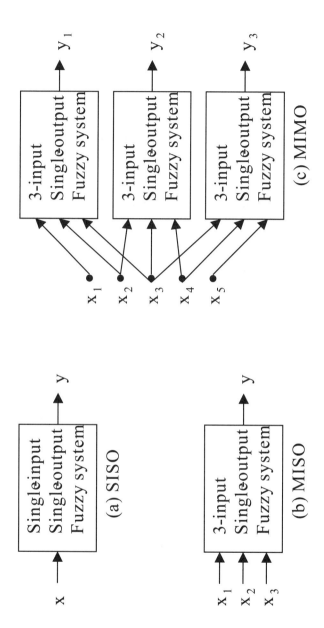

Figure 5.1 SISO, MISO, and MIMO fuzzy systems

To reduce the number of fuzzy rules for complex systems, the multistage fuzzy logic inference has been proposed [2]-[5]. In addition to input and output variables, intermediate variables are adopted in fuzzy rules to mimic human knowledge. The key advantage of using hierarchical structure (multistage) is that the number of fuzzy rules will increase quadratically ($O(N^2)$) with the number of input variables and (or) membership functions [2, 3]; for example, if a six-input and single-output fuzzy control system uses seven fuzzy values for each input variable, and the system is divided into five-stage in which instead of 7^6. In this multistage inference system shown in Fig. 5.2, there are two input variables and each stage has two inputs and one output. The number of fuzzy rules is reduced to $5 * 7^2$ intermediate output variables in the first stage; from the second to fourth stage, there are one input variable, one intermediate input variable and one intermediate output variable; in the final stage, there are one input variable, one intermediate input variable and one output variable. Thus, comparing the fuzzy rule number and the developing efforts between the single stage and multistage fuzzy systems, the multistage systems for complex applications will require less efforts in developing the fuzzy rules and less computation time. Before reviewing the related studies, the multistage fuzzy systems are briefly introduced in the following.

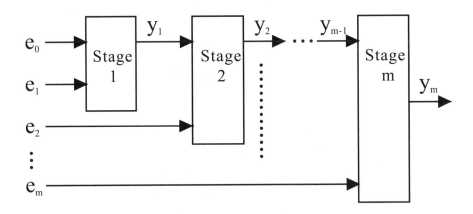

Figure 5.2   The architecture of multistage fuzzy logic inference

5.1.1   Multistage fuzzy systems

For large-scale systems, which are composed of interconnected subsystems, the essential problem is the interactions between the subsystems. Many approaches have been proposed to control complex interconnected systems such as the decomposition-coordination approach, and the decentralized control approach [6]-[9]. Since the decentralized control approach is reliable and practical in view of the implementation, it is the most popular approach which attempts to design control schemes where each subsystem is controlled independently based on local information. Considering a control system, a generic fuzzy controller can be implemented as

$$Y_i = (X_1 \times X_2) \ o \ R_f,$$

where R_f denotes the controller input/output fuzzy relation in $V \times V \times W$, V is the input space and W is the output space, X_1 and X_2 are the fuzzy variables obtained from the tracking error variable and its derivative, e_i and $\dot{e}_i$, respectively, Y_i is the fuzzy output of the controller, $\times$ denotes the Cartesian product and o denotes the maximum-minimum compositional rule of inference. When e_i and $\dot{e}_i$ are calculated as fuzzy singletons as I_1 and I_2, respectively, and R_f is converted into the form of a look-up decision matrix Φ, the defuzzified controller output of the i-th subsystem can be expressed as

$$u_i = GU_i * \Phi(I_1, I_2)$$

where $\Phi(I_1, I_2)$ is the element of Φ at the position $\Phi(I_1, I_2)$, I_1 and I_2 are converted into index values of the decision matrix and GUi is the output scaling factor. When a large-scale system has more than two input variables, it may be controlled by using multistage fuzzy controllers.

Definition 1.1 A multistage fuzzy system is defined as follows:
In a multistage fuzzy system, the fuzzy rules use three kinds of linguistic variables. They are input variables, output variables, and intermediate variables. The input variables only appear in the antecedent part (i.e., IF-part) of fuzzy rules. While the output variables are found only in the consequent part (i.e., THEN-part) of fuzzy rules. Only intermediate variables can appear in both parts of fuzzy rules.

Therefore, if a set of fuzzy rules contain intermediate variables, the rules are called multistage fuzzy rules. From a systematic point of view, intermediate variables refer to approximate outputs in current stage when humans are engaged in a complex activity such as decision-making. In rule representation, intermediate variables are included in THEN-parts in the current stage and in IF-parts of the next stage; the IF-parts variables in the current stage include the intermediate variable(s) of the previous stage and input variables. When facts are given, fuzzy rules in the present stage (except the final stage) are inferred; the consequence of an intermediate variable in the inference stage is passed to the next stage as a fact. Finally, the conclusions of the output variables are obtained from the final stage. Thus, in mimicking human knowledge by using intermediate variables, approximate concepts, which in some way are related to the system goals, are created in hierarchical structure. These approximate, qualitative concepts are hierarchically organized to provide

concept association and reasoning. Other possible architectures of multistage
fuzzy logic inference are shown in Fig. 5.3 and Fig. 5.4.

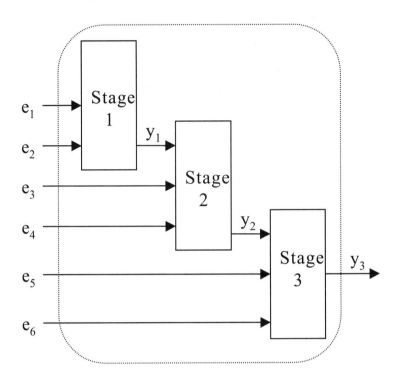

Figure 5.3   The skew-tree architecture of multistage fuzzy logic inference

The architectures of Fig. 5.3 and Fig. 5.4 can support various structures
involving skew tree and ternary tree, respectively. Assuming that there are five
input variables, the architecture may have two stages with three input variables
and single output for each stage, where every variable is characterized by seven
fuzzy membership functions. When the number of input variables increases by
one, the architecture can be designed as either skew-tree structure (e.g., Fig.
5.3) or ternary tree structure (e.g., Figure 5.4). Considering the architecture
shown in Figure 5.3, there are six inputs and a single output, which then can
be partitioned into three stages. The first inference stage has two inputs and
single output while the second stage and the third stage have three inputs. The
outputs of the first stage and the second stage are intermediate variables, which
are passed on to their next stages as input facts. Thus, the total complete rule
number in Fig. 5.3 has $1 \times 7^2 + 2 \times 7^3 = 735$.

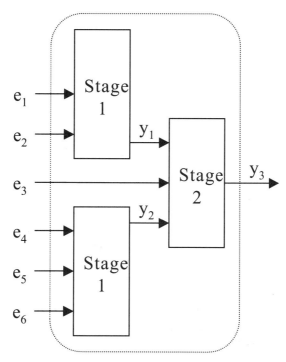

Figure 5.4 The ternary-tree architecture of multistage fuzzy logic inference

Architecture	Rule number
Suggested structure in Fig. 5.2	$5 \times 7^2 = 245$
Skew-tree structure in Fig. 5.3	$1 \times 7^2 + 2 \times 7^3 = 735$
Ternary-tree structure in Fig. 5.4	$1 \times 7^2 + 2 \times 7^3 = 735$

Table 5.1 Comparison of the complete rule number from Fig. 5.2 to Fig. 5.4

For the architecture shown in Fig. 5.4, it can be partitioned into two stages. In the first inference stage, there are two fuzzy inference modules. One has two inputs *and* single output and another one has three inputs. The second stage has three inputs. The first stage has two outputs as intermediate variables, which are passed on to the second stages as input facts. Thus, the total complete rule number in Fig. 5.4 has $1 \times 7^2 + 2 \times 7^3 = 735$. As a result from Fig. 5.2 to Fig. 5.4, the comparisons of the complete rule number are shown in Table 5.2.

5.1.2   Related studies and problems

To tackle complex multivariable control problems, the decomposition of multivariable control systems is preferable because it alleviates the complexity of the problem. Shakouri et al. suggested a fuzzy control algorithm for a multivariable system which was represented by a typical state space model [10]. Trojan and Kiszka proposed an approach to obtain solutions of multivariable fuzzy equations [11]. Gupta *et al.* introduced a fuzzy control algorithm where the multivariable fuzzy system was decomposed into a set of one-dimensional systems [12]. Linkens and Nyongesa proposed learning with genetic algorithms to construct a hierarachical (multistage) multivariable fuzzy system [13]. Kuo et al. proposed a three-layered parallel fuzzy inference model called reinforcement fuzzy neural network with distributed prediction scheme [14].

The multistage fuzzy system can be constructed by simply cascading a number of single-stage fuzzy inference units. Typical examples are: Ichihashi [15] and Tong [16] have proposed the ideas of constructing Multi-Stage Fuzzy Controllers based on hierarchies of fuzzy rules and strategic knowledge; Qian and Lu [17] have proposed a fuzzy reasoning network. Based on this fuzzy reasoning network, they have built a fuzzy expert system for fault diagnosis in a fluidized catalytic cracking unit. Also, Clymer [18] have successfully built a discrete event fuzzy airport control using a fuzzy-logic expert-system controller. From the above works, we can predict that multi-stage fuzzy systems will play an important role in future complex systems.

Although fuzzy logic control can encode expert knowledge in a direct and easy way using rules with linguistic labels and achieve much practical success, there are some drawbacks in the design approach. First, the design of fuzzy logic control has relied on **a priori** knowledge of the human expert and thus the controller performance is dependent on the quality of his/her expertise. Second, a reliable linguistic model of the expert operator's control strategy may not always be obtainable. Also, some significant process changes may be outside the operator's experience, and the design procedure appears to be limited by the elucidation of the heuristic control rules [16]. Third, it often takes much time to design and tune the membership functions, and wrong fuzzy rules or membership functions may lead to poor controller performance and possibly to stability.

To improve such an abnormal working condition, the parameters of a fuzzy controller should be adjusted to meet the unexpected cases. Therefore, multistage fuzzy controllers with a learning algorithm, which provides a means of automatically training the multistage inference network, have been proposed to solve control problems [4, 14]. This kind of controller has a learning algorithm and is capable of generating and modifying control rules based on the evaluation of the error information. The modification of control rules is achieved by using the back-propagated approach. However, the problem of the self-organizing multi-stage fuzzy controller is that the convergent time of the control action is tedious since there are many parameter needed to be adjusted and the convergence of the control action is not guaranteed.

5.1.3 Multistage approach

If the complex multivariable fuzzy system cannot be decomposed into some subsystems, the multistage fuzzy control is adopted to control such a complex multivariable problem. In this chapter, we propose a systematic methodology to the design of a Multistage Fuzzy Logic Controller (MFLC) for large scale nonlinear systems. A new general method, which is based on a performance index of tracking errors, is used to generate a fuzzy control rule base. Input variables obtained from tracking errors are adopted as input variables of the fuzzy controller and the determination of scale factors of the MFLC are suggested by genetic algorithms [19]. Moreover, a fast inference approach is adopted to shorten inferring time [5, 20, 21]. In this approach, the reduced computations are performed for input, output, and intermediate variables. For input variables, the fuzzy set operations are reduced by applying rules: (1) the input fact is not broadcast to IF-parts of fuzzy rules to evaluate match-degrees. Match-degree computations are evaluated only on the common ranges of the fact and fuzzy values for the same input variables; (2) the computed match-degrees are broadcast to IF-parts to evaluate firing strengths of fuzzy rules. The redundant match-degree calculations are removed in common if-clauses. For output variables, the calculations of the same fuzzy value in the THEN-parts of different rules can be omitted to reduce fuzzy set operations. If some fuzzy rules have the same then-clause, only the result derived with maximum firing strength among them is effective. These techniques save many fuzzy set operations for input and output variables.

5.2 Multistage inference fuzzy systems

To reduce the complexity of multivariable fuzzy rules, the architecture of Fig. 5.2 is adopted because its complete fuzzy rule number can reach minimum (the proof is left as an exercise). In the general multistage fuzzy system, which is shown in Fig. 5.2, the fuzzy rules use three kinds of linguistic variables. They involve input variables, output variables, and intermediate variables. The input variables only appear in the antecedent part (i.e., IF-part) of fuzzy rules, while the output variables are found only in the consequent part (i.e., THEN-part) of fuzzy rules. Only intermediate variables can appear in both parts of fuzzy rules. If a set of fuzzy rules contains intermediate variables, the fuzzy rules are called multistage fuzzy rules.

To construct a multistage inference fuzzy system, the most influential pa-

rameters of input variables are usually organized in the first stage, then the
next important input parameters in the second stage, and so on. In this work,
we consider the case where the fuzzy rule base consists of M stages in the
following forms:

$$
\textit{Stage } 1: \quad
\left|
\begin{array}{l}
\text{IF } x_0 \text{ is } A_{1,0}^1 \wedge \cdots \wedge x_{L_1} \text{ is } A_{1,L_1}^1 \\
\text{THEN } y_1 \text{ is } B_1^1 \\
\qquad\qquad\qquad \cdots \\
\text{IF } x_0 \text{ is } A_{n,0}^1 \wedge \cdots \wedge x_{L_1} \text{ is } A_{n,L_1}^1 \\
\text{THEN } y_1 \text{ is } B_n^1
\end{array}
\right| \;\Rightarrow (\textit{output to 2nd stage})
$$

$$
\textit{Stage } 2: \quad
\left|
\begin{array}{l}
\text{IF } y_1 \text{ is } A_{1,1}^2 \wedge \cdots \wedge x_{L_2} \text{ is } A_{1,L_2}^2 \\
\text{THEN } y_2 \text{ is } B_1^2 \\
\qquad\qquad\qquad \cdots \\
\text{IF } y_1 \text{ is } A_{n,1}^2 \wedge \cdots \wedge x_{L_2} \text{ is } A_{n,L_2}^2 \\
\text{THEN } y_2 \text{ is } B_n^2
\end{array}
\right| \;\Rightarrow (\textit{output to 3rd stage})
$$

$$
\textit{Stage } m: \quad
\left|
\begin{array}{l}
\text{IF } y_{m-1} \text{ is } A_{1,m-1}^m \wedge \cdots \wedge x_{L_m} \text{ is } A_{1,L_m}^m \\
\text{THEN } y_m \text{ is } B_1^m \\
\qquad\qquad\qquad \cdots \\
\text{IF } y_{m-1} \text{ is } A_{n,m-1}^m \wedge \cdots \wedge x_{L_m} \text{ is } A_{n,L_m}^m \\
\text{THEN } y_m \text{ is } B_n^m
\end{array}
\right| \;\Rightarrow (\textit{to control input})
$$

where $\wedge$ is 'and' operator, $A_{j,k}^i$ and B_j^i are linguistic terms characterized by
fuzzy membership functions $\mu_{A_{j,k}^i}(x)$ and $\mu_{B_j^i}(y_i)$, respectively, $(i=1,2,...,m;$
$j=1,2,...,n;\ k=0,1,...,L_i)$; x_k and y_i $(i=1,...,m-1)$ in the IF-parts are input
and intermediate variables, respectively, and y_m in the THEN-parts is the
output variable.

5.2.1 Multistage fuzzy inference engine

The multistage fuzzy inference engine is decision-making logic, which employs
fuzzy rules from the fuzzy rule bases, to determine a mapping from the fuzzy
sets in the input universe of discourse U_x to the fuzzy set in the output universe

of discourse U_y. For the i-th inference stage, let A_x^i be an arbitrary fuzzy set in U_x; then each rule R_j^i in the i-th stage determines a fuzzy set $A_x^i \circ R_j^i$ based on the t-norm operator:

$$
\begin{aligned}
\mu_{A_x^i \circ R_j^i}(y) &= \sup_{X \in U} [\mu_{A_x^i}(X) * \mu_{A_{1,j}^i} * \cdots * \mu_{A_{L_{i,j}}^i} \to \mu_{B_j^i}(X, y_i)] \\
&= \sup_{X \in U} [\mu_{A_x^i}(X) * \mu_{A_{1,j}^i} * \cdots * \mu_{A_{L_{i,j}}^i} * \mu_{B_j^i}(y_i)]
\end{aligned}
\tag{5.1}
$$

When facts are given, the fuzzy rules in the first stage are inferred, and then the consequences of the intermediate variables in the inference stage are formulated before they are passed on to the next stage as facts. This can easily be illustrated by an example with two inputs and one output at inference stage 1, and three fuzzy rules. The general scheme and reasoning structure of multistage inference are shown in Fig. 5.5 and Fig. 5.6, respectively.

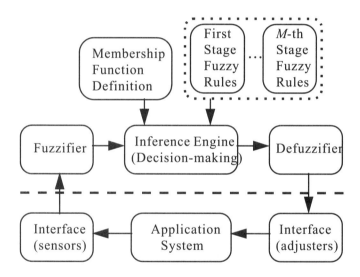

Figure 5.5 A general scheme of multistage fuzzy inference system

5.2.2 Multistage fuzzy inference procedure

In general, the fuzzy inference procedure consists of the following steps:

1. Read inputs and fuzzify inputs into input facts.
2. Perform match-degrees among inputs and those if-clauses of fuzzy rules that involve input variables.
3. Compute the firing strengths of the fired fuzzy rules.

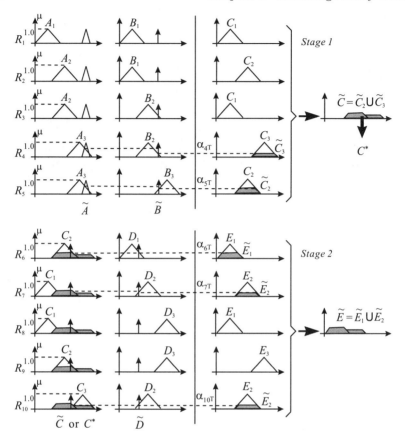

Figure 5.6   The architecture of multistage fuzzy logic inference

4. Calculate the conclusion by deriving the consequences of intermediate output variables of the i-th stage, where i is not the final one,
and normalize these derived consequences.

5. Pass the conclusions in the i-th stage onto the next stage as input
facts. By the similar process, the conclusion may be defuzzified and
then passed onto the next stage as a fact when the conclusion is too
fuzzy in the reasoning. Repeat step 1 to step 5 until the multi-stage
fuzzy rules in all inference stages are inferred.

6. Perform the conclusions of output variables of the final stage when
all fuzzy rules in every stage have been inferred.

7. Calculate defuzzification to obtain a singleton to be the control
input.

An algorithmic description of the above procedure is expressed as follows:

```
Algorithm multistage fuzzy logic inference(){
  // inputs: input variable (tracking errors)
  // output: obtained control input
  Do while (not halt){
    Input-fuzzy();
      // Fuzzification process for input data to
      // obtain input facts
    If-clause-evaluate();
      // input facts are broadcasted to all
      // if-clauses to compute match-degrees
    If-part-evaluate();
      // Match-degrees are taken as inputs
      // to evaluate firing strengths

    // intermediate variable derived as follows:
    for stage 2 to stage m {
      Then-part-evaluate();
        // deriving then-part fuzzy values and
        // normalizing them (sometimes defuzzifying them)
        // to obtain consequence (except final stage)
      If-clause-evaluate();
        // Either the fuzzy set conclusion or the
        // defuzzified singleton value are
        // broadcasted to all if-clause
      If-part-evaluate();
        // Match-degrees are taken as inputs
        // to evaluate firing strength
    } // end for
    Then-part-evaluate();
      // Deriving then-part fuzzy values and normalizing
      // then at the final stage to obtain consequence
    Defuzzy-output();
      // perform defuzzification to obtain control
      // input for the output variable
  } // end do while
} // end multistage fuzzy logic inference
```

5.3   Methodology of fuzzy rule generation

The fuzzy rule base is the heart of a fuzzy control system in the sense that all other design parameters are used to assist and interpret these fuzzy rules and make them usable to design a fuzzy controller for a specific control problem.

The fuzzy IF-THEN rules provide a very convenient framework for human experts to express their domain knowledge. Thus most of fuzzy rules come from human experts. However, the linguistic fuzzy rules may not always be obtainable. In this section, we propose an alternative method to generate fuzzy rules.

5.3.1 Fuzzy rule generation for multi-stage fuzzy inference systems

If the control problem is to get the state $X=[x_0, x_1, \cdots, x_m]^T$ to track a specific state $X_d=[x_{d_0}, \cdots, x_{d_m}]^T$ for the system, then the error signal vector can be represented as $E=X-X_d =[e_0, e_1, \cdots, e_m]^T$. The goal is to find a control action y(t) obtained from a multistage inference fuzzy controller, which satisfies $|E(t)|_\infty \leq \varepsilon$, and the tracking error asymptotically to zero as $t \to \infty$ for arbitrary initial conditions. As we indicated in the previous section, the knowledge base of the fuzzy controller involves a relationship between the input and output variables. For the multiple inputs, $e_0, e_1, \cdots, e_m$, the formally fuzzy controller is represented as a function

$$y_m = f_m(e_0, e_1, \cdots, e_m) \tag{5.2}$$

The function f_m is in general a complex ill-defined nonlinear relationship between the inputs and the output. In [22], an alternative form of the output of the rules was suggested by Yeh:

$$\text{IF } e_0 \text{ is } A_{I_0} \text{ and } e_1 \text{ is } A_{I_1} \text{ and } \cdots \text{ and } e_m \text{ is } A_{I_m}$$
$$\text{THEN } y_m \text{ is } B_{f(I_0,I_1,\cdots,I_m)} \tag{5.3}$$

where $f : I^{M+1} \to I$ is the rule-generated function and $I = \{-n, \cdots, -1, 0, 1, \cdots, n\}$, I_0, I_1, and I_m are the indices of fuzzy sets. However, when the number of system variables increases, the total number of fuzzy rules is increased in an exponential function. To overcome this problem, a multi-stage inference fuzzy control structure is used where the most influential parameters are chosen as the input variables in the first stage, the next most influential parameters are chosen as the input variables in the second stage, and so on.

For simplicity, the fuzzy rules with two inputs and one output in the first stage are of the form:

$$\text{IF } e_0 \text{ is } A_{I_0} \text{ and } e_1 \text{ is } A_{I_1} \text{ THEN } y_1 \text{ is } B_{f_1(I_0,I_1)} \tag{5.4}$$

The rules in the j-th stage (i.e., $j = 2, 3, \cdots, m$) are of the form:

$$\text{IF } y_{j-1} \text{ is } A_{I_{j-1}} \text{ and } e_j \text{ is } A_{I_j} \text{ THEN } y_j \text{ is } B_{f_j(I_{j-1},I_j)} \tag{5.5}$$

The multistage inference structure is shown in Fig. 5.2. From the above model, the key problem is how to determine the function $f_j(\cdot)$ to generate the multi-stage fuzzy rules.

Assuming that the control input is bounded, a performance index (cost function) J_j of the system can then be measured in the items of the tracking error E. Based on the optimal control, the gradient approach is to change the control input in the direction of the negative gradient of the performance index J_j. Then the control input to make J_j small is obtained. The parameters of the performance index$(i = 0, 1, ...m)$ are organized in Eq. (5.6),

$$
\begin{aligned}
J_j &= \sum_{k=1}^{n} \sqrt{e_0^2(k) + \cdots + e_m^2(k)} \\
&= \sum_{k=1}^{n} \sqrt{u_{m-1}^2(k) + e_m^2(k)}
\end{aligned}
\tag{5.6}
$$

where $u_{m-1} = \sqrt{u_{m-2}^2 + e_{m-1}^2}, \cdots, u_2 = \sqrt{u_1^2 + e_2^2}, \; u_1 = \sqrt{e_0^2 + e_1^2}$.

J_j is the performance index, k is the k-th time interval, and n is the total number of time intervals. Let the objective of the controller here be to force tracking errors E to slide to the origin for the system. This can be realized by minimizing the performance index J_j which is defined as a function of tracking errors e_i. The partial derivatives of J_j with respect to e_m and u_{m-1} can be obtained as follows:

$$
\begin{aligned}
\frac{\partial J_j}{\partial e_m(k)} &= \frac{e_m(k)}{\Delta} \\
\frac{\partial J_j}{\partial u_{m-1}(k)} &= \frac{u_{m-1}(k)}{\Delta}
\end{aligned}
\tag{5.7}
$$

where $\Delta = \sqrt{u_{m-1}^2 + e_m^2}$.

The negative gradient for the optimal performance can be expressed as

$$
-|\nabla J_j| = \left[-\frac{|e_m(k)|}{\Delta} \quad -\frac{|u_{m-1}(k)|}{\Delta} \right]
\tag{5.8}
$$

Based on optimal control, the control input of the fuzzy controller in the last stage is chosen as

$$
\begin{aligned}
y_m(k) &= GU_m(-|\nabla I_j|) \left[\begin{array}{c} e_m(k) \\ u_{m-1}(k) \end{array} \right] \\
&= GU_m(-\frac{|e_m(k)| e_m(k)}{\Delta} - \frac{|u_{m-1}(k)| u_{m-1}(k)}{\Delta}) \\
&= GU_m * f_m(e_m, u_{m-1}),
\end{aligned}
\tag{5.9}
$$

where GU_m is the output scale factor of the m-th stage and $f_m(e_m, u_{m-1})$
$= -\frac{|u_{m-1}|u_{m-1}+|e_m|e_m}{\Delta}$. The rule-generated function of the m-th stage is obtained from $f_m(e_m, u_{m-1})$ in which e_m and u_{m-1} are replaced by their index I_m and I_{m-1} of the fuzzy subsets A_{I_m} and $A_{I_{m-1}}$ in Eq. (5.5), respectively,

$$f_m(I_m, I_{m-1}) = sat(n, -\frac{|I_m| I_m + |I_{m-1}| I_{m-1}}{\Delta'}) \tag{5.10}$$

where $\Delta' = \sqrt{I_m^2 + I_{m-1}^2}$, and $sat(n, x)$ stands for a saturation function:

$$\begin{aligned} Sat(n, x) &= n, && \text{if } x \geq n \\ &= round(x), && \text{if } -n < x < n \\ &= -n, && \text{if } x \leq -n \end{aligned} \tag{5.11}$$

where n is the maximum index of fuzzy linguistic terms and $round(x)$ can truncate x into an integer.

From Eq. (5.8), the most negative gradient $-|\nabla I_j|$ implies that u_{m-1} is maximum. Thus we take the positive gradient of u_j for the j-th stage as

$$|\nabla u_j| = \left[\frac{|e_j(k)|}{\Delta_j} \quad \frac{|u_{j-1}(k)|}{\Delta_j}\right] \tag{5.12}$$

where $\Delta_j = u_j$. Using a similar method, the output of the j-th stage is chosen as

$$\begin{aligned} y_j(k) &= GU_j(|\nabla u_j|) \left[\begin{array}{c} e_j(k) \\ u_{j-1}(k) \end{array}\right] \\ &= GU_j(\frac{|e_j(k)| e_j(k)}{\Delta_j} + \frac{|u_{j-1}(k)| u_{j-1}(k)}{\Delta_j}) \\ &= GU_j * f_j(e_j, u_{j-1}) \end{aligned} \tag{5.13}$$

The rule-generated function of the j-th stage is obtained from $f_j(e_j, u_{j-1})$ in which e_j and u_{j-1} are replaced by their index I_j and I_{j-1} of the fuzzy subsets A_{I_j} and $A_{I_{j-1}}$, respectively,

$$f_j(I_j, I_{j-1}) = sat(n, \frac{|I_j| I_j + |I_{j-1}| I_{j-1}}{\Delta_j}). \tag{5.14}$$

For example, assume that the fuzzy set F in which every fuzzy subset is associated with an integer is expressed as $F = \{NB_{-3}, NM_{-2}, NS_{-1}, ZO_0, PS_1, PM_2, PB_3\}$. One fuzzy rule in the j-th subsystem with two inputs and single output can be coded with the form of an IF-THEN clause: IF y_{j-1} is NB_{-3} and e_j is NB_{-3} THEN y_j is PB_3, where the integer 3 of the fuzzy subset PB_3 is obtained from the Equation $f(-3, -3) = sat(3, \frac{-|-3|*(-3) - |-3|*(-3)}{\Delta'}) = 3$ (Eq. 5.14), where $\Delta' = \sqrt{(-3)^2 + (-3)^2}$.

5.3.2 Fast multi-stage fuzzy logic inference

The graphic representation of the proposed method for illustrating multi-stage fuzzy logic inference is shown in Fig. 5.7.

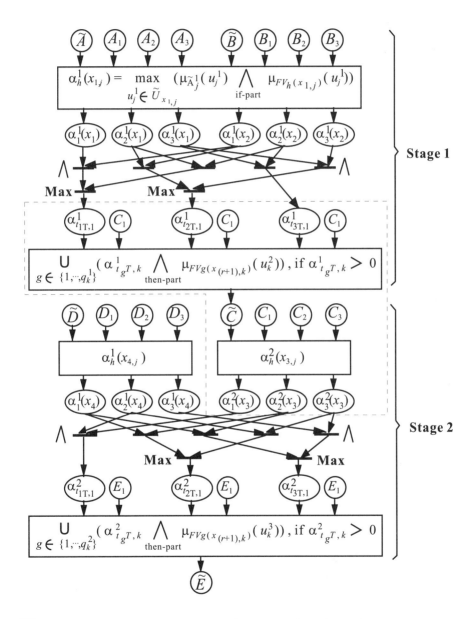

Figure 5.7   The graphic representation of multistage fuzzy logic inference

The key advantage of using multi-stage structure of fuzzy logic is that the number of rules will increase only linearly (not exponentially) with the number of variables. But the latency time (i.e., inferring time) of the multi-stage fuzzy logic inference, the number of fuzzy set operations of input, output, and intermediate variable must be reduced as much as possible. This can be solved by pre-computing the fuzzy set operations on several multi-stage fuzzy rules to shorten the latency time. Thus, the number of the match-degree calculations for input variables may decrease as well as the numbers of the conclusion formulations and defuzzification operations for output variables may decrease. For the intermediate variables, the fuzzy set operations can be pre-computed at compiling time; besides, the numbers of *intersection* and *union* scalar operations can be reduced in order to speed up reasoning at execution time. Therefore, the latency time involved in multi-stage fuzzy logic inference can be effectively reduced.

If-part evaluations of fuzzy rules at any stage

To describe the method, the notation of fuzzy values of variables is adopted in which the fuzzy values of the intermediate variable y_{i-1} are {*Fuzzy-Value$_h$*} of the intermediate variable y_{i-1} in the i-th stage, which are denoted by $\{FV_h^i(y_{i-1})\}$, $1 \le i \le m$, $h \in \{1, \cdots, l_i\}$, and the linguistic terms of IF-part are expressed as

$$A_{j,k}^i \in \{FV_h^i(y_{i-1})\}, \tag{5.15}$$
$$1 \le i \le m, \ j \in \{1, \cdots, n_i\}, \ 1 \le k \le m-1, \ h \in \{1, \cdots, l_i\}$$

where n_i is the number of the i-th stage fuzzy rules, and l_i is the number of fuzzy values of the intermediate variable y_{i-1} in the i-th stage. When an input fact or an inferred one occurs, the match-degrees among $FV_h^i(y_{i-1})$s in the i-th stage are performed with the fact as follows:

$$\alpha_h^i(y_{i-1}) = \max_{u^{i-1} \in U_{y_{i-1}}} \left(\mu_{FV_h^i(y_{i-1})}(u^{i-1}) \bigwedge \mu_{\tilde{A}^i}(u^{i-1}) \right) \tag{5.16}$$
$$1 \le i \le m, \ h \in \{1, \cdots, l_i\}$$

where $\bigwedge$ means a *T-norm* operator. The *T-norm* operators commonly chosen for the *intersection* operations are the **logical, algebraic, bounded, and drastic** *product* operators, whereas the *S-norm* operators for the corresponding *union* operations are the **logical, algebraic, bounded, and drastic** *sum* operators.

When these non-zero match-degrees are evaluated, they are broadcasted to those if-clauses which involve the fuzzy value $FV_h^i(y_{i-1})$. So the firing strength of rule R_j^i can also be derived from Eq. (5.17):

$$\alpha_{jT}^i = \bigwedge \alpha_h^i(y_{i-1}), \ 1 \le i \le m, \ j \in \{1, \cdots, n_i\}, \ h \in \{1, \cdots, l_i\} \tag{5.17}$$

Then-part derivations of fuzzy rules at any stage

Assume that in the i-th stage the fuzzy values of the variable y_i in then-part are $\{Fuzzy\text{-}Value_g\}$ of the then-part variable y_i in the i-th stage, which are denoted by $\{FV_g^i(y_i)\}$, $1 \le i \le m$, $g \in \{1, \cdots, q_i\}$. Then,

$$B_j^i \in \{FV_g^i(y_i)\}, \ 1 \le i \le m, \ j \in \{1, \cdots, n_i\}, \ g \in \{1, \cdots, q_i\} \quad (5.18)$$

where q_i is the number of fuzzy values of the then-part variable y_i in the i-th stage. In the i-th stage, we can get

$$\mu_{\tilde{B}_j^i}(u^i) = \alpha_{jT} \bigwedge \mu_{B_j^i}(u^i), \ u^i \in U_{y_i}, \ 1 \le i \le m, \ j \in \{1, \cdots, n_i\} \quad (5.19)$$

Note that the fuzzy value $FV_g^i(y_i)$ can appear in the then-clauses of different rules. By Equation (5.18), we have

$$B_j^i = FV_g^i(y_i), \ 1 \le i \le m, \ j \in \{1, \cdots, n_i\}, \ g \in \{1, \cdots, q_i\} \quad (5.20)$$

Then the conclusion $\mu_{\tilde{B}^i}(u^i)$ is secured by uniting the derived results $\alpha_{t_gT}^i \bigwedge \mu_{FV_g^i}(y_i)(u^i)$, which can be obtained according to the following theorem:

Theorem 1 [5, 20]: The conclusion of the then-part variable y_i in the i-th stage is formulated by

$$\mu_{\tilde{B}^i}(u^i) = \bigcup_{g \in \{1, \cdots, q_i\}} (\alpha_{t_gT}^i \bigwedge_{\text{then-part}} \mu_{FV_g^i(y_i)}(u^i)), \ u^i \in \tilde{U}_{y_i}, \ \text{if} \ \alpha_{t_gT}^i > 0 \quad (5.21)$$

$$\alpha_{t_gT}^i = \max_{i \in T_g^i} \alpha_{jT}^i, \ 1 \le i \le m, \ j \in \{1, \cdots, n_i\}, \ g \in \{1, \cdots, q_i\} \quad (5.22)$$

where the $\alpha_{t_gT}^i$ is the maximum firing strength of those rules which involve the same fuzzy value in the then-part in the i-th stage. Note that there exists only the distribution of T_i, $i \in \{0, \cdots, 3\}$ operator, to S_0 operator [5, 20]. For an intermediate variable in then-part of fuzzy rules, the conclusion $\mu_{\tilde{B}^i}(u^i)$ is passed on to the next stage as an inferred fact which is denoted by $\mu_{\tilde{A}^{i+1}}(u^i)$. When fuzzy logic operators of the same type are used in if-part and then-part, the pre-computations of fuzzy values can be done.

Pre-computations of fuzzy values for intermediate variables

In pre-computing the match-degrees of intermediate variables, the non-zero pre-computed value exists only for the two adjacent fuzzy values which are defined as having overlapped with each other. As a result, the fuzzy set operations in both if-part and then-part of intermediate variables are pre-computed. In inferring multistage fuzzy rules, the consequence $\mu_{\tilde{B}^i}(u^i)$, $1 \le i \le (m-1)$, of the i-th then-part variable y_i in the i-th stage is passed on to the $(i+1)$-th stage as an inferred fact. When the intermediate variable y_i (in if-part) in the $(i+1)$-th stage equals the y_i variable (in then-part) in the i-th stage, the match-degree $\alpha_h^{i+1}(y_i)$, $1 \le i \le (m-1)$, $h \in \{1, \cdots, l_i\}$, $j \in \{1, \cdots, n_i\}$ of the h-th fuzzy value of the variable y_i can be pre-computed according to the following theorem:

Theorem 2 [5, 20]: The consequence $\mu_{\tilde{B}^i}(u^i)$ of the then-part variable y_i in the i-th stage is passed on to the $(i+1)$-th stage as an inferred fact, $\mu_{\tilde{A}^{i+1}}(u^i)$. The match-degree $\alpha_h^{i+1}(y_i)$, $1 \le i \le (m-1)$, $h \in \{1, \cdots, l_{i+1}\}$ of the h-th fuzzy value of the variable y_i in the $(i+1)$-th stage can be pre-computed as

$$\alpha_h^{i+1}(y_i) = \max_{g \in \{1, \cdots, q_{i+1}\}} (\alpha_{t_g T}^i \wedge \beta_{h,g}), \text{ if } \beta_{h,g} > 0 \qquad (5.23)$$

$$\beta_{h,g} = \max_{u^i \in \tilde{U}_{y_i}} (\mu_{FV_h^{i+1}(y_i)}(u^i) \wedge \mu_{FV_g^i(y_i)}(u^i)) \qquad (5.24)$$

where $\alpha_{t_g T}^i = \max_{i \in T_g^i} (\alpha_{jT}^i)$, $1 \le i \le m$, $j \in \{1, \cdots, n_i\}$. Note that the T_i, $i \in \{0, \cdots, 3\}$, operators in if-part and then-part must be of the same type as T-norm operators, and the S-norm operator is only the S_0 operator [5]. When the intermediate variable y_i, $1 \le i \le m - 1$ (in if-part), in the $(i+1)$-th stage is the same as the one (in then-part) in the i-th stage, the $\beta_{h,g}$s are easily obtained from the membership function definitions of variable y_i. Meanwhile, the match-degree $\alpha_h^{i+1}(y_i)$ is broadcasted to the if-part of fuzzy rules. Then the firing strength of rule R_j^{i+1}, $1 \le i \le m$, $j \in \{1, \cdots, n_{i+1}\}$ can also be derived from the following:

$$\alpha_{jT}^{i+1} = \alpha_{h'}^{i+1}(x_{i+1,k}) \wedge \alpha_h^{i+1}(y_i),$$
$$k \in \{0, 1, \cdots, L_i\}, \ h \in \{1, \cdots, l_{i+1}\}, \ h' \in \{1, \cdots, l'_{i+1}\} \qquad (5.25)$$

For example, if fuzzy logic operators which are of the same type are used in the if-part and then-part for intermediate variable x_3, the computations are enclosed by the dotted line in Fig. 5.7. Then their pre-computations are detailed in Fig. 5.8. Pre-computation values $\beta_{h,g}, 1 \le h \le 3, 1 \le g \le 3$ are easily obtained from the membership functions of the variable x_3. Therefore, during inferring fuzzy rules, the computation of match-degrees $\alpha_h^2(x_3), 1 \le h \le 3$ is a scalar operation. Since fuzzy values C_1 and C_3 do not overlap with each other, $\beta_{1,3}$ and $\beta_{3,1}$ are zero in Fig. 5.9. Therefore, pre-computations of $\beta_{1,2}$ and $\beta_{2,3}$ are necessary because fuzzy value C_1 overlaps with C_2 and C_2 overlaps with C_3.

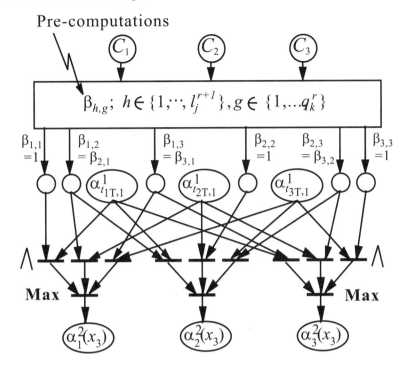

Figure 5.8 Pre-computing of intermediate variable x_3

5.4 An illustrative example

To demonstrate the effectiveness of the MFLC controller, the two-trailer-and-truck backer-parking problem is used as an illustrative example. Figure 5.10 shows the simulated two-trailer-and-truck system.

The position of the two-trailer-and-truck system can be determined by the five state variables ϕ_{1t}, ϕ_{1c}, ϕ_{2c}, x, and y, and the coordinate pair (x, y) specifies the position of the rear center of the trailer. The state variable ϕ_{1t} specifies the angle of the second trailer with the horizontal (ranging from -270° to 90°), whereas ϕ_{1c} specifies the relative cab angle with respect to the center line along the first trailer (ranging from -90° to 90°); ϕ_{2c} specifies the relative cab angle with respect to the center line along the second trailer (ranging from -90° to 90°). The objective of the multi-stage inference fuzzy controller is to make the two-trailer-and-truck system arrive at the loading dock at a right dock ($\phi_f = $ -90°) and to align the position (x, y) of the trailer with the desired loading dock (x_f, y_f). This control system contains four input variables and one output variable. The input variables are defined by using fuzzy variables e_x, $e_{\phi_{1t}}$, $e_{\phi_{1c}}$, and $e_{\phi_{2c}}$, where $e_x = x - x_f$, $e_{\phi_{1t}} = \phi_{1t} - \phi_f$, $e_{\phi_{1c}} = \phi_{1c} - 0°$,

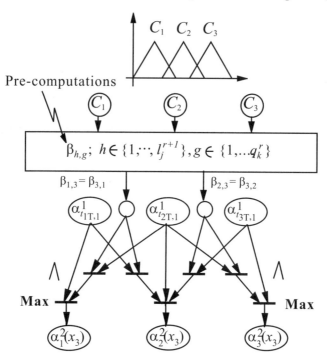

Figure 5.9   Considering overlapped fuzzy value pairs only

and $e_{\phi_{2c}} = \phi_{2c} - 0°$, whereas the output variable is defined by using θ. In this work, the fuzzy term sets with the integer indices of input/output variables are given by

$A_{\phi_{1t}} = \{LB_{-3}, LU_{-2}, LV_{-1}, VE_0, RV_1, RU_2, RB_3\}$,
$A_{\phi_{1c}} = A_{\phi_{2c}} = \{NE_{-3}, NU_{-2}, NV_{-1}, ZR_0, PV_1, PU_2, PO_3\}$,
$A_x = \{LE_{-2}, LC_{-1}, CE_0, RC_1, RI_2\}$,
$B_\theta = \{NB_{-3}, NM_{-2}, NS_{-1}, ZO_0, PS_1, PM_2, PB_3\}$,

where the fuzzy terms are defined in the Figure 5.11.

To construct the multistage fuzzy controller, the intermediate variables u_1 and u_2, which mean the desired angles of rotation for the intermediate variables in the different inference stage, are introduced in the following rule forms:

$$
\begin{aligned}
&\text{Stage 1:}\quad \text{IF } e_x \text{ is } LE_{-2} \text{ and } e_{\phi_{1t}} \text{ is } RB_{-3}\\
&\qquad\qquad \text{THEN } u_1 \text{ is } z1_{f_1(-2,-3)}\\
&\text{Stage 2:}\quad \text{IF } u_1 \text{ is } z1_{f_1(-2,-3)} \text{ and } e_{\phi_{1c}} \text{ is } NE_{-3}\\
&\qquad\qquad \text{THEN } u_2 \text{ is } z2_{f_2(f_1(-2,-3),-3)}\\
&\text{Stage 3:}\quad \text{IF } u_2 \text{ is } z2_{f_2(f_1(-2,-3),-3)} \text{ and } e_{\phi_{2c}} \text{ is } NE_{-3}\\
&\qquad\qquad \text{THEN } \theta \text{ is } z3_{f_3(f_2(f_1(-2,-3),-3),-3)}
\end{aligned}
\tag{5.26}
$$

where the fuzzy term sets of the intermediate variables u_1 and u_2 are de-

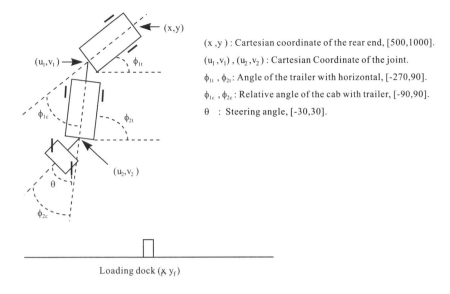

(x, y) : Cartesian coordinate of the rear end, [500,1000].

(u_1, v_1) , (u_2, v_2) : Cartesian Coordinate of the joint.

ϕ_{1t} , ϕ_{2t}: Angle of the trailer with horizontal, [-270,90].

ϕ_{1c} , ϕ_{2c} : Relative angle of the cab with trailer, [-90,90].

θ : Steering angle, [-30,30].

Figure 5.10   Diagram of simulated two-trailer-and-truck system

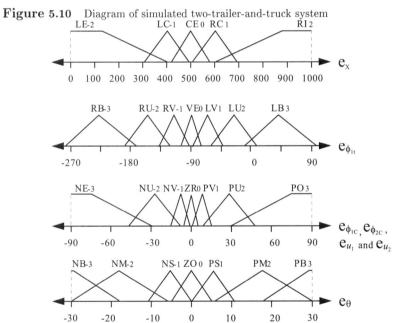

Figure 5.11 Fuzzy term sets with the integer indices of fuzzy variables $\phi_{1t}, \phi_{1c}, \phi_{2c}, x, \theta, u_1, u_2$

fined as $A_{u_1} = A_{u_2} = \{ILB_{-3}, ILU_{-2}, ILV_{-1}, IVE_0, IRV_1, IRU_2, IRB_3\}$, respectively, $z1 \in A_{u_1}, z2 \in A_{u_2}y$, and $z3 \in B_\theta$. The two input variables e_x and $e_{\phi_{1t}}$ determine the intermediate status u_1 of the two-trailer-and-truck system as well as the input variable $e_{\phi_{1c}}$ and the intermediate status u_1 determine the intermediate status u_2. Then the input variable $e_{\phi_{2c}}$ and the intermediate variable u_2 determines the steering-angle θ, with the latter one deciding the position of the two-trailer-and-truck system.

To determine the rule-generated function $f_i(\cdot)$, (i.e., $i=1,2,3$), the performance index is defined and organized in the following Equation:

$$
\begin{aligned}
J_j &= \sum_{k=1}^{n} \sqrt{\rho_2(\rho_1(e_x^2(k) + e_{\phi_{1t}}^2(k)) + e_{\phi_{1c}}^2(k)) + e_{\phi_{2c}}^2(k)} \\
&= \sum_{k=1}^{n} \sqrt{\rho_2 u_2^2(k) + e_{\phi_{2c}}^2(k)}
\end{aligned}
\tag{5.27}
$$

where $u_2 = \sqrt{\rho_1 u_1^2 + e_{\phi_{1c}}^2}, u_1 = \sqrt{e_x^2 + e_{\phi_{1t}}^2}, \rho_1 = \rho_2 = 1$ are weighting factors. The negative gradient for the performance index can be expressed as

$$
-|\nabla J_j| = \left[-\frac{|e_{\phi_{2c}}(k)|}{\Delta} \quad -\rho_2 \frac{|u_2(k)|}{\Delta} \right]
\tag{5.28}
$$

where $\Delta = \sqrt{\rho_2(\rho_1(e_x^2 + e_{\phi_{1t}}^2) + e_{\phi_{1c}}^2) + e_{\phi_{2c}}^2} = \sqrt{\rho_2 u_2^2 + e_{\phi_{2c}}^2}$

By the Eq.(5.7)-(5.9), the control input of the fuzzy controller in the last stage is chosen as

$$
\begin{aligned}
\theta(k) &= GU_3(-|\nabla J_j|) \left[\begin{array}{c} e_{\phi_{2c}}(k) \\ u_2(k) \end{array} \right] \\
&= GU_3(-\frac{|e_{\phi_{2c}}(k)| e_{\phi_{2c}}(k)}{\Delta} - \rho_2 \frac{|u_2(k)| u_2(k)}{\Delta}) \\
&= GU_3 * f_3(e_{\phi_{2c}}, u_2)
\end{aligned}
\tag{5.29}
$$

where $\Delta = \sqrt{\rho_2 u_2^2 + e_{\phi_{2c}}^2}$, $f_3(e_{\phi_{2c}}, u_2) = -\frac{|e_{\phi_{2c}}| e_{\phi_{2c}} + \rho_2 |u_2| u_2}{\Delta}$, and GU_3 is the output scale factor. The rule-generated function for determining the steering-angle θ is obtained from $f_3(e_{\phi_{2c}}, u_2)$ in which $e_{\phi_{2c}}$ and u_2 are replaced by their index $I_{\phi_{2c}}$ and I_{u_2} of the fuzzy subsets, respectively,

$$
f_3(I_{\phi_{2c}}, I_{u_2}) = sat(n, -\frac{|I_{\phi_{2c}}| I_{\phi_{2c}} + \rho_2 |I_{u_2}| I_{u_2}}{\Delta_3'})
\tag{5.30}
$$

where $\Delta_3' = \sqrt{I_{\phi_{2c}}^2 + I_{u_2}^2}$. For example, if one of the fuzzy rules is "IF u_2 is ILU_{-2} and $e_{\phi_{2c}}$ is NE_{-3} THEN θ is $z3_{f_3(-2,-3)}$", then this rule implies that the index $I_{\phi_{2c}} = -3$, $I_{u_2} = -2$, and $z3_{f_3(-2,-3)} = PB_3$.

By the Eq.(5.12) and (5.13), the intermediate output of the second stage is chosen as

$$
\begin{aligned}
u_2' &= GU_2(|\nabla u_2|) \begin{bmatrix} e_{\phi_{1c}} \\ u_1 \end{bmatrix} \\
&= GU_2(\frac{|e_{\phi_{1c}}| e_{\phi_{1c}}}{u_2} + \frac{|u_1| u_1}{u_2}) \\
&= GU_2 * f_2(e_{\phi_{1c}}, u_1)
\end{aligned}
\tag{5.31}
$$

and the intermediate output of the first stage is chosen as

$$
\begin{aligned}
u_1' &= GU_1(|\nabla u_1|) \begin{bmatrix} e_{\phi_{1t}} \\ e_x \end{bmatrix} \\
&= GU_1(\frac{|e_{\phi_{1t}}| e_{\phi_{1t}}}{u_1} + \frac{|e_x| e_x}{u_1}) \\
&= GU_1 * f_1(e_{\phi_{1t}}, e_x)
\end{aligned}
\tag{5.32}
$$

The rule-generated function for the intermediate outputs is obtained from $f_2(e_{\phi_{1c}}, u_1)$ and $f_1(e_{\phi_{1t}}, e_x)$ in which $e_{\phi_{1c}}, u_1, e_{\phi_{1t}}$, and e_x are replaced by their corresponding indices $I_{\phi_{1c}}, I_{u_1}, I_{\phi_{1t}}$, and I_{e_x} of their fuzzy subsets, respectively,

$$
f_2(I_{\phi_{1c}}, I_{u_1}) = sat(n, -\frac{|I_{\phi_{1c}}| I_{\phi_{1c}} + \rho_1 |I_{u_1}| I_{u_1}}{\Delta_2'})
\tag{5.33}
$$

$$
f_1(I_{\phi_{1t}}, I_x) = sat(n, -\frac{|I_{\phi_{1t}}| I_{\phi_{1t}} + |I_x| I_x}{\Delta_1'})
\tag{5.34}
$$

where $\Delta_2' = \sqrt{I_{\phi_{1c}}^2 + \rho_1 * I_{u_1}^2}$ and $\Delta_1' = \sqrt{I_{\phi_{1t}}^2 + I_x^2}$.

To take care of all the conditions, the fuzzy rule sets must be complete. The complete fuzzy rules can be determined by the rule-generated functions f_1, f_2, and f_3, and the corresponding three fuzzy rule bases are expressed in Figures 5.12, 5.13 and 5.14. The fuzzy set values of $e_{\phi_{1t}}, e_{\phi_{1c}}, e_{\phi_{2c}}, e_x, u_1, u_2$, and θ are shown in Fig. 5.11. These rule base sets are shown in Figures 5.12, 5.13 and 5.14, in which the fuzzy variables of the first stage are $e_{\phi_{1t}}, e_x$, and u_1, the fuzzy variables of the second stage are $e_{\phi_{1c}}, u_1$, and u_2, and the fuzzy variables of the last stage are $e_{\phi_{2c}}, u_2$, and θ. The output scaling factors are chosen as $GU_3 = GU_2 = 1$.

$$f_1(e_{\phi_{1t}}, e_x)$$

$e_{\phi_{1t}}$ \ e_x	LE-2	LC-1	CE0	RC1	RI2
RB-3	IRB	IRB	IRB	IRB	IRV
RU-2	IRB	IRU	IRU	IRV	IVE
RV-1	IRU	IRV	IRV	IVE	ILV
VE0	IRU	IRV	IVE	ILV	ILU
LV1	IRV	IVE	ILV	ILV	ILU
LU2	IVE	ILV	ILU	ILU	ILB
LB3	ILV	ILB	ILB	ILB	ILB

Figure 5.12 Rule generated function f_1

The simple kinematic equations replace the two-trailer-and-truck simulator, which has been discussed by S.-G. Kong [23]. The simulator method of [23] is to measure the angle, which is defined as the output variable of fuzzy rules. The steering-angle output θ is then computed. Our kinematic equations, which give an intuitive description of the moving behavior of the two-trailer-and-truck system, are refined from [23]. The steering-angle output θ is directly inferred from the firing set of fuzzy rules. If the two-trailer-and-truck moved backward from (x, y) to (x', y') at an iteration, then

$$f_2(\ \phi_{1c}\ ,\mathbf{u}_1\ )$$

$\mathbf{u}_1$ $\mathbf{e}_{\phi_{1c}}$	IRB-3	IRU-2	IRV-1	IVE0	ILV1	ILU2	ILB3
NE-3	IRB	IRB	IRB	IRB	IRB	IRV	IVE
NU-2	IRB	IRB	IRU	IRU	IRV	IVE	ILV
NV-1	IRB	IRU	IRV	IRV	IVE	ILV	ILB
ZR 0	IRB	IRU	IRV	IVE	ILV	ILU	ILB
PV 1	IRB	IRV	IVE	ILV	ILV	ILB	ILB
PU 2	IRV	IVE	ILV	ILU	ILU	ILB	ILB
PO 3	IVE	ILV	ILB	ILB	ILB	ILB	ILB

Figure 5.13   Rule generated function f_2

$$\phi'_{c,h} = \phi'_{c,h} + \theta$$
$$u'_2 = u_2 + r\,\cos(\phi'_{c,h})$$
$$v'_2 = v_2 + r\,\sin(\phi'_{c,h})$$
$$\phi'_{2t} = \tan^{-1}(\frac{v_1 - v'_2}{u_1 - u'_2})$$
$$u'_1 = u'_2 + l\,\cos(\phi'_{2t})$$
$$v'_1 = v'_2 + l\,\sin(\phi'_{2t})$$
$$\phi'_{1t} = \tan^{-1}(\frac{y - v'_1}{x - u'_1})$$

$$f_3(e_{\phi_{2c}}, u_2)$$

$e_{\phi_{2c}}$ $\diagdown$ u_2	IRB-3	IRU-2	IRV-1	IVE0	ILV1	ILU2	ILB3
NE-3	PB	PB	PB	PB	PB	PS	ZO
NU-2	PB	PB	PM	PM	PS	ZO	NS
NV-1	PB	PM	PS	PS	ZO	NS	NB
ZR 0	PB	PM	PS	ZO	NS	NM	NB
PV 1	PM	PS	ZO	NS	NS	NM	NB
PU 2	PS	ZO	NS	NM	NM	NB	NB
PO 3	ZO	NS	NB	NB	NB	NB	NB

Figure 5.14 Rule generated function f_3

$$x' = u'_1 + l \cos(\phi'_{1t})$$
$$y' = v'_1 + l \sin(\phi'_{1t})$$
$$\phi'_{2c} = \phi'_{c,h} - \phi'_{2t}$$

where θ is produced through the reasoning of the fuzzy rules; $\phi'_{c,h}$ denotes the cab angle with the horizontal; r denotes the moving distance at an iteration; l denotes the length of the trailer and is set at 100.

With the first, second, and third stage fuzzy rule sets (Figure 5.8), Figures 5.15, 5.16 and 5.17 show the typical backing-parking trajectories of the two-trailer-and-truck fuzzy control system from different initial positions. The initial positions $(x, y, \phi_{1t}, \phi_{1c}, \phi_{2c})$ of the two-trailer-and-truck system, from case 1 to case 3, are (200, 200, 45, 0, 0), (200, 200, -90, 0, 0), and (800, 200, -45, 0, 0), respectively. In this simulation, the y-position coordinate y of the two-trailer-and-truck is ignored. For the intermediate variable u_1, the reduced numbers of operations of fuzzy logic inference based on the pre-computation method, compared with related methods [4, 24], are shown in Table 5.2.

Figure 5.15 Sample two-trailer-and-truck trajectories from the fuzzy control system for initial position $(x, y, \phi_{1t}, \phi_{1c}, \phi_{2c})$: (a) (200,200,45,0,0)

5.5 Conclusion

In this chapter, we developed a general method to generate fuzzy rules for a multistage fuzzy controller from the performance index of the control system.

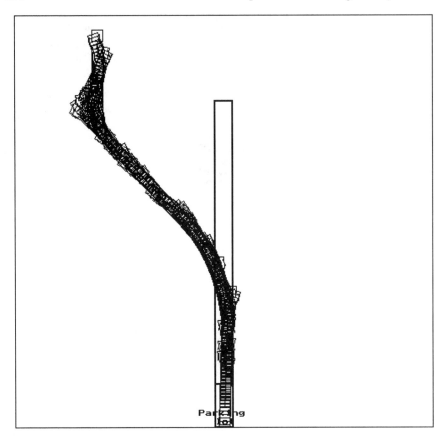

Figure 5.16   Sample two-trailer-and-truck trajectories from the fuzzy control system for initial position $(x, y, \phi_{1t}, \phi_{1c}, \phi_{2c})$: (b) (200,200,-90,0,0)

	Related Methods [4, 24]	Suggested Method
No. of *pre*−computations	$35 \times 49 = 1{,}715$	6
No. of ∧ operations	$35 \times 49 = 1{,}715$	12
No. of *max* scalar operations	49	7

Table 5.2   Comparison of two methods for intermediate variable u_1

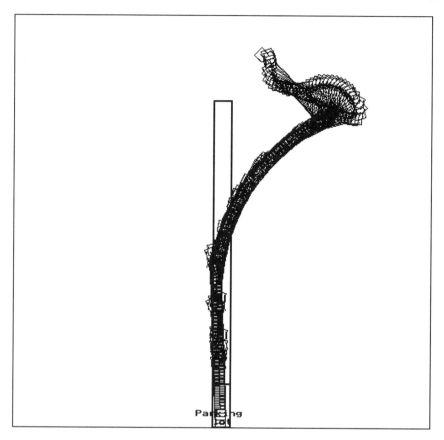

Figure 5.17 Sample two-trailer-and-truck trajectories from the fuzzy control system for initial position $(x, y, \phi_{1t}, \phi_{1c}, \phi_{2c})$: (c) (800,200,-45,0,0)

This method can be used as an alternative way to generate a complete rule base when a reliable linguistic model of the expert operator's control strategy may not be obtainable. This method also can reduce the design cycle time. We also presented a method of fast multi-stage fuzzy logic inference. When T-norm operators which are of the same type are used in both IF-parts and THEN-parts for intermediate variables, a method for precomputing the match-degrees of fuzzy values is proposed. The number of operations that must be carried out at execution time is significantly reduced. The complexity of the algorithms is much smaller than the related works [4, 24]. The simulation results using three-stage fuzzy inference showed that the good performance of the two-trailer-and-truck applications can be achieved.

5.6   References

[1] C. von Altrock, B. Krause and H.-J. Zimmermann, "Adavanced fuzzy logic control of a model car in extreme situations," *Fuzzy Sets and Systems*, Vol. 48,(1992) 41-52.

[2] G. V. S. Raju, J. Zhou and R. A. Kisner, "Hierarchical Fuzzy Control," *International Journal of Control*, Vol. 54, No. 5, (1991) 1201-1216.

[3] G. V. S. Raju and J. Zhou, "Adaptive Hierarchical Fuzzy Controller," *IEEE Trans. on Systems, Man and Cybernetics*, Vol. 23, No. 4,(1993) 973-980.

[4] K. Uehara and M. Fujise, "Multistage Fuzzy Inference Formulated as Linguistic-Truth-Value Propagation and Its Learning Algorithm Based on Back-Propagating Error Information," *IEEE Trans. on Fuzzy Systems*, Vol. 1, No. 3,(1993) 205-221.

[5] H. P. Chen and T. M. Parng, "A new approach of multi-stage fuzzy logic inference," *Fuzzy Sets and Systems*, Vol. 78, (1996) 51-72.

[6] M. S. Mahmoud, M. F. Hassan, and M. D. Darwish, "Large-scale Control System: Theories and Technique," New York: Marcel Dekker.

[7] R. A. DeCarlo, et al., "Variable structure control of nonlinear multivariable systems: A tutorial," *Proc. IEEE*, Vol. 76(3), (1988).

[8] D. T. Gavel and D. D. Siljak, "Decentralized adaptive control: structural conditions for stability," *IEEE Trans. Automat. Contr.*, Vol. 34(4), (1989) 413-426.

[9] L. Shi and S. K. Singh, "Decentralized adaptive controller design for large-scale systems with higher order interconnections," *IEEE Trans. Automat. Contr.*, Vol. 37(8), (1992) 1106-1118.

[10] A. Shakouri, et el., "Fuzzy control for multivariable systems,"in *Proc. 2nd IFAC Symp. Compt.-Aided Design Multivariable Tech. Syst.*, (1982).

[11] G. M. Trajan and J. B. Kiszka, "Solution of multivariable fuzzy equations," *Fuzzy Sets and Syst.*, Vol. 23, (1987) 271-279.

[12] M. M. Gupta, J. B. Kiszda, and G. M. Trojan, "Multivariable structure of fuzzy control systems," *IEEE Trans. Syst., Man, Cybern.*, Vol. 16, no. 5, (1986) 638-655.

[13] Derek A. Linkens and H. Okola Nyongesa, "A hierarchical multivariable fuzzy controller for learning with genetic algorithms," *INT. J. CONTROL*, Vol. 63(5), (1998) 865-883.

[14] Y. H. Kuo, J. P. Hsu, and C. W. Wang, "A parallel Fuzzy Inference Model with Distributed Prediction Scheme for Reinforcement Learning," *IEEE Trans. Syst., Man, Cybern.*, Vol. 28, No. 2, (1998) 160-172.

[15] I. Ichihashi, "Iterative fuzzy model and a hierachical network," in Proc. 4th IFSA World Congress, of Engineering (Brussels, Belgium), (1991) 49-52.

[16] R.M. Tong, "A retrospective view of fuzzy control systems," *Fuzzy Sets and Systems*, Vol. 14, (1984) 199-210.

[17] D.-q. Qian and Y.-z. Lu, "A strategy of problem solving in a fuzzy reasoning network," *Fuzzy Sets and Systems*, Vol. 33, (1989) 137-154.

[18] J. R. Clymer, P. D. Corey, and J. A. Gardner, "Discrete Event Fuzzy Airport Control," *IEEE Trans. on Systems, Man and Cybernetics*, Vol. 22, No. 2, (1992) 343-351.

[19] Zong-Mu Yeh, "A Systematic Method for Design of Multivariable Fuzzy Logic Control Systems," *IEEE Transactions on Fuzzy Systems*, (In press).

[20] Zong-Mu Yeh and H. P. Chen, "A Novel Approach for Multi-Stage Inference Fuzzy Control," *IEEE Transactions on Systems, Man, Cybernetics*, Vol. 28, No. 6, (1998) 935-946.

[21] Zong-Mu Yeh and H. P. Chen, "Multi-Stage Inference Fuzzy Logic Control," *Proceedings of 6th IEEE Conference on Fuzzy Systems*, (1997).

[22] Zong-Mu Yeh, "A Performance Approach to Fuzzy Control Design for Nonlinear Systems," *Fuzzy Sets and Systems*, Vol. 64, (1994) 339-352.

[23] S.-G. Kong and B. Kosko, "Adaptive Fuzzy Systems for Backing up a Truck-and-Trailer," *IEEE Trans. on Neural Networks*, Vol. 3, No. 2, (1992) 211-223.

[24] A. Bugarin and S. Barro, "Fuzzy Reasoning Supported by Petri Nets," *IEEE Trans. on Fuzzy Systems*, Vol. 2, No. 2, (1994) 135-150.

6

Learning Fuzzy Systems

Ahmad Lotfi

School of Engineering and Advanced Technology, Staffordshire University
PO Box 333, Stafford, ST18 ODF,
U.K. - Email: lotfi@mail.com

0-8493-2269-3/00/$0.00+$.50
© 2001 by CRC Press LLC

Learning Fuzzy Systems

Abstract

The main advantage of a fuzzy system is its ability to utilise information expressed in linguistic form. The design of a fuzzy system is very much an art. The designer considers the knowledge accumulated and crafts the membership function(s) and/or the inference mechanism in the system. Often, these membership functions are fixed once the design process has terminated. It would be desirable to have a fuzzy system whose membership function parameters can be "adapted"' or "learned" from input and output data. This will facilitate the design process much easier. In this chapter, a review of techniques available for updating/learning the parameters of a fuzzy system is presented.

6.1   Introduction

One of the superior capabilities of fuzzy systems is that they can use the information expressed in a linguistic pattern. Though most fuzzy systems have been formed to emulate human decision making behaviour, the linguistic information stated by an expert may not be precise, or it may be difficult for the expert to articulate the accumulated knowledge to encompass all circumstances. Hence, it is essential to provide a learning capability for fuzzy systems, namely, to generate or modify the expert rules based on experiences.

There are, essentially, two different approaches in the definition of fuzzy rules. The rules are either defined using an empirical experience or applying an adaptive/learning scheme to adjust the free parameters of the fuzzy system commencing with some arbitrary initial values. The learning fuzzy systems can be implemented using parameter adjustment algorithms and, in most cases, the gradient of a cost function with respect to each adjustable parameter is calculated and the parameters will be updated accordingly. There are also some derivative-free optimisations such as genetic algorithms (GAs) and random search methods. GAs have been successfully applied to generate fuzzy rules and adjust membership functions of fuzzy systems [6, 9, 22]. The readers are referred to [15] for a review of using GAs to tune the membership functions of fuzzy systems.

In the literature, the parameter adjustment procedure in fuzzy systems is called variously, e.g., adaptive [7, 25], tuning [3, 19, 29], and learning fuzzy systems [11, 12, 20, 28]. Nevertheless, we intend to clearly differentiate the goals of adaptation from those of learning. A model that treats each operating situation independently is limited to *adaptive or tuning* operation, whereas a system that correlates past experiences with current situations is capable of *learning* [1]. It is to be noted that, because of the multidisciplinary nature of the fuzzy system, it is known by numerous other names such as fuzzy rule-based system (FRBS), fuzzy model [26, 27], fuzzy associative memory (FAM) [13] and fuzzy logic controller (FLC)[18]. In this chapter simply the term "fuzzy system" will be used.

The structure of this chapter is as follows: fuzzy systems will be introduced in the next section followed by a history and description of learning fuzzy systems. An application of the learning fuzzy system to non-linear function approximation is employed as an illustration example. The preservation of the integrity of fuzzy systems is presented in section 6.5.

6.2 Fuzzy Systems

There are many different types of fuzzy systems, such as those first proposed by (and named after) Mamdani [17], and Takagi and Sugeno [27]. The one which will be utilised in this chapter is a special case of the Mamdani type in which the rules always have crisp consequents. This model has been used extensively to express the relationship between output and input variables either for control or for system modelling.

R^i: If x_1 is $\tilde{A}_1^i$ and ... x_j is $\tilde{A}_j^i$ ... and x_p is $\tilde{A}_p^i$ then y is B^i ⋆

The label of the ith rule is R^i. The jth input variable is $x_j : j = 1, 2, \ldots, p$ and y is the output. $\tilde{A}_j^i$ ($i = 1, 2, \ldots, n$ and $j = 1, 2, \ldots, p$) are fuzzy labels, and B^i are real numbers. n and p are the numbers of rules and input variables, respectively. The number of distinguishable membership functions for a specific input variable x_j ($\tilde{A}_j^1, \tilde{A}_j^2, \ldots, \tilde{A}_j^i, \ldots, \tilde{A}_j^n$) is K_j. It is assumed that the universe of input variables is limited to lower limit (LL) and upper limit (UL) bounds, i.e., $x_j \in [LL_j, \; UL_j], \; j = 1, \ldots, p$.

The output y, as a function of input variables $x_j : j = 1, 2, \ldots, p$, is given in the following equation [28]:

$$y = \sum_{i=1}^{n} B^i f^i \tag{6.1}$$

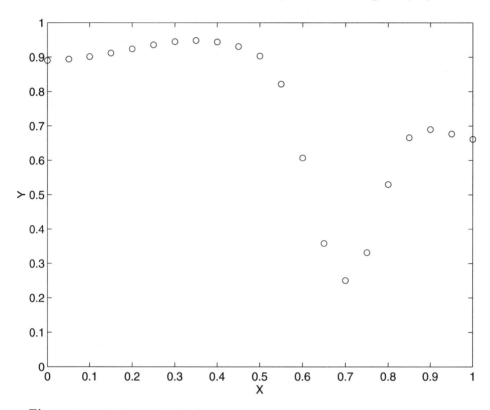

Figure 6.1   Arbitrary training data.

$$f^i = \frac{\prod_{j=1}^{p} \mu_{\tilde{A}_j^i}(x_j)}{\sum_{i=1}^{n} \prod_{j=1}^{p} \mu_{\tilde{A}_j^i}(x_j)} \tag{6.2}$$

Different shape of fuzzy values, $\tilde{A}_j^i$, can be employed, e.g., triangular or Gaussian. The Gaussian membership functions are a good choice for learning fuzzy systems as the first and second derivative of the function are continuous functions. They can be written as follow:

$$\mu_{\tilde{A}_j^k}(x_j) = exp\left(-\left(\frac{x_j - c_{j,k)}}{\sigma_{j,k)}}\right)^2\right) \quad j = 1, 2, ..., p \quad k = 1, 2, K_j \tag{6.3}$$

where $c_{j,k} : j = 1...p, k = 1...K_j$ and $\sigma_{j,k} : j = 1...p, k = 1...K_j$ are respectively the offset from the origin and the width of the Gaussian hump. The free parameters,i.e., $c_{j,k}$ and $\sigma_{j,k}$, and the consequent parameters of rules, B^i, can be set manually or using a learning method.

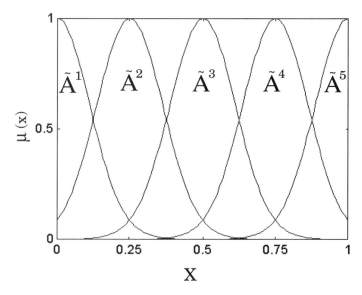

Figure 6.2 Initial membership function of linguistic term $\tilde{A}^i$, $i = 1, 2, 3, 4, 5$.

6.2.1 Example 1: Fuzzy Systems

Before explaining learning fuzzy system, in this section a simple example is presented to explain the terminology used for a fuzzy system. Consider a set of input-output pairs data $(x^t, y^t):t = 1, 2, \ldots, 20$ in the space $[0 \quad 1] \times [0 \quad 1]$ are given as shown in Figure (6.1).

The problem is to approximate the non-linear input-output relation in Figure (6.1) by a set of fuzzy if-then rules. A set of 5 rules of the following form is produced empirically.

If x is *Very Low* then y is 0.9 else
If x is *Low* then y is 0.8 else
If x is *Medium* then y is 0.7 else
If x is *High* then y is 0.2 else
If x is *Very High* then y is 0.6

Alternatively the rules can be written as follows:

If x is $\tilde{A}^1$ then y is B^1 else
If x is $\tilde{A}^2$ then y is B^2 else
If x is $\tilde{A}^3$ then y is B^3 else
If x is $\tilde{A}^4$ then y is B^4 else

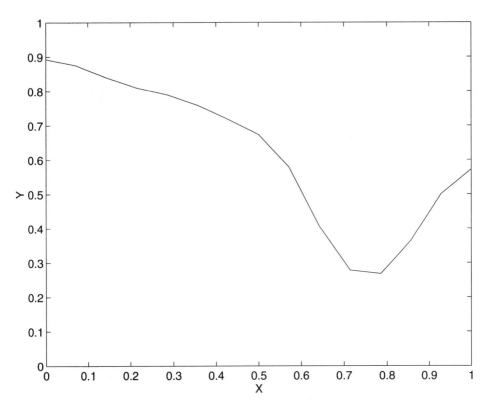

Figure 6.3   Initial function approximation for the arbitrary training data.

If x is $\tilde{A}^5$ then y is B^5

The initial MFs of linguistic terms, $\tilde{A}^i$: $i = 1, 2, 3, 4, 5$, are shown in Figure (6.2). The MFs are of Gaussian shape with the parameters σ and c given in Table (6.1). The initial consequent parameters, B^i:$i = 1, 2, 3, 4, 5$, are 0.9, 0.8, 0.7, 0.2 and 0.6 respectively. The results of the initial function approximation for the arbitrary training data are shown in Figure (6.3).

To minimise the difference between the approximated function and actual data set, the initial parameters assigned for each fuzzy value must be altered. In the following sections, learning fuzzy system are explained.

MFs	Linguistic Terms	σ	c
$\tilde{A}^1$	Very Low	0.16	0.0
$\tilde{A}^2$	Low	0.16	0.25
$\tilde{A}^3$	Medium	0.16	0.5
$\tilde{A}^4$	High	0.16	0.75
$\tilde{A}^5$	Very High	0.16	1.0

TABLE 6.1 Parameters of membership functions.

6.3 Learning Fuzzy Systems

6.3.1 History

A very first introduction of learning fuzzy systems was in 1979 when Procyk and Mamdani [23] proposed a Self-Organising Control (SOC) policy for fuzzy controllers which was able to develop and improve as more data became available. There were some further studies exploring the concept of SOC [5]. The other method to aggregate the learning ability of fuzzy systems is to use the learning ability of Neural Networks (NNs) [8]. The combined system is known as a *neural-fuzzy system* [2, 12, 10, 28]. The advantage of this method is that we are able to use the properties and training algorithms developed for neural networks in "learning" the underlying parameters of a neural-fuzzy system.

6.3.2 Neural-fuzzy Systems

A strong synergetics relationship between fuzzy system and neural network exists that has been exploited to integrate fuzzy and neural systems. There are mainly two ways that the integration of these two systems can work. Either the neural network is used to realise a fuzzy system or the fuzzy system is used to influence the dynamics of a neural network. When a fuzzy concept is used to assist a neural system it is referred to as a *fuzzy-neural system*. When a neural network assists a fuzzy system to induce rules or tune the membership functions it is referred to as a *neural-fuzzy or neuro-fuzzy system* [21]. It is to be noted that the terminologies neural-fuzzy and fuzzy-neural are widely used interchangeably in the literature, though we insist on using the term neural-fuzzy for learning fuzzy systems where the neural network is used to emulates fuzzy system features, such as rules, membership functions and inference mechanism.

One of the main advantages of learning fuzzy systems over classical learning systems and neural networks is their ability to utilise intuitive knowledge, which may be presented in a linguistic form. Though, once the membership functions and rules of the system are stored, it is desirable to preserve the

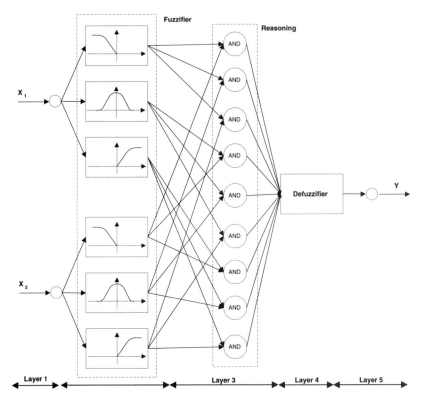

Figure 6.4   Neural network representation of a fuzzy system with 2 inputs, 3 membership functions for each input, 9 rules and 1 output

linguistic information. That is, one would like to be able to use the same intuitive understanding, which was used to create the fuzzy system, to interpret its behaviour at all times in the future. In general, this ideal cannot be guaranteed in a learning fuzzy system.

A neuro-fuzzy model is built using a multilayer neural network and it has a total of five layers [14]. A neuro-fuzzy model with two inputs and a single output is considered here for convenience and it is shown in Figure (6.4). Accordingly, there are two nodes in layer 1 and one node in layer 5. Nodes in layer 1 are input nodes that directly transmit input signals to the next layer. Layer 5 is the output layer. Nodes in layer 2 and 4 are "term nodes" and they act as membership functions to express the fuzzy values of linguistic variables. Each node of layer 3 is a "rule node" and represents a single fuzzy rule [6]. In total, there are $K_1 \times K_2$ nodes in layer 3. K_1 and K_2 are the number of individual membership functions for each input.

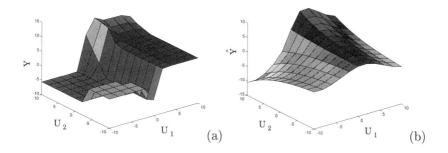

Figure 6.5 Decision surface (a) initial (b) desired.

6.3.3   Example 2: Neuro-fuzzy Systems

Consider the following non-linear function.

$$y = \left[3e^{\frac{x_2}{10}} - 1\right] tanh(\frac{x_1}{2}) + \frac{2}{30}\left[4 + e^{\frac{x_2}{10}}\right] sin\frac{(x_1 + 4)\pi}{10} \qquad (6.4)$$

If we want to use a fuzzy system as a function approximator to predict the output y for any given inputs x_1 and x_2, then a set of fuzzy rules is required. A fuzzy system with $p = 2$ inputs, $K_j = 3, j = 1, 2$ membership functions for each input, $q = 1$ output and $n = 9$ rules is given below. The universe U_1 and U_2 are both set to $[-10 \ 10]$. Based on some understanding from the desired surface, the initial values for the membership function parameters are assigned.

$$\text{If } x_1 \text{ is } \tilde{A}_1^1 \text{ AND } x_2 \text{ is } \tilde{A}_2^1 \text{ then } y \text{ is } B^1 = 0 \text{ else}$$
$$\text{If } x_1 \text{ is } \tilde{A}_1^1 \text{ AND } x_2 \text{ is } \tilde{A}_2^2 \text{ then } y \text{ is } B^2 = 5 \text{ else}$$
$$\text{If } x_1 \text{ is } \tilde{A}_1^1 \text{ AND } x_2 \text{ is } \tilde{A}_2^3 \text{ then } y \text{ is } B^3 = -10 \text{ else}$$
$$\text{If } x_1 \text{ is } \tilde{A}_1^2 \text{ AND } x_2 \text{ is } \tilde{A}_2^1 \text{ then } y \text{ is } B^4 = 5 \text{ else}$$
$$\text{If } x_1 \text{ is } \tilde{A}_1^2 \text{ AND } x_2 \text{ is } \tilde{A}_2^2 \text{ then } y \text{ is } B^5 = 0 \text{ else}$$
$$\text{If } x_1 \text{ is } \tilde{A}_1^2 \text{ AND } x_2 \text{ is } \tilde{A}_2^3 \text{ then } y \text{ is } B^6 = 10 \text{ else}$$
$$\text{If } x_1 \text{ is } \tilde{A}_1^3 \text{ AND } x_2 \text{ is } \tilde{A}_2^1 \text{ then } y \text{ is } B^7 = 10 \text{ else}$$
$$\text{If } x_1 \text{ is } \tilde{A}_1^3 \text{ AND } x_2 \text{ is } \tilde{A}_2^2 \text{ then } y \text{ is } B^8 = 10 \text{ else}$$
$$\text{If } x_1 \text{ is } \tilde{A}_1^3 \text{ AND } x_2 \text{ is } \tilde{A}_2^3 \text{ then } y \text{ is } B^9 = 10$$

The adaptive fuzzy system explained in this section can be shown in a neural-network style format. Figure (6.4) illustrates a neuro-fuzzy system for the above rules. The approximated surface for the neural-fuzzy system is depicted in Figure (6.5-a). Figure (6.5-b) illustrates the actual surface from the non-linear function given in the expression (6.4).

6.3.4   Parameter Adjustment

The initial fuzzy labels assigned to a linguistic variable are not entirely capable of incorporating the human experience into the fuzzy if-then rules. Obviously, a designer, with experience, can produce a membership function which suits a particular situation. However, this is explicitly excluded here, as the experience by the designer in handcrafting the membership functions for one system does not in general carry over to the design of another system. A learning ability for membership functions in fuzzy systems can make the incorporation between the membership functions of fuzzy rules and human experience more effective.

For a given fuzzy system, it is obvious that altering the following parameters will affect the overall input-output mapping of the system.

1. The membership function of linguistic values,
2. Fuzzy reasoning methods,
3. The number of rules.

Assignment of a membership function to each fuzzy value is, in general, non-unique. However, there has been some research for giving a systematic approach in this direction [4, 24]. It depends, to a certain extent, on the designer in the choice of the membership functions, as well as the interpretation of the "fuzziness" of the variables concerned. Altering the membership functions has a dominant effect on the other two (fuzzy reasoning and number of rules). It can be seen that for a fixed number of rules in the rule set, changing the membership function can achieve the same input-output mapping, to a particular degree of approximation, regardless of the fuzzy reasoning method. Alternatively, for a fixed fuzzy reasoning method, we can attain to the same degree of approximation, the same input-output mapping with a different number of rules and different membership functions.

In the next section the gradient-descent or backpropagation algorithm which is also used for neural networks is employed to adapt the parameters of a fuzzy system.

6.4   Learning Rule

If the correct output, corresponding to a particular set of inputs to a fuzzy system, is known, then it is possible to adjust the free parameters of a fuzzy system by means of error backpropagation. The method by which this is done is the same as the way that multilayer perceptron are trained, that is:

1. For each known input/output relation, a cost, J, is calculated by:

$$J = \frac{1}{2}\epsilon^2 \tag{6.5}$$

where $\epsilon = y_d - y$, y_d is desired (i.e., known) output, and y is the output of the fuzzy system.

2. The partial derivatives, $\frac{\partial J}{\partial c_{j,k}}$, $\frac{\partial J}{\partial \sigma_{j,k}}$, and $\frac{\partial J}{\partial B_i}$ for each of the free parameters, are calculated using the chain-rule; they are:

$$\frac{\partial J}{\partial B_i} = -\frac{\epsilon f^i}{\sum_{\ell=1}^{n} f^\ell} \tag{6.6}$$

$$\frac{\partial J}{\partial c_{j,k}} = -\frac{2\epsilon(x_j - c_{j,k}) \left[\sum_{i=1}^{n} d_{i,j,k} f^i (B^i - y)\right]}{(\sigma_{j,k})^2 \sum_{i=1}^{n} f^i} \tag{6.7}$$

$$\frac{\partial J}{\partial \sigma_{j,k}} = -\frac{2\epsilon(x_j - c_{j,k})^2 \left[\sum_{i=1}^{n} d_{i,j,k} f^i (B^i - y)\right]}{(\sigma_{j,k})^3 \sum_{i=1}^{n} f^i} \tag{6.8}$$

where $d_{i,j,k}$ is 1 if the ith rule is dependent on the kth membership function of the jth input or 0 if it is not dependent.

3. The free parameters B^i, $c_{j,k}$, and $\sigma_{j,k}$ are then adjusted by:

$$B_i' = B_i - \eta \frac{\partial J}{\partial B_i} \tag{6.9}$$

$$c_{j,k}' = c_{j,k} - \eta \frac{\partial J}{\partial c_{j,k}} \tag{6.10}$$

$$\sigma_{j,k}' = \sigma_{j,k} - \eta \frac{\partial J}{\partial \sigma_{j,k}} \tag{6.11}$$

where B_i', $c_{j,k}'$, and $\sigma_{j,k}'$ are the new values of the free parameters and η is the "learning rate" which determines the size of the adjustments made.

6.4.1 Example 3: Learning Fuzzy Systems

Consider the example 1 presented in section 6.3. Following the training algorithm explained in the previous section, the result of function approximation for the given non-linear input-output data after 150 epochs of training is depicted in Figure (6.6). The learning rate, η, was 0.01. The final membership functions after training is depicted in Figure(6.7).

Allowing the membership functions to change can violate the interpretation in that the meaning initially assigned to the linguistic values can be lost. This

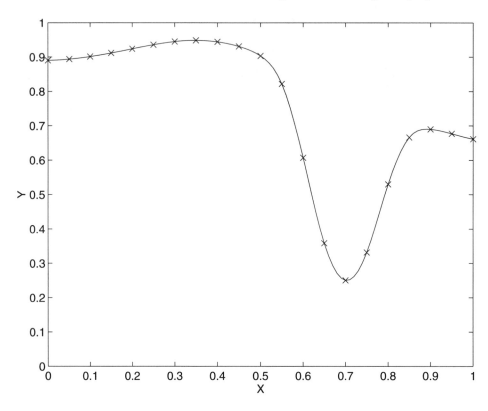

Figure 6.6 Function approximation with a learning fuzzy system after N=150 epochs training.

danger is evident, if the initial membership functions given in Figure (6.2) are contrasted with the membership functions after training. In Figure (6.7) membership function $\tilde{A}^1$ has moved to the right and $\tilde{A}^3$ is completely contained within $\tilde{A}^2$.

6.5 Interpretation Preservation

If allowed to adapt freely, the membership functions of a learning fuzzy system may lose the meaning which was initially assigned to them. They may change their relative positions such that, for example, "low" may become greater than "high", or the range of their activations may become excessively wide or narrow [7, 11, 12, 28].

Although the adapted membership functions may have attained a new significance, after the original meaning has been lost, it may be very difficult or

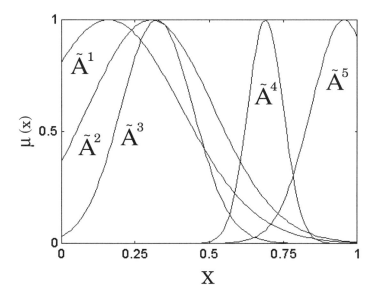

Figure 6.7 Membership functions $\tilde{A}^i$: $i = 1, 2, 3, 4, 5$ after $N = 150$ epochs training without constraints.

otherwise undesirable to interpret this. In some cases a learning fuzzy system may have changed to such a degree that a conventional linguistic interpretation is no longer possible. In such a case, the learning fuzzy system may be viewed as a "black box" function approximator similar in function to a neural network. All these possibilities make a conventional learning fuzzy system unsuitable for many industrial applications in which maintainability and reliability are of importance, despite their likely performance superiority.

6.5.1 Constraint Learning

In [16], a constrained training algorithm, which maintains the interpretation of learning fuzzy system during training, is proposed. It is a paradigm which will enable the learning fuzzy controller to adapt and optimise itself while still remaining conceptually comprehensible to a human expert. This may be achieved at the cost of a slight degradation of the performance of the learning fuzzy system, in the sense that the error function may attain a higher value than if the membership functions are allowed to adapt freely. In most cases, this trade-off is acceptable, as it is often more important to be able to interpret the behaviour of the learning fuzzy system than to achieve a lower minimum in the cost function.

The membership function assigned to a fuzzy value should not exceed certain maximum and minimum limits of fuzziness after adaptation. If the similarity between the initial membership function and the membership function during training is measured, when the similarity measure exceeds its limit, the linguistic meaning assigned to the membership function is said to be lost.

6.5.2   Constraint Learning Rule

Consider the updating rules given in Equations (6.6-6.8). They can be modified for constraint learning by updating the parameters after each iteration using the following update rule.

$$B_i' = B_i - \eta \frac{\partial J}{\partial B_i} \times \Re_{B_i} \tag{6.12}$$

$$c_{j,k}' = c_{j,k} - \eta \frac{\partial J}{\partial c_{j,k}} \times \Re_{c_{j,k}} \tag{6.13}$$

$$\sigma_{j,k}' = \sigma_{j,k} - \eta \frac{\partial J}{\partial \sigma_{j,k}} \times \Re_{\sigma_{j,k}} \tag{6.14}$$

The restriction functions, $\Re_\sigma$, $\Re_c$ and $\Re_B$, are introduced to limit the freedom of updating the parameters and they are governed by the following equations.

$$\Re_\sigma = \frac{1}{1 + e^{-\left(\frac{\sigma - \underline{\sigma}}{\nu_\sigma}\right)}} - \frac{1}{1 + e^{-\left(\frac{\sigma - \bar{\sigma}}{\nu_\sigma}\right)}} \tag{6.15}$$

$$\Re_c = \frac{1}{1 + e^{-\left(\frac{c - \underline{c}}{\nu_c}\right)}} - \frac{1}{1 + e^{-\left(\frac{c - \bar{c}}{\nu_c}\right)}} \tag{6.16}$$

$$\Re_B = \frac{1}{1 + e^{-\left(\frac{B - \underline{B}}{\nu_B}\right)}} - \frac{1}{1 + e^{-\left(\frac{B - \bar{B}}{\nu_B}\right)}} \tag{6.17}$$

where ν_σ, ν_c and ν_B are respectively dispersion parameters of σ, c and B. These are introduced so that a "gentle roll off" is achieved. As the parameters approach their predefined maximum and minimum limits, smaller and smaller updates are performed. By controlling the parameter ν, this can be controlled.

Hence, regardless of whether or not a minimum solution for the cost function, J, is achieved or not, the restriction bounds do not permit the free parameters to move beyond the defined limits. It preserves the interpretation at the possible expense of yielding a less optimal solution.

6.5.3   Example 4: Interpretation Preservation of Learning Fuzzy Systems

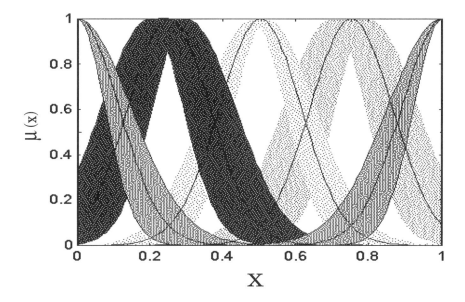

Figure 6.8 Limit bounds for initial membership function of linguistic terms $\tilde{A}^i$, $i = 1, 2, 3, 4, 5$.

The function approximation problem explained earlier in Examples 1 and 3 is repeated here taking into account the effect of constraint training. The upper and lower limits for the parameters σ and c are given in Table 6.2. Figure 6.8 shows the initial membership functions with their acceptable limits. The membership functions of linguistic terms after $N = 150$ epochs of training with $\nu_\sigma = 0.07$ and $\nu_c = 0.07$ are shown in Figure 6.9.

In contrast the membership functions achieved from the constrained training methods depicted in Figure 6.9 resemble the initial membership functions shown in Figure 6.2 while the result of function approximation is almost identical to the results of function approximation without any constraints.

MFs	σ	c	$\underline{\sigma}$	$\underline{c}$	$\bar{\sigma}$	$\bar{c}$
$\tilde{A}^1$	0.16	0.0	0.11	0.0	0.21	0.0
$\tilde{A}^2$	0.16	0.25	0.13	0.2	0.19	0.3
$\tilde{A}^3$	0.16	0.5	0.13	0.48	0.19	0.52
$\tilde{A}^4$	0.16	0.75	0.13	0.7	0.19	0.8
$\tilde{A}^5$	0.16	1.0	0.11	1.0	0.21	1.0

TABLE 6.2 Parameters of membership functions.

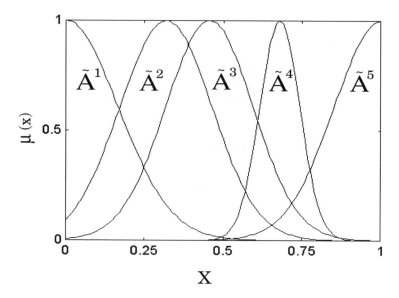

Figure 6.9   Final membership functions after 150 epochs of training with limit bounds.

6.6   Conclusions

In this chapter, reviews of fuzzy and learning fuzzy systems are presented followed by a gradient descent method to update the parameters of a fuzzy system. It has been shown that the integrity of learning fuzzy systems can be preserved by using a constrained training algorithm. There is a trade-off between obtaining the minimum of cost function and the preservation of integrity in the sense of the interpretability of the learning fuzzy systems.

6.7 References

[1] P. A. Antsaklis and K. M. Passino. *An introduction to intelligent and autonomous control.* Kluwer Academic Publishers, 1993.

[2] C. L. Chen and W. C. Chen. Fuzzy controller design by using neural network techniques. *IEEE Trans. on Fuzzy Systems*, 2(3):235–244, Aug., 1994.

[3] Chih-Hsun Chou and Hung-Ching Lu. A heuristic self-tuning fuzzy controller. *Fuzzy Sets and Systems*, 61:249–264, 1994.

[4] Byeong Mook Chung and Jhu Ho Oh. Tuning method of linguistic membership function. pages 706–711, Orlando, Florida, June, 1994.

[5] S. Daley and K. F. Gill. A design study of self-organising fuzzy logic controller. *Proc. Instn. Mech. Engrs (IMechE)*, 200(C1):59–69, 1986.

[6] Wael A. Farag, Victor H. Quintana, and Germano Lambert-Torres. A genetic-based neuro-fuzzy approach for modeling and control of dynamical systems. *IEEE Transaction on Neural Networks*, 9(5):757–767, September 1998.

[7] Pierre Yves Glorennec. Adaptive fuzzy control. In R. Lowen and M.Roubens, editors, *Fuzzy Logic, State of the Art*, pages 541–551. Kluwer Academic Publishers, 1993.

[8] John Hertz, Anders Krogh, and Richard G. Palmer. *Introduction to the Theory of Neural Computation.* —Addison—, 1990.

[9] A. Homaifar and E. McCormick. Simultaneous design of membership function and rule sets for fuzzy controllers using genetic algorithms. *IEEE Transactions on Fuzzy Systems*, 3(2):129–139, May 1995.

[10] S. Horikawa, T. Furuhashi, and Y. Uchikawa. On fuzzy modeling using fuzzy neural networks with the back-propagation algorithm. *IEEE Trans. on Neural Networks*, 3(5):801–806, Sept., 1992.

[11] Hisao Ishibuchi, Ken Nozaki, and Hideo Tanaka. Empirical study on learning in fuzzy systems by rice taste analysis. *Fuzzy Sets and Systems*, 64:129–144, 1994.

[12] J.-S.R. Jang, C.-T. Sun, and E. Mizutani. *Neuro-Fuzzy and Soft Computing: A Computational Approach to Learning and Machine Intelligence.* Prrentice hall, Upper Saddle River, NJ, 1997.

[13] Bart Kosko. Fuzzy function approximation. *Proc. of IEEE Int. Joint Conference on Neural Networks (IJCNN-92)*, 1:209–213, June, 1992.

[14] Chin Teng Lin and C. S. George Lee. Neural-network-based fuzzy logic control and decision system. *IEEE Tranaction on Computers*, 40(12):1320–1336, December 1991.

[15] D. A. Linkens and H.O. Nyongesa. Genetic algorithms for fuzzy control; part i: Offline system development and application. *IEE Proc. Control Theory Application*, 142(3):161–175, May 1995.

[16] A. Lotfi, H. C. Andersen, and A. C. Tsoi. Interpretation preservation

of adaptive fuzzy inference systems. *International Journal of Approximate Reasoning*, 15(4):379–394, 1996.

[17] E. H. Mamdani. Application of fuzzy algorithm for control of simple dynamic plant. *Proc. IEE*, 121(12), December, 1974.

[18] E. H. Mamdani and S. Assilian. An expriment in linguistic synthesis with a fuzzy logic controller. *Int. Journal Man Machine Studies*, 7(1):1–13, 1974.

[19] M. Naeda and S. Murakami. A self-tuning fuzzy controller. *Fuzzy Sets and Systems*, 51:29–40, 1992.

[20] H. Nomura, I. Hayashi, and N. Wakami. A learning method of fuzzy inference rules by descent method. pages 203–210, San Diego, CA, March, 1992.

[21] H. O. Nyongesa. Neuro-fuzzy or fuzzi-neural: case studies of fuzzy neural computation. In *Fifth UK Workshop on Fuzzy Systems, Recent Advances in and Practical Applications of Fuzzy Systems*, volume 1, pages 24–25, Sheffield, UK, May 1998.

[22] D. Park, A. Kandel, and G. Langholz. Genetic-based new fuzzy reasoning models with application to fuzzy control. *IEEE Transactions on System, Man and Cybernetics*, 24(1):39–47, January 1994.

[23] T. J. Procyk and E. H. Mamdani. A linguistic self-organising process controller. *Automatica*, 15:15–30, Jan., 1979.

[24] B. G. Song, R. J. Marks, S. Oh, P. Arabshahi, T. P. Gaudell, and J. J. Choi. Adaptive membership function fusion and annihilation in fuzzy if-then rules. pages 961–967, San Francisco, CA, April, 1993.

[25] C. Y. Su and Y. Stepanenko. Adaptive control of a class of nonlinear systems with fuzzy logic. *IEEE Trans. on Fuzzy Systems*, 2(4):285–294, November, 1994.

[26] M. Sugeno and G. T. Kang. Structure identification of fuzzy model. *Fuzzy Sets and Systems*, 28:15–33, 1988.

[27] T. Takagi and M. Sugeno. Fuzzy identification of systems and its application to modelling and control. *IEEE Trans. on Systems, Man, and Cybernetics*, 15(1):116–132, Jan., 1985.

[28] Li-Xin Wang. *Adaptive Fuzzy Systems and Control: Design and Stability Analysis*. Prentice-Hall, Englewood Cliffs, NJ, 1994.

[29] Li Zheng. A practical computer-aided tuning technique for fuzzy control. pages 702–707, San Francisco, CA, April, 1993.

7

An Application of Fuzzy Modeling to Analysis of Rowing Boat Speed

Kanta Tachibana
Dept. of Computational Science and Engineering, Nagoya University, Furou-cho Chikusa-ku, Nagoya, 464-8603, Japan
kanta@cmplx.cse.nagoya-u.ac.jp

Takeshi Furuhashi
Dept. of Information Electronics, Nagoya University, Furou-cho Chikusa-ku, Nagoya, 464-8603, Japan

Manabu Shimoda, Yasuo Kawakami, Tetsuo Fukunaga
Dept. of Life Sciences (Sports Sciences), The University of Tokyo, 3-8-1, Komaba, Meguro, Tokyo, Japan

0-8493-2269-3/00/$0.00+$.50
© 2001 by CRC Press LLC

An Application of Fuzzy Modeling to Analysis of Rowing Boat Speed

Abstract

Fuzzy modeling has distinct features, which are applicability to nonlinear systems and ability to extract knowledge. Fuzzy neural network (FNN) enables automatic acquisition of knowledge. The authors have proposed an uneven division of input space for the FNN which reduces the number of fuzzy rules without sacrificing the precision of the model.

In many sports, nonlinear factors affect the performance. In rowing competitions, the performance criterion is the boat speed. In this chapter, fuzzy modeling is applied to reveal the relationships between the supplied power and the boat speed.

The forces and the angles of on-water rowing are measured. The subjects are candidates of Japanese national team rowers. The total propulsive work, consistency and uniformity of the propulsive power were calculated from the force and the angle data. The relationships between these factors and the performance were identified with fuzzy modeling. Compared to linear regression, a more precise and simpler model was obtained.

7.1   Introduction

Fuzzy modeling [1] is a method to describe the characteristics of nonlinear systems using fuzzy rules. For automatic acquisition of fuzzy rules, combinations of fuzzy logic and neural networks have been studied [2]. The Fuzzy Neural Network (FNN) in [2] is capable of identifying fuzzy rules and tuning the membership functions by means of back propagation learning. This FNN has been applied to the fuzzy modeling of nonlinear systems.

The authors have proposed a method of input space division [3]. The proposed method divides the input space unevenly according to the input-output relationships of the data. This method works effectively in reducing the number of fuzzy rules without sacrificing the precision of the FNN. It is easy to understand a concise model with a smaller number of fuzzy rules.

Many sports contain nonlinear problems. Nonlinear modeling is necessary to analyze the relationships between the performance and its influential factors. A precise and simple model of the performance will provide coaches and athletes with effective feedback.

This chapter presents the study of a fuzzy modeling of rowing boat speed. Discriminant analysis of biomechanical factors was done for ergometer rowing [4]. This analysis obtained linear equations to classify novice, good and elite rowers. But, there is nonlinearity in the rowers-boat system. The proposed fuzzy modeling technique is applied to the analysis of rowing performance. In rowing races except for those of single scull, many rowers propel a boat together. The ultimate purpose is to run the boat faster than everyone else. Forces exerted by the rowers accelerate the boat. The boat speed is not linear to the sum of the forces. Hydrodynamic and aerodynamic resistances, which do not have linear characteristics, slow the boat down. There are nonlinear relationships between water, air, rowers' motions and the boat speed.

We have developed a measuring device of on-water rowing motions. It measures forces exerted on oars and angles of oars. Candidates of national team rowers participated the experiments. Three factors, which are total propulsive work, consistency of the power and uniformity of the power, are prepared for the fuzzy modeling from the measured data. The relationships between these factors and the boat speed are identified by a fuzzy model in this chapter.

7.2 Complexities in rowing

In rowing competitions, maximizing the boat speed is the purpose of coaches and rowers. The boat speed is the result of the following complex factors:

1. Rowers propel the boat with oars. This process has nonlinearities because the body of a rower has multiple segments.

2. Opposite direction force is generated to the boat when a rower moves forward or backward. The shift of the mass on the boat generates another complexity.

3. Hydrodynamic and aerodynamic resistances decelerate the boat. These negative forces also have nonlinear characteristics.

These effects are too complicated to analyze as a whole. This chapter focuses on the relation between the power supplied to the boat and the average speed of the boat. The forces exerted on oars and the angles of oars are measured during on-water rowing.

Fuzzy modeling uses the following three kinds of data as its inputs to infer the boat speed: total work provided to the boat during the test, the consistency of the power and the uniformity of the power. It is natural to regard the propulsive work as an important determinant of the boat speed. It is said that the volume of supplied power in a stroke should be kept the same as the other strokes for effective run of the boat. The uniformity of the power is the most distinctive character of rowing from any other sports.

The relationships between the three factors and the boat speed are considered to be nonlinear. Fuzzy Modeling is applied to identify the relationships.

7.3 Fuzzy modeling

Distinct advantages of fuzzy modeling are linguistic expression with fuzzy rules and applicability to nonlinear systems.

This section describes fuzzy modeling. Fuzzy neural network described in subsection 7.3.1 is a combination of fuzzy inference and neural network. This combination enables automatic acquisition of fuzzy models. Uneven division of input space described in subsection 7.3.2 reduces the number of fuzzy rules. This allows constructing a comprehensive fuzzy model.

7.3.1 Fuzzy neural network

The FNN presented by the authors is a multi-layered back-propagation model with a specially designed structure for easy extraction of fuzzy rules from the trained FNN. We use Type I of the FNNs in [2]. Fig. 7.1 shows an example of the FNN.

This is a case where the FNN has two inputs x_1 and x_2, one output y and three membership functions for each input. The Back Propagation (BP) learning algorithm can be applied to modify the connection weights w_c, w_g, and w_b. Suppose the model has M-inputs and N-outputs; the following simplified fuzzy inference can be extracted from this type of FNN:

$$R^i : \quad \text{IF } x \text{ is } \boldsymbol{A^i} \quad \text{THEN } y \text{ is } \boldsymbol{B^i} \tag{7.1}$$

$$\begin{aligned} \boldsymbol{x} &= (x_1, x_2, \cdots, x_M), & \boldsymbol{y} &= (y_1, y_2, \cdots, y_N), \\ \boldsymbol{A^i} &= (A_1^i, A_2^i, \cdots, A_M^i), & \boldsymbol{B^i} &= (B_1^i, B_2^i, \cdots, B_N^i) \end{aligned} \tag{7.2}$$

$$\mu^i(\boldsymbol{x}) = \prod_{m=1}^{M} A_m^i(x_m) \tag{7.3}$$

$$\widehat{\mu^i(\boldsymbol{x})} = \frac{\mu^i(\boldsymbol{x})}{\sum_{j=1}^{NOR} \mu^j(\boldsymbol{x})} \tag{7.4}$$

$$y_n^*(\boldsymbol{x}) = \sum_{i=1}^{NOR} \widehat{\mu^i(\boldsymbol{x})} b_n^i \tag{7.5}$$

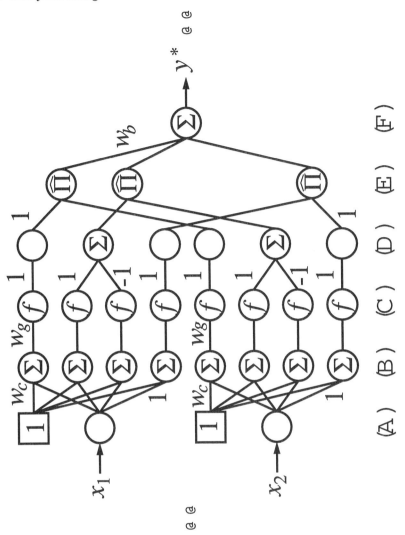

Figure 7.1 Fuzzy Neural Network

where input variables $x_m (m = 1, \cdots, M)$ and output variables $y_n (n = 1, \cdots, N)$ are real numbers, A_m^i is the membership function for i-th rule for m-th input variable and B_n^i is the membership function for i-th rule for n-th output variable. In this type of FNN, B_n^i are singletons. Let us represent them by b_n^i. NOR is the number of fuzzy rules, μ^i is the activation value of R^i, $\widehat{\mu^i}$ is the normalized activation value, and y_n^* is the inferred value.

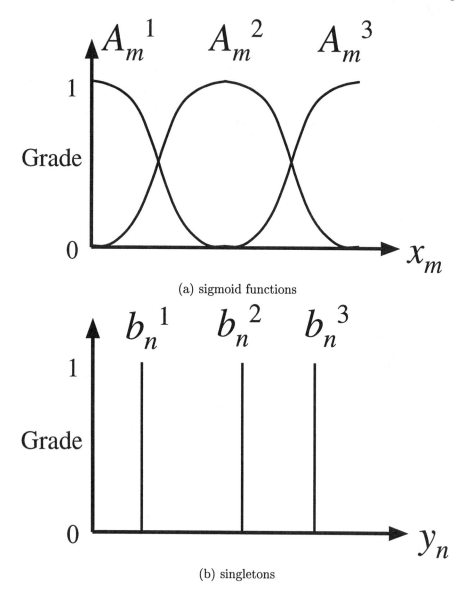

(a) sigmoid functions

(b) singletons

Figure 7.2   Membership Functions

Fig. 7.2(a) shows an example of membership functions in the antecedent formed in (A)-(D)-layers. The connection weights w_c, w_g determine the positions and slopes of the sigmoid functions f in the units in the (C)-layer, respectively. Each membership function consists of one or two sigmoid functions. The outputs of the units in the (D)-layer are the values of membership functions. The products of these values are the inputs to the units in the (E)-layer and the outputs of the units are the normalized activation value in the antecedent $\widehat{\mu^i}$ in eq.(7.4). The output of the unit in the (F)-layer is the sum of the products of the connection weights w_b and the normalized activation values. The connection weights w_b correspond to the singletons in the consequence b_n^i as shown in figure 7.2(b). The output in the (F)-layer is, therefore, the inferred value y_n^* in eq.(7.5).

The model infers $y^*(x^s) = (y_1^*(x^s), \cdots, y_N^*(x^s))$ for a supervised signal (x^s, y^s). Error e^s for this supervised signal is given by:

$$e^s = (e_1^s, e_2^s, \cdots, e_N^s)$$
$$\forall n(n = 1, \cdots, N)\ e_n^s = y_n^*(x^s) - y_n^s. \tag{7.6}$$

The parameters of FNN is updated so that

$$minimize \quad E = \sum_n^N \sum_s^{NOD} (e_n^s)^2 \tag{7.7}$$

where NOD is the number of sample data.

Since the center-of-gravity method is used in the (E)-layer, the updating method of connection weights, *i.e.*, BP algorithm, needs some modifications. The learning algorithm for the FNN is well described in [2].

The feature of this FNN is that fuzzy rules can be extracted easily from the trained FNN. The three layered neural network can identify the input-output relationships. However, it is hard to extract rules from the three layered neural network.

7.3.2 Uneven division of input space

The uneven division of input space for the fuzzy modeling in [3] is described in this subsection. The input space is divided so that the variances of data outputs across the subspaces are minimized. The procedure of input space division is as follows:

1. If the given data have M input variables, M dimensional input space is divided. The input space initially has no division, *i.e.*, the number of subspaces equals to 1. A fuzzy rule is assigned to one subspace, so the number of rules NOR is the same as the number of subspaces. Initially, NOR is also 1. The subspace, which covers the whole input space, is denoted by S^1. Figure 7.3 shows a case where two inputs x_k, x_l are given. The top figure shows the initial division of input space. A fuzzy model with one rule is made with an FNN and trained. The training of the FNN here is only to adjust the singleton in the consequence for efficient training.

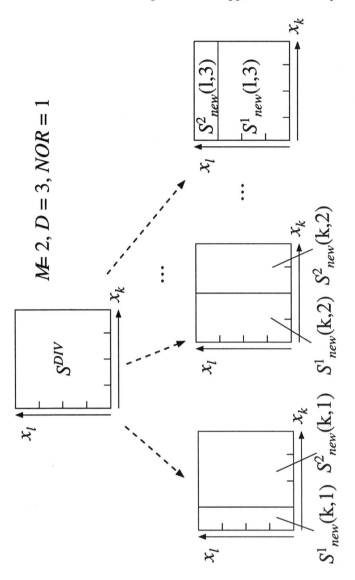

Figure 7.3   Division of Input Space

2. The data are divided into NOR data sets. If the input vector is in the r-th subspace, the data belong to the r-th data set. A subspace is divided. The divided subspace S^{DIV} is decided as:

$$S^{DIV} = \arg \max_{r=1,\cdots,NOR} V(S^r) \tag{7.8}$$

where $V(S^r)$ is the variance of outputs of the r-th data set.
S^{DIV} is divided into two new subspaces, S^1_{new} and S^2_{new}. Number
of possible dividing point on each axis D is given *a priori*. Possible
dividing points are allocated evenly on the axis. Figure 7.3 shows
that it has three possible division points, $D = 3$. Divided axis m_{DIV}
and dividing point d_{DIV} are decided as:

$$\begin{aligned}
&[m_{DIV}, d_{DIV}] \\
&= \arg \min_{\substack{m=1,\cdots,M \\ d=1,\cdots,D}} \sum_{s=1}^{2} V(S^s_{new}(m,d))
\end{aligned} \tag{7.9}$$

$S^1_{new}(m,d)$ and $S^2_{new}(m,d)$ are generated subspaces by dividing
S^{DIV} at the d-th dividing point on the m-th axis. The sum of the
variances of output data in the generated subspaces is the criterion.
NOR is increased by 1, *i.e.*, $NOR := NOR + 1$.
An FNN with NOR rules is generated and trained. The training
of the FNN is only to adjust the singletons in the consequence for
efficient training.

3. Go to step 2 unless the number of rules becomes equal to the pre-
   determined number. Figure 7.4 shows an example of dividing input
   space which has two subspaces. The right hand side subspace has
   the larger variance of outputs and it is divided as described in step 2.

4. The FNN is trained after the division of input space. Connection
   weights w_g and w_c in the antecedent as well as w_b in the consequence
   are adjusted by the BP learning algorithm.

Figure 7.5 shows an example of uneven division of the input space x_k, x_l,
and the membership functions constructed by the FNN. It has five subspaces.
Five fuzzy rules are extracted from this FNN. The membership functions are
easy to interpret into linguistic expressions.

7.4 Experiments

Six female and three male rowers participated the experiments. All of them
were candidates for the Japanese national team. First, two of the female rowers
rowed a double scull. They undertook a series of tests, which comprised 100
m rowing at 20 strokes per minute, 100 m at 24 spm, 100 m at 26 spm and
100 m at 28 spm. Another four pairs of female rowers and two pairs of male
rowers undertook the same tests.

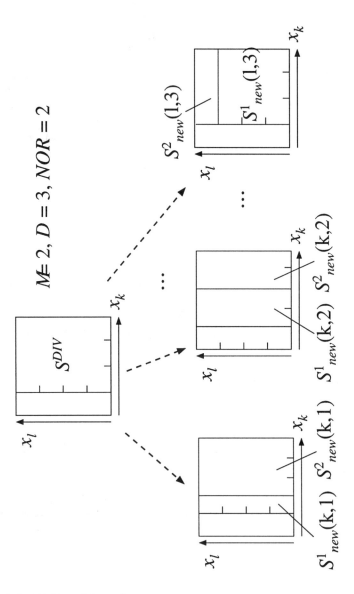

Figure 7.4 Division of Input Space

A double scull has four oars. The force and the angle of each oar were
measured with the sampling frequency at 50 Hz. The data were low pass
filtered with the cut-off frequency at 12.5 Hz. Times taken to row 100 m were

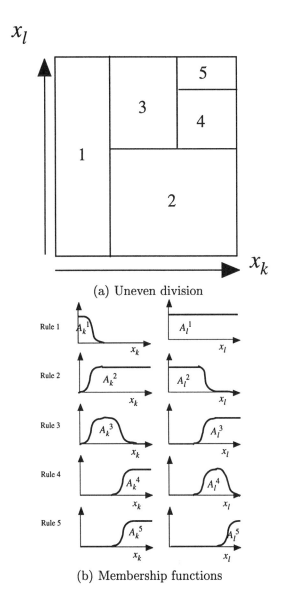

(a) Uneven division

(b) Membership functions

Figure 7.5   Obtained division and membership functions

also measured. The average speed of the boat y were given by:

$$y = 100/time. \tag{7.10}$$

Three factors, the total propulsive work, the consistency of power and the uniformity of power, were derived as follows:

Propulsive power is the product of the propulsive force and the angular velocity of the oar. For the i-th oar ($i = 1, \cdots, 4$), the propulsive force F_{ip} is the product of the force F_i and cosine of the oar angle θ_i, given by the following equation:

$$F_{ip}(t) = F_i(t)\cos(\theta_i(t)) \tag{7.11}$$

where t represents the time step. Angular velocity ω_i is the difference of the oar angle:

$$\omega_i(t) = \theta_i(t) - \theta_i(t-1). \tag{7.12}$$

The propulsive power of i-th oar is:

$$P_{ip}(t) = F_{ip}(t)\omega_i(t), \tag{7.13}$$

omitting the oar outboard length. The total propulsive power at the t-th time step $P(t)$ is the sum of those of the four oars:

$$P(t) = \sum_{i=1}^{4} P_{ip}(t). \tag{7.14}$$

The total work given to the boat is the sum of the total power during the 100 m test:

$$\text{Total Work} = \sum_{t} P(t) \tag{7.15}$$

The consistency of power was given by the coefficient of variation of the supplied power for each stroke:

$$\text{Power Consistency} = 100(1 - \sigma(P_j)/\bar{P}_j) \tag{7.16}$$

where P_j is the power supplied during the j-th stroke. $\sigma(P_j)$ and $\bar{P}_j$ represent the standard deviation and the average of supplied power for strokes, respectively.

The uniformity of power is the similarity of four oars on transition of supplying the propulsive power. The power uniformity at the t-th time step is given by the following equation:

$$\text{Power Uniformity}(t) = 100(1 - \sigma_i(P_{ip}(t))/\max_t(\bar{P}_{ip}(t))) \tag{7.17}$$

where $\sigma_i(P_{ip}(t))$ is the standard deviation of propulsive power for oars at the time step t. Average power for the four oars at the time step t is represented by $\bar{P}_{ip}(t)$. Maximal value of $P_{ip}(t)$ normalizes the standard deviation of power at each time step. The average of Power Uniformity(t) during the test is used as the third factor.

7.5   Modeling results

Seven crews rowed the four tests each. The number of data was 28. It was not large. So, to prevent the model from over-fitting to the data, two factors out of three were used to infer the average boat speed.

First, x = (Total Work, Power Consistency) were used as the inputs. The input and output data were normalized in the range [0,1]. Table 7.1 shows the result obtained by the linear regression. Table 7.2 shows the result of the fuzzy modeling. In this table, the membership functions and the singletons in the consequent were labeled with S for Small, M for Medium, L for Large. These linguistic rules are easy to understand for coaches and athletes. The rules were reasonable. The more the total work was given, the faster the boat speed became. In the case where the total work was large and the consistency was high, the boat speed was very high. Nonlinear relationships were revealed by this model. The consistency did not affect the boat speed if the total work was not large. It had an effect only if the total work was large.

MSE	0.035
Knowledge	$y = 0.84x_1 + 0.36x_2$

Table 7.1   Result of Linear Regression

MSE	0.016
Knowledge	If x_1 is S, then y is MS.
	If x_1 is MS, then y is ML.
	If x_1 is ML, then y is ML.
	If x_1 is L and x_2 is Not L, then y is L.
	If x_1 is L and x_2 is L, then y is Very L.

Table 7.2   Result of Fuzzy Modeling

Figure 7.6 shows the division of the input space. Figures 7.7 and 7.8 show the membership functions for the total work and the power consistency, respectively.

Next, x = (Total Work, Power Uniformity) were used as the inputs. Table 7.3 shows the result obtained by the linear regression. Table 7.4 shows the result of the fuzzy modeling. These rules were also reasonable. The more the total work was given, the faster the boat speed became. But, the fourth rule

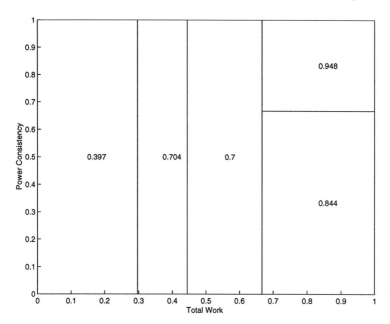

Figure 7.6 Obtained Division of Input Space

did not coincide with our intuition well. It says that in the case where the total work was large, and the power uniformity was high, then the boat speed was high. This was not very high. The reason for this discrepancy was due to the small number of data.

MSE	0.045
Knowledge	$y = 0.84x_1 + 0.38x_2$

Table 7.3 Result of Linear Regression

Figure 7.9 shows the division of the input space. Figures 7.10 and 7.11 show the membership functions for the total work and the power consistency, respectively.

7.6   Conclusion

In this paper, fuzzy modeling was applied to identification of the relationships between the propulsive work, the consistency of the power, the uniformity of

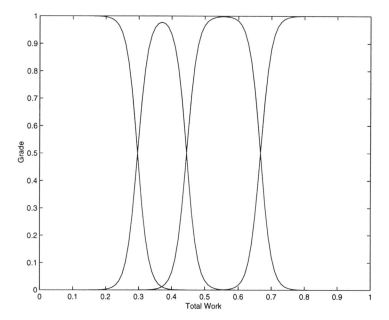

Figure 7.7 Membership Functions for Total Work

MSE	0.017
Knowledge	If x_1 is S, then y is MS.
	If x_1 is M, then y is ML.
	If x_1 is L and x_2 is Not Very L,
	then y is Very L.
	If x_1 is L and x_2 is Very L, then y is L.

Table 7.4 Result of Fuzzy Modeling

the power and the boat speed. The nonlinear relationships were revealed.

The obtained rules were generally reasonable. But, they were not exact because:

- The number of data was small.
- The subjects were in the same ability level.

Future direction of this study is to do more experiments including other levels of rowers and to construct a more informative model.

The relation of the supplied power and the boat speed does not explain all of the rowing boat speed. Analysis of how the rowers provide power to the oars using their multi-link bodies is another interesting issue to study.

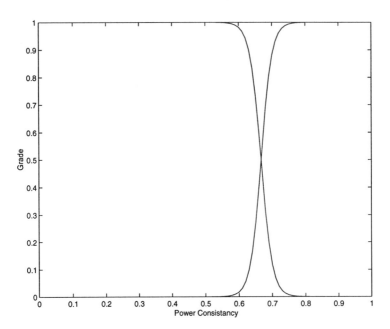

Figure 7.8   Membership Functions for Power Consistency

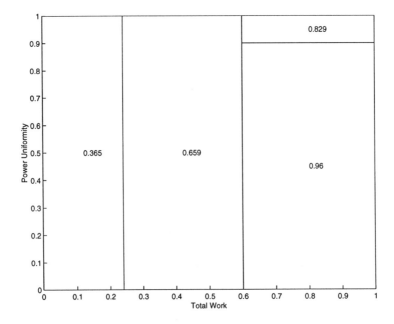

Figure 7.9   Obtained Division of Input Space

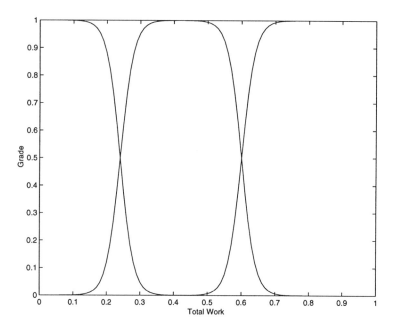

Figure 7.10 Membership Functions for Total Work

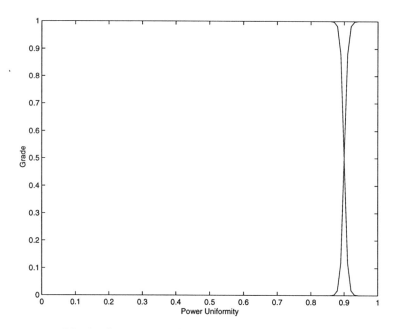

Figure 7.11 Membership Functions for Power Uniformity

7.7   References

[1] T. Takagi and M. Sugeno, "Fuzzy Identification of Systems and Its Applications to Modeling and Control", IEEE Trans. on Syst., Man, and Cybern., Vol.15, No.1, pp.116–132, 1985.

[2] S. Horikawa, T. Furuhashi and Y. Uchikawa, "On Fuzzy Modeling Using Fuzzy Neural Networks with the Back-Propagation Algorithm", IEEE Trans. on Neural Networks, Vol.3, No.5, 801–806, 1992.

[3] K. Tachibana and T. Furuhashi, "A Hierarchical Fuzzy Modeling Using Fuzzy Neural Networks which Enable Uneven Division of Input Space", The 14th Fuzzy System Symposium, pp.305–308, 1998.

[4] R. Smith and W. L. Spinks, "Discriminant Analysis of Biomechanical Differences between Novice, Good and Elite Rowers", Journal of Sports Sciences, 13, pp.377–385, 1995.

8

A Novel Fuzzy Approach to Hopfield Coefficients Determination

Salvatore Cavalieri

Institute of Informatic and Telecommunications, University of Catania, V.le A.Doria 6, 95125 Catania, Italy. E-mail: cavalieri@iit.unict.it

Marco Russo

M.Russo is with INFN Section of Catania - ITALY and with the Dept. of Physics, Univ. of Messina, Contrada Papardo, Salita Sperone 31, 98166 ME - ITALY. E-mails: marco.russo@ai.unime.it, marco.russo@ct.infn.it, marco.russo@ieee.org

A Novel Fuzzy Approach to Hopfield Coefficients Determination

Abstract

The Hopfield-type neural model is a suitable tool for the solution of optimization problems featuring NP-hard computational complexity. The solution of such problems using a Hopfield model requires determination of the values of a certain number of coefficients linked to the surrounding conditions of the optimization problem itself. It is quite difficult to determine these values, because a heuristic search is necessary. This is not only time-consuming, but may lead to the determination of a set of coefficients which provide neural solutions that are far from optimal, or even non-valid ones. So far there have been no reported research in literature offering a general method for the search for coefficients which will guarantee optimal or close to optimal solutions. This chapter proposes a method which allows automatic determination of Hopfield coefficients. The results obtainable can be user-defined. It is, in fact, possible to specify whether the user wishes high quality solutions or prefers greater robustness, i.e., a high percentage of valid solutions.

8.1   Introduction

In literature there exists a category of combinatorics problems which are extremely complex, due to the need to explore all the possible solutions.

For this reason heuristic solutions are often preferred; although they do not always guarantee optimal solutions, the computation times involved are limited.

The autoassociative memory model proposed by Hopfield [1] has attracted considerable interest as a method for solving difficult optimization problems. Its particular capacity to solve NP-hard combinatorics problems in a very short time has led to the successful application of Hopfield networks to a large number of real problems [2–8].

Many researchers have studied the properties of Hopfield networks for solving optimization problems [9, 10]. It has generally been found that although these networks do produce some useful results, a great drawback is that at times they provide non-valid solutions, or solutions referring to local minima (the valid solutions found may be very far from the global minimum value).

The quality and percentage of valid solutions (henceforward referred to as robustness) of the solution provided by a Hopfield network essentially depends on the choice of the energy function, which must fully take into account all the surrounding conditions of the optimization problem itself. Once the energy function is fixed, an important role for improving the quality and robustness of the solution is played by the choice of the coefficients which link the energy function to the surrounding conditions of the combinatorics problem to be solved.

No methods that allow unambiguous determination of the Hopfield Coefficients (HCs) are currently available in literature.

In effect, in [11] the authors propose an analytical method for determination of the HCs, but the approach seems too tied to the Travelling Salesman Problem (TSP) and is difficult to extend to different applications.

The lack of a general method for automatic determination of HCs makes a heuristic search inevitable. This search consists of manual variation of the values of the coefficients and empirical evaluation of their effect on the solution to the problem. Obviously this method is inconvenient, not only because it is excessively time-consuming but also because it does not guarantee HCs which correspond to optimal or close to optimal solutions.

Our aim was to devise software that would autonomously search for HCs such as to ensure high percentages of valid and/or close to optimal solutions.

The software we present is based on the attempt to reproduce artificially experience on the use of Hopfield network, in particular on the heuristic search of HCs we have acquired in various applications in several fields (see [6–8,12–14] for example).

The core of the software proposed is a system based on fuzzy inferences, the aim of which is to reproduce human experience. Fuzzy Logic (FL) was used as opposed to other approaches such as Neural Networks (NNs) for two reasons. The first relates to the learning phase needed to acquire the method for HCs tuning. We preferred to use an approach based on FL rather than NNs (e.g., backpropagation) because as the former is linguistic in nature the representation of the knowledge base it provides is easier for a human to interpret. The second reason was that in the course of our scientific experience [15] [16] we have become convinced that FL usually provides very interesting results from the point of view of robustness. We are of the opinion that this is due to the fact that FL was deliberately conceived of to deal in a formal manner with the imprecise and/or uncertain information typical of human reasoning. As the chapter will show, this property of FL allows to obtain HCs which guarantee, when requested from the user, extremely robust neural solutions.

The fuzzy system was trained using the FuGeNeSys program [16–18] which adopts a supervised learning technique, the core of which is based on Genetic

Algorithms (GAs). The examples used in the learning phase were provided by the authors on the basis of their experience.

The software presented in the chapter is based on the following algorithm. In a preliminary phase, as we will show in the chapter, the user fixes some constants that are required for the problem to be solved with our approach. After the random initialization of the HCs for the specific optimization problem, the fuzzy rules vary these HCs as we would do manually. The coefficient tuning process ends within a maximum predefined number of iterations, during which our algorithm tries to improve the quality and/or the robustness of the Hopfield solution as requested by the user.

In some applications the quality of the solution provided is important, even at the cost of reaching a solution after a large number of invalid trials. In other applications, on the other hand, the robustness of the solution is much more important, i.e., the possibility of obtaining valid solutions immediately, without attaching great importance to their quality. By appropriately setting certain parameters governing the automatic HC tuning procedure, it is possible to obtain separate sets of HCs, each of which provides solutions of better quality or greater robustness.

It is important to point out that the computational complexity of the algorithmic solution here proposed is the same of the Hopfield's model, i.e., a polynomial one. In fact, the algorithm calculates the stable solution of the Hopfield network a predefinite, user defined maximum number of times. This number is not linked to the complexity of the problem to be solved, as will be shown in the paper, but only to the required quality and/or robustness of the solution.

We will describe the fuzzy heuristic approach to HC tuning in detail, showing its general validity and applicability to any optimization problem.

Then several examples of the application of the algorithm solution proposed will be presented. These examples will highlight the capability of our approach to find solutions featuring robustness and/or quality.

8.2   Hopfield-Type Neural Network

The use of neural networks to solve optimization problems was first proposed by Hopfield and Tank [1, 2]. They devised a neural model, known as the Hopfield model, which is able to offer valid solutions to discrete combinatorics optimization problems. The computational capacity offered by the Hopfield model was first demonstrated by application to the TSP. Since then, several researchers have made contributions to both the neural model itself and its application to various optimization problems [3, 4, 7, 8, 14, 19, 20]. The Hopfield model is based on a single-layer architecture of neurons, the outputs of which are fed back towards the inputs. The output of the i-th neuron, O_i, which assumes values ranging between 0 and 1, is linked to the input of the same neuron, U_i, by a sigmoidal monotonic increasing function g_i. Each feedback between the output of the j-th neuron and the input of the i-th neuron has an associated weight, w_{ij}, which determines the influence of the j-th neuron on the i-th neuron. An external bias current, I_i, is then supplied to the i-th neuron. The dynamics of the Hopfield network for the i-th neuron, O_i, are described by:

$$\frac{dU_i}{dt} = -\frac{U_i}{\tau} + \sum_j w_{ij}O_j + I_i \tag{8.1}$$

where τ is a user-selected decay constant. Hopfield [21] showed that if the weights matrix $W = [w_{ij}]$ is symmetrical and if the function g_i is a steep-like curve, the dynamics of the neurons described by (8.1) follow a gradient descendent of the quadratic energy function, also known as the Lyapunov function:

$$E = -\frac{1}{2}\sum_{i,j} w_{ij}O_iO_j - \sum_i I_iO_i \tag{8.2}$$

Under the same hypothesis, Hopfield [21] showed that the minima of the energy function (8.2) coincide at the corners of the hypercube defined by $O_i \in \{0, 1\}$.

8.3 Fuzzy Logic

The aim of this section is to describe the approach adopted to calculate the fuzzy rules trained (see section 8.7) for automatic modification of the Hopfield network coefficients.

In classical set theory, given a value $x \in X$ and a subset A of X ($A \subseteq X$) the element x either belongs to the set A or not. So it is possible to associate a Boolean numerical value (that is, one belonging to the set $\{0, 1\}$) to each of the elements of X, specifying whether it belongs to A or not.

However, the human way of thinking does not reproduce classical theory: in the human mind sets have much less clear outlines.

Considering, for instance, some commonly used adjectives such as *tall, intelligent, tired, ill* and so on, it is obvious that their outlines are not at all clear. The point is that we do not refer to these properties in terms of classical binary logic but in terms of a generalization with multiple values.

The concept of a fuzzy set is a step towards this generalization. As introduced by Zadeh [22], a fuzzy set is a set whose membership function can take any value within the closed interval $[0, 1] \subseteq \Re$. A fuzzy subset A, called the Universe of Discourse, has a membership function of:

$$\mu_A : X \to [0,1] \qquad (8.3)$$

which associates each element, x, of X with a number $\mu_A(x)$ ranging from 0 to 1, representing the degree of membership of x in A.

In general a fuzzy conditional rule is made of a *premise* and a *conclusion*:

$$\text{if premise then conclusion} \qquad (8.4)$$

The premise is made up of a number of fuzzy predicates P_i (henceforward also called antecedents) of the general form (Tom IS speed) that are eventually negated or combined by different operators such as AND or OR computed with t-*norms* or t-*conorms* (which according to Zadeh are minimum and maximum respectively).

In the latter example Tom is the value of the linguistic variable defined in the Universe of the Discourse of men and speed is one of the names of the term set of the linguistic variable (for example slow, normal, speed).

The following is an example of a fuzzy conditional rule using such operators:

$$\text{if } P_1 \text{ and } P_2 \text{ or } P_3 \text{ then } P_4 \qquad (8.5)$$

where, for example:

$$P_1 = (\text{car IS light}),$$
$$P_2 = (\text{power IS medium}),$$
$$P_3 = (\text{power IS high}),$$
$$P_4 = (\text{car IS fast}).$$

To apply an inference method to the conclusion, it is first necessary to assess the degree of membership θ of the premise, through assessment of the degrees of membership α_i of each predicate $P_i = (X_i \text{ IS } A_i)$ in the premise. The membership degree α_i is calculated by assessing the degree of membership of a generic value of X_i in the fuzzy set A_i. If X_i is made up of a fuzzy set, its degree of membership α_i is determined by making an intersection between the fuzzy value of X_i and the fuzzy set A_i and choosing the maximum value of membership; if X_i is a crisp value, its degree of membership in the fuzzy set A_i is made up of the value the membership function of A assumes corresponding to X_i. The degree of membership, θ, of the premise can thus be calculated by assessing the fuzzy operations on the predicates. We recall that according to Zadeh the operator AND corresponds to the minimum operation between two degrees of membership, while OR corresponds to the maximum. Once the value of θ is known, an inference method can be applied to assess the conclusion.

Finally, having obtained the output fuzzy set, defuzzification is performed to transform the fuzzy information obtained into numerical values.

Recently some defuzzification methods have been introduced which considerably simplify calculation of the output value: the rules are aggregated and defuzzification is performed in a single operation, bypassing calculation of the fuzzy output set [23].

Let us see the equations used to calculate the fuzzy inferences in greater detail.

Each rule has I antecedents. For the generic r-th rule, the i-th antecedent, P_{ir}, has the following form:

$$P_{ir} = X_i \text{ IS } FS_{ir} \tag{8.6}$$

X_i is the i-th input and is crisp. That is, X_i is the particular fuzzy set that is always null except for a precise numerical value x_i. FS_{ir} is a fuzzy set. It has a Gaussian membership function $\mu_{FS_{ir}}(x)$, univocally determined by a centre, c_{ir}, and a parameter, γ_{ir}, linked to the variance according to the following equation:

$$\mu_{FS_{ir}}(x) = e^{-\gamma_{ir}^2 (x - c_{ir})^2} \tag{8.7}$$

Considering the crisp nature of the inputs, the degree of truth, α_{ir}, of the generic antecedent P_{ir} is:

$$\alpha_{ir} = e^{-\gamma_{ir}^2 (x_i - c_{ir})^2} \tag{8.8}$$

We always used the connector AND, as calculated by Zadeh, between the various antecedents. So the degree of truth, θ_r, of the r-th rule is the lowest of all the degrees of truth, α_{ir}, of the antecedents belonging to the rule:

$$\theta_r = \min_{i=1}^{I}(\alpha_{ir}) \tag{8.9}$$

As regards the conclusion of the rules, a numerical output value, C_r, is associated with each rule.

The analytical expression of the defuzzification method adopted, called Weighted Sum (WS) defuzzification [23], is:

$$y = \sum_{r=1}^{R} C_r \theta_r \tag{8.10}$$

Figure 8.1 shows a practical example of calculation of a fuzzy inference made up of only two rules.

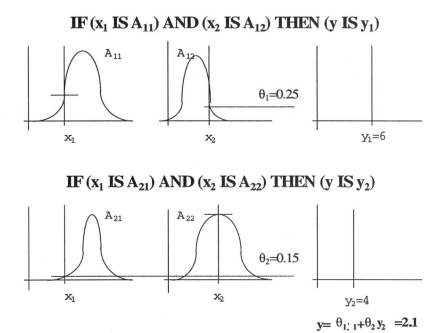

$$\text{IF } (x_1 \text{ IS } A_{11}) \text{ AND } (x_2 \text{ IS } A_{12}) \text{ THEN } (y \text{ IS } y_1)$$

A_{11} A_{12} $\theta_1=0.25$

x_1 x_2 $y_1=6$

$$\text{IF } (x_1 \text{ IS } A_{21}) \text{ AND } (x_2 \text{ IS } A_{22}) \text{ THEN } (y \text{ IS } y_2)$$

A_{21} A_{22} $\theta_2=0.15$

x_1 x_2 $y_2=4$

$$y= \theta_{1;\,1}+\theta_2 y_2 \ =2.1$$

Figure 8.1   Practical inferencing

8.4   The Fuzzy Tuning of Hopfield Coefficients

The aim of this section is to give a detailed description of the method we propose for automatic determination of HCs. It is based on close integration of the Hopfield Model and Fuzzy Inferences, as shown in Fig. 8.2.

The neural output (Hopfield Solution) is represented by the solution provided by the neural model, which can be valid or non-valid. The Solution_Check module has the task of assessing the validity of the neural solution and, if it is valid, its quality.

In any optimization problem it is possible to identify the surrounding conditions (and therefore the associated HCs) which determine the validity of the neural solution. Each valid solution has a certain degree of quality depending on the value of the solution determined as compared with the optimal solution. Even in such cases it is generally possible to identify the surrounding conditions (and the HCs) which will guarantee close to optimal solutions. Checking the validity of a neural solution of a generic optimization problem is quite straightforward as it consists of checking the value taken by each of the surrounding conditions. Verification of the quality of the solution, on the

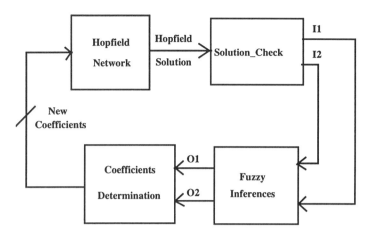

Figure 8.2 Integration of neural and fuzzy modules

other hand, is much more difficult as the global minimum in any combinatorics problem is never known. In order to assess the quality of the solution, we consider a LowerBound parameter (defined as the one possible lower bound of the optimal solution) and a Tolerance parameter. If the minimum of the energy function determined by the Hopfield network is lower than the Tolerance·LowerBound value, then the valid solution is also considered to be good. The Solution_Check module therefore has the task of checking the validity and quality of the solution provided by the neural network following the strategies outlined above.

The output of the Solution_Check module is made up of two parameters, indicated in the figure as I1 and I2. The first corresponds to the HC value determining non-validity of the solution or, if the solution is valid, the HC which mainly makes its quality poor. Parameter I2 is set as equal to the average of the remaining HCs. On the basis of these parameters the Fuzzy Inference module determines a new coefficient value for I1 (output O1) and varies the average of the remaining coefficients (output O2). Choice of the inputs I1 and I2 was due to two reasons. The first depends on experience. In a heuristic, manual approach, the HCs are varied by determining the coefficient which has caused the solution to be non-valid or of poor quality. Its value is then increased according to the values assumed by the remaining coefficients; so input I2 was considered to be significant. The second reason lies in the generalization of the approach presented. This choice allows the fuzzy approach to be applied to any optimization problem, as the inputs I1 and I2 and the outputs O1 and O2 are not directly linked to the number of coefficients in the problem to be solved.

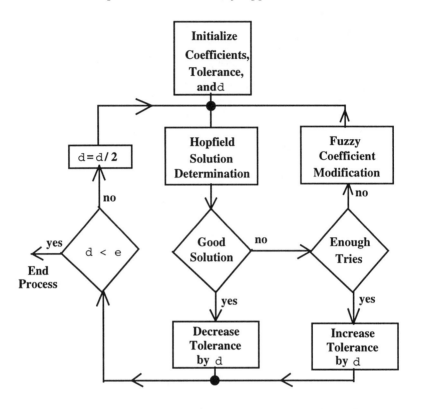

Figure 8.3   The procedure for determining a suitable set of coefficients

Fig. 8.3 illustrates the general procedure for determining a suitable set of coefficients. The Tolerance parameter is initially set at a reasonable high value and is lowered by a pre-defined amount indicated with δ, if the network reaches a valid, good solution. If it does not succeed in providing a valid good solution with a certain Tolerance value, the latter is increased, still by an amount δ. Following each increase or decrease in the Tolerance parameter, δ is halved. Increases and decreases in the Tolerance parameter are therefore made on the basis of a binary search in order to speed the search process up.

The Enough Tries test refers to the attempt to find a valid, good solution with a certain Tolerance value. If no valid good solution is found after a pre-defined maximum number of iterations the Tolerance value is increased by δ.

Vice versa, if after this maximum number of tries at least one valid good solution is found, then the Tolerance value is decreased by δ.

The process of increasing or decreasing the Tolerance value ends when the parameter δ is lower than a previously defined threshold indicated with ϵ, guaranteeing the end of our procedure in a finite time interval. In this way it is possible to identify the minimum Tolerance values below which no good solution can be found.

8.4.1 A Detailed Description of the Algorithm for Coefficient Determination

The flow-chart shown in Fig. 8.4 and named main() is a detailed description of the algorithm used to determine a suitable set of HCs for a generic Hopfield problem. The algorithm comprises a cycle, which is terminated by a comparison between δ and ϵ, as explained above. Within this cycle there is another one which modifies the coefficients and checks up on quality. This second cycle ends when a valid good solution is reached or when too many consecutive non-valid solutions have been found (i.e., Iterations$\geq$IterDelta).

If the cycle has ended because a valid good solution has been found, the Tolerance is decreased by δ; otherwise it is increased by the same amount. In any case, δ is halved.

As seen in Fig. 8.4, at each iteration, the validity and the quality of the neural solution is tested. This is done by the GoodSolution() function, whose representative flow-chart is shown in Fig. 8.5. Essentially its dual task is to determine the Hopfield solution and evaluate it.

Determination of the Hopfield solution is easily performed by iteration of the Hopfield network until it reaches a stable output.

Evaluation of the Hopfield solution consists of testing whether the solution is valid and, if it is, whether it is a good one. If the solution is not valid, the cause of non-validity is evaluated. A variable, c, is considered, whose admissible values fall within the integer range of [0,Coefficients], where Coefficients represents the number of HCs involved in the optimization problem to be solved. It was assumed that all the surrounding conditions are numbered from 1 to Coefficient, so if c takes a positive value it identifies the surrounding condition which has caused the neural solution to be non-valid or, if the solution is valid but not good, the surrounding condition which has led to poor quality. If the solution is both valid and good, $c = 0$.

It is often possible, depending on the initial conditions, that two or more consecutive solutions correspond to two totally different minima. We therefore decided to evaluate the neural solution considering a number of consecutive solutions. This number is indicated in Fig. 8.5 with IterMaxGood. We then considered a percentage of this value (indicated as PercIterMaxGood): if the number of valid good solutions (i.e., ones for which $c = 0$) is higher than this value, the set of coefficients determined is considered to be both valid and good. In this case, the set of HCs found is saved.

As can be seen from Fig. 8.5, there is a cycle which ends either when the number of neural solutions determined (CountFuzzy) is equal to IterMaxGood

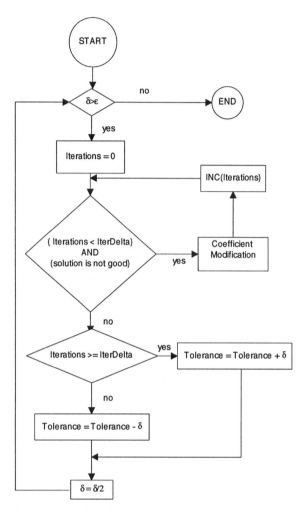

Figure 8.4   main() algorithm flow-chart

or when the number of valid good solutions (CountFuzzyOK) is higher than PercIterMaxGood.

In this cycle the CauseDetection() function gives the value of the variable c. If c is equal to zero, the CountFuzzyOK variable is increased. If, on the other hand, c is positive a global vector of Coefficient elements (called cause[] in the algorithm) stores the number of times each surrounding condition c is violated. This information is then used to modify the HC related to the condition which has not been met most frequently, as it will be shown later.

Figure 8.6 shows the representative flow-chart of the CauseDetection() func-

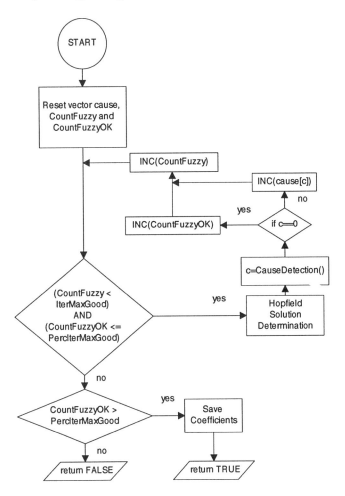

Figure 8.5 GoodSolution() function flow-chart

tion, which returns the c value.

The first operation performed is the determination of the validity of the neural solution.

If the solution is valid, its quality is tested. This is achieved by comparing the value the energy function assumes in correspondance of the solution with the LowerBound·Tolerance. If the quality is not sufficiently good, c is set to the surrounding condition which more than others affects the quality of solution (this value is indicated as goodnessHC in Fig. 8.6). To do so, first each surrounding condition related to the quality is assessed corresponding to the solution obtained. Then the values obtained for each of these surrounding conditions are compared.

If the quality of the solution is good according to the current Tolerance value, the variable c is set to 0.

Lastly, if the solution is not valid, the surrounding condition which has contributed more than the others to this non-validity is identified. As done before, this is performed by assessing each surrounding condition related to validity in correspondence to the solution obtained. Then the values obtained for each surrounding condition are compared.

On the basis of what was previously said, the algorithm we propose is characterized by the comparison between the values of the surrounding conditions related to the quality or to the validity of the solution. These values are not directly comparable, because they fall into different ranges for example.

Let Cause(c) be the value taken by the c-th surrounding condition corresponding to the solution obtained. In order to compare these values a fuzzy set indicated as invalid(c) is defined with a membership function $\mu_{\text{invalid}(c)}(\text{Cause}(c))$. This function provides for a measure of the influence of the c-th surrounding conditions on the quality or on the validity of the solution.

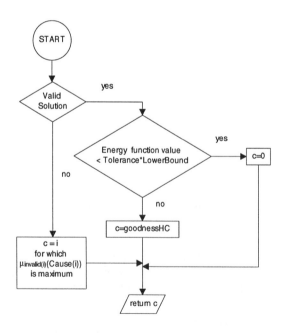

Figure 8.6   CauseDetection() function flow-chart

The degree of invalidity or not goodness of Cause(c) is specified by the clause:

$$(\text{Cause}(c) \; \text{IS} \; \text{invalid}(c))$$

The membership function $\mu_{\text{invalid}(c)}(\text{Cause}(c))$ (see Fig. 8.7) has only three values - $m(c)$, $t(c)$ and $M(c)$ - where $m(c) \leq t(c) \leq M(c)$. If the value of the c-th surrounding condition calculated for the neural solution is equal to the desired one (i.e., Cause(c) = $t(c)$) the truth value is null. If the surrounding condition takes a value outside the interval $]m(c), M(c)[$, the truth value will be unitary, thus indicating a great contribution to the not goodness or to the invalidity of the solution. Finally, when the Cause(c) values fall within the interval $[m(c), M(c)]$, the c-th surrounding condition makes a less decisive contribution to the not goodness or to the invalidity of the solution. The value of this contribution is weighed by the slope of the function.

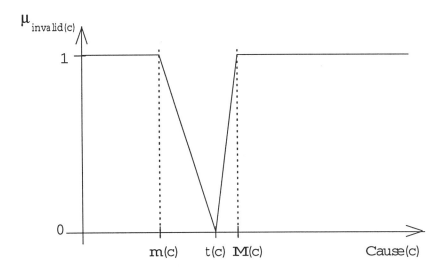

Figure 8.7 The invalid(c) membership function

The last algorithm to be described in this section is the one which modifies the coefficients, as can be seen in main(), where the block Coefficient Modification is present (see Fig. 8.4). The procedure we used first identifies the cause which has made the solution non-valid or has not guaranteed sufficient quality. As explained above, this is done using the global cause[] vector which specifies the number of times each surrounding condition has been violated.

The surrounding condition which has been violated most often is chosen.

Then the two fuzzy system inputs I1 and I2 are set respectively to the coefficient of the surrounding condition previously determined and the mean of the remaining conditions. The fuzzy rules trained are evaluated and the two defuzzified outputs O1 and O2 are obtained. The coefficient of the surrounding condition assumed to be the cause of invalidity or insufficient quality takes the value O1, while the others are each multiplied by $\frac{O2}{I2}$.

If the network offers a valid solution whose quality is insufficient, i.e., higher than the Tolerance·LowerBound value, but not very far from this value, in practice it has been seen that by leaving the coefficients almost unaltered the next solution provided by the Hopfield network will be of better quality.

We therefore decided that if the surrounding condition most violated is related to quality, the percent difference between the solution and the Tolerance·LowerBound product is calculated. If the difference remains within a pre-established threshold, coefficient modification will only involve the HC found, leaving the others unaltered. According to the algorithm outlined above, this was obtained by not multiplying each coefficient by $\frac{O2}{I2}$.

If the surrounding condition most violated is related to quality and the percent difference between the solution and the Tolerance·LowerBound product exceeds the pre-established threshold, the coefficients are all modified in the attempt to force the network to provide better solutions.

Let E be the value of the energy function calculated in correspondence of the neural solution. In order to realize the HC modification when the solution is valid but not good, a new membership function, $\mu_{\text{NotGood}}(E)$, again is considered. The degree of goodness of E is specified by the clause:

$$(E \text{ IS NotGood})$$

The membership function μ_{NotGood} (see Fig. 8.8) is characterized by only two parameters t_e and M_e, where $M_e \geq t_e$. If E is greater than the value of M_e, then the truth value is unitary. This value leads in our algorithm to the modification of all coefficients in the attempt to force the network to provide better solutions. On the other side, if the value E is in the range $]t_e, M_e[$, the membership function degree will be less than 1. According to our algorithm, this value leads to a smooth modification of the HC parameter linked to the quality of solution, leaving the others unchanged.

8.4.2   Membership Function Tuning

Two membership function classes were presented in the previous section, one used in order to directly compare the values of Cause(c) obtained for each surrounding condition and the other to realize the HC modification when the solution is valid but not good. Both the membership function classes play an

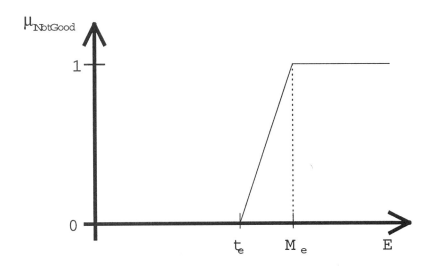

Figure 8.8 The membership function μ_{NotGood}

important role in our algorithm. For this reason the authors feel it is important to give some guidelines about the choice of their parameters.

Membership function $\mu_{\text{invalid}(c)}$ When the membership function is applied to the c-th surrounding condition linked to the validity of solution, the choice of the value of the parameter $t(c)$ is very simple: it is exactly equal to the value expected for the surrounding condition c. The choice of the values the other two parameters $m(c)$ and $M(c)$ must assume is more free. In general for the generic c-th surrounding condition linked to the validity of the solution it is possible to foresee an admissibility range for the value of Cause(c). This interval contains the value of $t(c)$ and corresponds to the values of the c-th surrounding condition which led to a soft degrade of the validity of the solution. The values of Cause(c) which led to a heavy degrade into the validity of the solution fall outside the foreseen interval. The values of $m(c)$ and $M(c)$ correspond to the boundary of the foreseen interval of validity around $t(c)$.

For example, let us suppose that a certain condition regarding the validity of the solution requires that only one output neuron must be excited among a fixed subset n_s of all neurons. A number of ones greater than 1 and that do not exceed 10-30% of n_s feature a solution whose validity may be reasonably considered softly degraded. Otherwise, we are in the presence of a heavy degradation. In this example, it is clear that $t(c) = 1$, $m(c)$ could be set to 0 and $M(c)$ may be assumed whatever value ranging from $0.1n_s$ to $0.3n_s$.

Membership function μ_{NotGood} Similar considerations can be done with regard to the choice of the values of t_e and M_e. The choice of t_e

is very easy, as it corresponds to the value desired for the quality of the solution. As said in the previous section, this value must be set equal to Tolerance·LowerBound.

If the quality of the solution, E, is lower than t_e, then the membership function is not used, because it was obtained as a good solution (i.e., the variable c is set to zero in function CauseDetection()).

Otherwise, if E is higher than the product Tolerance·LowerBound, then the membership function must be used in order to determine the modification the surrounding conditions which has mainly affected the quality of solution must undergo. On the basis of what was said, it is clear that M_e must be fixed equal to the value of the pre-established threshold previously explained. In the practical use of our algorithm, this parameter was always set to twice or three times the value of Tolerance·LowerBound. In the examples the authors will present in the following section, the parameter M_e is set three times the previous product.

Conclusive Remarks about Membership Function Tuning On the basis of what was previously said, it appears clear that the choice of the values of $t(c)$ and t_e is very easy, but the choice of the values of $m(c)$, $M(c)$ and M_e may be less easy. This choice is, in fact, based on qualitative consideration about the optimization problem to be solved, and may require an experience from the user of our algorithm. However we made a lot of tests in order to verify the impact of a wrong choice of $m(c)$, $M(c)$ and M_e parameters in the membership functions. It was seen that the result given by our approach (i.e., the set of HCs the algorithm is able to find) is not influenced by this choice, but only the time needed to obtain it may be lengthened. This result appears very interesting because it allows the use of our algorithm to a not very expert user.

8.5 Examples of Application of the Proposed Method

The aim yof this section is to show some examples of application of the algorithm we propose. The examples will refer to NP-hard optimization problems: the well-known Traveling Salesman Problem and the Flexible Manufacturing System Performance Optimization. The examples feature characteristics very different from each other, pointing out in this way the general validity of the approach proposed in the paper.

8.5.1 The Traveling Salesman Problem

The TSP consists of finding the shortest closed path by which every city out of a set of n cities is visited once and only once. It can be demonstrated that the problem is an NP-hard one, since the number of permutations to be considered in order to determine a solution is at most equal to $\frac{n!}{2n}$. Several solutions to this problem by Hopfield-type neural network are well known in literature. In the following the original work by Hopfield and Tank [2] and by Szu [5] will be shown.

TSP: Hopfield and Tank's Solution by the Hopfield Network

In order to solve the TSP using a Hopfield network, a model with n^2 neurons was considered by Hopfield and Tank [2]. The neurons were logically subdivided into n groups of n neurons each. Henceforward we will identify each neuron with a double index, xi (where the index $x = 1..n$ relates to the group corresponding to the city x, whereas the index $i = 1..n$ refers to the neurons in each group representing the order in which the city x is visited), its output with O_{xi}, the weight for neurons xi and yj with $w_{xi,yj}$, and the external bias current for the xi-th neuron with I_{xi}. The grid of neurons can be seen as constituting a matrix in which each row corresponds to a group x and each column corresponds to the visiting order index i. According to this convention, the Lyapunov energy function becomes:

$$E = -\frac{1}{2} \sum_{x,i,y,j} w_{xi,yj} O_{xi} O_{yj} - \sum_{x,i} I_{xi} O_{xi} \qquad (8.11)$$

If the output of the generic xi-th neuron, O_{xi}, assumes a value of 1, it indicates whether the optimal solution determined is such that i is the order in which the city x is visited. Determination of the optimal solution by the Hopfield network requires the definition of a suitable energy function, based on the conditions surrounding the problem. Below we will describe these surrounding conditions and the relative energy function terms.

1. As each city x $(x = 1,..,n)$ can be visited only once, there can be at most one output set to 1 in each row x.
2. Likewise, as each visiting order refers exclusively to a single city, the number of 1s in each column i $(i = 1,...,n)$ has to be 1.
3. As the number of cities to be visited must be n, the total number of 1s must be n.
4. Finally, it is necessary to introduce a term which will take into account the distance to be covered.

On the basis of these conditions, the energy function is characterized by the following:

$$E = \frac{A}{2} \sum_{x,i,j \neq i} O_{xi} O_{xj} +$$

c	$m(c)$	$t(c)$	$M(c)$	Cause(c)
1	0	1	$0.3n$	OnesPerRow()
2	0	1	$0.3n$	OnesPerColumn()
3	$n-1$	n	$1.5n$	TotalOnes()

Table 8.1   The Fuzzy sets defined in $1 \le c \le 3$

$$+ \ \frac{B}{2} \sum_{i,x,y \neq x} O_{xi}O_{yi} + \frac{C}{2} (\sum_{x,i} O_{xi} - n)^2 \ +$$

$$+ \ \frac{D}{2} \sum_{x,y \neq x,i} d_{xy}O_{xi}(O_{y,i+1} + O_{y,i-1}) \qquad (8.12)$$

where each coefficient (A, B, C, D) (HCs) refers to the surrounding conditions in the order in which they are described, and the term d_{xy} represents the distance between the generic adjacent cities x and y. The values of weights and bias currents, determined on the basis of a comparison between the energy function and the Lyapunov function, are expressed by:

$$\begin{aligned} w_{xi,yj} \ = \ & -A\delta_{xy}(1 - \delta_{ij}) - B\delta_{ij}(1 - \delta_{xy}) - C \ + \\ & -Dd_{xy}(\delta_{j,i+1} + \delta_{j,i-1}) \end{aligned} \qquad (8.13)$$

$$I_{xi} \ = \ C \quad \forall x, i, y, j \qquad (8.14)$$

where $\delta_{ij} = 1$ if $i = j$ and is 0 otherwise.

Membership Function Choice   The aim of this subsection is to give a practical example of membership functions $\mu_{\text{invalid}(c)}(\text{Cause}(c))$ choice with reference to the TSP solved by the original Hopfield and Tank's model.

The TSP has four surrounding conditions, so the variable c takes four positive values. If the solution is not valid, and the cause of invalidity is that the condition requiring a single 1 in each row is not met, $c = 1$. If the cause of invalidity is that the condition requiring a single 1 in each column is not met, $c = 2$, while if the cause of invalidity is that the condition requiring n 1s is not met, $c = 3$. The surrounding condition responsible for the quality of the solution, indicated previously as goodnessHC, corresponds to the value $c = 4$.

In order to define the 4 membership functions $\mu_{\text{invalid}(c)}(\text{Cause}(c))$ the values Cause(c), $m(c)$, $t(c)$ and $M(c)$ have to be specified for each surrounding condition. Table 8.1 shows these values for each HC related to the non-validity of the solution (i.e., $c = 1, 2, 3$). Note that the value of Cause(c) is defined by the functions OnesPerRow(), OnesPerColumn() and TotalOnes(). These functions respectively determine the maximum number of 1s per row, the maximum number of 1s per column and the total number of 1s.

The $t(c)$ values have to be $t(1) = 1$, $t(2) = 1$, and $t(3) = n$. The choice of the values of $m(c)$ and $M(c)$ was largely dictated by experience. It was assumed that $M(1) = M(2) = 0.3n$, because we know that if there are fewer 1s in each row or column it is not necessary to make great modifications in the HCs for the first two surrounding conditions. Vice versa, if the number of 1s in each row or column is greater than $0.3n$, there is a great violation of the invalidity condition and robust tuning of the relative HCs is needed. The same considerations hold for $M(3) = 1.5n$.

TSP: Szu's Solution by Hopfield Network

The Hopfield and Tank's paper [2] has stirred a great deal of interest in solving the TSP. Many researchers have investigated both modifications to the Hopfield and Tank's network energy function, and other architectures to solve the problem. David Van den Bout and T.K.Miller [24] did work with a Hopfield network that had a simpler energy function but relied on a simulated annealing schedule to ensure good itineraries. Durbin and Willshaw [25] came up with an elastic net method. This method was further refined by D.J.Burr [26] by adding an annealing schedule to the elastic net method, which generates good solutions more quickly. H. Szu [5] suggested a modification to the Hopfield and Tank's original net. In the following, this modification will be clearly explained.

Szu's modification to the Hopfield and Tank's network is to change the C term in the energy function so that there is a separate excitation on a per row and per column basis. Thus all the neurons in a row or column will get excited whenever no neurons are firing in the respective row/column. In the Hopfield and Tank's solution the excitation is on entire network basis. By exciting just the row or column, only the appropriate neurons can possibly turn on.

The Szu's energy function is characterized by the following five terms:

$$
\begin{aligned}
E \;=\; & \frac{A}{2} \sum_{x,i,j\neq i} O_{xi}O_{xj} + \frac{B}{2} \sum_{i,x,y\neq x} O_{xi}O_{yi} + \\
& + \frac{C}{2} \sum_{x} (\sum_{i} O_{xi} - 1)^2 + \frac{C}{2} \sum_{i} (\sum_{x} O_{xi} - 1)^2 + \\
& + \frac{D}{2} \sum_{x,y\neq x,i} d_{xy}O_{xi}(O_{y,i+1} + O_{y,i-1})
\end{aligned}
\tag{8.15}
$$

where, as seen before, each coefficient (A, B, C, D) (HCs) refers to the surrounding conditions in the order in which they are described, and the term d_{xy} represents the distance between the generic adjacent cities x and y.

Membership Functions Choice The TSP solution by Szu features four surrounding conditions. The meaning of the values of the variable c (c can ·be equal to 1,2,3 or 4) was previously described. Table 8.2 shows the values of the parameters $m(c)$, $t(c)$, $M(c)$ and Cause(c) for each HC related to the

c	$m(c)$	$t(c)$	$M(c)$	Cause(c)
1	0	1	$0.3n$	OnesPerRow()
2	0	1	$0.3n$	OnesPerColumn()
3	$-\infty$	0	0.75	AverageError()

Table 8.2   The fuzzy sets defined in $1 \leq c \leq 3$

validity of the solution.

Note that the function OnesPerRow() and OnesPerColumn() were described in the previous subsection. The values of $m(c)$, $t(c)$ and $M(c)$ for the causes $c = 1$ and 2 are the same seen before. Regarding the cause $c = 3$, Cause(c) value is now given by the function AverageError(). It provides for the average absolute error, calculated as the average for all rows and for all columns of the difference between the number of 1s in each row or in each column and the expected number of 1s (i.e., one 1 in each row and in each column). In this case, the choice of $m(3)$ is not important as the error is positive defined (in our work it was chosen equal to $-\infty$, but other values could be given). The choice of $M(3)$ was done on the basis of empirical considerations.

8.5.2   Flexible Manufacturing System Performance Optimization

The aim of this section is to give another example of the application of the method described above. The example refers to the performance optimization problem of a Flexible Manufacturing System (FMS). This example is widely treated in [27–29], where it is shown that it is a NP-hard problem. In the following a brief overview of the problem itself will be given.

A FMS is an interconnected system of resources (machine tools, robots, etc.) capable of automatically processing a wide variety of products simultaneously and under computer control [30]. Each product (called also part type) is the result of a sequence of processes (called production cycle) according to its technological requirements. In a FMS several parts of the same type (i.e., of the same kind of product) may be simultaneously processed in each production cycle.

Full exploitation of available resources is extremely important to optimize the productivity (or performance) of the FMS as a whole. One of the parameters on which to act in order to maximize exploitation of the resources is the number of parts processed in the same production cycle. Too low a number of parts processed underexploits the available resources, while too high a number causes conflicts between resources which slow down the productivity of the system. The aim to be reached is to determine a number of parts to be simultaneously processed in each production cycle such as to optimize the productivity of the FMS as a whole.

One of the most known theoretical solutions to this problem is presented in [31]. The approach proposed is based on the use of Event Graphs, which is a Petri Net [32,33] in which each place (graphically represented by a circle) is connected with only one output transition (graphically represented by a thin bar) by means of an arc going from the place to the transition and with only one input transition by means of an arc going from the transition to the place. Like Petri Nets, in a Event Graph each transition can have an associated firing time, in which case the Event Graph is called timed, and each place can contain one or more tokens (graphically represented by black dots). The arrival of a token in a place enables firing of the output transition for that place. Firing may occur in null time, if the transition is immediate, or in the time associated with the transition if it is timed. When the fire occurs, the token is removed from the input place and transferred to the output place for the transition which fired.

Modelling an FMS by Event Graphs is very easy and consists of representing each FMS resource (buffer, machine, robot, etc.) by a place and each activity performed by a resource by a transition, to which the time required to complete the activity is associated [31] [32] [34].

An Event Graph is said to be strongly connected if there is a sequence of transitions connecting any pair of places in the graph.

In a strongly connected event graph we can identify elementary circuits, each of which is a sequence of transitions that goes from one place back to the same place, while any other place is not repeated. A particular elementary circuit is called the command circuit, and specifies the operations sequentially performed by a single resource. For a more detailed explanation of the theory related to strongly connected event graph, the reader is suggested to refer to [31] [34].

Let Γ be the set of elementary circuits in the Event Graph, $M(\gamma)$ the number of tokens in the generic elementary circuit $\gamma \in \Gamma$, $\mu(\gamma)$ the sum of all the firing times of the transitions belonging to the elementary circuit γ, Γ^c the set of command circuits, γ^c the generic command circuit $\in \Gamma^c$, $\Gamma^* = \Gamma - \Gamma^c$ and γ^* the generic elementary circuit $\in \Gamma^*$.

As shown in [31], the FMS optimization problem, for a strongly connected Event Graph, can be formulated as:

$$\text{minimize}(\sum_{i=1}^{n} u_i \cdot x_i) \qquad (8.16)$$

where u_i are positive integer numbers, called P-Invariants [32] [33], x_i represents the number of tokens in place P_i, and n is the number of places of the Event Graph. Condition (8.16) must be constrained by:

$$M(\gamma^c) = 1 \quad \forall \gamma^c \in \Gamma^c \tag{8.17}$$

$$M(\gamma^*) \geq \lceil \alpha \cdot \mu(\gamma^*) \rceil \quad \forall \gamma^* \in \Gamma^* \tag{8.18}$$

where $\lceil l \rceil$ is defined as the smallest integer number greater or equal than the real number l and where α is the FMS performance index required [31] [34]. As can be seen, condition (8.17) fixes the number of tokens in each command circuit equal to 1. Condition (8.18) fixes a lower bound for the number of tokens in each elementary circuit, which is not a command circuit.

Finding a solution to such a problem usually involves the solution of an integer linear problem where at least as many constraints as the elementary circuits in the Event Graph have to be considered. Actually, this represents a major drawback of such an approach, since it requires the explicit enumeration of all such circuits. In [27–29] one of the authors presented an alternative to these algorithms, based on use of a Hopfield neural network. In the following the neural solution will be clearly described.

FMS Performance Optimization: Solution by the Hopfield Network

The solution of the FMS performance optimization problem, by the Hopfield neural model, may be achieved by the following steps:

Step1: Modelling the FMS by Event Graphs. The FMS is first modelled by means of Event Graphs. As said previously, modelling an FMS by Event Graphs is very easy and consists of representing each FMS resource (buffer, machine, robot, etc.) by a place and each activity performed by a resource by a transition, to which the time required to complete the activity is associated.

Step 2: Mapping the Event Graph onto the Neural Model. Once the FMS has been modelled by the Event Graph, it is transformed into a Hopfield neural model. This is achieved by making each place, P_i, in the Event Graph correspond to the neuron, O_i, in the neural network. The value (1 or 0) of the output of each neuron O_i models the presence or absence of a token in the place P_i modelled: if the output O_i is 1 the place P_i corresponding to the neuron contains a token, if O_i is 0 the place P_i contains no tokens. It is clear that the proposed coding of the neural output is based on the necessary assumption that each place in the Event Graph contains at most one token. This does not represent a limit, as it is demonstrated in [34] that it is always possible to modify a generic Event Graph into an equivalent one in which each place possesses at most one token. The mapping between the Event Graph modelling the FMS and the novel neural model allows the number of neurons it contains to be defined.

Step 3: Determination of Energy Function of the Hopfield Neural Model. Once the number of neurons and their relationship with the Event Graph modelling the FMS has been fixed, the next step is to obtain the energy function of the Hopfield model linked to the FMS optimization problem.

The energy function must be made up by three terms, one for the first surrounding condition (8.16), which refers to the quality of solution, and the other two for the surrounding conditions (8.17) and (8.18), which refers to the validity of the solution.

The energy function term relating to the quality of the solution can be obtained by considering that condition (8.16) can also be expressed in the following form:

$$\text{minimize}(\sum_{i=1}^{n} u_i \cdot x_i) = \text{minimize}(\sum_{i=1}^{n} u_i \cdot x_i)^2 =$$
$$= \text{minimize}(\sum_{i=1}^{n} \sum_{j=1}^{n} u_i \cdot u_j \cdot x_i \cdot x_j) \qquad (8.19)$$

where n, as said, is the number of places in the Event Graph, i.e., the number of neurons in the Hopfield neural model. This condition can be formalized by the following term of the Lyapunov energy function:

$$\frac{A}{2} \sum_{i=1}^{n} \sum_{j=1}^{n} u_i \cdot u_j \cdot O_i \cdot O_j \qquad (8.20)$$

based on the consideration that each x_i corresponds to O_i, according to the mapping between the Event Graph and the neural model, as outlined previously. The aim of the real coefficient A is to weight the influence of condition (8.20) on the solution to the problem.

The energy function term relating to the validity of the solution has to impose a certain number of tokens in each elementary circuit γ of the Event Graph, according to (8.17) and (8.18). The corresponding term of the Lyapunov energy function has to be of the following kind:

$$\frac{\text{Constant}}{2} \cdot \sum_{\gamma} (\sum_{i:P_i \in \gamma} O_i - M_t(\gamma))^2 \qquad (8.21)$$

where the first sum is extended to every elementary circuit γ, the second sum is extended to $\forall i \in [1,..,n]$ such that the place P_i belongs to the elementary circuit γ, and $M_t(\gamma)$ represents the number of tokens desired in each circuit γ. The term (8.21) is minimized when the number of activated neurons in each circuit γ is equal to $M_t(\gamma)$. The value of $M_t(\gamma)$ is given by conditions (8.17) and (8.18), as it will be shown in the following.

Condition (8.17) imposes a single token in each of the command circuits γ^c. It corresponds to the Lyapunov function term:

$$\frac{B}{2} \cdot \sum_{\gamma^c} (\sum_{i:P_i \in \gamma^c} O_i - 1)^2 \qquad (8.22)$$

where B, like A, weights the influence of condition (8.22) on the solution to the problem. As can be seen term (8.22) is minimized when a single token is present in each command circuit γ^c.

Let us consider the Lyapunov energy function term:

$$\frac{C}{2} \cdot \sum_{\gamma^*} (\sum_{i:P_i \in \gamma^*} O_i - \lceil \alpha \cdot \mu(\gamma^*) \rceil)^2 \qquad (8.23)$$

where C performs the same role as A and B. As can be verified, condition (8.23) determines a constant bias current value, fixing the number of tokens in each non-command elementary circuit γ^* as $\lceil \alpha \cdot \mu(\gamma^*) \rceil$. In this way, condition (8.18) may not be respected, because a valid solution may feature the presence of some circuits in which the number of tokens is strictly greater than $\lceil \alpha \cdot \mu(\gamma^*) \rceil$. In order to have condition (8.18) respected, in [27–29] the Lyapunov energy function term (8.23) is still considered but a dynamic modification of bias current values during the neural iteration is considered. This modification is able to cause the number of tokens in each circuit γ^* to be no less than $\lceil \alpha \cdot \mu(\gamma^*) \rceil$. The reader is referred to the papers [27–29] to have the dynamic modification of the bias currents explained in great detail.

Membership function choice   Once the energy function has been determined, the Hopfield neural model can provide a solution constrained to satisfy the surrounding conditions (8.16), (8.17) and (8.18) of the FMS performance optimization problem, only if the coefficients A,B,C are well defined. In the following the use of the fuzzy method for the tuning of the coefficients A,B and C will be clearly described. In particular this section will focus on the choice of the membership function $\mu_{invalid(c)}(\text{Cause}(c))$. The FMS performance optimization problem features three surrounding conditions; so the variable c takes three prositive values. If the solution is valid but is not good, then the variable c assumes the value 1. In other words, the condition goodnessHC corresponds to the value $c = 1$. If the solution is invalid and the cause of invalidity is that condition (8.17), requiring that $M(\gamma^c)=1 \ \forall \gamma^c \in \Gamma^c$, is not

c	$m(c)$	$t(c)$	$M(c)$	Cause(c)
2	0	1	4	ones_per_command_circuit()
3	$\lceil \alpha \cdot \mu(\gamma^*) \rceil - 1$	$\lceil \alpha \cdot \mu(\gamma^*) \rceil$	$+\infty$	ones_per_elementary_circuit()

Table 8.3   The fuzzy sets defined in $2 \leq c \leq 3$

met then the value c is equal to 2. Finally if the solution is invalid and the
cause of invalidity is that condition (8.18), requiring that $M(\gamma^*) \geq \lceil \alpha \cdot \mu(\gamma^*) \rceil$
$\forall \gamma^* \in \Gamma^*$, is not met, then the value of c is 3. Table 8.3 shows the values
Cause(c), $m(c)$, $t(c)$ and $M(c)$ in the CauseDetection() function, for each surrounding condition relating to the non-validity of the solution (i.e., $c = 2$ and
3).

Note that the value of Cause(c) is defined by the functions
ones_per_command_circuit() and ones_per_elementary_circuit(), which determine the number of 1s in each command circuit and the number of 1s in each
elementary circuit, respectively. It is clear that $t(2) = 1$ because the desired
number of 1s in each command circuit is 1. About the value of $t(3)$ it was
fixed to $\lceil \alpha \cdot \mu(\gamma^*) \rceil$ because this value is the minimum desired number of 1s
in each elementary circuit. About the choice of the value of $m(c)$ and $M(c)$,
shown in Table 8.3, there was no particular criterion adopted, but only reasonable values were adopted. In particular, it is clear that $M(3)$ must be $+\infty$
as a value of $M(\gamma^*)$ greater than $\lceil \alpha \cdot \mu(\gamma^*) \rceil$ is allowed by condition (8.22).
Finally, the LowerBound() in CauseDetection() function was assumed equal
to the value of the energy function to be minimized when the number of 1s
in each circuit is equal to that desired minus one and the 1s are placed in the
places characterized by lower p–invariants values.

8.6   Remarks on the Tuning of the Parameters

The HC determination process described in the previous section is quite automatic, once certain parameters have been fixed. It is therefore necessary
to make a few remarks about the way in which these parameters are to be
established.

As mentioned previously, the LowerBound can be determined according to
various criteria which are irrelevant to the algorithm itself. The only condition
that has to be met is that the LowerBound be lower than the global minimum
of the function to be minimized. It can be demonstrated that for any optimization problem it is always possible to determine a value that will satisfy
this condition.

Choice of the parameters Tolerance, ϵ and δ is quite straightforward and
not critical for the effects of the algorithm. More specifically, Tolerance has
to be set to a reasonably high value to ensure that at least one good solution

is reached. ϵ has to be as low as possible to make the search for an optimal set of HCs as exhaustive as possible. It should be noted, however, that too low an ϵ value could make the calculation time too long. Lastly, δ has to be chosen according to the Tolerance value, bearing in mind that it represents the first increase or decrease performed on Tolerance (0.5·Tolerance is a cautious choice).

The only three parameters that really affect the results of the method proposed are IterDelta, IterMaxGood and PercIterMaxGood. According to their value they can affect the set of HCs determined as they are evidently correlated with the quality and robustness of the solutions.

More specifically, as IterDelta increases a greater number of attempts are made to find a good solution before increasing δ. This parameter thus directly affects the quality of the neural solution and an increase in it means trying to obtain better-quality solutions.

The other two parameters - IterMaxGood and PercIterMaxGood - are decisive in determining the robustness of the solution. As the ratio $\frac{PercIterMaxGood}{IterMaxGood}$ tends towards 1, in fact, HCs which make the neural network converge are always sought. It should be pointed out that an increase in PercIterMaxGood may cause a degradation in the quality of the solution. Asking for a large number of valid good solutions, in fact, may lead to a search for such a "flat" energy function minimum as to guarantee a large number of valid good solutions. But this minimum, which is difficult to get out of, may also turn out to be a local one.

The parameter IterMaxGood also affects the quality of the solution on its own. The greater the number of solutions found, the higher the probability of finding one very close to optimal.

Being able to set these parameters arbitrarily is, in our opinion, very important, as the user of an optimizer based on a Hopfield model may prefer a close to optimal solution obtained in a few attempts to the optimal one that can be obtained with a much larger number of tries. Vice versa, he may require the best solution whatever the price in terms of time.

8.7   Description of the Fuzzy Inferences trained

With FuGeNeSys we trained two separate fuzzy inferences. The first, which we called Fuzzy Worst Case Modifier (FWCM), refers to modification of the Hopfield Network coefficient which has caused the solution to be non-valid or not good. The second inference, called the Fuzzy Mean Modifier (FMM), refers to modification of the mean of the remaining coefficients. It should be pointed out that the fuzzy approach proposed behaves differently according to whether the FWCM refers to a coefficient causing non-validity or poor quality. In the former case, the FMM output is used to modify all the remaining coefficients.

In the latter, on the other hand, the FMM output is not used and consequently the other coefficients remain unchanged. As mentioned earlier, each of the two inferences comprises two inputs and one output. The inputs are the same for both inferences - the Hopfield coefficient which has caused a non-valid or not good solution, and the average of the other coefficients. Fig. 8.9 shows the two inferences obtained after the learning phase. The root mean square normalized errors made on the learning patterns were 4.46% for the FWCM and 4.87% for the FFM.

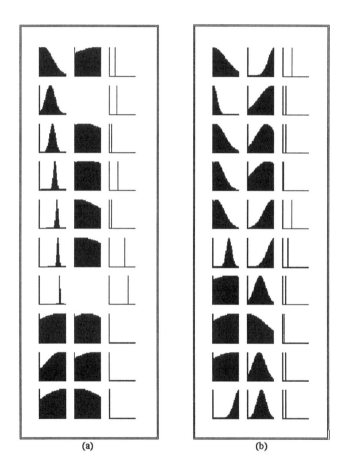

Figure 8.9   FWCM and FMM

In both part (a) and part (b) of Fig. 8.9 we find the rules in the rows, the fuzzy sets referring to the first input in the first column, those referring to the second input in the second column, and the output singletons in the last column. As regards the axes, on the ordinate we have the truth value interval [0,1] while on the abscissa the interval for the first columns is [100,1010] and for the second columns [0,960]. For the FWCM outputs, values range in the interval [0,930] while for the FMM we have [0,810].

8.8   Fuzzy Approach versus Heuristic Determination of HCs

The aim of this section is a dual one. First of all we want to show how the method we propose allows us to determine solutions which are much closer to optimal and much more robust than those provided by HC determination based on a classical heuristic search.

Secondly, we aim to demonstrate that appropriate use of the parameters IterDelta, IterMaxGood and PercIterMaxGood allows us to establish a priori the quality and robustness of the neural solution.

The results presented in this section refer to the optimization problems seen before: the TSP solved by the Hopfield and Tank's original energy function, the TSP solved by the Szu's energy function and the FMS performance optimization.

8.8.1   TSP by Hopfield and Tank's Original Energy Function

The fuzzy logic-based algorithm was applied to a TSP featuring 10 cities with random distances between them. The minimum distance in the scenario was 0.05, so the LowerBound was set to $n \cdot 0.05 = 0.5$. The Tolerance was set to 5, δ to 4 and ϵ to 0.01. For the three parameters IterDelta, IterMaxGood and PercIterMaxGood the following three sets of values were chosen:

$$\left\{ \begin{array}{lcl} \text{IterDelta} & = & 100 \\ \text{IterMaxGood} & = & 10 \\ \text{PercIterMaxGood} & = & 1 \end{array} \right. \qquad (8.24)$$

$$\left\{ \begin{array}{lcl} \text{IterDelta} & = & 100 \\ \text{IterMaxGood} & = & 10 \\ \text{PercIterMaxGood} & = & 7 \end{array} \right. \qquad (8.25)$$

$$\left\{ \begin{array}{lcl} \text{IterDelta} & = & 300 \\ \text{IterMaxGood} & = & 10 \\ \text{PercIterMaxGood} & = & 1 \end{array} \right. \qquad (8.26)$$

This choice was dictated by a desire to assess the influence of IterDelta on the quality of the solution and the influence of PercIterMaxGood on its robustness, as explained in Section 8.6. For each set of parameters IterDelta,

IterMaxGood and PercIterMaxGood the fuzzy-logic based coefficient tuning algorithm gave a set of HCs. The HCs determined were as follows:

$$HCs\#2 = \begin{cases} A & = & B = 768 \\ C & = & 171 \\ D & = & 334 \end{cases} \tag{8.27}$$

$$HCs\#3 = \begin{cases} A & = & B = 893 \\ C & = & 134 \\ D & = & 444 \end{cases} \tag{8.28}$$

$$HCs\#4 = \begin{cases} A & = & B = 832 \\ C & = & 151 \\ D & = & 482 \end{cases} \tag{8.29}$$

The solutions obtained on the basis of these three sets of HCs were then compared with those presented by Hopfield and Tank in [2], based on the following set of HCs:

$$HCs\#1 = \begin{cases} A & = & B = 500 \\ C & = & 200 \\ D & = & 500 \end{cases} \tag{8.30}$$

Below the comparisons between the four sets of HCs will be shown from two points of view: the robustness and the quality of the neural solution provided.

In Fig. 8.10 we give the comparative results of robustness performance with varying numbers of cities. Two different TSPs were considered, one with 5 and one with 10 cities. 10 different random distance scenarios were considered for each problem and for each distance scenario 10 consecutive neural solutions were found. The tests were repeated for the four different sets of HCs seen previously, thus giving a total of 800 tests. In order to make the results as significant as possible, for each set of HCs the graphs show the percentage of non-valid solutions found in all the tests performed, both for the 10-city TSP and for the 5-city one.

An analysis of Fig. 8.10 shows that all three sets of coefficients determined using the fuzzy approach are more robust than those determined using the classical heuristic approach. It can also be seen that the most robust solutions are reached with HCs #3 and #4, which have the highest values for the $\frac{PerIterMaxGood}{IterMaxGood}$ ratio and the IterDelta parameter respectively. In particular set #3 has the greatest robustness. This was to be expected since HC set #3 features the highest $\frac{PercIterMaxGood}{IterMaxGood}$ ratio.

The aim of Fig. 8.11 is to compare the quality of the solutions obtained with the four sets of coefficients. For each of the 10 distance scenarios considered the figure shows the average percentage of optimal solutions found in 10 consecutive neural iterations. Alongside the 10 percentages the figure gives the mean of the 10 percentages for each set of HCs.

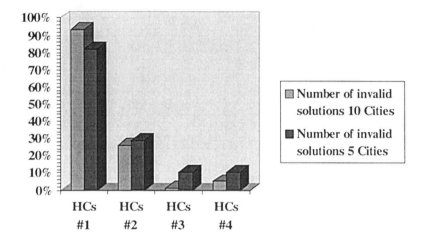

Figure 8.10   Robustness

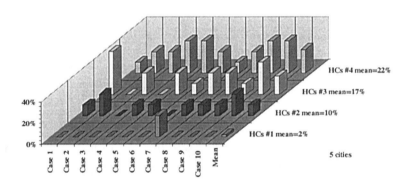

Figure 8.11   Quality

Here again the solutions obtained using the fuzzy approach are better than those reported in literature. More specifically, the percentage of optimal solutions reached with the parameters suggested by Hopfield and Tank is 2%, while with our coefficients we reached 10%, 17% and 22% respectively for HC #2, HC#3 and HC#4. It should be noted that the set of coefficients HC #4 has the highest IterDelta value and the highest percentage of optimal solutions. It should also be pointed out that the search for more robust solutions (set HC #3) causes on average a degradation in the quality of the solutions obtained (as compared with set HC #4). This was to be expected, as explained in 8.6.

8.8.2 TSP by Szu's Energy Function

The fuzzy logic-based algorithm was applied to a TSP featuring 15 cities with random distances between them.

The minimum distance in the scenario was 0.05, so the LowerBound was set to 0.75. The Tolerance was set to 10, δ to 5 and ϵ to 0.01.

The sets of IterDelta, IterMaxGood and PercIterMaxGood values are the same shown in (8.26). This choice was made to assess the influence of IterDelta on the quality of the solution, as done in the previous section.

On the basis of this set of parameters, the fuzzy-logic algorithm gave the HCs:

$$\text{HCs} = \begin{cases} A & = & B = 317 \\ C & = & 888 \\ D & = & 766 \end{cases} \qquad (8.31)$$

Unfortunately in [5] Szu did not specify the set of HCs that he used in his energy function. For this reason we can not compare the solutions obtained using (8.31) with those featured by the original Szu's work for the same scenarios, as done in the previous section with the Hopfield and Tank's solution. The comparison between the two approaches may be done only on the basis of the percentage of optimal solutions obtained in TSPs featuring certain number of cities, as only this information is available in the Szu's work [5] and in [35].

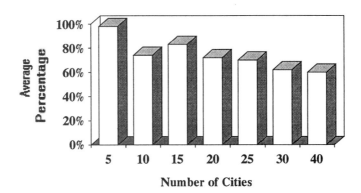

Figure 8.12 Quality of solution

In Fig. 8.12 the percentage of optimal solutions obtained with the set of coefficients (8.31) is shown, considering TSPs featuring 5, 10, 15, 20, 25, 30 and 40 cities.

As said in the previous section, 10 different random distance scenarios were considered for each TSP (i.e., for each number of cities) and for each distance scenario 10 consecutive neural solutions were found. For each TSP, Fig. 8.12 shows the average percentage of optimal solutions found in 10 consecutive neural iterations. As the TSP is a NP-hard optimization problem, the optimal solutions for very complicated problems featuring a number of cities greater than 15 could not be calculated. For this reason the goodness of the solution provided by the Hopfield network related to TSPs featuring number of cities greater than 15 was evaluated on the basis of the smallest observed tour length, as defined in [36].

As can be seen from Fig. 8.12, now the average values of optimal solution percentage features higher values if compared with those shown in Fig. 8.11, highlighting the important role played by the energy function.

From Fig. 8.12 it is clear that the percentage of optimal solution ranges from 60% to 90%, featuring high values for very complicated problems (20–40 cities), too. This is a very remarkable result, above all on account of the high percentage values obtained for large TSPs. For similar complex problems the the Szu's approach seldom gives close-to-optimal solution, as is reported in [5] and [35].

8.8.3   FMS Performance Optimization

No example of FMS performance optimization solved by the Hopfield neural network is available in literature. For this reason the authors can not compare the performance of the neural solution obtained using the coefficients found by the fuzzy approach versus the performance obtained using some other set of coefficients. What it is possible to say is that the choice of the values of the HCs was very hard. By using an heuristic approach (i.e., by manually varying the coefficients), the authors were not able to find a set of coefficients which guarantee valid solutions. The use of the Fuzzy method described in the previous section allowed to identify a set of coefficients which guarantee a high percentage of valid solutions. The set of coefficients that were found is

$$\text{HCs} = \begin{cases} A &=& 80 \\ B &=& 385 \\ C &=& 295 \end{cases} \qquad (8.32)$$

and the percentage of valid and optimal solution can be assessed about at 25%.

8.9 Conclusions

The chapter has presented the use of fuzzy inferences for the automatic determination of the coefficients of the energy function linked to the surrounding conditions of the problem to be solved. Until now the only methodology known for this tuning is manual heuristic search, essentially based on the know-how of the human operator. This procedure is not only very time-consuming but it cannot assure optimal solutions. In fact, the set of coefficients determined could provide solutions which are very far from the optimal solution to the problem.

The chapter has focused on the possibility of using the automatic HC search algorithm to reach two different goals. As has been stressed, it is, in fact, possible to force the automatic search towards coefficients which provide robust or good-quality solutions.

This feature is particularly interesting as it allows us to meet the different requirements that arise when optimization methods are used. It is possible to find HCs that provide optimal solutions or coefficients which allow good solutions but of not such high quality, in exchange for a lower computational effort.

The results reported in the chapter effectively show that the approach proposed features a search for the set of coefficients which guarantees valid solutions very close to the global minima of the energy function, or ones which guarantee very robust solutions. The robustness and quality features obtained were much higher than those provided by classical heuristic approaches.

Due to the inherent features of this automatic tool based on fuzzy logic, we believe that it greatly enhances the real use of the Hopfield network for solving very complex optimization problems.

8.10   References

[1] J.J.Hopfield, "Neural Networks and Physical Systems with Emergent Collective Computational Abilities," *Proceedings National Accademy of Sciences*, vol. 79, pp. 2554–2558, Apr. 1982.

[2] J.J.Hopfield and D.W.Tank, "Neural Computations of Decisions in Optimization Problems," *Biol. Cyber.*, vol. 52, pp. 141–152, 1986.

[3] M.M.Ali and H.T.Nguyen, "A Neural Network Implementation of an Input Access Scheme in a High-Speed Packet Switch," in *Globecom*, (Dallas), pp. 1192–1196, Nov. 1989.

[4] D.W.Gassen and J.D.Carothers, "A Hopfield Network for Solving a Complex Scheduling Problem in Behavioral Synthesis," in *IJCNN 1993*, pp. 1537–1540, 1993.

[5] H.Szu, "Fast TSP Algorithm based on Binary Neuron Output and Analog Neuron input using the zero-diagonal Interconnected Matrix and Necessary and Sufficient Constraints of the Permutation Matrix," in *First International Conference on Neural Networks*, (San Diego, CA), pp. 259–266, June 1987.

[6] S.Cavalieri and O.Mirabella, "Using Neural Networks to Reduce Schedules in Time-Critical Communications Systems," in *7-th Italian Workshop on Neural Nets*, (Salerno, Italy), May 1995.

[7] S.Cavalieri, A.Di Stefano, and O.Mirabella, "Neural Strategies to Handle Routing in Computer Networks," *International Journal of Neural Systems*, vol. 4, pp. 269–289, Sept. 1993.

[8] S.Cavalieri, A.Di Stefano, and O.Mirabella, "Optimal Path Determination in a Graph by Hopfield Neural Network," *Neural Networks*, vol. 7, no. 2, pp. 397–404, 1994.

[9] S.Abe, "Theories on the Hopfield Neural Networks," in *IJCNN*, pp. 557–564, 1989.

[10] G.A.Tagliarini and E.W.Page, "Solving Constraints Satisfaction Problems with Neural Networks," in *Proceedings of the International Conference on Neural Networks*, pp. 741–747, 1987.

[11] S.V.B.Aiyer, M.Niranjan, and F.Fallside, "A Theoretical Investigation into the Performance of the Hopfield Model," *IEEE Transactions on Neural Networks*, vol. 1, no. 2, pp. 204–215, 1990.

[12] S.Cavalieri and M.Martini, "Solving an End-Effector Positioning Problem by Hopfield Neural Network," in *International Workshop on Artificial Neural Networks*, (Malaga, Costa del Sol, Spain), June 1995.

[13] S.Cavalieri, "A Solution to the End-Effector Position Optimization Problem in Robotics using Neural Networks," *Journal on Neural Computing & Applications*, vol. 5, pp. 45–47, 1997.

[14] S.Cavalieri and O.Mirabella, "Neural Networks for Process Scheduling in Real-Time Communication Systems," *IEEE Transactions on Neural*

Networks, vol. 7, no. 5, pp. 1272–1285, 1996.

[15] T.Yamakawa, "Stabilization of an Inverted Pendulum by a High-Speed Fuzzy Logic Controller Hardware System," *Fuzzy Sets and Systems*, pp. 161–180, 1989.

[16] F.Beritelli, S.Casale, and M.Russo, "Robust Phase Reversal Tone Detection Using Soft Computing," in *IEEE Proceedings of the Third International Symposium on Uncertainty Modeling Analysis and Annual Conference of the North American Fuzzy Information Processing Society, ISUMA-NAFIS '95*, (College Park, Maryland, USA), pp. 589–594, Sept. 1995.

[17] M.Russo, *Metodi Hardware e Software per Logiche di Tipo non Tradizionale*. PhD thesis, University of Catania, Catania, Italy, Feb. 1996. Ph.D. thesis in Italian.

[18] V.Catania, N.Fiorito, M.Malgeri, and M.Russo, "A Framework for Codesign based on Fuzzy Logic and Genetic Algorithms," in *Proceedings of the Eighth International Conference on Industrial and Engineering Applications of Artificial Intelligence and Expert Systems, IEA/AEI '95*, (Melbourne, Australia), pp. 797–804, June 1995.

[19] M.A.Cohen and S.G.Grossberg, "Absolute Stability of Global Pattern Formation and Parallel Memory Storage by Competitive Neural Networks," *IEEE Transactions on Systems, Man and Cybernetics*, vol. 13, pp. 915–926, 1983.

[20] R.Hecht and Nielsen, *Neurocomputing*. Reading, MA: Addison-Wesley, first ed., 1990.

[21] J.J.Hopfield, "Neurons with Graded Response Have Collective Computational Properties Like Those of Two-State Neurons," in *National Academy of Science*, pp. 3088–2092, May 1984.

[22] L. A.Zadeh, "Fuzzy Sets," *Information and Control*, pp. 338–353, 1965.

[23] Y.Lin and G.A.Cunningham III, "A New Approach to Fuzzy-Neural System Modeling," *IEEE Transactions on Fuzzy Systems*, vol. 3, pp. 190–198, May 1995.

[24] T.D.E.Van den Bout, "A Traveling Salesman Objective Function that Works," in *First International Conference on Neural Networks*, (San Diego, CA), pp. 299–303, June 1987.

[25] D.R.Durbin, "An Analogue Approach to the Traveling Salesman Problem using an Elastic Net Method," *Nature*, vol. 326, pp. 689–691, 1987.

[26] D.J.Burr, "An Improved Elastic Net Method for the Traveling Salesman Problem," in *First International Conference on Neural Networks*, (San Diego, CA), pp. 69–76, June 1987.

[27] S.Cavalieri, "Performance Optimization of Flexible Manufacturing Systems using Artificial Neural Networks," in *Ninth International Conference on Industrial & Engineering Applications of Artificial Intelligence & Expert Systems, IEA/AIE 96*, (Fukuoka, Japan), pp. 479–486,

June 1996.

[28] S.Cavalieri, "Application of Neural Networks to Factory Automation Performance Optimization," in *Computational Engineering in Systems Applications, CESA 96*, (Lille, France), pp. 240–245, June 1996.

[29] S.Cavalieri, "A Novel Neural Network Model for the Performance Evaluation of Flexible Manufacturing Systems," in *22nd Annual International Conference on Industrial Applications, IECON96*, (Taipei, Taiwan), Aug. 1996.

[30] J.R.Pimentel, *Communication Networks for Manufacturing*. Prentice-Hall international Editors, 1990.

[31] J.H.P.Hillion, "Performance Evaluation of Job-Shop Systems using Timed Event Graphs," *IEEE Transaction on Automatic Control*, vol. 34, no. 1, pp. 3–9, 1989.

[32] R.Zurawski, "Petri Nets and Industrial Application: A Tutorial," *IEEE Transaction on Industrial Electronics*, vol. 41, no. 6, pp. 915–926, 1994.

[33] G.M.Ajmone, G.Conte, *Performance Models of Multiprocessor Systems*. Computer System Series, 1986.

[34] X.S.Lafit, J.M.Proth, "Optimization of Invariant Criteria for Event Graphs," *IEEE Transaction on Automatic Control*, vol. 37, no. 5, pp. 547–555, 1992.

[35] NeuralWare, *Neural Computing: A Technology Handbook for Professional II/PLUS and NeuralWorks Explorer*, pp. 191–208. NeuralWare, Inc. Technical Publications Group, 202 Park West Drive, Pittsburg, PA 15275, USA: NeuralWare, Inc., 1995.

[36] E.Aarts and Jan Korst, *Simulated Annealing and Boltzmann Machines*, ch. 9, pp. 153–179. John Wiley & Sons, 1990.

9

Fuzzy control of a CD player focusing system

L.Fortuna[*]

G.Muscato[*]

R.Caponetto[*]

(*) DEES, University of Catania, V.le A.Doria 6, 95125 Catania, Italy. E-mail: gmuscato@dees.unict.it.

M.G.Xibilia[+]

(+) Dept. of Mathematics - Salita Sperone 31 I-98166 Messina (ME) - Italy email: mxibilia@ingegneria.unime.it

Fuzzy Control of a CD Player Focusing System

Abstract

The main aim of this chapter is to present the fuzzy control of a CD player focusing system. The fuzzy controller is a classical Sugeno type Fuzzy-PD. A practical implementation on a real system using fuzzy microcontroller validates the superiority of this approach.

9.1   Introduction

Soft computing strategies have been widely used in the last decade for the automatic control of nonlinear systems [1], [2], [3]. The main advantage offered by Soft Computing-based controller design is the possibility of merging the knowledge of an expert and the use of optimization strategies in designing the controller. In this chapter the design of an optimized fuzzy controller for the focusing system of a CD player is presented. The proposed approach is also suitable for designing controllers for DVD systems. The problem of CD-ROM control has been widely investigated in the last few years. Among the relevant works on CD-ROM control it is possible to cite [4]- [14]. In [4] and [5] a μ-synthesis is adopted to design a robust controller for the radial servo system, [6] and [7] use a parametric identification scheme for both radial and focus loop, [8] introduces adaptive control of the radial servo system, [9] introduces adaptive repetitive control of the radial servo mechanism, and [10] proposes an iterative learning scheme. In [11] an adaptive speed algorithm to control the spindle motor of a CD-ROM drive is described. QFT methods are used in [12] and [13], while an H_∞ control approach is described in [14].

In this work the controller design is mainly based on Soft Computing strategies. First, the model of the system is determined using traditional identification techniques and a controller is designed in the frequency domain. To improve the results, an optimized fuzzy controller is obtained by using two different strategies. The first strategy mainly consists of directly designing an optimal fuzzy controller using a genetic algorithm to find the shape of the membership functions and the consequents which minimize a suitable performance index. The number of fuzzy sets and rules is selected previously. This strategy, which for simple non-linear systems usually leads to good fuzzy controller performance, does not give suitable results in the case being considered. The second strategy is based on two steps: in the first step the traditional controller is interpolated with a set of fuzzy rules by using a suitable learning algorithm. The fuzzy controller obtained gives almost the same performance as the traditional one. Once the fuzzy controller is determined, it is optimized using a genetic algorithm to improve its performance. The outlined procedure was developed to design a fuzzy controller for the focus system of a Philips ROM 65200.

9.2 The CD player

A Compact Disk (CD) is a widely-used support for digitally coded systems and requires an optical decoding device (CD player) [15, 16].
The basic scheme of a CD system is shown in Fig. 9.1.

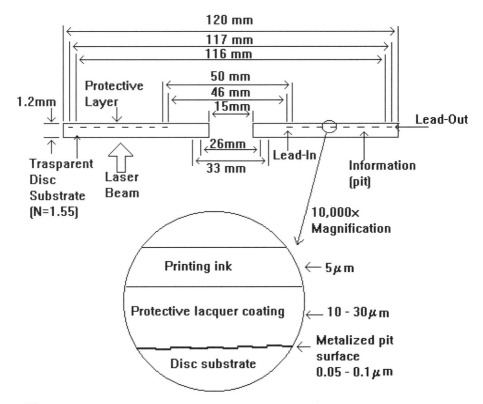

Figure 9.1 Scheme of a CD

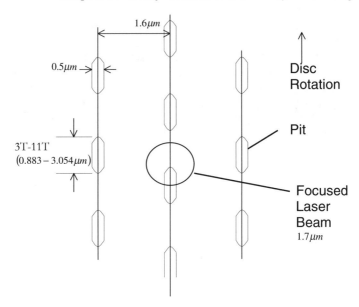

Figure 9.2   A section of the physical track

Each physical track on the disk forms a 360 degree turn in a continuous spiral line and consists of a succession of depressions, called pits, in the reflective layer. The encoded information is represented by variations in the pit length and by variation in the distance between pits. The physical track spirals outward when the disk rotates counter-clockwise as seen by the optical stylus. The scanning velocity during recording is between 1.2 m/s and 1.4 m/s with a channel bit rate of 4.3218 $Mbit/s$. The information in the reflective layer is read by an optical beam from an optical stylus focusing on this layer through the transparent substrate. During reading, the scanning light spot is diffracted by the pits of the reflective information layer. The optical power that is diffracted back into the lens of the optical system is modulated according to the encoded digital information. A section of the track is shown in Fig. 9.2.

Due to the uniformity of the linear dimension of the pits along the whole of the spiral line, the revolution speed of the CD must depend on the pickup position, in order to have a constant bit rate. The revolution speed gradually decreases from 500 rpm to 200 rpm when the pickup moves from inside to outside. The optical apparatus is maintained on the track by a servomechanism. Disk irregularities cause a focal plane movement that should be taken into account. It is therefore necessary to use a servo focusing system that is able to keep the focal plane at the optimal distance, with a maximum error of 1μm. The servo focusing system is represented in Fig. 9.3.

The signal which identifies the focal point position is called *focus error* and

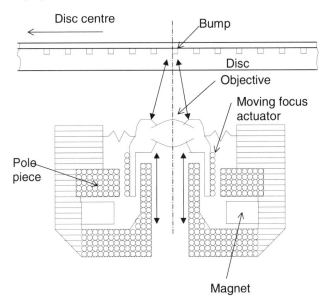

Figure 9.3   The focusing system

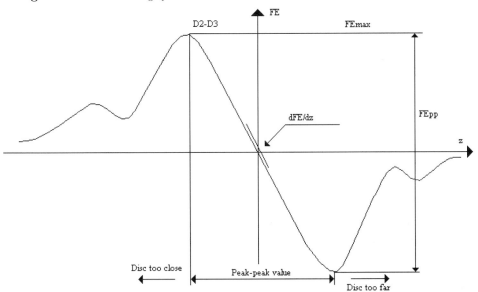

Figure 9.4   The focus error signal

is detected with the Single Foucault method. Fig. 9.4 shows the theoretical trend of the focus error.

From the figure it is possible to observe that the error is linear if the distance

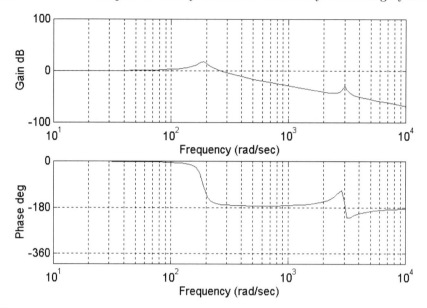

Figure 9.5   The theoretical frequency responce

between the focal point and the lens position remains small. The signal becomes useless if the error is too large. More complete information is obtained from the CAsum signal, which is a two-level signal: the high level indicates correct focalization.

9.3   System identification

In order to determine a model of the focusing system in the linear zone, the frequency response was experimentally determined.

The Bode diagrams were obtained by applying a set of sinusoidal input signals (voltage of the focusing system coil) to the system and measuring the corresponding focus error signal. An offset was considered to maintain the system close to the correct distance so that linearity is guaranteed. The theoretical and measured frequency response are shown in Figs. 9.5 and 9.6 respectively.

Looking at the Bode diagram, the corresponding transfer function was approximately computed as:

$$G(s) = \frac{1.197 * 10^{-7}s^2 + 0.000117s + 1}{3.111 * 10^{-12}s^4 + 4.504 * 10^{-10}s^3 + 0.0000284s^2 + 0.000713s + 1}$$

(9.1)

The resulting transfer function represents a model of the system close to the correct position. The system's nonlinearity was identified by using a ramp

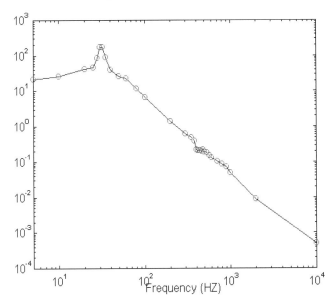

Figure 9.6 The measured frequency responce

input capable of driving the system far from the correct position and performing a set of input/output measurements. Interpolating the obtained Input/Output values, the system's nonlinearity (focus error versus displacement) was obtained, as shown in Fig. 9.7.

9.4 Traditional controller synthesis

The aim of the controller is to keep the focus error close to zero even in the presence of disturbances acting on the system. The signal being controlled is therefore the focus error, while the output of the controller is the voltage across the focusing coil. The disturbances should be carefully considered during design of the controller. In particular four kinds of disturbances were considered:

- a set of step signals;
- a Gaussian white noise with zero mean and unit variance;
- a band-limited white noise;
- a sequence of sinusoidal signals, which simulate the disturbance due to the disk rotations.

The full controller is made up of 3 different parts:

- a start-up controller, which, when the system is turned on, takes

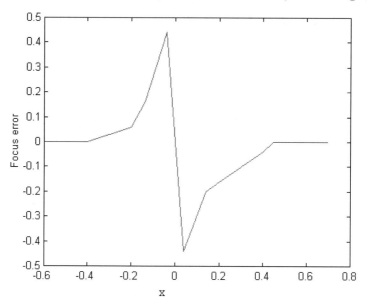

Figure 9.7   The focus error nonlinearity

the system to the correct focus position starting from a given initial condition;

- a first-level closed loop controller which, after the start-up phase, keeps the system in the desired position;
- a second-level controller which takes large deviations from the correct position into account.

The start-up controller and the second-level controller only act during particular conditions and were implemented using traditional controllers. The most important part is the first-level closed-loop controller, which is active during most of the operating phases.

The following is a description of the design of the closed-loop first-level controller. At first a classical control system was built in the frequency domain in order to meet the following requirements:

- step error $\leq 1\mu m$
- phase margin $\phi \geq 60^o$
- rise time $t_r \geq 0.01s$

The designed controller is:

$$C(s) = \frac{1.5(1 + 0.0044s)}{(1 + 0.000317s)} \tag{9.2}$$

It can be observed that this controller can be well approximated by a PD-type controller given by:

$$C(s) = 1.5(1 + 0.0044s) \qquad (9.3)$$

The computed control system was tested in the presence of the disturbances described previously, and performed well.

In order to obtain a further improvement, a fuzzy PD controller was designed with two different strategies. The synthesis of the fuzzy controller is illustrated in the following sections.

9.5 Optimized fuzzy controller: the direct method

In this section the first approach used to design the fuzzy controller of the focusing system is described. Taking into account the results obtained with the frequency domain approach, a PD fuzzy controller was considered. A fuzzy PD controller for a SISO system requires two input variables:

- *error*;
- error derivative, denoted as *derror*;

A set of fuzzy rules in the Sugeno form [17], with constant consequents, was derived via an optimization strategy. A rule therefore assumes the following form:

$$IF \ (error \ IS \ A) \ AND \ (derror \ IS \ B) \ THEN \ u \ IS \ k \qquad (9.4)$$

where A and B are fuzzy sets, u is the output of the controller and k is a constant value. At a first attempt the set of fuzzy rules which represents the controller is built by directly using a Genetic Algorithm as the optimization strategy. As is well known, Genetic Algorithms (GAs) are global optimization strategies, based on emulation of natural selection, widely used in multimodal minimization problems. When GAs are used to optimize a fuzzy controller, several strategies can be considered, differing according to the type of optimized variables (i.e., number of rules, number of fuzzy sets, shape of the membership functions), the performance index and the coding of the chromosomes. In this application the number of fuzzy sets for each variable and the number of rules is maintained fixed and the optimization algorithm is only used to design the membership function shape and the consequences. The complete set of fuzzy rules which defines the controller is fixed as follows:

$R1:$ IF $error$ IS A_{11} AND $derror$ IS A_{12} $THEN$ u IS k_1
$R2:$ IF $error$ IS A_{11} AND $derror$ IS A_{22} $THEN$ u IS k_2
$R3:$ IF $error$ IS A_{11} AND $derror$ IS A_{32} $THEN$ u IS k_3
$R4:$ IF $error$ IS A_{21} AND $derror$ IS A_{12} $THEN$ u IS k_4
$R5:$ IF $error$ IS A_{21} AND $derror$ IS A_{22} $THEN$ u IS k_5
$R6:$ IF $error$ IS A_{21} AND $derror$ IS A_{32} $THEN$ u IS k_6
$R7:$ IF $error$ IS A_{31} AND $derror$ IS A_{12} $THEN$ u IS k_7
$R8:$ IF $error$ IS A_{31} AND $derror$ IS A_{22} $THEN$ u IS k_8
$R9:$ IF $error$ IS A_{31} AND $derror$ IS A_{32} $THEN$ u IS k_9

The defuzzified controller output is computed as:

$$u^* = \frac{\sum_{i=1}^{9} \mu_i * k_i}{\sum_{i=1}^{9} \mu_i} \tag{9.5}$$

where:
$\mu_i = min(A_{j1}(error), \ A_{k2}(derror))$ for $j, k, i = 1, 2, 3$.

A classical genetic algorithm was used in order to minimize the sum of the quadratic error between the reference signal (which in this case is zero) and the output of the closed-loop controlled system when the considered set of disturbances is applied to the system for $T_f = 0.1 \ sec.$. The initial conditions are set to zero for each simulation. Each fuzzy set was coded by 2 binary substrings (8 bit per substring) which identify the 2 break points of a symmetric triangular membership function. A population of 40 individuals was selected. For the variable *error* the range is $[-0.01, \ 0.01]$ while for the error derivative the bound is $[-0.001, \ 0.001]$. The output of each rule can belong to the set $[-0.03, \ 0.03]$. The maximum number of generations is $MAXGEN = 45$. The membership functions and consequents obtained are given in Fig. 9.8.

In Fig. 9.9 a comparison is made between the output of the system controlled with the classical PD regulator and the fuzzy controller when band-limited white noise disturbance acts on the system.

As can be observed from the figure, the controllers' performance is quite similar. Moreover, if the whole set of disturbances is considered, the classical PD controller outperforms the fuzzy controller. The proposed strategy, which for simpler systems usually gives good results, is therefore not suitable for the CD focusing system. In the following section it will be shown that, by using a slightly different optimization procedure, an efficient fuzzy controller can be built. The improvement introduced by the fuzzy controller is also discussed.

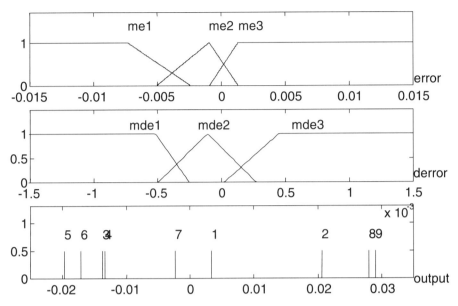

Figure 9.8 Membership functions and consequents of the optimized fuzzy controller

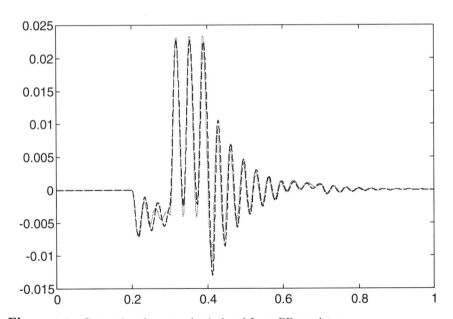

Figure 9.9 Comparison between classical and fuzzy PD regulators

9.6   The indirect optimization strategy

In this section a different optimization strategy is used to design the fuzzy controller for the focusing system. More specifically a 2-step optimization strategy is adopted. The first step uses a genetic optimization strategy to derive a fuzzy controller which approximates the classical PD. The classical PD controller described in Section 4 was discretized as follows:

$$y(k) = a \ e(k) + b \ de(k) \qquad (9.6)$$

where y is the controller output, e is the error signal (difference between the reference and the output of the system) and de is the error derivative. The controller output was then computed for a number of $(e, \ de)$ values and the patterns obtained were used as training patterns for a neuro-fuzzy network. At the end of the training a set of fuzzy rules which interpolates the classical PD controller is obtained (FC1). The FC1 rules do not introduce any improvement with respect to the classical PD. The FC1 rules were then used as a starting point for a second optimization phase, i.e., the initial population for a GA was built allowing a variation of 10% around the membership function and the consequents of the FC1 rules. A GA was therefore used to minimize the quadratic performance index used in the direct approach. Finally, a set of optimized fuzzy rules representing the fuzzy controller was obtained (FC2).

9.6.1   Approximation of the classical controller by a set of fuzzy rules

In order to perform the desired approximation, the classical controller is simulated using a white noise as input. The simulation allows us to obtain the set of I/O values which can be used to identify the fuzzy model of the controller. After a trial and error phase, five fuzzy sets were chosen for each of the input variables. Both the membership functions and the consequences were maintained symmetrical with respect to the origin. The number of fuzzy sets and rules was selected a priori and a genetic algorithm was used to train the neurofuzzy network to minimize the quadratic error between the target and the output of the fuzzy controller on the whole set of learning patterns. The genetic algorithm parameters were fixed as follows:

- population size: 40;
- number of generations: 60;
- range of the *error* variable: $[-0.01, \ 0]$;
- range of the *error derivative* variable: $[-0.001, \ 0]$;
- range of the consequents: $[-0.03, \ 0]$

The fuzzy rules obtained are given in Fig. 9.10.

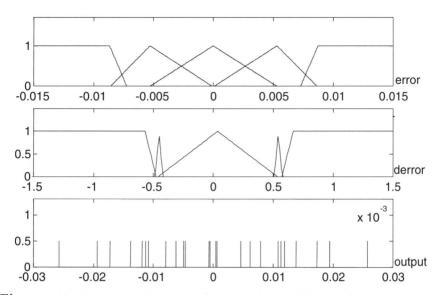

Figure 9.10   Fuzzy rules which approximate the classical PD controller

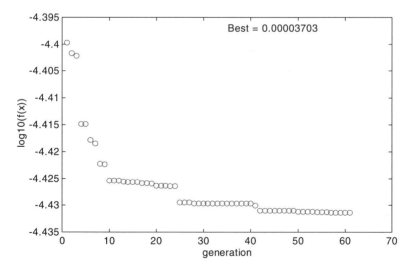

Figure 9.11   Fitness function trend

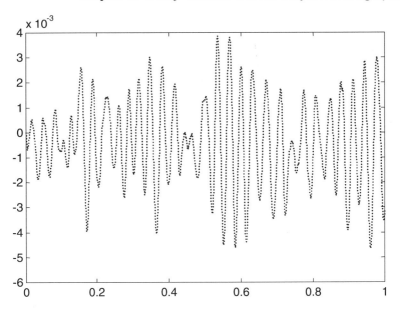

Figure 9.12 Comparison of the behaviour of the controllers with a band-limited white noise. The dashed line is the fuzzy controller

Fig. 9.11 shows the fitness function values versus the number of generations.

The performance of the fuzzy controller can be illustrated by Figs. 9.12 and 9.13 where the system responses with the fuzzy and classical controllers are compared, with band-limited white noise and a step function disturbance. As can be observed, the performance of the controllers is quite similar, even if the classical controller gives again better performance.

9.6.2   Optimization of the fuzzy controller

Starting from the previously determined fuzzy controller, a 10% variation was considered for each parameter of the controller and a genetic algorithm was used, as in direct optimization. The fitness function and the genetic algorithm parameters were fixed as in Section 5. The performance of the optimized fuzzy controller is shown in Figs. 9.14, 9.15 and 9.16.

Similar results were obtained for the whole set of disturbances. Performance analysis indicates the great improvement introduced by the fuzzy PD controller. A detailed explanation of the reasons which allow to obtain a performance improvement with a fuzzy controller is given in the following section.

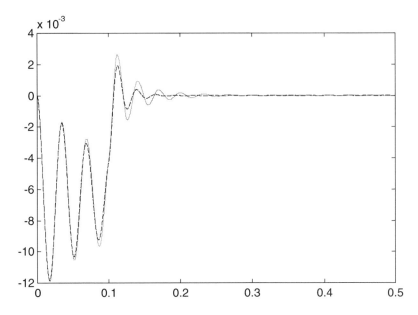

Figure 9.13 Comparison of the behaviour of the controllers with a step noise (dashed line = optimized)

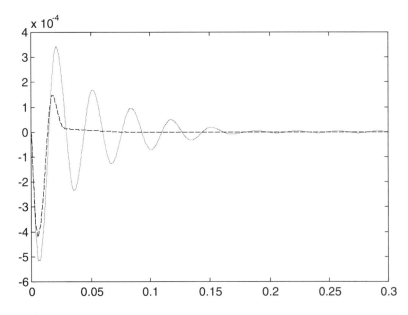

Figure 9.14 Comparison of the behaviour of the controllers with a step disturbance (dashed line = optimized)

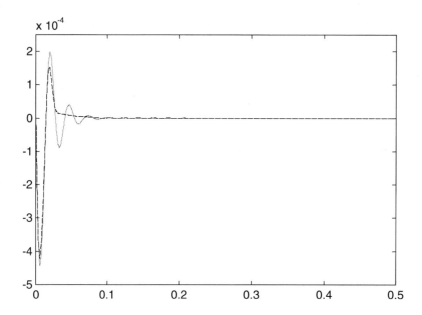

Figure 9.15   Comparison of the behaviour of the controllers with a step disturbance (dashed line = optimized)

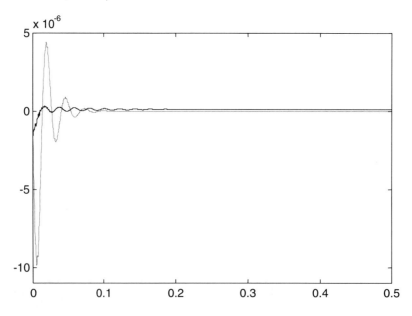

Figure 9.16   Comparison of the behaviour of the controllers with a step disturbance (dashed line = optimized)

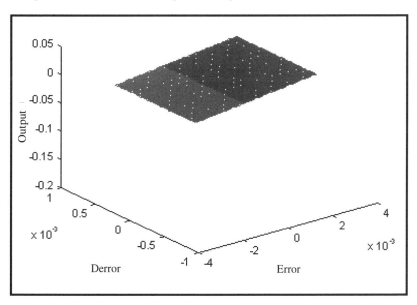

Figure 9.17 Classical controller output surface

9.7 Improvements introduced by the fuzzy controller

Let us compare the classical and fuzzy PD controllers by representing the surfaces of the controller output as a function of the *error* and *error derivative* variables. The surfaces considered are illustrated in Figs. 9.17 and 9.18 respectively.

A simpler understanding is given by the corresponding level curves in Figs. 9.19, 9.20, 9.21, 9.22.

The level curves in Fig 9.18 are parallel lines; their angle is given by the proportional gain K_p of the PD controller. The trend of Fig. 9.19 is due to the fact that the derivative gain K_d is lower than the proportional gain. Figs. 9.20 and 9.21 clearly show the versatility of the fuzzy controller. In particular, the plane *error-error derivative* has been divided into 16 regions, so that the fuzzy controller can be seen as 16 different PD controllers, as represented in Figs. 9.23 and 9.24, thus justifying the performance improvement introduced by the fuzzy controller.

The K_p and K_d values are computed by considering the four corner values of the 3 variables for each region of the surface and solving the following system of equations with the least square algorithm:

$$U_i = K_p \ e_i + K_d \ de_i \tag{9.7}$$

where $i = 1, 2, 3, 4$.

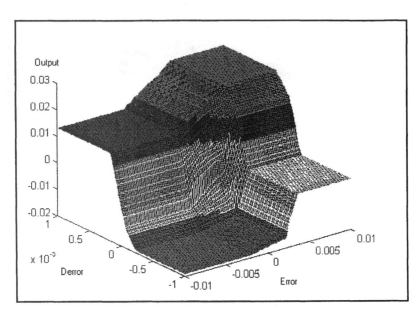

Figure 9.18   Fuzzy controller output surface

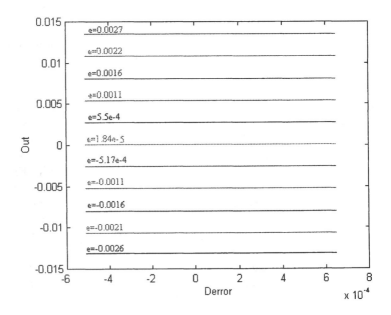

Figure 9.19   Level curves of the classical controller output: output versus the error derivative

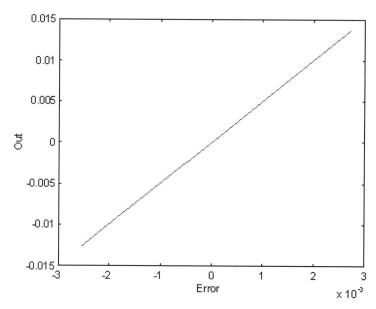

Figure 9.20 Level curves of the classical controller output: output versus the error

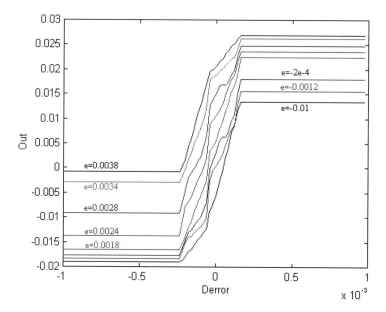

Figure 9.21 Level curves of the fuzzy controller output: output versus the error derivative

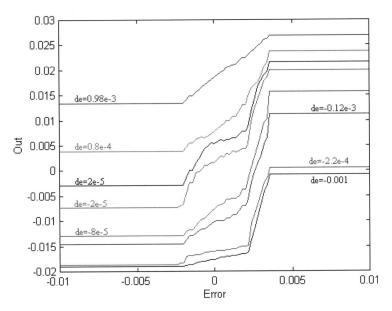

Figure 9.22   Level curves of the fuzzy controller output: output versus the error

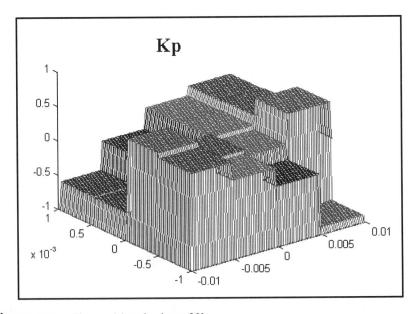

Figure 9.23   The partitioned values of Kp

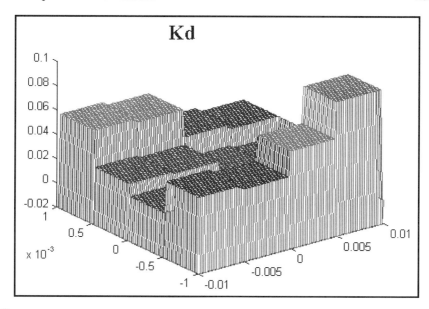

Figure 9.24 The partitioned values of Kd

9.8 Implementation details

The designed Fuzzy controller was implemented using an ST52 microcontroller manufactured by STMicroelectronics and was tested on the Philips ROM65200 CD-ROM system. ST52 is a microcontroller that executes Boolean and fuzzy algorithms. The versatility of the I/O configuration of this microcontroller allows it to interface with a wide set of external devices such as D/A converters, power control devices (SCR, TRIAC) and external sensors. The ST52 is supported by the software tool Fuzzystudio 3.0 which develops each project graphically and automatically converts it into an optimized microcode. The fundamental component of the chip is the fuzzy core, which consists of four 8-bit input channels, 16 membership functions for each input and two 8-bit outputs.

Fig. 9.25 shows the control algorithm implemented in FuzzyStudio 3.0.

Once the ST52 was programmed the microcontroller was inserted on a small board. The input of the ST52 was connected to the focus system output (focus error) while the output was connected to a suitable driver for the coil of the focus system. A set of measurements was performed validating the controller performance obtained in simulation.

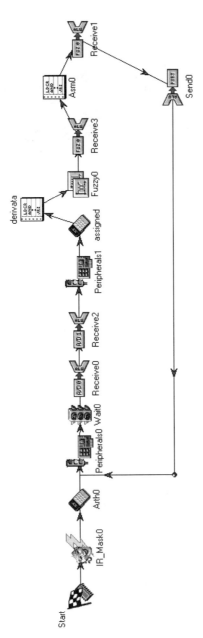

Figure 9.25   Scheme of the Fuzzy controller in FuzzyStudio 3.0

9.9 Conclusion

This chapter has described the fuzzy control design of the focus system of a CD player. The fuzzy controller is a classical Sugeno type Fuzzy-PD. The system was tuned in two different ways, based on optimization, by means of a simulator, of the membership function shape and of the consequents. The first method consisted of direct optimization of the controller, using a genetic algorithm to minimize the mean square error of the output. In this case the performance obtained was comparable with that of a classical PD. The second method consisted of two steps. The aim of the first step was to learn the behaviour of a classically-designed linear controller, using a fuzzy controller. Then in the second step the parameters of the fuzzy controller were optimized. In this case the results showed that this controller outperforms the linear one. In particular it was shown that the fuzzy controller is equivalent to a set of several PD controllers. A practical implementation on a real system was performed using a fuzzy microcontroller and the measurements confirmed the results obtained in simulation.

9.10   References

[1] L.A.Zadeh, "What is Soft Computing", Soft Computing, (Springer-Verlag), Vol. 1,N.1, March 1997.

[2] Lofti A Zadeh, "Outline of a New Approach to the Analysis of Complex System and Decision Processes", IEEE Trans. on Syst. Man and Cyb., volSMC 3, no. 1, 1973.

[3] R.M.Tong, "A Control Engineering Review of Fuzzy System", Automatica, vol.13, pp.559-569, 1997.

[4] Steinbuch, M., G. Schootstra and O.H. Bosgra. "Robust control of a Compact disc Player." IEEE 1992 Conference on Decision and Control, 1992, Tucson, Arizona, pp. 2596-2600.

[5] Steinbuch, M., P.J.M. van Groos, G. Schootstra, P.M.R. Wortelboer and O.H. Bosgra. "μ-Synthesis for a Compact disc Player" Int. Journal of Robust and Nonlinear Control, 1997.

[6] Callafon, R.A. de, P.M.J. van den Hof and M. Steinbuch. "Control relevant identification of a compact disc pick-up mechanism." 1993 IEEE Conference on Decision and Control, San Antonio, Dec. 1993, pp. 2050-2055.

[7] Dotsch, H.G.M., P.M.J. van den Hof, O.H. Bosgra and M. Steinbuch. "Identification in view of control design of a CD Player". Selected topics on Identification, Modelling and Control, Delft, vol. 9 (1996), pp. 25-30.

[8] Draijer, W., M. Steinbuch and O.H. Bosgra. "Adaptive control of radial servo system of a Compact disc player." IFAC Automatica, vol.28 (1992), pp. 455-462.

[9] Dotsch, H.G.M., P.M.J. van den Hof and T. Smakman. Adaptive Repetitive Control of a Compact Disc Mechanism. 1995 IEEE Conference on Decision and Control, New Orleans, LA- Dec. 1995, pp.1720-1725.

[10] Jung-Ho Moon, Moon-Noh Lee, and Myung Jin Chung. "Track-Following Control for Optical Disk Drivers using an Iterative Learning Scheme.", IEEE Trans. on Consumer Electronics, vol. 42, no. 2, May 1996, pp 192-198.

[11] Stan, S.G. and J.L. Bakx. "Adaptive speed algorithms for CD-ROM system". IEEE Trans. on Consumer Electronics, vol. 42 (1996), no. 1, pp. 43-51.

[12] Park, M.S., Y. Chait and M. Steinbuch. "Inversion-free design algorithms for multivariable quantitative feedback theory: An application to robust control of a CD-ROM.", IFAC Automatica, vol 33 (1997), no. 5.

[13] Chait, Y., M.S. Park and M. Steinbuch. "Design and implementation of a QFT controller for a Compact disc Player". Journal of Systems Engineering, vol. 4 (1994), pp. 107-117.

[14] M.Steinbuch, M.L. Norg, "Industrial feedback", in Plenary Lectures and mini-courses of 1997 European Control Conference, Brussels, 1997.

[15] International Standard ISO/IEC Standard 10149, "Information Technology- Data interchange on read-only 120mm optical data disks (CD-ROM)", Yellow Book. 1989.

[16] Bouwhuis, G. et al. "Principles of optical disk system". Adam Hilger Ltd., 1984, Bristol, UK.

[17] Sugeno, "Fuzzy Identification of System and Its Application to Modeling and Control", IEEE Trans. on System, Man and Cybernetics, vol. SMC-15, no.1, 1985.

10

A Neuro-Fuzzy Scheduler for a Multimedia Web Server

Zafar Ali

Arif Ghafoor
email:ghafoor@ecn.purdue.edu

C.S.G.Lee
School of Electrical & Computer
Engineering, Purdue University, West
Lafayette, Indiana 47907

0-8493-2269-3/00/$0.00+$.50

A Neuro-Fuzzy Scheduler for a Multimedia Web Server

Abstract

In this chapter, we consider the problem of multimedia synchronization in a Web environment. The work-load generated by the multimedia server during a Web session exhibits variations that are quite different from the traffic fluctuation offered by a single media stream, e.g., a Variable Bit Rate (VBR) video source. We propose a set of parameters that can be used to characterize the work-load generated by the multimedia server in a Web-type browsing environment. Specifically, three parameters: *Required Amortized Capacity* (RAC), *Pre-fetch Activity Ratio* (PAR) and *Capacity Deviation* (CD) factor are proposed. The work-load characterization scheme is subsequently used in designing a server-based synchronization scheme. The problem of scheduling multimedia information to ensure media synchronization in a Web environment is identified as a multi-criteria scheduling problem which is NP-hard.

The ability of fuzzy control to deal with multi-variables makes it a good alternative for the multi-criteria scheduling problem considered in this chapter. Consequently, we propose a *Neuro-Fuzzy Scheduler (NFS)* that makes an intelligent compromise among multi-criteria by properly combining some elementary scheduling heuristics. To evaluate the effectiveness of the proposed methodology, an extensive set of simulations is conducted and the performance of the neuro-fuzzy scheduler is compared against widely used heuristics and a branch and bound algorithm. Various test cases representative of the networking environment and the work-load profile are used for this purpose. The results show that the proposed neuro-fuzzy scheduler can dynamically adjust to the varying work-load quite well. The results also demonstrate the effectiveness of RAC, PAR and CD parameters in characterizing the work-load generated by a multimedia server in a Web environment.

10.1   Introduction

During the last few decades, we have witnessed a trend in which digital convergence— combining communication and computing became a driving force for producing a new spectrum of computing and telecommunication services and a new medium of communication: the *Internet* and *Intra-nets*. Most of the applications/ services of the Internet and corporate networks use stored information in one form or the other. For example, tele-shopping, news-on-demand, digital libraries, etc. types of application are already available, in a primitive form, on the *World Wide Web* (WWW). The trend shows emergence of a *multimedia Web* which will allow users to interactively author, store and share multimedia information.

In the perceived multimedia Web environment, a multimedia server manages access to several *Web pages* it stores. Each Web page is typically composed of a number of *Multimedia Documents* (MMDs). User interaction, in a multimedia Web page, can be characterized by a two level browsing graph, with vertices pointing towards various MMDs and edges representing the logical links among documents. A Web user follows these links to retrieve some explicit MMD. Fig. 10.1 shows an example of hypermedia model for a manufacturing system containing related MMDs.

Conceptually an MMD is a composite unit of information consisting of various types of multimedia objects, including video clips, audio segments, images, or text. The playout schedule for the MMD is generally specified by its author at the time of document composition. This process is known as *pre-orchestration* of the MMD. An example of temporal relations is depicted in Fig. 10.1(b), where document level description of a particular node *Side Plate Assembly Document* is expanded on a time-line. This MMD describes the side plate assembly process, in the form of a multimedia presentation. The presentation starts with a concurrent playout of a video along with music. This is immediately followed by the presentation of an animation sequence with a video object, which is later joined by the other media objects as depicted in the figure.

A meaningful presentation of multimedia information requires synchronous playout of the component objects according to the specified temporal relations [1–3]. That is why it is necessary to maintain continuity of individual objects and to preserve the pre-defined temporal relationships among the objects composing the MMD. These requirements are known as *intra-object* and *inter-object synchronizations* respectively [4–6].

The issues involved in ensuring synchronized presentation in a multimedia Web are quite different from the ones that are faced in transporting a single media object. In particular, information browsing in a multimedia Web is a perfect example of non-stationary work-load. These variations are quite different from work-load variations in a single media stream, e.g., traffic generated by a Variable Bit Rate Video source. For the transport of a single media object, attributes of the channel can be set up to fulfill *Quality Of Service* (QOS) requirements of the media streams [7]. On the other hand, effective characterization of user interactions in multimedia Web applications may not be possible. Furthermore, a multimedia Web browsing process exhibits dynamically changing data rates both at the object level as well as at the document

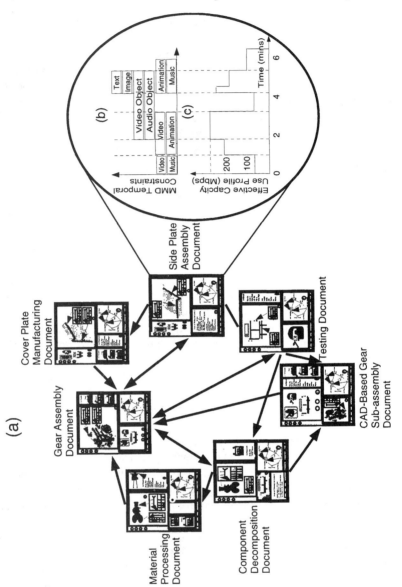

Figure 10.1   Two-level conceptual model of browsing in a multimedia Web: (a) A browsing graph, (b) Time line representation of temporal constraints of MMD represented by node Side Plate Assembly Document in (a), and (c) Capacity use profile of MMD in (b).

level. Object level variations are due to inter-frame compression employed to reduce object size. The document level variations are due to changing level of concurrency and characteristics of the member objects with an MMD. This is depicted in Fig 10.1(c), where *effective capacity use profile* for MMD of Fig 10.1(b) is plotted.

Existing synchronization schemes can be broadly classified as feedback based, resource controlled, and deadline based. Feedback technique proposed in [8] runs at the application level and is effective to maintain synchronization among continuous media streams across remote user stations in the absence of globally synchronized clocks. As clock drift is a very slowly varying phenomenon, the scheme addresses the case where multimedia objects have long presentation duration, e.g., in video-on-demand services and is not suitable to multimedia Web applications. Transport level resource controlled schemes [7,9,10] use an independent channel for communication of each object. In these schemes, synchronization is achieved by controlling resources for these channels. In a multimedia Web environment, the use of an independent channel for each component object is expensive in terms of signaling and routing overheads [11,12]. This is because Web applications typically involve MMDs consisting of a large number of small objects [13]. Consequently, a large number of channels need to be released and re-established as a user hops from multimedia document to multimedia document during browsing. Support for standard VCR-type operations further complicates the problem. Hence, it is desirable to re-use the same channel for the transport of several multimedia objects during a Web session. The deadline based synchronization schemes [14–16], on the other hand, can re-use the same channel for the transport of several multimedia objects during a Web session. However, such schemes do not address dynamically changing resource requirements of a multimedia Web session.

The earlier proposed synchronization schemes also assume that the underlying networking infrastructure provides *hard* QOS guarantees. The synchronization problem becomes more acute when QOS guarantees provided by the network are *soft* and can vary during the course of a multimedia session. Examples of such networking environments include *Reservation Setup Protocol* (RSVP) running on an *IP* network [17]. *Available Bit Rate* (ABR) channels in ATM networking [18] and RF channels in mobile networking [19] are also examples of such networking environments.

For distributed multimedia Web systems, light-weight synchronization protocols that can readily adapt to the non-stationary work-load of the browsing process and changing network configurations are needed. In this chapter, we propose a framework that allows multimedia servers to *intelligently* adapt to the changing work-load generated by the Web browsing environment of Fig. 10.1 and to variations in the availability of network resources. This goal is achieved by using a *dynamic scheduler* based on a *neuro-fuzzy* framework.

In particular, the following are the main contributions of this chapter:

- *Characterization of Work-Load Generated by a Multimedia Web Server*: To quantify non-stationary work-load offered by the browsing process, we use a dynamic interval-based approach where the scheduling problem is divided into small intervals called *Scheduling Intervals* (SI). The SIs are based on the limited a priori knowledge about the stored information being retrieved. Consequently, we propose a set of parameters that are used to characterize the work-load of a given interval.

- *Neuro-Fuzzy Scheduler*: Multimedia Web server's work-load characterization scheme is used for designing a server-based synchronization scheme where server adapts to the offered work-load by intelligently switching to the scheduling mechanism which is expected to yield best *Quality Of Presentation* (QOP) for the current *Scheduling Interval (SI)*. For a given SI, we identify the problem of scheduling of multimedia data as a multi-criteria scheduling problem in a parallel machine environment, which is NP-hard. Consequently, we propose a set of heuristic scheduling algorithms. A Neuro-Fuzzy Scheduler (NFS) which makes an intelligent compromise among multi-criteria by properly combining these scheduling algorithms is proposed. For this purpose, the underlying *fuzzy adaptive learning control network* of the neuro-fuzzy scheduler automatically generates a fuzzy rule base by learning the training examples. The rule base is later used by the scheduler in selecting the appropriate scheduling algorithm to adapt to the current system state as well as the SI's work-load.

Performance of the NFS is compared with several known heuristics and a branch and bound algorithm that provides an optimal solution. Various test cases representative of the network environment and multimedia information characteristics have been used for training as well as observing the performance of scheduling algorithms under different conditions. The results show that the proposed NFS can dynamically adjust resource management parameters based on the network resources including attributes of communication channels and destination buffers, and nature of the work-load generated by the multimedia Web server.

The organization of this chapter is as follows: Section 10.2 discusses the quality and synchronization requirement of multimedia information. Section 10.3 outlines the networking challenges encountered in supporting multimedia Web type applications. In section 10.4, we present a set of parameters that is used to characterize work-load generated during browsing in a multimedia Web. The problem of ensuring best QOP within an SI is formulated as a *multi-criteria dynamic scheduling* problem in Section 10.5. Section 10.6 presents a detailed discussion of the proposed NFS. In Section 10.6.2, we propose four scheduling algorithms that are tailored to yield best performance in a given work-load and resource setup. Section 10.7 presents the learned fuzzy logic rule base and membership functions. This section also evaluates the performance of the neuro-fuzzy scheduler. Section 10.8 concludes the chapter and outlines future research tasks. Table 10.1 summarizes the notations used in the following discussion. The meaning of these parameters will become clear as we proceed through the chapter.

10.2 Quality and Synchronization Requirement of Multimedia Information

In contrast to live data, the multimedia Web applications provide more flexibility in enforcing synchronization. This is because the multimedia server can regulate the transmission rates of data streams. In this Section we elaborate on the synchronization and presentation requirements of multimedia information in a multimedia Web environment.

10.2.1 Synchronization Requirements

Synchronous playback of multimedia information at the client site requires enforcing intra and inter-object temporal relationships. Intra-object synchronization mechanisms are required to smoothen the delivery of multimedia objects and to minimize the impact of jitter delay over the presentation process. Failure of such synchronization can cause unacceptable interruptions at the time of presentation. For example, for NTSC quality video transmission, we must ensure a delivery rate of 30 frames per second to avoid unpleasant interruptions. On the other hand, inter-object synchronization needs to be observed to avoid the so called *lip-sync* problem [20].

In a networked environment, synchronization is typically observed by segmenting each media object into a stream of some generic *Atomic Unit of Synchronization* (AUS). The transmission of an object then implies the transmission of a stream of AUSs. The playout duration of an AUS is the atomic time unit used by the presentation process. To facilitate inter-object synchronization, all objects are segmented into AUSs of equal presentation duration. Let Δ be the presentation duration of an AUS. For example, in Fig. 10.2, the $\Delta = \frac{1}{30}th$ second duration of a video frame is selected as the synchronization period for concurrent presentation of a video and an audio along with an image object. In this fashion, concurrent AUSs can be considered belonging to a group, say $\mathcal{G}_i$, with all $AUS_j \in \mathcal{G}_i$ having the same presentation deadline. For example, in Fig. 10.2 the group set $\mathcal{G}_1$ consists of AUS_1 and AUS_2 with deadline $\frac{1}{30}$ second.

As mentioned earlier, in contrast to live data, the multimedia Web appli-

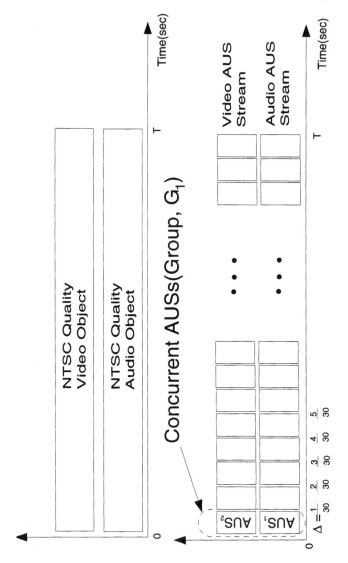

Figure 10.2   Temporal segmentation of multimedia objects into AUSs.

cations provide more flexibility in enforcing synchronization. The primary
reason is that the multimedia server can regulate the transmission of AUSs
according to their presentation deadlines. For example, in a resource sufficient
environment where a separate channel is used for the transport of each multimedia object involved in the presentation, synchronization can be provided
by controlling the AUS transmission rate at the server [10]. In particular, con-

sider transmission of AUS_i over channel C_j. Let d_i and s_i be the presentation deadline and size of the AUS_i. Clearly, on time delivery of the AUS_i can be ensured by starting its transmission on or before the following deadline:

$$d_i^s = d_i - \frac{s_i}{c_j} - J_j, \tag{10.1}$$

where d_i^s denotes the transmission start deadline of the AUS_i at the server site, $\frac{s_i}{c_j}$ represents the time it takes to pump AUS_i onto the available channel C_j and J_j is the worst case propagation and jitter delays. Similarly, transmission start deadline for all AUSs can be computed and observed.

The synchronization problem becomes more acute in a multimedia Web environment considered in this chapter. Specifically, due to non-stationary work-load of the browsing process and varying level of network resources, availability of a channel at around the transmission start deadline of an AUS given by Equation 10.1 cannot be guaranteed. Section 10.3 elaborates more on these issues.

10.2.2 QOP Requirements

Synchronization failures cause degradation of perceivable quality of multimedia information. In practice, the related object streams may still give the effect that the data is *in sync* and gives some constraints under which skew among related media streams may be tolerated [21]. A detailed study on human perception to multimedia synchronization presented in [21] shows that the quality requirements of multimedia presentation are quite soft. Nonetheless, for a given resource setup, the goal of a multimedia system is to provide the best possible Quality Of Presentation (QOP) to the end users.

In the following we discuss some parameters that affect the quality of a multimedia presentation.

• **Deadline Misses**: Strict presentation requirements demand that multimedia objects be played out with zero skew [20]. *Deadline miss* by an AUS may cause considerable *skew* among concurrent data streams, as streams with missed deadlines start lagging while the data on other streams is continuously used up during presentation.

• **Buffer Overflow**: Pre-fetched and the early arrived AUSs need to be buffered at the client site. How early a transmission is to be scheduled depends on the availability of buffers at the client site. Care must be taken in pre-fetching data since extensive pre-fetching can also result in synchronization failure due to client's buffer overflow. This can be a serious problem since data lost due to buffer overflow cannot be recovered. Retransmission strategies to overcome such failures are not feasible in real-time multimedia applications.

• **Resolution**: Video, audio and images are more bandwidth intensive media than plain text. Some applications may require high resolution images and high fidelity sound while for other applications low resolution may be acceptable. A user can specify another quality parameter dictating the desired and acceptable resolution for a media object. For example, for audio objects, several levels of resolution are possible, such as telephone quality, mono CD quality, stereo quality, etc. Similarly, for video data numerous multi-resolution hierarchical compression techniques are available that can provide the user with a wide range of options for resolution. For example, hierarchical codes offer scalable resolution mechanisms that allow partitioning of compressed data into multi-resolution groups. In this case, one group acts as the base group while others provide quality enhancement to the base group [22]. Most of the standard compression schemes including MPEG-4 are based on this concept and offer multi-resolution and hierarchical partitioning of compressed data [19].

• **Presentation Rate Ratio**: *Presentation Rate Ratio* is defined as the ratio of the actual presentation rate to the minimum acceptable presentation rate for a continuous media object such as video and audio. For the continuous media objects, in addition to reducing resolution, Presentation Rate Ratio can also be adjusted to cope with a constrained resource setup.

10.3   Synchronization in a Multimedia Web Environment

In this section, we discuss issues that are involved in observing synchronization in a multimedia Web environment. Note that the issues involved in ensuring synchronized presentation in a multimedia Web are quite different from the ones that are faced in transporting a single media object. We start our discussion by establishing the fact that the traffic generated by a multimedia Web server is non-stationary in nature.

10.3.1   Non-stationary Work-Load

Traffic patterns observed in a multimedia Web environment are quite different from the traffic variations experienced in communicating a single media stream, e.g., *Variable Bit Rate* (VBR) video source. In particular, traffic variations within a multimedia object are due to inter-frame compression employed to reduce object size, etc. On the other hand, traffic generated by a multimedia server contains not only intra-object variations but also variations due to browsing and changing level of concurrency and characteristics of the member objects within an MMD, etc. This is exemplified in Fig 10.3 which plots a work-load trace observed during browsing in the hypermedia system of Fig. 10.1. Fig. 10.3(b) plots the capacity requirement profile for a MMD of Fig 10.3(a). In the following we make use of this figure to illustrate different phenomena constituting towards non-stationarity of work-load generated by a

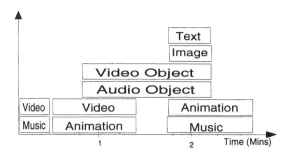

(a) Temporal Constraints

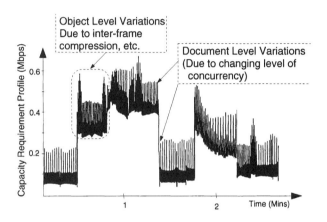

(b) Capacity Requirement Profile

Figure 10.3   A work-load profile generated during browsing in a hypermedia system: (a) Time line representation of temporal constraints need to be observed during presentation, (b) Capacity requirement (work-load) profile.

multimedia web server.

• **Browsing Level Variations**: The browsing level variations are caused by the user's interactions, as modeled by the browsing graph of Fig. 10.1. The browsing graph represents browsing options available to the user. The expected access pattern of navigation can be modeled using fuzzy relations among MMDs represented by nodes in the browsing graph. This concept is exemplified in Fig. 10.4 where a fuzzy graph is used to represent expected browsing in the hypermedia system of Fig. 10.1. In other words, given a node

being viewed (say x_i), the user can only view access nodes (say $y_i's$) which
are incident with the current node, x_i. Furthermore, based on the membership grade $\mu_R(x_i, y_i)$ relative possibility of visiting y_i can be quantified. For
example, $\mu_R(1, 3) = 0.25$ and $\mu_R(1, 4) = 0.45$ in the fuzzy graph in Fig. 10.4.
Note that, $\mu_R(x_i, y_i)$ in a browsing environment can be based on an expert's
knowledge to specify a relative frequency of traversing from the node x_i to the
node y_i. Note that the browsing process is asynchronous in nature, i.e., during
browsing, a multimedia Web user can request different MMDs at an arbitrary
time. Furthermore, users can also perform standard operations such as pause,
skip, and fast-forward, etc. at any point during the presentation.

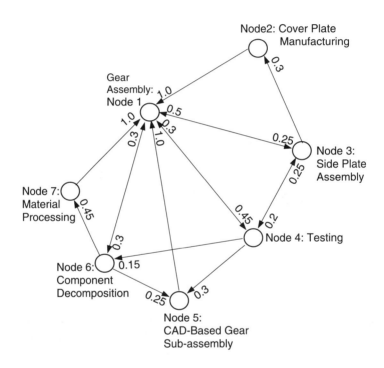

Figure 10.4 A Fuzzy graph representation of browsing in hypermedia system of
Fig. 10.1.

• **Document Level Variations**: The document level variations are due
to a changing level of concurrency and characteristics of the member objects
within an MMD. This is exemplified in Fig 10.3(b) where a capacity requirement profile for an MMD of Fig 10.3(a) is plotted.

• **Object Level Variations**: As mentioned earlier, object level variations are due to inter-frame compression employed to reduce the object sizes. These variations are also exemplified in Fig 10.3(b). Such variations are known to be non-stationary in nature [23, 24].

In summary, asynchronous nature of the browsing process, changing level of concurrency and characteristics of the member objects within an MMD, user interaction, etc. make the work-load generated by the server non-stationary in nature. This poses a new set of challenges in supporting multimedia Web applications that are quite different from the one faced in transporting a single object. Specifically, for single media stream, attributes of the channel can be set up to fulfill the effective capacity requirements of the media streams [10, 25]. In Section 10.4 we present a set of parameters that can be used to characterize work-load generated by a multimedia Web server.

10.3.2 Dynamic Bandwidth and Resource Constraints

In some networking scenarios, multiple independent channels for each object involved in multimedia Web application may not be available. An example of such a situation is multimedia Web delivery to a residential user who may only have a single ISDN line or a Web TV connection with a limited bandwidth. Another example of such applications is Web service to a mobile user where we are restricted to a limited number of independent channels. Furthermore, even if the bandwidth restriction does not exist and channels can be requested on-the-fly (e.g., in an ATM network), use of an independent channel for the transport of each object is expensive from the signaling and routing point of view. This is because Web applications typically involve documents that consist of a large number of small objects [13]. Consequently, a large number of channels needs to be released and re-established as a user hops from an MMD to an MMD during browsing. Support for standard VCR-type operations further complicates the problem. Hence, it is desirable to re-use the same channel for the transport of several multimedia objects in a Web session.

The problem of supporting multimedia Web applications becomes more challenging when QOS guarantees provided by the network are *soft* and may vary drastically during the course of a multimedia session. An example of such a networking scenario is the *Reservation Setup Protocol* (RSVP) running on an *IP* network [17]. *Available Bit Rate* (ABR) channels in ATM networking [18] and RF channels in mobile networking [19] are also examples of such networking environments. In RSVP, the resources are guaranteed for a short time and need to be refreshed on a periodic basis. Similarly, resource availability on an ABR channel depends on the congestion state of the network and resource availability in a mobile networking environment is affected by hand-off, etc. In short, in a number of networking scenarios, network resource availability may vary during the course of a multimedia Web session.

In this chapter, we assume that resources are only guaranteed for a short interval. In this interval, we assume that m channels represented by the set $\mathcal{C} = \{\mathcal{C}_1, \mathcal{C}_2, \ldots, \mathcal{C}_m\}$ are available. We also assume that each channel $\mathcal{C}_j$ provides guaranteed effective capacity c_j and bounded jitter J_j and client's site(s) is equipped with a buffer of a fixed size K. Channel aggregation in wireless networking to get high throughput connections for multimedia communication is an example of the multi-channel environment. Use of multiple heterogeneous channels in a packet switching network, where each channel is tailored to satisfy QOS some desired requirements of a particular media type, e.g., audio, video, etc., is also an example of a multi-channel environment. The multi-channel model is further generalized to the case where guarantees are made for a short period.

Due to the unpredictable nature of the browsing process, in certain intervals, the cumulative capacity $C_{\text{total}} = \sum_{j=1}^{m} c_j$ and destination buffers K may not be sufficient for retrieving multimedia information. An example of a resource constrained networking environment is multimedia Web delivery to a residential user who may only have a single ISDN line with a limited bandwidth. Another example of resource constrained environment is mobile Web service when the system has a limited number of independent channels. The following subsection elaborates more on a resource constrained environment.

10.3.3   AUS Filtering Process

When resources are severely constrained, the presentation of multimedia information to the end user cannot be supported without degrading the performance. In such cases, the goal of a multimedia data scheduler is to degrade performance in a graceful manner. Different *AUS filtering* mechanisms, such as dropping AUSs at the server site, can be employed for this purpose. For example, for an MPEG encoded video data, an *AUS filter* may drop several B- and P- frames, thus reducing the overall capacity requirement of the video stream.

For discrete media objects like multi-resolution images, the resolution level can be adjusted based on the availability of resources [19]. For isochronous objects such as video and audio, in addition to reducing resolution, the presentation rate ratio can also be adjusted. However, the rate adjustment process needs to take into account the type of the media object being transmitted. For example, audio objects are more sensitive to AUS losses; therefore, the presentation rate ratio for audio streams should be set to a high value, if possible, close to one. On the other hand, for video objects the presentation rate ratio can be set to a low value [19].

The AUS-filtering algorithm proposed in this chapter achieves this objective by assigning an *Importance Index* I_i with AUS_i, where I_i represents the relative importance of the AUS_i with respect to other AUSs of the MMD. For example, importance index in an MPEG coded video stream can be set to a high value for the I-frames and to a medium to low value for B- and P- frames. Similarly, for resolution adjustment, the AUS-filter further divides an AUS into several complementary AUSs with base AUS defining the lowest resolution object and other AUSs complementing the base AUS to enhance the presentation quality. Clearly, the importance index can be set to a high value for the base AUSs and medium to low values for the complementing AUSs.

The assignment of an importance factor and AUS partitioning based on the relative importance is tightly coupled with the the underlying compression methodology used. To facilitate AUS-filtration at the run time, the process of AUS partitioning and importance assignment can be observed off-line at the time when the multimedia information is stored at the server.

10.3.4   Interval Based Dynamic Scheduling

To deal with the unpredictable nature of the work-load generated by a multimedia Web server and to adapt to dynamically varying network resources, we propose an interval based dynamic scheduling methodology. The scheduling problem is divided into small intervals called *Scheduling Intervals* (SI). The selection of an SI is based on the duration over which resources are reserved and/ or the period for which limited a priori knowledge about the information requested by the user is available. For the scheme proposed in this chapter, the minimum of the two intervals is used to define SIs. The SIs selected in this fashion have varying durations. In general, determination of size of an SI presents a trade-off among various factors. In particular, if SI is too small, it cannot make use of the capacity averaging effect of the MMDs. On the other hand, a large SI can cause erroneous behavior for the scheduler while it tries to adapt to the changing state of the system. Furthermore, at any time, an interactive operation performed by a user, e.g., skip, pause, rewind, etc., is regarded as the start of a new SI. Some alternate methodology, e.g., a neural network based scheme, which can optimize the SIs selection process using reinforcement learning, can also be used to further improve the system performance. Note that the dynamic scheduling methodology presented in this chapter is not restricted by the specifics of the SI selection process.

The interval based dynamic scheduling concept is proposed using a neuro-fuzzy system. The proposed neuro-fuzzy scheduler adapts to the offered work-load and the available resources by intelligently switching to the scheduling mechanism which is expected to yield the best QOP for the given SI. For this purpose, the SI's work-load and information about the system resources are used by the neuro-fuzzy scheduler.

In the following section, we present a set of parameters that are used to characterize an SI's work-load. These parameters are later used by the proposed neuro-fuzzy scheduler to perform scheduling decision.

10.4   Work-Load Characterization

As mentioned above, to deal with the unpredictable nature of the work-load offered by the browsing process, we use a dynamic interval based approach where SIs are based on the limited a priori knowledge about the resource availability and the stored information being retrieved. In this section, we propose a set of three parameters that are used to characterize the capacity requirement profile of an SI; these include *Required Amortized Capacity (RAC)*, *Pre-fetch Activity Ratio (PAR)* and *Capacity Deviation (CD)*. RAC quantifies the capacity requirement of an SI while PAR and CD represent the destination buffering requirement. The algorithm (1) computes these parameters. In the following, we elaborate more on these parameters and the working of algorithm (1).

RAC corresponds to the minimum capacity requirement of an SI to ensure synchronization. It is important to recognize that RAC is not an arithmetic mean of the capacity requirement computed over the SI; as in an SI, AUSs can be scheduled earlier but cannot be made late. In fact, capacity averaging effect within an SI can only be achieved based on the SI's work-load profile. Algorithm (1) uses a priori knowledge about the temporal relationships among the AUSs to compute the RAC value. In the following, we first outline details of algorithm (1) for the computation of RAC value.

Recall, from Section 10.2, that in order to facilitate synchronization, objects are segmented into AUSs of equal duration Δ. In algorithm (1), the term $\frac{s_i}{\Delta}$ represents the capacity requirement of an AUS_i with size s_i. Also, AUSs with the same presentation deadline are logically grouped together, as shown in Fig. 10.2. Let an SI consist of L such groups represented by the set $\{\mathcal{G}_1, \mathcal{G}_2, \cdots, \mathcal{G}_L\}$ with $\mathcal{G}_i$ denoting the group of AUSs that belong to the temporal period $[(i-1)\Delta, i\Delta)$. The capacity requirement of group $\mathcal{G}_i$ is given by $\displaystyle\sum_{AUS_j \in \mathcal{G}_i} \frac{s_j}{\Delta}$. Algorithm (1) analyses the L groups of AUSs within the SI and computes RAC_i which denotes the minimum capacity required to ensure a timely delivery of all AUSs up to the ith period (or over time interval $[0, i\Delta)$). At the $(i+1)$st iteration, based on the value for RAC_i, the algorithm checks whether or not the AUSs belonging to group $\mathcal{G}_{i+1}$ can be transported with RAC_i capacity. In other words, it compares the value for RAC_i with the capacity requirement of $\mathcal{G}_{i+1}$. If $\mathcal{G}_{i+1}$ does not demand an increase in the overall capacity requirement, the value for RAC_{i+1} is set to RAC_i. Otherwise, RAC_{i+1} is updated, by allowing pre-fetching of relevant information of the $(i+1)$st period, as detailed in algorithm (1).

The RAC parameter can be further explained using the SI profiles observed

Initialize:
$$RAC_1 = \sum_{AUS_j \in \mathcal{G}_1} \frac{s_j}{\Delta}; \ PAD = 0; \ PAP = 1;$$

for $i := 2$ **to** L

/* Does group $\mathcal{G}_i$'s AUSs increase value of traffic parameter RAC, if yes, update the parameter accordingly */

$$RAC_i = \max\left(RAC_{i-1}, \frac{RAC_{i-1}\Delta(i-1) + \displaystyle\sum_{AUS_j \in \mathcal{G}_i} s_j}{i \cdot \Delta} \right);$$

/* Is this a pre-fetching period?, if yes, update Pre-fetching Activity Period (PAP) and Pre-fetching Activity Density (PAD) values. */

if $RAC_i ! = RAC_{i-1}$

/* First update the PAD value. */
$PAD_i = (RAC_i - RAC_{i-1})i\Delta;$
/* Now update the PAP */
$PAP = i;$

end

end

/*RAC is based on averaging effect up to PAP */
$RAC = RAC_{PAP};$
/* Now compute Pre-fetching Activity Ratio PAR, which is a normalized version of the PAP */
$PAP = \frac{PAP}{L};$
/* Capacity Deviation (CD) is proportional to the value of Pre-fetching Activity Density (PAD) value and is given by the following expression: */

$$CD = \frac{\displaystyle\sum_{i=1}^{PAP} PAD_i}{PAP_\Delta};$$

Figure 10.5 Computation of parameters characterizing an SI's work-load.

during browsing of the manufacturing hypermedia system example of Figure 10.1. Figure 10.6 depicts the capacity requirement profile of these SIs. In this figure, each SI is composed of eight multimedia objects. For a better illustration, the SI of Fig. 10.6(b) is produced as a result of the reverse playout of SI of Fig. 10.6(a) . Such reversal does not change the arithmetic mean of the capacity requirement profiles for both SIs. However, SI of Fig. 10.6(a) contains relatively high activity at the beginning of the presentation. Hence, the minimum capacity requirement to transport this SI cannot be reduced by pre-fetching AUSs beyond time point a as indicated in the figure. On the other hand, the SI of Fig. 10.6(b) starts with low activity and AUSs can be transmitted earlier to reduce the overall value of RAC. Consequently, for the SI of Fig. 10.6(a) $RAC = 0.56$ Mbps while the temporal inverse of the SI, as depicted in Fig. 10.6(b) , yields $RAC = 0.4$ Mbps.

The algorithm (1) also computes the Pre-fetch Activity Period (PAP) parameter that characterizes the shape of an SI's capacity requirement profile by identifying whether the SI contains higher activity at its beginning or at its end. For this purpose it keeps track of a pre-fetch activity index that stores the time up to which pre-fetch is possible. The PAP value of the SIs of Fig. 10.6 is also indicated in the figure. Note, since the SI of Fig. 10.6(a) has a relatively higher capacity activity at the beginning of the SI, pre-fetching is viable up to point a, as shown in this figure. Hence, PAP value for this example is given by a. The SI of Fig. 10.6(b) has relatively higher activity towards the end; the PAP extends towards the end of the SI. The algorithm then normalizes the PAP value and computes the Pre-fetch Activity Ratio (PAR) which is defined as $PAR = \frac{PAP}{L}$, where L represents the length of the SI. Note that $PAR = 0.34$ for the SI of Fig. 10.6(a) that has a relatively higher capacity activity at the beginning of the SI and $PAR = 1$ for the SI of Fig. 10.6(b) which has relatively higher activity towards the end.

The Capacity Deviation (CD) factor characterizes the deviation of an SI's capacity requirement profile above the RAC value. The algorithm (1) computes the value for CD based on Pre-fetch Activity Density (PAD) factor for each pre-fetching Δ period. In algorithm (1), for the pre-fetching period Δ_i, $RAC_i \neq RAC_{i-1}$. The density of the pre-fetch data during period i is given by the deviation of RAC_i value from RAC_{i-1} value. In particular, $PAD_i = (RAC_i - RAC_{i-1})i\Delta$. Hence, given $PAD_i \forall i = 1, 2, \cdots, L$, we can compute

$$CD = \frac{\sum_{i=1}^{PAP} PAD_i}{PAP\Delta}$$

Clearly, the SI of Fig. 10.6(b) has much more deviation from the RAC value as compared with the SI of Fig. 10.6(a) . The value of CD is $0.12Mbps$ in the formal case while it is $10kbps$ for the later.

In Section 10.6, parameters RAC, PAR and CD are used to describe the work-load of an SI. We provide fuzzy logic rules for selecting a scheduling mechanism that is expected to yield the best results for the given work-load and system state. In the following, we elaborate on the requirement of the neuro-fuzzy scheduler.

10.5 Dynamic Scheduling at the Server

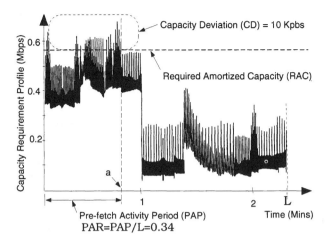

(a) Example SI with High RAC value

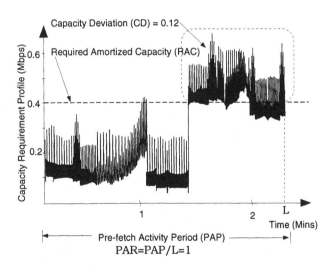

(b) Example SI with Low RAC value

Figure 10.6   SI profiles observed during browsing in Hypermedia System of 10.1.

Pre-orchestrated and stored nature of information, the presence of a large number of small objects and soft delivery requirements make multimedia Web

applications quite flexible to the networking scenarios. In this section, we
formulate a dynamic scheduling problem where, at each SI, the multimedia
server dynamically adapts to the non-stationary work-load. The objective is
to minimize a multi-variable function for QOP degradation due to AUS losses.
The scheduling problem is formally presented in the following subsection.

10.5.1   A Multi-criteria Scheduling Problem

The main functionality of the scheduler is to determine the order and time
at which the AUSs should be transmitted over the given m channels. If the
resources are severely constrained, the multimedia server needs to invoke an
AUS filtering process. For this purpose, as discussed in Section 10.3.3, each
AUS_i is assigned an importance factor I_i which quantifies the relative importance of the AUS_i within a group of AUSs. To formulate an objective function
for the AUS filter, first define a *filtering factor*($\mathcal{F}_i$) as follows:

$$F_i = \begin{cases} 0 & \text{if } AUS_i \in \mathcal{S}, \\ 1 & \text{otherwise.} \end{cases}$$

Here $\mathcal{S}$ represents the schedule obtained after observing AUS-filtering. In
other words, $I_i\mathcal{F}_i$ represents the cost incurred when an AUS_i is dropped at
the server.

In addition of minimizing the number of AUSs dropped, the scheduler also
needs to minimize the AUS losses due to deadline miss or destination buffer
overflow. Let $\sum \mathcal{L}_d$ and $\sum \mathcal{L}_b$, respectively, represent the total number of AUSs
lost due to deadline misses and destination buffer overflow. Note that $\sum \mathcal{L}_d$
and $\sum \mathcal{L}_b$ are two conflicting objectives. Specifically, $\sum \mathcal{L}_d$ can be minimized
by pre-fetching as much AUSs as possible. However, extensive pre-fetching
may yield extremely high data (AUSs) losses due to buffer overflow.

For a given Scheduling Interval (SI), the scheduler's objective depends on
the state of the system (resource availability) and the SI's work-load. For example, based on the state of the system and work-load of the SI, the scheduler
needs to identify when to follow the AUS-filtering process, i.e., minimization
of $\sum I_i\mathcal{F}_i$ objective. Similarly, if the SI's work-load is significantly less than
the total capacity of the m channels, and the scheduler selects minimization
of $\sum \mathcal{L}_d$ as the objective. Such a selection will yield a high number of losses
due to buffer overflow condition. Hence, the objective of the scheduler is to
minimize all types of AUS losses for every SI considered. In other words, the
objective is to minimize the following:

$$\sum_{SI} \left\{ \sum_{AUS_i \in SI} \left(\underbrace{\mathcal{L}_d}_{O_1} + \underbrace{\mathcal{L}_b}_{O_2} + \underbrace{I_i\mathcal{F}_i}_{O_3} \right) \right\}. \tag{10.2}$$

In the following, we map the multimedia information scheduling problem to a new type of parallel machine scheduling problem which has not been considered in the standard scheduling literature.

Consider the SI which consists of n AUSs represented by the set $AUS = \{AUS_1, AUS_2, \dots, AUS_n\}$. Given an SI, the problem of AUS scheduling onto communication channels can be mapped to an equivalent machine scheduling problems. Specifically, m heterogeneous channels can be modeled as m uniform machines with different processing speeds. A set of AUS's is equivalent to a set of independent tasks. The processing time of a task is given by the size of an AUS. Furthermore, to facilitate the synchronization at the client's site, the server transmits an AUS on a designated channel without interruption, which corresponds to a non-preemptive environment. Similarly, the objective given by Equation(10.2) can also be mapped to objectives commonly used in the scheduling literature.

In standard scheduling terminology, an AUS that misses its deadline can be considered as a tardy AUS. Specifically, define the term *tardiness* of an AUS_i in a schedule $\mathcal{S}$ as:

$$T_i = \max(0, a_i - d_i),$$

where a_i denotes the arrival time of an AUS at the destination. Define,

$$U_i = \begin{cases} 1 & \text{if } T_i > 0, \\ 0 & \text{otherwise.} \end{cases}$$

Clearly, $U_i = 1$ for a tardy AUS. Hence object O_i in Equation 10.2 is equivalent to minimize the total number of tardy AUSs. In other words the objective O_1 is to minimize $\sum_{SI} \left(\sum_{AUS_i \in SI} U_i \right)$.

As mentioned earlier, as objective O_1 is to minimize the number of deadline misses, it may result in extensive losses of AUSs due to buffer overflow. To control buffer overflow conditions, we need to consider earliness of AUSs. Specifically, first define the term *earliness* of AUS_i in a schedule $\mathcal{S}$ as:

$$E_i = \max(0, d_i - a_i).$$

Since early AUSs must be kept in memory until consumption, such AUSs may be a liability when destination buffers are close to being full. In these circumstances, it is desirable to control a weighted number of early AUSs. In particular, the objective O_2 in Equation(10.2) is to minimize $\sum_{SI} \left(\sum_{AUS_i \in SI} w_i E_i \right)$.

Here w_i's are inversely related to the size of the AUS_i. The idea is to complete transmission of *bigger* AUSs as close to their deadline as possible.

This in turns reduces the destination buffering requirement. When an *SI* uses objective O_2, the schedule follows the well known *Just-In-Time* (JIT) concept with *bigger* AUSs completing closer to their deadlines. It can be seen that objective O_2 certainly has its merit for the cases where total capacity of the available channel considerably exceeds the work-load requirement of the *SI*.

The objective O_3 is concerned with the cases for which the available resources are severely constrained for a given SI. In such a situation, it is desired to invoke an AUS-filtering mechanism. The objective of an AUS-filtering process is to minimize the weighted droppage of AUSs at the server site which is given as $\displaystyle\sum_{SI} \sum_{AUS_i \in SI} I_i \mathcal{F}_i$.

For the remainder of this chapter, we use the notation $\alpha \mid \beta \mid \gamma$ of [26] to refer to the scheduling problems in a concise manner. In our case, α denotes the number and type of channels. Q denotes the uniform parallel channel model where the channel capacities may differ. The word *uniform* indicates that an object's transmission time is affected by the capacity of a channel, but not by the object type. A subscript may be used to specify the number of channels. Peculiarities of the problem are described by β. For example, jitter bound J_j in this field indicate that channels are heterogeneous in their transit delay characteristics. Finally, γ indicates the objective function. Under this notational framework, for a given *SI*, objective function O_1 of Equation 10.2 can be represented as $\displaystyle\sum_i U_i$. Similarly, objective function O_2 of Equation 10.2 can be represented by $\displaystyle\sum_i w_i E_i$. Objective function O_3 of Equation 10.2 does not exist in standard scheduling terminology. We adapt the notation of $\displaystyle\sum_i I_i \mathcal{F}_i$ to represent this objective.

In light of the above, we map AUS scheduling in a multimedia Web to a new type of multi-criteria scheduling problem $Q_m \mid J_j \mid \displaystyle\sum_i U_i + \sum_i w_i E_i + \sum_i I_i \mathcal{F}_i$.
Most research concerning the parallel machine scheduling has been focused on developing scheduling algorithms for a single objective such as minimization of maximum tardiness, minimization of completion time (makespan), minimization of number of early/ late jobs, etc. To the best of our knowledge, the multi-criteria scheduling problem considered in this chapter has not been addressed earlier.

10.5.2 Computation Complexity of the Multi-criteria Scheduling Problem

In the following, we show that the problem $Q_m \mid J_j \mid \sum_i U_i + \sum_i w_i E_i + \sum_i I_i \mathcal{F}_i$ is NP-hard.

We start our discussion by showing $Q_m \mid J_j \mid \sum_i U_i$ is NP-hard. The following uses results from [26]. Note that $\alpha \mid \beta \mid C_{max} \propto \alpha \mid \beta \mid L_{max} \propto \alpha \mid \beta \mid \sum_i U_i$. Since $P_2 \mid\mid \sum_i U_i$ is a special case of $Q_m \mid\mid \sum_i U_i$, and $P_2 \mid\mid C_{max} \propto P_2 \mid\mid \sum_i U_i$. It is known that $P_2 \mid\mid C_{max}$ is NP-hard, because it is equivalent to PARTITION [27]. The NP-hardness of $Q_m \mid\mid \sum_i U_i$ follows.

In the following, we make use of NP-hardness of $Q_m \mid J_j \mid \sum_i U_i$ problem to prove that $Q_m \mid J_j \mid \sum_i U_i + \sum_i w_i E_i + \sum_i I_i \mathcal{F}_i$ is also NP-hard.

Let $f(\gamma_1, \gamma_2, \gamma_3) = \lambda_1 \gamma_1 + \lambda_2 \gamma_2 + \lambda_3 \gamma_3$. Clearly, $f(\gamma_1, \gamma_2, \gamma_3)$ is the objective function of the scheduling problem with $\lambda_1 = \lambda_2 = \lambda_3 = 1$, $\gamma_1 = \sum_i U_i$, $\gamma_2 = \sum_i w_i E_i$ and $\gamma_3 = \sum_i I_i \mathcal{F}_i$.

LEMMA 10.1   If $\alpha \mid \beta \mid \gamma_1$ is NP-hard, then $\alpha \mid \beta \mid f(\gamma_1, \gamma_2, \gamma_3)$ is also NP-hard.

PROOF 10.1   The proof is based on the fact that the existence of a polynomial time algorithm for $\alpha \mid \beta \mid f(\gamma_1, \gamma_2, \gamma_3)$ implies the existence of a polynomial algorithm for $\alpha \mid \beta \mid \gamma_1$, thus proving the result. In particular, a solution to $\alpha \mid \beta \mid f(\gamma_1, \gamma_2, \gamma_3)$ with $\lambda_1 = 1$ and $\lambda_2 = \lambda_3 = 0$ provides a solution to $\alpha \mid \beta \mid \gamma_1$.

THEOREM 10.1   *The problem* $Q_m \mid J_j \mid \sum_i U_i + \sum_i w_i E_i + \sum_i I_i \mathcal{F}_i$ *is NP-hard.*

The proof follows from Lemma(10.1) and the fact the $Q_m \mid\mid \sum_i U_i$ is NP-hard.

In fact, the problem $Q_m \mid J_j \mid \sum w_i E_i$ is also NP-hard [26]. Similarly, the NP-hard nature of the problem $Q_m \mid J_j \mid \sum I_i \mathcal{F}_i$ follows by mapping a relaxed version of the problem to a bin-packing problem.

10.6   The Proposed Neuro-Fuzzy Scheduler

The last Section formulates controlled transmission of AUSs in a multimedia Web session as a multi-criteria dynamic scheduling problem, $Q_m/J_j/\sum_i U_i + \sum_i w_i E_i + \sum_i I_i \mathcal{F}_i$. It also shows that even the static version of the problem is NP-hard for which polynomial time solutions are unlikely to exist. In this chapter, therefore, we are not interested in designing an *optimal scheduler* but a *dynamic and real-time* scheduler which can react to changing SI work-load and varying system resources in a timely fashion while maximally meeting the multi-criteria objective.

The ability of fuzzy systems to deal with multi-variables makes them attractive for the multi-criteria scheduling problem [28]. Neural networks, on the other hand, have been successfully used in designing real-time systems [12,18,23,25,29–37]. Furthermore, several contributions are made to show that fuzzy logic and neural computing are complementary techniques [38–42]. We also use a neuro-fuzzy framework to provide a heuristic approach to solve the scheduling problem $Q_m \mid J_j \mid \sum U_i + \sum w_i E_i + \sum I_i \mathcal{F}_i$. The neuro-fuzzy scheduler proposed in this chapter combines the scheduling algorithms proposed in Section 10.6.2. These scheduling algorithms are tailored to meet a particular objective and are suitable for a specific state of the system.

The input to the neuro-fuzzy scheduler consists of two state vectors, χ and ω_{SI} with χ describing the system's state and ω_{SI} summarizing the SI's work-load. All input parameters of the system are normalized so that the neuro-fuzzy scheduler can be used to solve scheduling problems at numerous scales (e.g., for channel capacities starting from Kbps to and ranging up to Gbps). In particular, the SI work-load vector ω_{SI} is defined as:

$$\omega_{SI} = [NAC_{SI}, PAR_{SI}, NCD_{SI}], \tag{10.3}$$

where NAC_{SI} represents required amortized capacity, RAC_{SI} value, normalized by the total capacity available for the SI. Similarly, NCD_{SI} is the capacity deviation factor CD_{SI} normalized by the RAC_{SI} value. In particular,

$$NAC_{SI} = \frac{RAC_{SI}}{C_{\text{total}}}, \quad NCD_{SI} = \frac{CD_{SI}}{RAC_{SI}}. \tag{10.4}$$

Recall that the SI related parameters, RAC_{SI}, PAR_{SI} and NCD_{SI}, are defined by the work-load determination algorithm presented in Section 10.4.

The system state vector χ is defined by the following parameters.

$$\chi = [\kappa, \delta],$$

where κ represents the size of destination buffer normalized by CD_{SI}, i.e.,

$$\kappa = \frac{K}{L \cdot CD_{SI}} \tag{10.5}$$

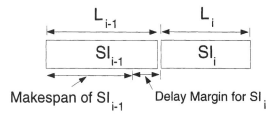

Figure 10.7 Delay Margin for SI_i.

Here L represents the length of the SI. δ is defined as normalized Delay Margin (DM). The meaning of the delay margin for an SI_i is illustrated in Fig 10.7 where two SIs, SI_{i-1} and SI_i are considered. In this example, makespan of SI_{i-1} is less than the length L_{i-1} of the SI_{i-1}. This difference is defined as delay margin for SI_i. Note that DM represents the earliest time at which multimedia data contained in SI_i can be transmitted. Furthermore, the delay margin is normalized by the length of the SI to get the value for the parameter δ, i.e., $\delta = \frac{DM}{L}$.

Output y of the neuro-fuzzy scheduler is the scheduling algorithm that is expected to yield the best QOP for an SI. In Section 10.6.2, we propose four scheduling algorithms that are tailored for different SI work-loads and system state. Section 10.6.2 elaborates more on these algorithms, In the following we first discuss the underlying structure of the neuro-fuzzy scheduler.

The neuro-fuzzy scheduler is in a form of a five layer network that realizes a fuzzy logic system [38]. As shown in Fig 10.8, nodes in layer L_1 are the input linguistic nodes which represent input linguistic variables. Layer L_5 is the output layer. Two kinds of output linguistic nodes are used in this layer L_5. One is for the training data (desired output) that needs to be fed into the net for training and the other is for decision signal (actual output). Nodes in layer L_2 and layer L_4 are the term nodes which act as membership functions of the input and output linguistic variables, respectively. Nodes in layer L_3 are the rule nodes. Each such node represents one fuzzy rule and all the nodes together form a fuzzy rule base. Links in layers L_3 and L_4 function collectively as a fuzzy inference engine, with L_3 links defining the preconditions of the rule nodes and L_4 links representing the consequence of the rule nodes. Links in layers L_2 and L_4 are fully connected between the linguistic nodes and their corresponding term nodes.

As shown in Fig 10.9, each node i in layer k, $n_i^{(k)}$, has a net input function $f_i^k(u_{ij}^{(k)})$ and an activation output function $a_i^{(k)}(f_i^{(k)})$ for node i in layer k. Here, $u_{ij}^{(k)}$ denotes the possible input to the node i in layer k from node j in layer $(k-1)$. The setting of the net input and output functions at each layer is described in the following:

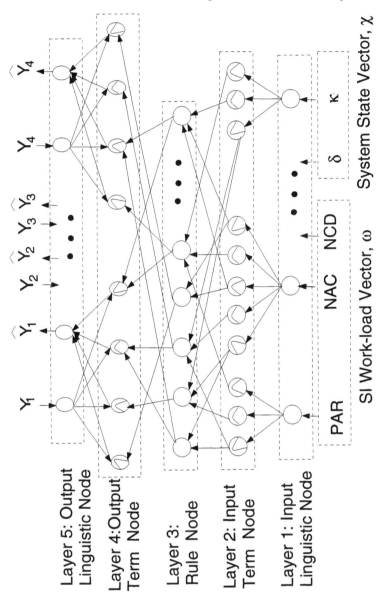

Figure 10.8   The neuro-fuzzy scheduler.

• **Layer L_1:** There are five input nodes; three of them feed the SI work-load related information while the rest inputs the system state vector (see Fig. 10.8). The nodes characterizing the system state vector have their respective input

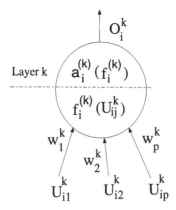

Figure 10.9 Node $n_i^{(k)}$.

linguistic variables of κ and δ. The SI's work-load describing nodes, on the other hand, input linguistic variables of *NAC*, *PAR* and *NCD*. All nodes at layer L_1 only transmit input values to the next layer directly, i.e.,

$$f_i^{(1)}(u_{ij}^{(1)}) = u_{ii}^{(1)} \text{ and } a_i^{(1)} = f_i^{(1)} , \qquad (10.6)$$

where $u_{11}^{(1)} = PAR$, $u_{22}^{(1)} = NAC$, $u_{33}^{(1)} = NCD$, $u_{44}^{(1)} = \delta$ and $u_{55}^{(1)} = \kappa$.

• **Layer** L_2: The nodes at this layer function as *fuzzifiers*. From our experience with the scheduling problem under consideration, the following term sets are used.

$$T(NAC) = \{VeryHigh(VH), High(H), Medium(M), Low(L), VeryLow(VL)\},$$
$$T(x) = \{High(H), Medium(M), Low(L)\}, x \in \{PAR, NCD, \delta, \kappa\},$$
$$T(y_i) = \{Suitable(S), Unsuitable(U)\}, y \in \{1, 2, 3, 4\}.$$

Each node at this layer performs a bell-shape membership function defined as follows:

$$f_i^{(2)}(u_{ij}^{(2)}) = M_{x_n}^j(m_{jn}^{(I)}, \sigma_{jn}^{(I)}) = -\frac{(u_{ij}^{(2)} - m_{jn}^{(I)})^2}{(\sigma_{jn}^{(I)})^2} \text{ and } a_i^{(2)} = e^{f_i^{(2)}} , \qquad (10.7)$$

where $u_{ij}^{(2)} = a_j^{(1)}$, $1 \leq i \leq k$. The index k is given by:

$$k = \mid T(PAR) \mid + \mid T(NAC) \mid + \mid T(NCD) \mid + \mid T(\delta) \mid + \mid T(\kappa) \mid = 17.$$

Here $\mid T(x) \mid$ denotes the number of terms in $T(x)$ and $j = \lceil \frac{i+1}{2} \rceil$. Furthermore, $m_{jn}^{(I)}$ and $\sigma_{jn}^{(I)}$ are the mean and the standard deviation of the bell-shape membership function of the nth term of the input linguistic variable from node j in input layer, respectively. Note that $n = 1$ if i is the odd node and $n = 2$ if i is the even node.

• **Layer** L_3: The links in this layer are used to perform precondition matching of fuzzy control rules. According to fuzzy set theory, the rule-base forms a fuzzy set with dimensions $| T(PAR) | \times | T(NAC) | \times | T(NCD) | \times | T(\delta) | \times | T(\kappa) |$. Thus, there are 405 rule nodes in the initial structure of the net. The number of rule nodes can be reduced later during supervised learning, as elaborated in Section 10.6.1.

Each rule node performs the fuzzy *AND* operation defined as:

$$f_i^{(3)}(u_{ij}^{(3)}) = \min(u_{ij}^{(3)}; \ \forall j \in Q_i) \ , \text{ and } \quad a_i^{(3)} = f_i^{(3)} \ , \tag{10.8}$$

where $u_{ij}^{(3)} = a_j^{(2)}$ and $Q_i = \{j \mid j \text{ is the precondition nodes of the } i\text{th rule }\}$, $1 \le i \le 405$.

• **Layer** L_4: The nodes in this layer have two operation modes: down-up and up-down. In the down-up operation mode, the links perform consequence matching of fuzzy control rules. We set eight nodes in this layer. Each node performs the fuzzy *OR* operation to integrate the firing strength of the rules which have the same consequence. Thus, we define:

$$f_i^{(4)}(u_{ij}^{(4)}) = \sum_i u_{ij}^{(4)} \ , \text{ and } \quad a_i^{(4)} = \min(1, f_i^{(4)}) \tag{10.9}$$

where $u_{ij}^{(4)} = a_j^{(3)}$ and $Q(i) = \{j \mid \text{all } j \text{ that have the same consequence of the } i\text{th term in the term set of } y_i, \ 1 \le i \le 4$. The up-down operation mode in this layer and the links in layer five have similar functions to those in layer L_2. Each node performs a bell-shape function defined as:

$$f_i^{(4)}(u_{ij}^{(4)}) = M_{x_n}^j(m_{jn}^{(O)}, \sigma_{jn}^{(O)}) = -\frac{(u_{ij}^{(4)} - m_{jn}^{(O)})^2}{(\sigma_{jn}^{(O)})^2} \ , \text{ and } \quad a_i^{(4)} = e^{f_i^{(4)}}(10.10)$$

where $u_{ij}^{(4)} = a_j^{(5)}$, $1 \le i \le k$ with $k = | T(PAR) | + | T(NAC) | + | T(NCD) | + | T(\delta) | + | T(\kappa) |$. Here $| T(y) |$ denotes the number of terms in $T(y)$ and $j = \lceil \frac{i+1}{4} \rceil$. Furthermore, $m_{jn}^{(I)}$ and $\sigma_{jn}^{(I)}$, respectively, represent the mean and the standard deviation of the bell-shape membership function of the nth term of the input linguistic variable from node j in the input layer. Note that $n = 1$ if i is the odd node and $n = 2$ if i is the even node.

• **Layer** L_5: For each y_i, there are two nodes in this layer. One of these nodes performs the down-up operation for the actual decision signal y_i. The node and its links act as the *defuzzifier*. The function used to simulate a center of area defuzzification method is approximated by:

$$f_i^{(5)}(u_{ij}^{(5)}) = \sum_j m_j^{(O)}\sigma_j^{(O)}u_{ij}^{(5)} \text{ , and } a_i^{(5)} = U\left(\frac{f_i^{(5)}}{\sum_j \sigma_j^{(O)}u_{ij}^{(5)}} - y_i\right) (10.11)$$

where $u_{ij}^{(5)} = a_j^{(4)}$, $i = 1$, y_i is the decision threshold, and,

$$U(x) = \begin{cases} 1 & \text{if } x \geq 0, \\ 0 & \text{otherwise.} \end{cases}$$

A hybrid learning algorithm is applied to train the neuro-fuzzy scheduler. The following subsection provides details about this process.

10.6.1 Hybrid Learning Algorithm

The learning algorithm is based on a two-phase learning scheme. In phase I, a self organizing learning scheme is used to construct the presence of the rule and to locate an initial membership function. In phase II, a supervised learning scheme is used to optimally adjust the membership functions for the desired outputs. To initiate the learning scheme, the size of the term set for each input/ output linguistic variable and training data are provided. The term set setting and the training data is based on the work-load profile observed during the browsing process of the hypermedia system of Fig. 10.1. An extensive set of training and testing data is generated using these profiles. To complement these profile based training examples, more profiles are randomly generated and used in training the neuro-fuzzy scheduler. The desired output for each of these training input parameter sets is obtained through simulation. Section 10.7 provides further details about the generation of the training and testing data. Note that in the following, we drop superscript (k) for layer L_k.

The problem for self-organized learning can be stated as follows: Given the training input data set for *PAR*, *NAC*, *NCD*, δ and κ, the corresponding desired output value $\hat{y}_i$, $1 \leq i \leq 4$, and the fuzzy partition for input and output term sets locate the membership functions and find the fuzzy logic rules. In this phase, the network operates in a dual manner. The nodes and links in the layer L_4 are set in the up-down transmission mode so that the training input and output data can be fed into the network from both sides.

In the self-organized learning phase, first the centers (or means) and the width (or variances) of the membership functions are determined. For this purpose, Kohonen's learning rule algorithm [39] is used. Once the centers of the membership functions are found, their widths are determined using the *N-nearest-neighbor* heuristic [39]. Once parameters of the membership functions are computed, the signal from both external sides can reach the output points of term nodes in layers L_2 and L_4. Furthermore, the outputs of term nodes in layer L_2 can be transmitted to rule nodes through the initial connection of layer L_3 links. In this manner, we can obtain the firing strength of each rule node. Based on these rule firing strengths (denoted as $o_i^{(3)}$) and the outputs of term nodes in layer L_4 (denoted as $o_j^{(4)}$), we need to determine the correct consequent links of layer L_4 of each rule node to find the existing fuzzy logic rule by competitive learning algorithms [39]. The links in layer L_4 are initially fully connected. We denote the weight of the link between the ith rule node and the jth output term node as w_{ji}. The following competitive learning law is used to update these weights for each training data set.

$$\dot{w}_{ji}(t) = o_j^{(4)}(-w_{ji} + o_i^{(3)}),$$

where $o_j^{(4)}$ serves as a win-loss index of the *jth* term node in layer 4. The essence of this law is *learn if win*. In the extreme case, if $o_j^{(4)}$ is a 0/1 threshold function, then this law indicates *learn only if win*.

After competitive learning involving the whole training data set, the link weights in layer L_4 represent the strength of the existence of the corresponding rule consequent. From the links connecting a rule node and the term nodes of an output linguistic node, at most one link is chosen and the others are deleted. Hence, only one term in an output linguistic variable's term set can become one of the consequents of a fuzzy logic rule.

After the fuzzy logic rules have been determined, the whole network structure is established. The network then enters the second learning phase to optimally adjust the parameters of the input and output membership functions. The problem for supervised learning can be stated as: Given the training input data $x_i(t)$, $i = 1, 2, ..., n$, the corresponding desired output value $y_i^d(t)$, $i = 1, 2, ..., m$, the fuzzy partitions $\mid T(x_i) \mid$ and $\mid T(y_i) \mid$ and the fuzzy logic rules, adjust the parameters of the input and output membership functions optimally. The fuzzy logic rules of this network are determined in the first-phase learning. In the second-phase learning, the network works in the feed-forward manner; that is, the nodes and the links in layers 4 and 5 are in the down-up transmission mode. The back-propagation algorithm is used for this supervised learning. Consider a single-output case for clarity; the goal is to minimize the error function

$$E = \frac{1}{2}(y^d(t) - y(t))^2,$$

where $y^d(t)$ is the desired output and $y(t)$ is the current output. For each training data set, starting at the input nodes, a forward pass is used to compute the activity levels of all the nodes in the network to obtain the current output $y(t)$. Then, starting at the output nodes, a backward pass is used to compute $\frac{\partial E}{\partial w}$ for all the hidden nodes. Assuming that w is the adjustable parameter in a node (e.g., $m_i j$ and σ_{ij} in our class), the general learning rule used is given by:

$$\Delta w \quad \propto \quad -\frac{\partial E}{\partial w},$$

$$w(t+1) \quad = \quad w(t) + \eta \left(-\frac{\partial E}{\partial w} \right),$$

where η is the learning rate and

$$\frac{\partial E}{\partial w} = \frac{\partial E}{\partial a}\frac{\partial a}{\partial w}.$$

10.6.2   NFS Heuristics

The neuro-fuzzy scheduler solves the scheduling problem by intelligently combining heuristics presented in this section. Note that such a selection is based on the current state of the system and the SI's work-load.

The first heuristic is based on the *Forward-Earliest Completion Time* (F-ECT) rule. F-ECT constructs a schedule by proceeding forward in time. It starts with the AUS needed at the beginning of the presentation and attempts to schedule each AUS on a channel that can transmit it at the earliest time. Let α_j denote the earliest time when channel C_j becomes idle. The values of α_j's are initially set to zero and are updated to $\alpha_j = \alpha_j + \frac{s_i}{c_j}$ whenever an AUS_i is assigned to channel C_j. Let S_j be the list of AUSs that are scheduled on channel C_j. The F-ECT algorithm computes $S_j, 1 \leq j \leq m$ as follows:

Forward-Earliest Completion Time (F-ECT) Algorithm

- **F_ECT.1** Sort AUSs to be scheduled during the SI in non-decreasing order of their playout deadlines. Put the sorted AUSs in a list W. If two AUSs have the same deadlines, then apply the longest processing time (LPT) rule, i.e., the AUS with larger size precedes the one with smaller size.
- **F_ECT.2** Initialize $S_j := \{\emptyset\}$ and $\alpha_j := 0$ for all channels, $1 \leq j \leq m$.
- **F_ECT.3** Starting from the head of the list, schedule each AUS in W on the channel that minimizes its arrival time at the client location, i.e., follow the earliest completion time (ECT) rule. In other words,

$$S_j \quad = \quad S_j \cup \{\mathrm{AUS}_i\} \quad \text{if} \quad j = \arg\min_{1 \leq k \leq m} \left\{ \alpha_k + \frac{s_i}{c_k} + J_k \right\}.$$

- **F_ECT.4** Update α_j, i.e., $\alpha_j = \alpha_j + \frac{s_i}{c_j}$
- **F_ECT.5** Repeat Steps 1 to 4 until all AUSs in *SI* have been scheduled.

Note that the F-ECT algorithm is geared towards meeting object O_1 in Equation(10.2). One disadvantage of the F-ECT heuristic is that it may schedule some AUSs too early causing data loss due to buffer overflow.

The *Backward-Earliest Completion Time* (B-ECT) heuristic attempts to correct the earliness liability of the F-ECT algorithm. In B-ECT algorithm, the AUSs are again scheduled in the order of their deadlines. However, B-ECT proceeds its analysis backward in time and tries to schedule an AUS with the largest playout deadline among unscheduled AUSs on the channel that yields the transmission start time of an AUS closest to its playout deadline. In this regard, B-ECT heuristic articulates a *controlled pre-fetching* of multimedia data. The B-ECT algorithm is outlined in the following, using the same set of notation as used earlier in describing F-ECT algorithm.

Backward-Earliest Completion Time (B-ECT) Algorithm

- **B-ECT.1** Sort AUSs to be scheduled during the SI in nondecreasing order of their playout deadlines. Put the sorted AUSs in a list $\mathcal{W}$. If two AUSs have the same deadlines, then apply the shortest processing time (SPT) rule, i.e., the AUS with a smaller size precedes the one with a larger size.
- **B-ECT.2** Initialize $\mathcal{S}_j := \emptyset$ and $\alpha_j := \max_{1 \le i \le n}\{d_i\}$ for all j.
- **B-ECT.3** Starting from the tail of the list, schedule each AUS on the channel that maximizes its start time, i.e.,

$$\mathcal{S}_j \;=\; \{\mathrm{AUS}_{(i)}\} \cup \mathcal{S}_j \text{ if } j = \mathrm{argmax}_{1 \le k \le m}\{\min\{d_{(i)}, \alpha_k\} - \frac{s_{(i)}}{c_k} - J_k\}.$$

- **B-ECT.4** Update α_j to $\alpha_j = A_{(i)} - \frac{s_{(i)}}{c_j}$.
- **B-ECT.5** Repeat Steps 1 to 4 until all AUSs in *SI* have been scheduled.

For the cases where resources are severely constrained and multimedia presentation cannot be supported without degrading the performance, both F-ECT and B-ECT algorithms result in uncontrolled data losses due to buffer overflow or deadline misses. In the following, we present an AUS-Filtering (AUS-F) algorithm that addresses a resource constrained setup by following a controlled droppage of AUSs, at the server site, based on the importance factor I_i. In other words, AUS-F algorithm is tailored to meet objective O_3 in Equation (10.2).

AUS-F Algorithm runs backward in time. The weight setting in the algorithm is based on a heuristic proposed and evaluated in [15]. The AUS-F algorithm maintains two lists: $S_j, 1 \leq j \leq m$ and $\mathcal{R}$. Here S_j is the list of AUSs that should be scheduled on channel $\mathcal{C}_j$ and $\mathcal{R}$ is the list of AUSs that should be dropped at the server site. Furthermore, AUS-F Algorithm runs backward in time. The AUS-F algorithm constructs these lists based on the following heuristic.

AUS-Filter (AUS-F) Algorithm

- **AUS-F.1** Sort *AUS*s in *SI* in non-decreasing order of the weights $(w_i = m \cdot d_i - m(m-1) \cdot \frac{s_i}{\sum_j c_j} I_i)$, and number them, $1 \cdots n$. Put the sorted AUSs in a list $\mathcal{W}$. If two *AUS*s have the same weight, then apply the LPT rule.
- **AUS-F.2** Initialize $S_j := \emptyset$ and $\alpha_j := \max_{1 \leq i \leq n}\{d_i\}$ for all j.
- **AUS-F.3** Starting from the tail of the list, schedule each AUS on the channel that maximizes its start time, i.e.,

$$S_j = S_j \cup \{\text{AUS}_i\} \quad \text{if} \quad j = \arg\min_{1 \leq k \leq m} \{\alpha_k + \frac{s_i}{c_k} + J_k\}.$$

  In this case, the expected arrival time of AUS_i is given by $A_i = \alpha_j + \frac{s_i}{c_j} + J_j$. If $d_i \leq A_i$, i.e., the deadline is already passed, put the AUS_i in list $\mathcal{R}$.
- **AUS-F.4** Repeat Steps 2–3 until all *AUS*s are processed. At this point, each *AUS* is either scheduled, or placed in $\mathcal{R}$.
- **AUS-F.5** Follow transmission of $AUS_i \in S_j$, based on its order in the list, on the channel $\mathcal{C}_j$. Drop all $AUS_i \in \mathcal{R}$ at the server site.

The last heuristic is geared towards meeting objective O_2 in Equation (10.2). Specifically, the AUSs are scheduled not only on the basis of their playout deadlines, but also their sizes. Completing transmission of *bigger* AUSs closed to their deadline results in better utilization of destination buffer resources. The weight setting in the algorithm is based on a heuristic proposed and evaluated in [15].

Weighted Just-In-Time (W-JIT) Algorithm

- **W-JIT.1** Sort AUSs in SI in non-decreasing order of the weight $m(m-1) \cdot \frac{s_i}{\sum_j c_j} + m \cdot d_i$. Put the sorted AUSs in a list $\mathcal{W}$. If two AUSs have the same weight, then apply the LPT rule.
- **W-JIT.2** Initialize $\mathcal{S}_j := \{\emptyset\}$ and $\alpha_j := 0$ for all channels, $1 \le j \le m$.
- **W-JIT.3** Starting from the head of the list, schedule each AUS in $\mathcal{W}$ to reach the destination at its deadline on the channel that results in ECT. If all channels are busy before the deadline then schedule it on the channel resulting in ECT.

$$\mathcal{S}_j \;=\; \mathcal{S}_j \cup \{\mathrm{AUS}_i\} \quad \text{if} \quad j = \arg \min_{1 \le k \le m} \left\{ \alpha_k + \frac{s_i}{c_k} + J_k \right\}.$$

- **W-JIT.4** Update α_j, i.e., $\alpha_j = \max\{(\alpha_j + \frac{s_i}{c_j}), d_i\}$.
- **W-JIT.5** Repeat Steps 1 to 4 until all AUSs in $\mathcal{W}$ have been scheduled.

10.7   Performance Evaluation

To evaluate the effectiveness of the proposed methodology, performance of the neuro-fuzzy scheduler is compared with several known heuristics and a branch and bound algorithm that provides an optimal solution to a restricted version of the multi-criteria scheduling problem considered in this chapter. For this purpose, we have implemented the neuro-fuzzy scheduler on a Sun SPARC platform. A learning rate of 0.05 and the error tolerance of 0.01 were used in our implementation. Various test cases that are representative of the network environment and multimedia information characteristics have been used for training as well as observing the performance of scheduling algorithm under different conditions.

10.7.1   The Learned Fuzzy Logic Rules

Recall, each node in layer L_3 of the underlying connectionist model of the neuro-fuzzy scheduler represents a fuzzy logic rule. As mentioned earlier, the connectionist model dynamically learns the fuzzy logic rules and reconciles the L_3 nodes accordingly. Tables 10.2 and 10.3 (at the end of the chapter) list the learned rules. The first three columns of the table represent the input linguistic variables quantifying the SI's work-load while the succeeding two columns depict input linguistic variables representing the system state. These linguistic variables are defined in Section 10.6. The last four columns of the table represent the results of these inputs indicating the scheduling algorithm that is expected to provide the best QOP for the given work-load and the state of the system. For example, the first row of the table indicates the fuzzy rule, R_1, that deals with an SI that has a *MEDIUM* value for NAC requirements and the case where possibility of pre-fetching multimedia information is low (i.e., PAR = *LOW*). Furthermore, in this case the system state is such that the destination is equipped with a large buffer (i.e., $\kappa = HIGH$) and delay requirements are medium to high (i.e., $\delta = MEDIUM/HIGH$). For this setup, the rule R_1 states that the F-ECT algorithm is expected to yield fewer AUS losses. Note that *NCD* has no impact on the selection of the scheduling algorithm under rule R_1. The reason is the presence of large buffers at the destination. The rule R_2 given by the second row of the table deals with a similar setup as for the rule R_1, except for in R_2 the SI's work-load is such that large amounts of data can be pre-fetched, i.e., PAR = *HIGH*. The rule R_2 states that under this setup B-ECT algorithm will yield a better QOP. The trend of favoring B-ECT algorithm for SI's with *HIGH* values of PAR parameter while preferring F-ECT for SI's with *LOW* values of PAR is quite common in the learned fuzzy rule base. This is intuitive since the LPT rule yields a better performance when the AUS's are scheduled forward in time and the SPT rule performs better when the AUS's are scheduled backward in time. Similarly, another trend that can be observed from the Table is the fact that for the cases when destination can only provide limited buffering ($\kappa = LOW$) and/ or enough capacity is available to enforce synchronization (i.e., $NAC = LOW/MEDIUM$), JIT scheduling is preferred. For example, R_3 states that when destination has low buffering capability and the other setup is as given by the third row of the Table, the JIT algorithm is a viable solution. This intuitively makes sense as in this case, F-ECT and B-ECT algorithms would pre-fetch large amounts of information which would cause extensive AUS losses due to buffer overflow. It can also be observed that for the cases where resources are severely constrained, the fuzzy rule base selects the AUS-F algorithm. An example of such selection is the 4th row of the learned rule base.

10.7.2 Learned Membership Functions

As mentioned in Section 10.6, the neuro-fuzzy scheduler automatically calibrates the parameters of the membership functions. Membership function learning is performed during the the self-organizing (unsupervised) learning phase as well as during the supervised learning. In both phases, the nodes at layer L_2 and L_4 try to optimally find the centers (or means) and the widths (variances) of the input and output parameters, respectively.

The results for the membership learning for the NAC input parameter are plotted in Fig 10.10. Fig 10.10(a) provides the learned membership function for each of these linguistic variables, obtained after the self-organizing learning phase. It can be noted from the figure that the NFS, during self-organizing

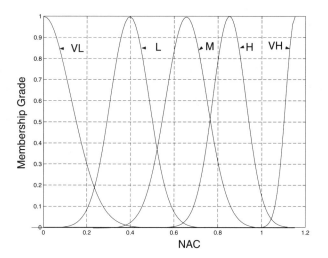

(a) μ_β after self-organized learning

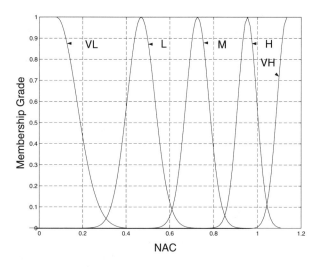

(b) μ_β after supervised learning

Figure 10.10   Learned Membership Functions for NAC: (a) after self-organized learning, (b) after supervised learning.

learning phase, finds an initial setting for the membership functions. Such a setting is based on the training data provided to the NFS. These membership functions are further tuned during the supervised learning phase. This can be seen from Fig. 10.10(b) which depicts the learned membership function after supervised learning. Note that these membership functions are more crisply defined in Fig. 10.10(b).

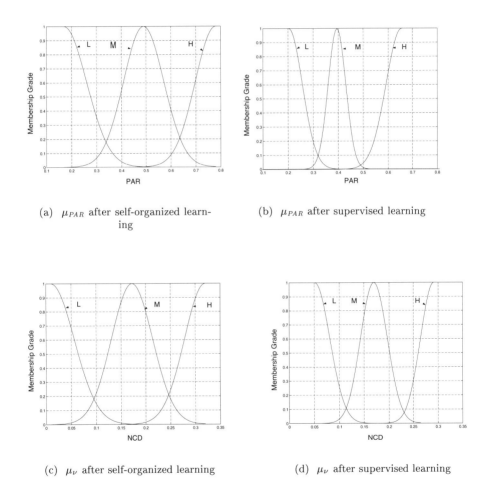

(a) μ_{PAR} after self-organized learning

(b) μ_{PAR} after supervised learning

(c) μ_{ν} after self-organized learning

(d) μ_{ν} after supervised learning

Figure 10.11 (a), (b) Learned Membership Functions for PAR Parameter and (c), (d) Learned Membership Functions for NCD parameter.

Membership learning process is further illustrated in Fig. 10.11 and
Fig. 10.12. Fig. 10.11 provides learned membership function for SI work-load
related parameters PAR and NC, while Fig. 10.12 depicts the similar results
for state parameters κ and δ. It can also be seen from these plots that much
of the membership learning is performed during the supervised learning.

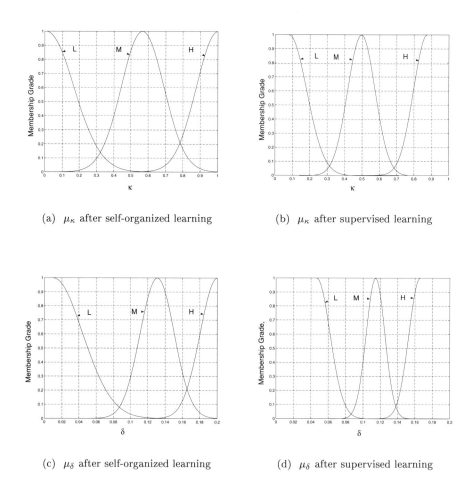

(a) μ_κ after self-organized learning   (b) μ_κ after supervised learning

(c) μ_δ after self-organized learning   (d) μ_δ after supervised learning

Figure 10.12   (a), (b) Learned Membership Functions for κ, and (c), (d) Learned Membership Functions for δ.

10.7.3 Performance Results

This section provides performance results for the neuro-fuzzy scheduler based on an extensive set of simulations. This section also provides details on how the test data are generated. The training data is also generated in the same fashion.

To evaluate the performance of the neuro-fuzzy scheduler, two sets of computational simulations are conducted. The objective of the first set of simulations is to measure the performance of the neuro-fuzzy scheduler relative to an optimal solution obtained using the branch and bound algorithm proposed in [16]. However, due to high time complexity of the branch and bound algorithm, we have to restrict the size of SIs in the first set to 8 to 16 groups of AUSs. In order words, the length of SIs in this set of simulation is restricted to about one second. More realistic SIs are considered in the second set of simulations where performance of the neuro-fuzzy scheduler is compared against the F-ECT, B-ECT, JIT and AUS-F heuristics. For the sake of better presentation, in the following, we first discuss the results obtained from the second set of simulation.

SI work-load defined by (NAC, PAR, NCD) and system state related information indicated by (κ, δ) are the input parameters of the neuro-fuzzy scheduler. This set of input parameters produces a multi-dimensional space of problem instances. To produce every point in this space is neither practical nor desirable. Therefore, we approach the comparison problem by taking several cuts of this space. We vary the NAC, PAP, NCD, κ and finally δ values one by one and evaluate neuro-fuzzy scheduler's performance for several settings for the other parameters. In other words, we explore the behavior of the neuro-fuzzy scheduler in several planes of the state space. To get higher confidence on the simulation results, it is necessary to generate a substantial number of problem instances. Each simulation result is based on the outcome of a 100 randomly generated problem instances. Note that a simulation result only states performance of the algorithm at a fixed point in the multi-dimensional problem space described above.

The second objective of the performance evaluation is to study the effectiveness of the NAC, PAR and NCD parameters for characterizing an SI's work-load. Two types of SIs are considered in our simulations. The first set is based on SI profiles observed in the example hypermedia system of Fig 10.1. Example profiles for this set are plotted in Figure 10.3 and Figure 10.6. In the second set, SI profiles are randomly generated. The Appendix (1) gives an algorithm that is used for generating SI profiles of the desired work-load characteristic. The Appendix (1) also describes how SI profile is used to generate data for the individual AUSs. Furthermore, in all the cases, parameter m, representing the number of channels, is randomly selected using a uniform distribution with parameters $U[2, 4]$. Jitter characteristic of a given channel is also assigned using a uniform distribution with parameters $U[200, 500]$ milliseconds.

For a given point in the multi-dimensional problem space spanned by vectors (NAC, PAR, NCD) and (κ, δ), the overall performance of an algorithm is defined in terms of the number of times it outperforms the other algorithms. For this purpose we simulated F-ECT, B-ECT, JIT, AUS-F and the proposed neuro-fuzzy scheduler algorithms for each problem instance. For each simulation run, i, the value for $\sum_k (I_k \mathcal{L}_d^k + I_k \mathcal{L}_b^k + I_k \mathcal{F}_k)(i)$ is recorded. Here, $\sum_k I_k \mathcal{L}_d^k(i)$, $\sum_k I_k \mathcal{L}_b^k(i)$ and $\sum_k I_k \mathcal{F}_k(i)$ represent the total weighted number of AUS losses due to deadline misses, destination buffer overflow and AUS-filtering, respectively. Note that, in order to use a unified performance measure, the importance factor is also associated with deadline miss and buffer overflow objective. Let $\mathcal{A}$ denote the set of algorithms considered here, i.e., $\mathcal{A} = \{$ F-ECT, B-ECT, JIT, AUS-F, NFS$\}$. Performance comparison is based on the *QOP factor* $Q(j)$, $j \in \mathcal{A}$ defined as follows:

$$Q(j) = \sum_{i=1}^{100} \mathcal{W}(j), \tag{10.12}$$

where i refers to the ith simulation run for a given fixed point of the multi-dimensional problem space. The winner function, $\mathcal{W}(j)$, is defined as follows:

$$\mathcal{W}(j) = \begin{cases} 1 & \text{if } \sum(\mathcal{L}_d + \mathcal{L}_b + \mathcal{F})(j) \leq \sum(\mathcal{L}_d + \mathcal{L}_b + \mathcal{F})(k) \forall k \in \mathcal{A}, \\ 0 & \text{otherwise.} \end{cases}$$

In order words, QOP factor $Q(j)$ represents the number of times algorithm j outperformed the other algorithms.

In the following we study the effect of various parameters on the performance of the proposed neuro-fuzzy scheduler. The performance comparison is based on the QOP factor defined in Equation 10.12.

Effect of Amortized Capacity

In this section, we investigate the performance of the neuro-fuzzy scheduler under various setting of the NAC parameter. Fig. 10.13 depicts the performance results for four different types of SI work-loads. Fig. 10.13(a) uses SI work-load trace depicted in Fig. 10.6(b) while Fig. 10.13(b) uses the example SI profile of Fig. 10.6(a) . Notice that the SI of Fig. 10.6(b) is computed by observing the reverse playout of SI of Fig. 10.6(a) . Hence, arithmetic means of the capacity requirement profiles for both SIs are the same. However, as can be noticed from Fig. 10.13 (a) and (b), the performance of various algorithms for the two profiles varies significantly. Specifically, the work-load of

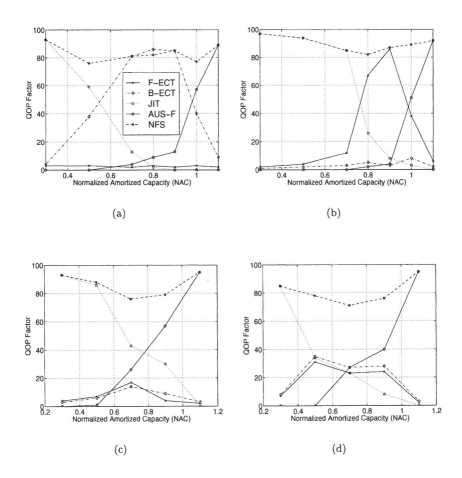

Figure 10.13 Effect of Amortized Capacity on Various Scheduling Algorithms: (a) For an SI Trace with $PAR = 1$, $NCD = 0.1$, $\kappa = U[0.5, 0.7]$, and $\delta = U[0, 0.2]$, (b) For an SI Trace with $PAR = 0.34$, $NCD = 0.4$, $\kappa = U[0.5, 0.7]$, and $\delta = U[0, 0.2]$, (c) For a randomly generated SI with $PAR = U[0.2, 0.6]$, $NCD = 0.2$, $\kappa = 0.3$, and $\delta = 0.2$, (d) For a randomly generated SI with $PAR = U[0.2, 0.6]$, $NCD = U[0, 0.3]$, $\kappa = U[0.2, 0.9]$, and $\delta = U[0, 0.3]$.

SI with higher values for PAR factor can be transported more efficiently using B-ECT algorithm. On the other hand, F-ECT outperforms B-ECT for the SIs with lower values for the PAR factor. As can be noted from Fig. 10.13(a) and Fig. 10.13 (b), the neuro-fuzzy scheduler learns this fact and adapts to the two profiles efficiently.

Figures 10.13(a) and (b) present the cases where SI's are randomly generated. The PAR parameter for these cases is also selected randomly. Therefore, the performance of F-ECT and B-ECT tend to remain closed to each other. However, it is observed that for low values of NAC, the JIT scheduling algorithm yields a better performance while for high values of NAC, AUS-F outperforms the other algorithms. This is intuitive as low values of NAC correspond to a system with sufficient capacity. In that case, the JIT schedule yields a better QOP. On the other hand, high values of NAC correspond to a capacity deficient system in which controlled filtering of AUSs reduces the overall impact of the QOP. The neuro-fuzzy scheduler learns this distinction effectively and outperforms the rest of the algorithms. Furthermore, the neuro-fuzzy scheduler consistently yields an overall good performance for various values of NAC. We also note that even for the cases in which the neuro-fuzzy scheduler fails to select the winner algorithm, it mostly selects the second best algorithm.

Effect of Pre-fetching Activity Ratio

In this section, we evaluate the effect of PAR on the performance of various algorithms including the neuro-fuzzy scheduler. Again the simulations were performed using SIs traces obtained from the hypermedia system shown in Fig. 10.1 as well as randomly generated SIs. Results of this set of experimentation are plotted in Fig 10.14.

To study the effect of changing PAP values onto various scheduling algorithms, we consider two separate sets of fixed parameters in Fig. 10.14(a) and Fig. 10.14(b). In this case, several problem instances are generated by using channels with different characteristics. It can easily be seen that F-ECT performs better for SI's with low PAR while B-ECT outperforms the F-ECT algorithms for high PAP values. Furthermore, the neuro-fuzzy scheduler recognizes this fact and most of the time selects the right algorithm. Plots given in Fig. 10.14(c) and Fig. 10.14(d) also validate this fact. These figures present results for randomly generated SIs.

Effect of Capacity Deviations, Buffering and Delay Margin

In this section we study the performance of the neuro-fuzzy scheduler under various values of NCD, κ and δ. Fig. 10.15(a) shows the result for an SI trace with a set of fixed parameters. In this case, several problem instances are generated by using channels of different characteristics. κ is also varied to study the impact of such variations on the scheduling problems. It can be noticed from the figure that when buffer resources are constrained, AUS-F outperforms the other algorithms. Furthermore, the neuro-fuzzy scheduler learns about this fact and yields consistent performance for various values of the destination buffer. The results are also complemented by Fig. 10.15(b) where a randomly generated SI is used.

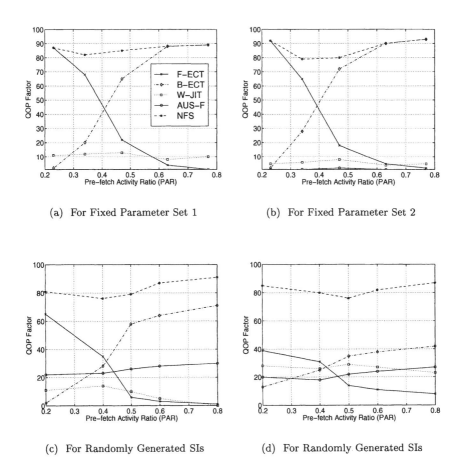

(a) For Fixed Parameter Set 1

(b) For Fixed Parameter Set 2

(c) For Randomly Generated SIs

(d) For Randomly Generated SIs

Figure 10.14 Effect of PAR on Various Scheduling Algorithms: (a) $NAC = 0.5$, $\kappa = 0.75$, $\delta = 0.18$, $NCD = 0.25$, (b) $NAC = 0.75$, $\kappa = 0.75$, $\delta = 0.18$, $NCD = 0.25$, (c) $NAC = 0.9$, $\kappa = 0.75$, $\delta = U[0,0.3]$, $NCD = U[0,0.3]$, $NAC = U[0.2,1.1]$, $\kappa = U[0.2,0.9]$, $\delta = U[0,0.3]$, $NCD = U[0,0.3]$.

Fig. 10.15(c) and Fig. 10.15(d) depict the performance of the neuro-fuzzy scheduler for changing values of capacity deviations and delay margin. The results show that the neuro-fuzzy scheduler adapts to such changes effectively.

In the following we evaluate the performance of the neuro-fuzzy scheduler in a restricted setting of the multi-criteria scheduling problem.

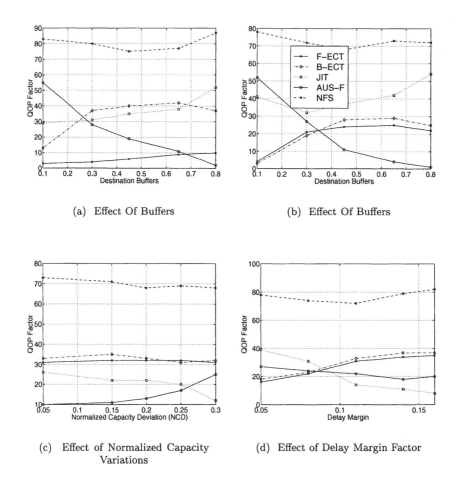

(a) Effect Of Buffers   (b) Effect Of Buffers

(c) Effect of Normalized Capacity   (d) Effect of Delay Margin Factor
     Variations

Figure 10.15   Effect of Pre-fetching Activity Ratio on Various Scheduling Algorithms:
(a) $NAC = 0.5$, $PAR = 0.63$, $\delta = 0.18$, $NCD = 0.25$, (b) $NAC = 0.75$, $\kappa = 0.75$,
$\delta = 0.18$, $NCD = 0.25$, (c) $NAC = 0.9$, $\kappa = 0.75$, $\delta = U[0, 0.3]$, $NCD = U[0, 0.3]$,
$NAC = U[0.2, 1.1]$, $\kappa = U[0.2, 0.9]$, $\delta = U[0, 0.3]$, $NCD = U[0, 0.3]$.

Neuro-Fuzzy Scheduler Compared With an Optimal Approach

In this section the performance of the neuro-fuzzy scheduler is compared
with a branch and bound algorithm presented in [16]. The branch and bound
algorithm provides an optimal solution to the $Q_m \mid J_j \mid \sum_i U_i$ problem. As
mentioned earlier, due to high time complexity of the branch and bound algorithm, we need to restrict the size of SIs in the first set to 8 to 16 groups

of AUSs with each group containing 2 or 4 AUSs. The reason is that the time consumed for scheduling using the branch and bound algorithm increases exponentially with number of AUSs in the SI, resulting in 33 hours on a Sun Ultra SPARC to solve an MMD with 32 AUSs in the worst case.

Complexity of the branch and bound algorithm also varies widely with the number of communication channels (m). For this set of simulations, we consider a system with two channels with different bandwidths and jitter delay characteristics. The bandwidth of one of the channels is set to 64 Kbits per second which is equivalent to the presentation rate of audio. The bandwidth of the second channel is assumed to be 4.8 Mbits per second. For the jitter delay of each channel, two different uniform distributions with ranges $[0, 0.05]$ and $[0.2, 0.4]$ were selected. The former corresponds to a route with few switching nodes, while the latter represents a long-haul connection through a relatively large number of switching nodes. A total of 240 multimedia document instances were tested by varying the structure of a multimedia document and by using different values for the transit delay of the given channels. To evaluate the results of simulations, we used the error ratio $e = \dfrac{\sum_i U_i(NFS) - \sum_i U_i(OPT)}{\sum_i U_i(OPT)}$ that represents the relative deviation of the neuro-fuzzy scheduler's solution ($\sum_i U_i(NFS)$) from the optimal value ($\sum_i U_i(OPT)$).

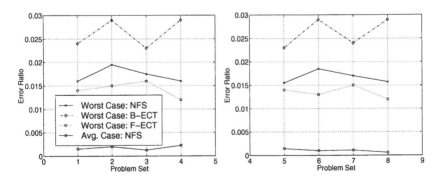

(a) Error Ratio for problem sets $1-4$ (b) Error Ratio for problem sets $5-8$

Figure 10.16 Performance of the NFS measured by error ratios compared with optimal solution: (a) P.1: SI with 8 AUSs and channel jitter $= U[0, 0.05]$, P.2: SI with 16 AUSs and channel jitter $= U[0, 0.05]$, P.3: SI with 24 AUSs and channel jitter $= U[0, 0.05]$, P.4: SI with 32 AUSs and channel jitter $= U[0, 0.05]$, (b) Poblem sets considered in (a) with channel jitter $= U[0.2, 0.4]$

The results of simulations are summarized in Figure 10.16 for different design parameters characterizing problem instances. In the figure, the average error ratio denotes the average value of the error ratios for all the proper subsets of problem instances. The worst error ratio is the largest value among all the error ratios in the subset.

It can be seen from the figure that the average error ratios for the neuro-fuzzy scheduler are quite low regardless of variations in design parameters. Furthermore, the worst case error is also reasonably low for all problem instances. In the problem instances considered in this set of simulation runs, we have found that the neuro-fuzzy scheduler consistently selects the algorithm which outperforms the others.

10.8   Conclusion

In this chapter, the problem of media synchronization in a multimedia Web environment is considered. We have presented work-load profiles generated by a multimedia Web server and elaborated how the work-load generated in a browsing environment is different from the work-load offered by a single media stream, e.g., traffic generated by a VBR source. In particular, the work-load generated by the multimedia server during a Web session exhibits variations due to the asynchronous nature of browsing process, the changing level of concurrency, the characteristics of the component objects within an MMD and the inter-frame compression employed to reduce the size of an object. We proposed three parameters, RAC, PAR, and CD for characterizing a work-load generated by the multimedia server in a browsing environment.

The work-load characterization scheme is used for designing a neuro-fuzzy scheduler to address the media synchronization problem and enforcing QOP. The problem of scheduling multimedia information to ensure media synchronization in a Web environment is identified as a multi-criteria scheduling problem: $Q_m \mid J_j \mid \sum U_i + \sum w_i E_i + \sum I_i \mathcal{F}_i$ which is shown to be NP-hard.

A neuro-fuzzy scheduler to heuristically solve the scheduling problem is proposed. We showed that the proposed scheduler has an ability to automatically learn fuzzy rules and membership functions. The results for learned membership functions are presented. We have also provided a fuzzy rule base learned by scheduler.

The effectiveness of the proposed methodology is evaluated using simulation. The performance of the neuro-fuzzy scheduler is compared against several known heuristics and a branch and bound algorithm. We have also studied the effect RAC, PAR and CD, parameters have on the performance of the neuro-fuzzy scheduler as well as scheduling algorithm based on the F-ECT, B-ECT, W-JIT and AUS-filtering heuristics. The results show that the proposed neural fuzzy scheduler can dynamically adjust to the varying work-load quite well. These results also demonstrate the effectiveness of RAC, PAR and CD parameters in characterizing the work-load generated by a multimedia server in a Web environment.

10.9 Appendix

This appendix outlines the approach that is used to randomly generate traffic profiles for a given set of parameters, *RAC, PAR* and *CD*. The appendix also describes how these profiles are used to generate data for AUS sizes.

The SI work-load generation is based on the fact that RAC represents average capacity requirement over time interval $[0, PAR \cdot L)$ [1]. Furthermore, CD quantifies the variation around the RAC value. Consequently, uniformly distributed random with distribution parameters set to meet RAC and CD. The work-load of the remainder of the SI is then generated using a truncated normal distribution. The parameters for the normal distribution are also selected randomly.

In the following, we outline how work-load profiles are used to determine sizes of individual AUSs. The work-load defines the cumulative capacity requirement of an SI for each Δ period. Let W_Δ be the capacity requirement for a given Δ period. Recall, a Δ period presents a group $\mathcal{G}_i$ of AUSs. The problem is to find sizes for each $AUS_j \in \mathcal{G}_i$. For this purpose, number of AUSs contained in $\mathcal{G}_i$ are generated using $U[1, 10]$. Let n be the total number of AUSs in group $\mathcal{G}_i$. The work-load W_Δ is distributed into n bins by observing the following procedure. First generate $n - 1$ uniformly distributed random numbers and sort them in ascending order. Let $\{r_1, r_2, \cdots, r_{n-1}\}$ be the set of sorted numbers. It can be seen that this set partitions W_Δ value into n bins. Given such partitioning, size of AUS_1 is given by $s_1 = r_1 \Delta$. Similarly, $s_2 = (r_2 - r_1)\Delta$, $s_n = (W_\Delta - r_{n-1})\Delta$, etc. are determined.

---

[1]Note that RAC is not the mean capacity requirement of the SI which spans $[0, L)$.

Symbol	Explanation
Resource Related Parameters	
$\mathcal{C}$	Set of available channels
m	number of available channels
c_j	Capacity of channel $\mathcal{C}_j \in \mathcal{C}, 1 \leq j \leq m$
C_{total}	Cumulative Capacity of m channels, $C_{\text{total}} = \sum_{i=1}^{m} c_j$
J_j	Bounded jitter for $\mathcal{C}_j \in \mathcal{C}, 1 \leq j \leq m$
K	Size of Destination Buffer
κ	Normalized Size of Destination Buffer
Synchronization Related Parameters	
SI	Scheduling Interval
AUS	Atomic Unit of Synchronization
s_i	Size of AUS_i
d_i	Presentation deadline of AUS_i
Δ	Presentation Duration of an AUS
$\mathcal{G}_i$	Group of AUSs with same Δ period
MMD	Multimedia Document
SI's Work-Load Related Parameters	
RAC	Required Amortized Capacity
NAC	Normalized Amortized Capacity
PAR	Pre-fetch Activity Ratio
CD	Capacity Deviation
NCD	Normalized Capacity Deviation
Multimedia Presentation Related Parameters	
QOP	Quality of Presentation
$\sum \mathcal{L}_d$	Total number of AUSs lost due to deadline misses
$\sum \mathcal{L}_b$	Total number of AUSs lost due to buffer overflow
$\sum \mathcal{F}$	Total number of AUSs dropped (filtered) at the server
I_i	Importance Factor for AUS_i
δ	Normalized Delay Margin
Neuro-Fuzzy Scheduler (NFS) Related Parameters	
μ_x	Membership Grade of linguistic variable x
$T(x)$	Term set for linguistic variable x
VH, H, M, L, VL	*Very High, High, Medium, Low, Very Low*
η	Learning Rate
Scheduling Algorithms Related Parameters	
NFS	Neuro-Fuzzy Scheduler
F-ECT	Backward-Earliest Completion Time Scheduling Algorithm
B-ECT	Forward-Earliest Completion Time Scheduling Algorithm
JIT	Just-In-Time Scheduling Algorithm
AUS-F	AUS-Filter Scheduling Algorithm

Table 10.1   Notation

SI's Work-Load			System State		Scheduling Algorithm			
NAC_{SI}	PAR_{SI}	NCD_{SI}	κ	δ	F-ECT	B-ECT	JIT	AUS-F
M	L	-	H	H/M	1	0	0	0
M	H	-	H	H/M	0	1	0	0
M	-	L	L	-	0	0	1	0
M	H	H	L	-	0	0	0	1
M	H	M	L	-	0	1	0	0
M	L	M	L	-	1	0	0	0
M	M	M	L	-	-	-	0	0
M	M	H	L	-	0	0	0	1
M	L	H	L	-	0	0	1	0
M	-	H	H	L	0	0	0	1
M	-	L	H	L	0	0	1	0
M	L	M	H	L	1	0	0	0
M	H	M	H	L	0	1	0	0
M	M	M	H	L	-	-	0	0
M	-	H	M	L	0	0	0	1
M	-	L	M	L	0	0	1	0
M	L	M	M	L	1	0	0	0
M	H	M	M	L	0	1	0	0
M	M	M	M	L	-	-	0	0
M	H	H	M	M/H	0	0	0	1
M	M	H	M	M/H	0	0	1	0
M	L	H	M	M/H	1	0	0	0
M	L	L/M	M	L	1	0	0	0
M	H	L/M	M	L	0	1	0	0
M	M	L/M	M	L	-	-	0	0

Table 10.2 The Learned Fuzzy Rule Base (Part I).

SI's Work-Load			System State		Scheduling Algorithm			
NAC_{SI}	PAR_{SI}	NCD_{SI}	κ	δ	*F-ECT*	*B-ECT*	*JIT*	*AUS-F*
L	-	L	L	-	0	0	1	0
L	-	H	L	-	0	0	0	1
L	-	M	L	-	0	0	-	-
L	M	H	M	-	0	0	1	0
L	M	M/L	M	-	-	-	0	0
L	M	H	M	-	0	0	1	0
L	H	H	M/H	-	0	1	0	0
L	L	H	M/H	-	1	0	0	0
L	M	-	H	-	0	0	1	0
L	L	-	H	-	1	0	0	0
L	H	-	H	-	0	-	-	0
L	M	H	H	-	-	-	-	0
L	-	M/L	H	-	0	0	1	0
H	H	H	L	L	0	0	0	1
H	L	L	L	M/H	1	0	0	0
H	L	M	L	M/H	0	0	0	1
H	H	L	L	M/H	0	1	0	0
H	H	H	L	M/H	0	0	0	1
H	M	L	L	M/H	-	-	0	0
H	M	M	L	M/H	0	0	0	1
H	H	M	L	M/H	0	0	0	1
H	H	H	M	L	0	0	0	1
H	H	H	M	M/H	-	-	0	-
H	L	L	M	M/H	1	0	0	0
H	H	L	M	M/H	0	1	0	0
H	M	L	M	M/H	-	-	0	0
H	H	M	M	M/H	0	0	0	1
H	L	M	M	M/H	1	0	0	0
H	M	M	M	M/H	-	0	0	-
H	-	H	H	L	0	0	0	1
H	H	L	H	M/H	0	1	0	0
H	L	L	H	M/H	1	0	0	0
H	M	L	H	M/H	-	-	0	0
H	L	M	H	M/H	1	0	0	0
H	H	M	H	M/H	0	0	0	1
H	M	M	H	M/H	-	-	0	-
VL	-	-	-	-	0	0	1	0
VH	-	-	-	-	0	0	0	1

Table 10.3 The Learned Fuzzy Rule Base (Part II).

10.10 References

[1] J. F. Gibbon and T. D. C. Little, "The use of network delay estimation for multimedia data retrieval," *IEEE Journal on Selected Areas in Communications*, vol. 14, no. 7, pp. 1376–1387, 1996.

[2] P. Senac, M. Diaz, A. Leger, and P. de Saqui-Sannes, "Modeling logical and temporal synchronization in hypermedia systems," *IEEE Journal on Selected Areas in Communications*, vol. 14, no. 1, pp. 84–103, 1996.

[3] S. V. Raghavan, B. Prabhakaran, and S. K. Tripathi, "Synchronization representation and traffic source modeling in orchestrated presentation," *IEEE Journal on Selected Areas in Communications*, vol. 14, no. 1, pp. 104–113, 1996.

[4] K. Ravindran and V. Bansal, "Delay compensation protocols for synchronization of multimedia data streams," *IEEE Transactions on Knowledge and Data Engineering*, vol. 5, no. 4, pp. 574–589, August 1993.

[5] M. C. Yuang, P. L. Tien, and S. T. Liang, "Intelligent video smoother for multimedia communications," *IEEE Journal on Selected Areas in Communications*, vol. 15, no. 2, pp. 136–146, 1997.

[6] Z. Ali, M. Woo, and A. Ghafoor, "A distributed architecture for synchronized multimedia services over the Internet," in *Proceedings of ICNP'94*, pp. 204 –211, IEEE Computer and Communications Society, 1994.

[7] K. Ravindran and R. Steinmetz, "Object-oriented communication structures for multimedia data transport," *IEEE Journal on Selected Areas in Communications*, vol. 14, no. 7, pp. 1360–1375, September 1999.

[8] S. Ramanathan and P. Rangan, "Adaptive feedback techniques for synchronized multimedia retrieval over integrated networks," *IEEE Transactions on Networking*, vol. 1, pp. 246–260, April 1993.

[9] A. Campbell, G. Coulson, F. Garcia, and D. Hutchison, "A continuous media transport and orchestration service," in *Proceedings of SIGCOMM*, pp. 99–110, ACM, Auegst 1992.

[10] M. Woo, N. U. Qazi, and A. Ghafoor, "A synchronization framework for communication of pre-orchestrated multimedia information," *IEEE Network Magazine*, vol. 8, no. 1, pp. 52–61, January/ February 1994.

[11] Z. Wang and J. Crowcroft, "Quality-of-service routing for supporting multimedia applications," *IEEE Journal on Selected Areas in Communications*, vol. 14, no. 7, pp. 1228–1234, 1996.

[12] E. Gelenbe, A. Ghanwani, and V. Srinivasan, "Improved neural heuristics for multicast routing," *IEEE Journal on Selected Areas in Communications*, vol. 15, no. 2, pp. 147–155, 1997.

[13] S. Baqai, M. Woo, and A. Ghafoor, "Network resource management for enterprise-wide multimedia services," *IEEE Communications*, vol. 34, pp. 78–83, January 1996.

[14] T. Little and A. Ghafoor, "Multimedia synchronization protocols for broadband integrated services," *IEEE Journal on Selected Areas in Communications*, vol. 9, no. 9, pp. 1368–1382, December 1991.

[15] S. Baqai, M. F. Khan, M. Woo, S. Shinkai, A. Khokhar, and A. Ghafoor, "Quality-based evaluation of multimedia synchronization protocols for distributed multimedia information systems," *IEEE Journal on Selected Areas in Communications*, vol. 14, pp. 1388–1403, September 1996.

[16] M. Woo, R. Uzsoy, and A. Ghafoor, "Multichannel scheduling for communication of pre-orchestrated multimedia information (heterogeneous channels case)," technical report, Purdue University, 1994.

[17] Internet Draft, *Resource ReSerVation Protocol (RSVP) - Version 1 Fuctional Specifications*, Internet Engineering Task Force, August 1996.

[18] A. Pitsillides, Y. A. Sekercioglu, and G. Ramamurthy, "Effective control of traffic flow in ATM networks using fuzzy explicit rate marking (ferm)," *IEEE Journal on Selected Areas in Communications*, vol. 15, no. 2, pp. 209–225, 1997.

[19] N. Yeadon, F. Garcia, D. Hutchison, and D. Shepherd, "Filters: QoS support mechanisms for multipeer communications," *IEEE Journal on Selected Areas in Communications*, vol. 14, pp. 1245–1263, September 1996.

[20] R. Steinmetz, "Human perception of jitter and media synchronization," *IEEE Journal on Selected Areas in Communications*, vol. 14, pp. 61–72, January 1996.

[21] G. Blakowski and R. Steinmetz, "A media synchronization survey: Reference model, specification, and case studies," *IEEE Journal on Selected Areas in Communications*, vol. 14, pp. 5–35, January 1996.

[22] S. Moni and S. Kashyap, "Multi-resolution representation scheme for multimedia databases." Accepted for Publication in ACM Multimedia System Journal.

[23] J. E. Neves, M. J. Leitao, and L. B. Almedia, "Neural networks in B-ISDN flow control: ATM traffic prediction or network modeling," *IEEE Communications Magazine*, vol. 33, no. 10, pp. 50–57, 1995.

[24] Z. Ali, E. K. P. Chong, and A. Ghafoor, "A scalable call admission control algorithm for ATM networks." to appear in IEEE Globecom to be held in Rio de Janeiro, December 5-9, 1999.

[25] I. W. Habib, A. A. Tarraf, and T. N. Saadawi, "Intelligent traffic control for ATM broadband networks," *IEEE Communications Magazine*, vol. 33, no. 10, pp. 76–85, 1995.

[26] M. Pinedo, *Scheduling: Theory, Algorithms, and Systems*. Series in Industrial and Systems Engineering, Englewood Cliffs, NJ: Prentice Hall, 1995.

[27] M. R. Garey and D. S. Johnson, *Computers and Intractability: A*

Guide to the Theory of NP-Completeness. W. H. Freeman and Company, 1979.

[28] G. I. Adamopoulos and C. P. Pappis, "A fuzzy-linguistic approach to a multi-criteria sequencing problem," *European Journal of Operational Research*, vol. 1, no. 92, pp. 628–636, 1996.

[29] S. A. Youssef, I. W. Habib, and T. N. Saadawi, "A neurocomputing controller for bandwidth allocation in ATM networks," *IEEE Journal on Selected Areas in Communications*, vol. 15, no. 2, pp. 191–199, 1997.

[30] A. Farago, J. Biro, T. Henk, and M. Boda, "Analog neural optimization for ATM resource management," *IEEE Journal on Selected Areas in Communications*, vol. 15, no. 2, pp. 156–164, 1997.

[31] P. K. Compbell, A. Christiansen, M. Dale, H. L. Ferra, A. Kowalczyk, and J. Szymanski, "Experiments with simple neural networks for real-time control," *IEEE Journal on Selected Areas in Communications*, vol. 15, no. 2, pp. 165–178, 1997.

[32] K. Uehara and K. Hirota, "Fuzzy connection admission control for ATM networks based on possibility distribution of cell loss ratio," *IEEE Journal on Selected Areas in Communications*, vol. 15, no. 2, pp. 179–190, 1997.

[33] Y. C. Liu and C. Douligeris, "Rate ragulation with feedback controller in ATM networks-a neural network approach," *IEEE Journal on Selected Areas in Communications*, vol. 15, no. 2, pp. 200–208, 1997.

[34] H. I. Fahmy, G. Develekos, and C. Douligeris, "Application of neural networks and machine learning in network design," *IEEE Journal on Selected Areas in Communications*, vol. 15, no. 2, pp. 226–239, 1997.

[35] E. Nordstrom, J. Carlstrom, O. Gallmo, and L. Asplund, "Neural networks for adaptive traffic control in ATM networks," *IEEE Communications Magazine*, vol. 33, no. 10, pp. 43–49, 1995.

[36] A. Hiramatsu, "Training techniques for neural network applications in ATM," *IEEE Communications Magazine*, vol. 33, no. 10, pp. 58–67, 1995.

[37] Y. K. Park and G. Lee, "Applications of neural networks in high-speed communication networks," *IEEE Communications Magazine*, vol. 33, no. 10, pp. 68–75, 1995.

[38] C.-T. Lin and C. S. G. Lee, "Neural-network-based fuzzy logic control and decision system," *IEEE Transactions in Computers*, vol. 40, no. 12, pp. 1320–1336, 1991.

[39] C.-T. Lin and C. S. G. Lee, *Neural Fuzzy Systems.* Prentice Hall, 1998.

[40] M. Russo, "Fugenesys-a fuzzy genetic neural system for fuzzy modeling," *IEEE Transactions on Fuzzy Systems*, vol. 6, no. 3, pp. 373 –388, August 1998.

[41] Z. Ali, C. S. G. Lee, and A. Ghafoor, "Media synchronization in multi-

media web using a neuro-fuzzy framework." to appear in IEEE JSAC, Specical Issue on Intelligent Techniques in High Speed Networks, 2000.

[42] R.-G. Cheng and C.-J. Chang, "A neural-net based fuzzy admission controller for an ATM network," in *Proceedings of INFOCOM '96*, pp. 777–782, IEEE Computer and Communications Society, 1996.

11

A Neuro-Fuzzy System Based on Logical Interpretation of If-Then Rules

Jacek Leski

email: jl@biomed.iele.polsl.gliwice.pl

Norbert Henzel

Institute of Electronics, Technical University of Silesia, Akademicka 16, 44-100 Gliwice, Poland. email: henzel@zeus.polsl.gliwice.pl

A Neuro-Fuzzy System Based on Logical Interpretation of If-Then Rules

Abstract

Initially, an axiomatic approach to the definition of fuzzy implication has been recalled in this chapter. Based on this definition several important fuzzy implications and their properties have been described. Then, the idea of approximate reasoning using generalized modus ponens and fuzzy implication is considered. The elimination of the non-informative part of a final fuzzy set before defuzzification plays the key role in this chapter. After reviewing well-known fuzzy systems, a new artificial neural network based on logical interpretation of if-then rules (ANBLIR) is introduced. Another novelty incorporated in the system is the moving fuzzy consequent in if-then rules. The location of this fuzzy set is determined by a linear combination of system inputs. Moreover, this system automatically generates rules from numerical data. The proposed system operates with Gaussian membership functions in thepremise part and triangular in the consequence part. Parameter estimation has been made by combination of both gradient and least squares methods. For initialization of unknown parameter values of premises, a preliminary fuzzy c-means clustering method has been employed. The applications of ANBLIR to pattern recognition on numerical examples using benchmark databases (FORENSIC GLASS, IRIS, WINE and MONKS) are shown.

11.1 Introduction

An investigation of inference processes when premises and/or conclusions in if-then rules are fuzzy is still a subject of many papers [2], [4], [6], [9], [11], [16], [20], [22], [28]. In such processes, a sound and proper choice of logical operators plays an essential role. The theoretical (mathematical) and the practical (computational) behavior of logical operators in inference processes has to be known before such a choice is made. Both types of the above mentioned knowledge related to well-known families of triangular norms and implications can also be found in the literature [9], [11], [28].

Some selected logical operators and fuzzy implications were also investigated with respect to their behavior in the inference processes. The fuzzy if-then rules have on one hand a conjunction interpretation and on the other hand the interpretation in terms of classical logical implication. The inference algorithms based on conjunctive implication interpretation of if-then rules were simpler and faster with relation on algorithms used for the logical interpretation of such rules. Additionally, applying conjunctive implication interpretation of if-then rules leads to intuitively better inference results. In the chapter we present an inference with specific defuzzification that leads to simpler, faster and intuitively acceptable results. An artificial neural network that automatically generates this kind of fuzzy if-then rules has been described.

In literature, several methods of automatic fuzzy rule generation from given numerical data have been described [3], [12], [14], [17], [21], [29]. The simplest method of rule generation is based on a clustering algorithm and estimation of proper fuzzy relations from a set of numerical data [17], [29]. Another type of method, which use the learning capability of neural networks and the fact that both fuzzy systems and neural nets are universal approximators, has been successfully applied to various tasks. The problem here is the difficulty in understanding the identified fuzzy rules since they are implicitly acquired into the network itself. Mitra et al. [21] have proposed a fuzzy multilayer perceptron generating fuzzy rules from the connection weights. Several methods of extracting rules from the given data are based on a class of radial basis function networks (RBFNs). The fact that there is a functional equivalence between radial basis function networks (RBFNs) and the fuzzy system has been used by Jang et al. [13] to construct a Sugeno type of adaptive network based fuzzy inference system (ANFIS) which is trained by the back propagation algorithm. More general fuzzy reasoning schemes in ANFIS are employed by Horikawa et al. [12]. Such developed radial basis function based adaptive fuzzy systems have been described by Cho and Wang [3] and applied to system identification and prediction. Another type of fuzzy system with moving fuzzy set in consequents of if-then rules is shown in [19].

The aim of this chapter is the theoretical description and structure presentation of a new artificial neural network based on logical interpretation of if-then rules (ANBLIR). The novelty of the system is the introduction of the logical interpretation of fuzzy if-then rules with moving fuzzy sets in that rules consequent. The described system is applied to benchmark pattern recognition problems.

The chapter is divided into 7 sections. Some introductory remarks are contained in Section 1. Section 2 presents a short review of the study concerning an axiomatic approach to the definition of a fuzzy implication with a location of fuzzy implications within the interval [0,1]. Section 3 recalls the main ideas of the fuzzy inference process. Section 4 introduces the basics of fuzzy systems. In Section 5 the structure of ANBLIR and the estimation of its parameters are shown. Sections 6 and 7 illustrate the theoretical considerations by means of application of the system to the pattern recognition problems. Finally, concluding remarks are presented in Section 8.

11.2   An approach to axiomatic definition of fuzzy implication

We start our considerations applying an axiomatic approach (formulated by Fodor [9], [10], [11]) to the definition of fuzzy implication, which considers an implication to be a connective and seems to possess its most general and characteristic properties.

DEFINITION 11.1   A fuzzy implication is a function $I : [0,1]^2 \longrightarrow [0,1]$ satisfying the following conditions:

  I1. If $x \leq z$ then $I(x,y) \geq I(z,y)$ for all $x,y,z \in [0,1]$,
  I2. If $y \leq z$ then $I(x,y) \leq I(x,z)$ for all $x,y,z \in [0,1]$,
  I3. $I(0,y) = 1$ (falsity implies anything) for all $y \in [0,1]$,
  I4. $I(x,1) = 1$ (anything implies tautology) for all $x \in [0,1]$,
  I5. $I(1,0) = 0$ (Booleanity).

Assuming that $N : [0,1] \longrightarrow [0,1]$ is a strictly decreasing continuous function (a strong negation; $N(0) = 1$, $N(1) = 0$, $N(N(x)) = x$ for all $x \in [0,1]$), the N - reciprocal of I defined by

$$\underset{x,y \in [0,1]}{\forall} I_N(x,y) = I(N(y), N(x)) \qquad (11.1)$$

is also considered to be a fuzzy implication.

Now let us recall further properties, in terms of function I, which could also be important in some applications:

  I6. $I(1,x) = x$ (tautology cannot justify anything) for all $x \in [0,1]$,
  I7. $I(x, I(y,z)) = I(y, I(x,z))$ (exchange principle) for all $x,y,z \in [0,1]$,
  I8. $x \leq y$ if and only if $I(x,y) = 1$ (implication defines ordering) for all $x,y \in [0,1]$,
  I9. $I(x,0) = N(x)$ for all $x \in [0,1]$ is a strong negation,
  I10. $I(x,y) \geq y$ for all $x,y \in [0,1]$,
  I11. $I(x,x) = 1$ (identity principle) for all $x \in [0,1]$,
  I12. $I(x,y) = I(N(y), N(x))$ with a strong negation N for all $x,y \in [0,1]$,

I13. I is a continuous function.

The two most important families of such implications are related either to the formalism of Boolean logic or to the residuation concept from intuitionistic logic. For the concepts mentioned above, a suitable definition is introduced below [11], [22], [27], [28]:

DEFINITION 11.2 An S-implication associated with a t-conorm S and a strong negation N is defined by

$$\mathop{\forall}_{x,y\in[0,1]} I_{S,N}(x,y) = N(x) *_S y. \tag{11.2}$$

DEFINITION 11.3 An R-implication associated with a t-norm T is defined by

$$\mathop{\forall}_{x,y\in[0,1]} I_T(x,y) = \sup_z \{z \mid x *_T z \le y\}. \tag{11.3}$$

The last expression can be justified by the following classical set-theoretic identities [11]:

$$\overline{A} \cup B = \overline{(A \setminus B)} = \bigcup \{Z \mid A \cap Z \subseteq B\}, \tag{11.4}$$

where $\setminus$ denotes the set-difference operator.

We can see that both $I_{S,N}$ and I_T satisfy conditions I1-I5 for any t-norm T, t-conorm S and strong negation N; thus they are fuzzy implications.

For the sake of completeness we mention a third type of implications used in quantum logic:

DEFINITION 11.4 QL-implication associated with a t-norm T, a t-conorm S and a strong negation N is defined by

$$\mathop{\forall}_{x,y\in[0,1]} I_{T,S,N}(x,y) = N(x) *_S (x *_T y). \tag{11.5}$$

Generally, $I_{T,S,N}$ violates property I1. However, conditions under which I1 is satisfied by a QL-implication can be found in [9].

Considering a connection between implications and negation we notice that $I(\cdot, 0)$ is non-increasing and continuos. However, it is neither strictly decreasing nor continuos in general. Continuity of the implication is sufficient but not necessary to obtain strong negation via residuation. As an example, a particular t-norm (called nilpotent minimum) and t-conorm (called onepotent maximum) are considered in [9], [16] and recalled below:

$$x \wedge_0 y = \min{}_0 (x, y) = \begin{cases} 0, & \text{if } x \leq N(y), \\ \min(x, y), & \text{if } x > N(y), \end{cases} \tag{11.6}$$

and

$$x \vee_1 y = \max{}_1 (x, y) = \begin{cases} 1, & \text{if } x \leq N(y), \\ \max(x, y), & \text{if } x > N(y) \end{cases} \tag{11.7}$$

Then the residuated implication is of the form:

$$I_{\min 0} (x, y) = I_{\text{Fo}} (x, y) = \begin{cases} 1, & \text{if } x \leq y, \\ \max(1 - x, y), & \text{if } x > y \end{cases} \tag{11.8}$$

Although $I_{\min 0}$ is not continuous, $I_{\min 0} (x, 0) = 1 - x$, $x \in [0, 1]$, is the standard strong negation. Fuzzy implication (11.8) has been introduced by Fodor [9], [11] and will be also taken into account in further considerations.

Since t-norms (e.g., M-, Π-, W-, Z- norms), t-conorms (e.g., M'-, Π'-, W'-, Z'- conorms) and strong negation (e.g., $N(x) = 1 - x$) are well-established models for AND, OR, NOT respectively, fuzzy implications should be regarded as closely related to those models. The most important fuzzy implications representing the classes of fuzzy implications discussed above are juxtaposed in Table 11.1.

We may also classify and order fuzzy implications using an integrated index obtained from the location of fuzzy implications versus fuzzy operations within the interval $[0, 1]$.

Let $\star_1, \star_2 : [0, 1]^2 \to [0, 1]$ be measurable functions treated as two-argument operations in $[0, 1]$. The distance between the operations $\star_1$ and $\star_2$ with respect to the values of their arguments is calculated as follows [6]:

$$d(\star_1, \star_2) = \int_0^1 \int_0^1 |x \star_1 y - x \star_2 y| \, dx dy, \tag{11.9}$$

where d is here a pseudometric distance.

For constant operations, i.e., for $x \star_1 y = 0$, $x \star_2 y = 1$, for all $x, y \in [0, 1]$ we get $d(\star_1, \star_2) = 1$. Because constant operations differ from drastic operations only by boundary conditions, the distance for drastic operations is obtained as follows:

$$d(\sqcap, \sqcup) = 1 \tag{11.10}$$

where $\sqcap$ and $\sqcup$ denote drastic product (Z-norm) and drastic sum (Z'-conorm), respectively.

Taking into account min ($\wedge$) (M-norm) and max ($\vee$) (M'-conorm) operations we can divide the $[0, 1]$ interval into three basic classes as follows:

Impl. Name	Implication Form	Imp. Type	Prop.
Lukasiewicz	$\min(1 - x + y, 1)$	R with $T = W$ S with $S = W'$ QL with $\begin{array}{l} T = \min \\ S = W' \end{array}$	I1-I13
Fodor	$\begin{cases} 1 & x \leq y \\ \max(1 - x, y) & x > y \end{cases}$	R with $T = \min_0$ S with $S = \max_1$ QL with $\begin{array}{l} T = \min \\ S = \max_1 \end{array}$	I1-I12
Reichenbach	$1 - x + xy$	S with $S = \Pi'$	I1-I7, I9, I10, I12, I13
Kleene-Dienes	$\max(1 - x, y)$	S with $S = \max$ QL with $\begin{array}{l} T = W \\ S = W' \end{array}$	I1-I7, I9, I10, I12, I13
Zadeh	$\max[1 - x, \min(x, y)]$	QL with $\begin{array}{l} T = \min \\ S = \max \end{array}$	I2, I3, I5, I6, I9, I13

Table 11.1   Selected fuzzy implications

- products $(\sqcap \leq \star_T \leq \wedge) \in [0, \frac{1}{3}]$,
- averages $(\wedge \leq \star_A \leq \vee) \in [\frac{1}{3}, \frac{2}{3}]$,
- sums $(\vee \leq \star_S \leq \sqcup) \in [\frac{2}{3}, 1]$.

As an example, let us locate two products (algebraic product $x \bullet y = xy$ and bold product $x \odot y = 0 \vee (x + y - 1)$) within the $[0, 1]$ interval according to the pseudometric distance. For the algebraic product the calculated distance is $d(\sqcap, \bullet) = \frac{1}{4}$ and for bounded product we get $d(\sqcap, \odot) = \frac{1}{6}$. By analogy, we get locations for the algebraic sum $x \dot{+} y = x + y - xy$ and bounded sum $x \oplus y = 1 \wedge (x + y)$ which are symmetric to the corresponding products with respect to $\frac{1}{2}$ in the $[0, 1]$ interval. These and some additional known results are illustrated in Figure 11.1(A).

We can also order other families of operations, which can be obtained using algebraic product and bounded product (e.g., Yager operations, Schweizer and Sklar operations, Frank operations, Hamacher operations and others).

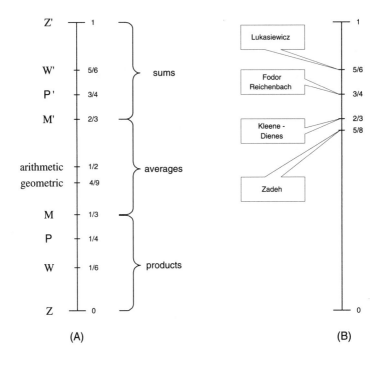

Figure 11.1   Location of t-norms (A) and fuzzy implications (B) within the $[0, 1]$ interval

Regarding a fuzzy implication as a two-argument function, we can find its location within the interval $[0, 1]$ using the above-mentioned pseudometric distance in the same way as for fuzzy operations. In Figure 11.1(B) we illustrate the computed distance $d(\sqcap, I)$ for the above considered fuzzy implications. Such determined distance may be also regarded as the volume under implication functions, which are shown in Figure 11.2 to Figure 11.6, respectively. However, the above mentioned distance is an integrated index characterizing a fuzzy implication; it also delivers indirectly information for the selection of other operations.

Below we will recall the idea of approximate reasoning by means of generalized modus ponens using fuzzy implications.

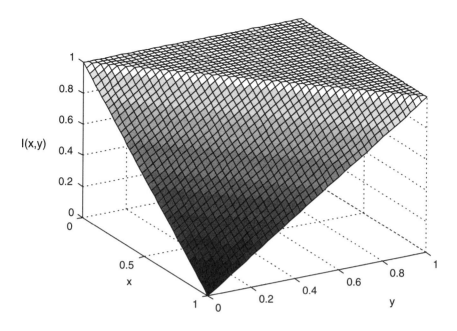

Figure 11.2   Graphical illustration of Lukasiewicz fuzzy implication

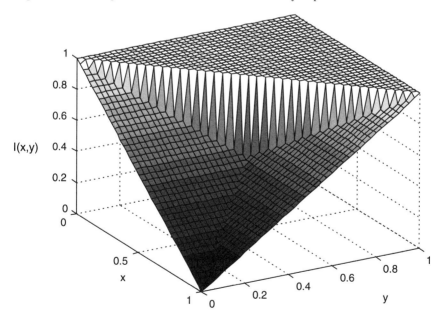

Figure 11.3   Graphical illustration of Fodor fuzzy implication

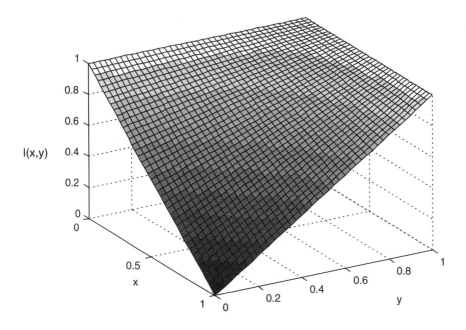

Figure 11.4   Graphical illustration of Reichenbach fuzzy implication

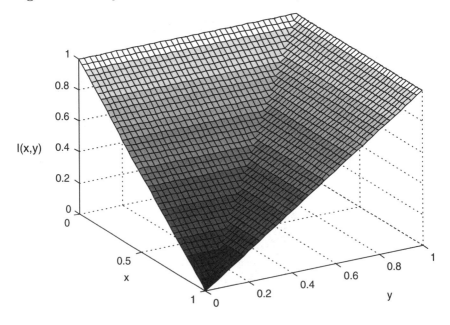

Figure 11.5   Graphical illustration of Kleene-Dienes fuzzy implication

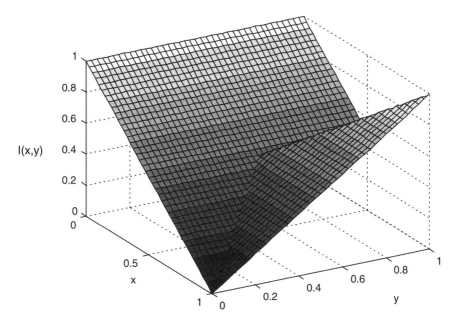

Figure 11.6 Graphical illustration of Zadeh fuzzy implication

11.3 Reasoning using fuzzy implications and generalized modus ponens

Fuzzy implications are mostly used as a way of interpretation of the if-then rules with fuzzy antecedent and/or fuzzy consequent. Such rules constitute a convenient form of expressing pieces of knowledge and a set of if-then rules forms a fuzzy rule base. Let us consider the canonical form of fuzzy if-then rule $R^{(k)}$, which includes other types of fuzzy rules and fuzzy proposition as special cases, in the (MISO) form:

$$R^{(k)} : \text{if } X_1 \text{ is } A_1^{(k)} \text{ and } ... \text{ and } X_n \text{ is } A_n^{(k)} \text{ then } Y \text{ is } B^{(k)}, \qquad (11.11)$$

where X_i and Y stand for linguistic variables of the antecedent and consequent and $A_i^{(k)}, B^{(k)}$ are fuzzy sets in universes of discourse $\mathbb{X}_i \subset \mathbb{R}$, $\mathbb{Y} \subset \mathbb{R}$ respectively.

Such a linguistic form of fuzzy if-then rules can be also expressed as a fuzzy relation:

$$R^{(k)} = \left(A_1^{(k)} \times ... \times A_n^{(k)} \Longrightarrow B^{(k)} \right) = \left(\underline{A}^{(k)} \Longrightarrow B^{(k)} \right), \qquad (11.12)$$

where $\underline{A}^{(k)} = A_1^{(k)} \times ... \times A_n^{(k)}$ is a fuzzy relation in $\mathbb{X} = \mathbb{X}_1 \times ... \times \mathbb{X}_n$ defined by

$$\left(A_1^{(k)} \times ... \times A_n^{(k)}\right)(x_1, ..., x_n) = A_1^{(k)}(x_1) *_T ... *_T A_n^{(k)}(x_n) = \underline{A}^{(k)}(\underline{x}),$$
$$(11.13)$$

where $*_T$ denotes respective t-norm T.

Fuzzy if-then rules may be interpreted in two ways: as a conjunction of the antecedent and the consequent (Mamdani combination) or as a fuzzy implication [6], [7], [8], [28], [30]. In this chapter we mainly exploit the second interpretation.

Approximate reasoning is usually executed in a fuzzy inference system, which performs a mapping from an input fuzzy set $\underline{A}'$ in $\mathbb{X}$ to a fuzzy set B' in Y via a fuzzy rule base. Two methods of approximate reasoning can be used: composition based inference (first aggregate then inference - FATI) and individual rule based inference (first inference then aggregate - FITA).

In composition based inference, a finite number of rules $k = 1, ..., K$ is aggregated via intersection or average operations, i.e.,:

$$R = \bigcap_{T,\Sigma}^{K} {}_{k=1} R^{(k)},$$
$$(11.14)$$

where $\bigcap_{T,\Sigma}$ denotes the symbol of aggregation operation using t-norm T or averages (e.g., normalized arithmetic sum) for aggregation of respective membership functions:

$$R(\underline{x}, y) = R^{(1)}(\underline{x}, y) \begin{bmatrix} *T \\ + \end{bmatrix} ... \begin{bmatrix} *T \\ + \end{bmatrix} R^{(K)}(\underline{x}, y).$$
$$(11.15)$$

Taking into account an arbitrary input fuzzy set $\underline{A}'$ in $\mathbb{X}$ and using the generalized modus ponens we obtain the output of fuzzy inference (FATI):

$$B' = \underline{A}' \circ R = \underline{A}' \circ \bigcap_{T,\Sigma}^{K} {}_{k=1} R^{(k)} = \underline{A}' \circ \bigcap_{T,\Sigma}^{K} {}_{k=1} \left(\underline{A}^{(k)} \Longrightarrow B^{(k)}\right)$$
$$(11.16)$$

or in terms of membership functions:

$$B'(y) = \sup_{\underline{x} \in \mathbb{X}} \left[\underline{A}'(\underline{x}) *_{T'} R(\underline{x}, y)\right] = \sup_{\underline{x} \in \mathbb{X}} \left[\underline{A}'(\underline{x}) *_{T'} \begin{bmatrix} \bigwedge_{k=1}^{K} T \\ \sum_{k=1}^{K} \end{bmatrix} R^{(k)}(\underline{x}, y)\right],$$
$$(11.17)$$

where $\wedge_T, *_{T'}$ denote t-norms T, T' for aggregation operation and composition respectively.

In individual rule based inference (FITA) each rule in the fuzzy rule base determines an output fuzzy set and after that an aggregation via intersection or average operation is performed. So the output fuzzy set is expressed by means of the formulas:

$$B'' = \bigcap_{\substack{k=1 \\ T,\Sigma}}^{K} \left\{ \underline{A}' \circ \left(\underline{A}^{(k)} \Longrightarrow B^{(k)} \right) \right\}$$ (11.18)

or:

$$B''(y) = \left[\frac{\overset{K}{\underset{k=1}{\bigwedge T}}}{\overset{K}{\underset{k=1}{\sum}}} \right] \sup_{\underline{x} \in X} \left[\underline{A}'(\underline{x}) *_{T'} R^{(k)}(\underline{x}, y) \right].$$ (11.19)

It can be proved that B' is more specified than B'', i.e.,:

$$B' \subseteq B'' \text{ or } \underset{y \in Y}{\forall} B'(y) \leq B''(y).$$ (11.20)

It means that the consequent B' is equal to or contained in the intersection of fuzzy inference results - B''. For simplicity of calculation the consequent B' is replaced by B'', under the assumption that the differences are not so big.

If the input fuzzy sets $A'_1, ..., A'_n$ or $(\underline{A}')$ are singletons in $x_{10}, ..., x_{n0}$ or $(\underline{x}_0)$, the consequence B' is equal to B'' $(B'(y) = B''(y))$. In that case we obtain:

$$B'(y) = B''(y) = \left[\frac{\overset{K}{\underset{k=1}{\bigvee S}}}{\overset{K}{\underset{k=1}{\sum}}} \right] [\underline{A}^{(k)}(\underline{x}_0) *_{T'} B^{(k)}(y)]$$ (11.21)

or with logical interpretation of fuzzy implication:

$$B'(y) = B''(y) = \left[\frac{\overset{K}{\underset{k=1}{\bigwedge T}}}{\overset{K}{\underset{k=1}{\sum}}} \right] I(\underline{A}^{(k)}(\underline{x}_0), B^{(k)}(y)).$$ (11.22)

11.4 Fundamentals of fuzzy systems

In approximate reasoning realized in fuzzy systems the if-then fuzzy rules play an essential role. Often they are also used to capture the human ability to make a decision or control in an uncertain and imprecise environment. In this section we will use such fuzzy rules to recall the important approximate reasoning methods which are basic in our further considerations. Assume that m numbers of n-input and one-output (MISO) fuzzy if-then rules are given. The k-th rule in which the consequent is represented by a linguistic variable Y may be written in the following forms:

$$R^{(k)} : \text{ if } X_1 \text{ is } A_1^{(k)} \text{ and } \dots \text{ and } X_n \text{ is } A_n^{(k)} \text{ then } Y \text{ is } B^{(k)} \qquad (11.23)$$

or in a pseudo-vector notation

$$R^{(k)} : \text{ if } \underline{X} \text{ is } \underline{A}^{(k)} \text{ then } Y = B^{(k)}, \qquad (11.24)$$

where:

$$\underline{X} = [X_1 X_2 \dots X_n]. \qquad (11.25)$$

$X_1, X_2, \dots, X_n$ and Y are linguistic variables which may be interpreted as inputs of a fuzzy system and the output of that system. $A_1^{(k)}, \dots, A_n^{(k)}$ are linguistic values of the linguistic variables $X_1, X_2, \dots, X_n$ and $B^{(k)}$ is a linguistic value of the linguistic variable Y.

A collection of the above written rules for $k = 1, 2, \dots K$ creates a rule base which may be activated (fired) under the singleton inputs:

$$X_1 \text{ is } x_{10} \text{ and } \dots \text{ and } X_n \text{ is } x_{n0} \qquad (11.26)$$

or

$$\underline{X} \text{ is } \underline{x}_0. \qquad (11.27)$$

It can easily be concluded from (11.22) that such a type of reasoning, where the inferred value of k-th rule output for crisp inputs (singletons), may be written for logical implication interpretation in the form:

$$B'^{(k)}(y) = R_k(\underline{x}_0) \Longrightarrow B^{(k)}(y) = I(R_k(\underline{x}_0), B^{(k)}(y)) \qquad (11.28)$$

and for conjunctive implication interpretation:

$$B'^{(k)}(y) = R_k(\underline{x}_0) *_T B^{(k)}(y) = *_T(R_k(\underline{x}_0), B^{(k)}(y)), \qquad (11.29)$$

where $\Longrightarrow$ stands for fuzzy implication, $*_T$ for t-norm T and

$$R_k(\underline{x}_0) = A_1^{(k)}(x_{10}) \text{ and } \dots \text{ and } A_n^{(k)}(x_{n0}) = \underline{A}^{(k)}(\underline{x}_0) \qquad (11.30)$$

denotes the degree of activation (the firing strength) of the k-th rule with respect to minimum ($\wedge$) or product ($\cdot$). The last represents explicit connective (AND) of the predicates X_i is $A_i^{(k)}; k = 1, 2, ..., K$ in the antecedent of an if-then rule.

A crisp value of the output we can get from the Modified Center of Gravity (MCOG) as defuzzification [5]:

$$\text{MCOG}\,[B(x)] = \frac{\int x\,[B(x) - \alpha]\,dx}{\int [B(x) - \alpha]\,dx}, \tag{11.31}$$

where α is constant.

The subtraction of value $\alpha \in [0, 1]$ eliminates the non-informative part of the membership function $B(x)$. For $\alpha = 0$ we get well known COG defuzzification. A final crisp value of the system output for sum as aggregation and MCOG defuzzification can be evaluated from formula:

$$y_0 = \frac{\int y \sum_{k=1}^{K} \left\{ \Psi\left[R_k(\underline{x}_0), B^{(k)}(y)\right] - \alpha_k \right\} dy}{\int \sum_{k=1}^{K} \left\{ \Psi\left[R_k(\underline{x}_0), B^{(k)}(y)\right] - \alpha_k \right\} dy} = \frac{\int y \sum_{k=1}^{K} [B'^{(k)}(y) - \alpha_k]dy}{\int \sum_{k=1}^{K} [B'^{(k)}(y) - \alpha_k]dy}, \tag{11.32}$$

where Ψ stands for fuzzy implication I or t-norm T for logical or conjunctive implication interpretation, respectively.

A method of determination, the values α will be described later. Now we introduce symbol $B^{*(k)} := B'^{(k)} - \alpha_k$. Membership functions of fuzzy sets $B^{*(k)}$ can be represented by the parameterized functions:

$$B^{*(k)} \frown f^{(k)} \left[\text{Area}\left(B^{*(k)}\right), y^{(k)} \right], \tag{11.33}$$

where $y^{(k)}$ is the center of gravity (COG) location of the fuzzy set $B^{*(k)}$:

$$y^{(k)} = \text{COG}\left(B^{*(k)}\right) = \frac{\int y B^{*(k)}(y)dy}{\int B^{*(k)}(y)dy}. \tag{11.34}$$

A general form for final output value can be put in the form:

$$y_0 = \frac{\sum_{k=1}^{K} y^{(k)}\,\text{Area}\left(B^{*(k)}\right)}{\sum_{k=1}^{K}\,\text{Area}\left(B^{*(k)}\right)}, \tag{11.35}$$

where $B^{*(k)}$ is a resulting conclusion for the k-th rule before aggregation.

Now we note that fuzzy systems with Larsen's product operation as conjunctive "fuzzy implication" of the if-then rules and symmetric triangle (isosceles triangle) membership functions for consequents $B^{*(k)}$ we can write in well known from literature formula [15]:

$$y_0 = \frac{\sum\limits_{k=1}^{K} \frac{w^{(k)}}{2} R_k\left(\underline{x}_0\right) y^{(k)}}{\sum\limits_{k=1}^{K} \frac{w^{(k)}}{2} R_k\left(\underline{x}_0\right)}, \tag{11.36}$$

where $w^{(k)}$ is the width of the triangle base for k-th rule.

It should be noted that the $\frac{w^{(k)}}{2}$ factor may be interpreted as a respective weight of k-th rule or its certainty factor.

Another very important fuzzy system is called Takagi-Sugeno-Kang. Assume that m numbers of n-input and one-output (MISO) fuzzy implicative rules or fuzzy conditional statements are given. The k-th rule may be written in the following forms:

$$R^{(k)} : \text{if } X_1 \text{ is } A_1^{(k)} \text{ and ... and } X_n \text{ is } A_n^{(k)} \text{ then } Y = f^{(k)}\left(X_1, ..., X_n\right) \tag{11.37}$$

or in a pseudo-vector notation

$$R^{(k)} : \text{if } \underline{X} \text{ is } \underline{A}^{(k)} \text{ then } Y = f^{(k)}\left(\underline{X}\right). \tag{11.38}$$

A crisp value of the output for Larsen's fuzzy relation (product) and aggregation (normalized sum) can be evaluated from [3]:

$$y_0 = \frac{\sum\limits_{k=1}^{K} A_k\left(\underline{x}_0\right) f^{(k)}\left(\underline{x}_0\right)}{\sum\limits_{k=1}^{K} A_k\left(\underline{x}_0\right)}. \tag{11.39}$$

Take into account that function $f^{(k)}$ is of the form:

$$f^{(k)}\left(\underline{x}_0\right) = p_0^{(k)} \tag{11.40}$$

where $p_0^{(k)}$ is crisply defined constant in the consequent of the k-th rule.

Such a model is called a zero-order Sugeno fuzzy model. The more general first-order Sugeno fuzzy model is of the form:

$$f^{(k)}\left(\underline{x}_0\right) = p_0^{(k)} + p_1^{(k)} x_{10} + ... + p_n^{(k)} x_{n0}, \tag{11.41}$$

where $p_0^{(k)}, p_1^{(k)}, ..., p_n^{(k)}$ are all constants.

In vector notation it takes the form:

$$f^{(k)}(\underline{x}_0) = \underline{p}^{(k)T}\underline{x}_0', \qquad (11.42)$$

where $\cdot^T$ stands for transposition and $\underline{x}_0'$ denotes an extended input vector:

$$\underline{x}_0' = \begin{bmatrix} 1 \\ \underline{x}_0 \end{bmatrix}. \qquad (11.43)$$

Notice that in both models the consequent is crisp.

In equation (11.35) the value describing the location of COG's consequent fuzzy set in if-then rules is constant and equals $y^{(k)}$ for k-th rule. A natural extension of the above-described situation is an assumption that the location of the consequent fuzzy set is a linear combination of all inputs for k-th rule:

$$y^{(k)}(\underline{x}_0) = \underline{p}^{(k)T}\underline{x}_0'. \qquad (11.44)$$

Hence we get the final output value in the form:

$$y_0 = \frac{\displaystyle\sum_{k=1}^{K} \operatorname{Area}\left(B^{*(k)}\right) \underline{p}^{(k)T}\underline{x}_0'}{\displaystyle\sum_{k=1}^{K} \operatorname{Area}\left(B^{*(k)}\right)}, \qquad (11.45)$$

where $B^{*(k)}$ is the conclusion for the k-th rule before aggregation.

11.5 Fuzzy system with logical interpretation of if-then rules

We assume that premises of if-then rules $A_1^{(k)}, ..., A_n^{(k)}$ have Gaussian membership functions:

$$A_j^{(k)}(x_{j0}) = \exp\left[-\frac{\left(x_{j0} - c_j^{(k)}\right)^2}{2\left(s_j^{(k)}\right)^2}\right], \qquad (11.46)$$

where $c_j^{(k)}, s_j^{(k)}; j = 1, 2, ..., n; k = 1, 2, ..., K$ are the parameters.

On the basis of (11.30) and for explicit connective AND taken as product we get:

$$\underline{A}^{(k)}(\underline{x}_0) = \prod_{j=1}^{n} A_j^{(k)}(x_{j0}). \qquad (11.47)$$

Using (11.46) we obtain:

$$R_k(\underline{x}_0) = \exp\left[-\sum_{j=1}^{n} \frac{\left(x_{j0} - c_j^{(k)}\right)^2}{2\left(s_j^{(k)}\right)^2}\right].\tag{11.48}$$

Additionally, we assume that consequents $B^{(k)}$ of k-th if-then rule have symmetric triangle (isosceles triangle) membership functions with the width of the triangle base $w^{(k)}$. For computing the system output we must calculate Area $\left(B^{*(k)}\right)$. From (11.28) and (11.32) we have:

$$B^{*(k)}(y) = I[R_k(\underline{x}_0), B^{(k)}] - \alpha_k.\tag{11.49}$$

For implication satisfying condition I9 we assume:

$$\alpha_k = 1 - R_k(\underline{x}_0).\tag{11.50}$$

For example if we use the Reichenbach implication we get:

$$\text{Area}\left(B^{*(k)}\right) = 2\int_{y^{(k)}-\frac{w^{(k)}}{2}}^{y^{(k)}} \left\{I\left[R_k(\underline{x}_0), B^{(k)}\right] - \alpha_k\right\} dy =$$

$$2\int_{y^{(k)}-\frac{w^{(k)}}{2}}^{y^{(k)}} \left[1 - R_k(\underline{x}_0) + R_k(\underline{x}_0)B^{(k)} - 1 + R_k(\underline{x}_0)\right] dy =$$

$$2R_k(\underline{x}_0)\int_{y^{(k)}-\frac{w^{(k)}}{2}}^{y^{(k)}} \left[\frac{2\left(y-y^{(k)}\right)}{w^{(k)}} - 1\right] dy = \frac{w^{(k)}}{2}R_k(\underline{x}_0) := g\left[R_k(\underline{x}_0), w^{(k)}\right].$$

$$\tag{11.51}$$

This situation is graphically illustrated in Figure 11.7.

The respective formulas for $g\left[R_k(\underline{x}_0), w^{(k)}\right]$ for other implications are presented in Table 11.2 (for simplicity, the abbreviated forms are used: $R \triangleq R_k(\underline{x}_0), w \triangleq w^{(k)}$). If we use symbols from the table, formula (11.45) has the form:

$$y_0 = \frac{\sum_{k=1}^{K} g\left[R_k(\underline{x}_0), w^{(k)}\right] \underline{p}^{(k)T}\underline{x}_0'}{\sum_{k=1}^{K} g\left[R_k(\underline{x}_0), w^{(k)}\right]}.\tag{11.52}$$

For n inputs and K if-then rules we have to establish the following unknown parameters:

- $c_j^{(k)}, s_j^{(k)}; j = 1, 2, ..., n; k = 1, 2, ..., K$ the parameters of membership functions of input sets,

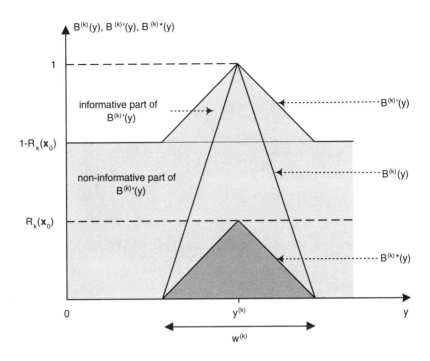

Figure 11.7 Informative and non-informative parts for the resulting conclusion before aggregation using the Reichenbach fuzzy implication

- $p_j^{(k)}$; $j = 0, 1, ..., n$; $k = 1, 2, ..., K$ the parameters determining the location of output sets,
- $w^{(k)}$; $k = 1, 2, ..., K$ the parameters of output sets.

Obviously, the number of if-then rules is unknown. Let us observe that equation (11.48) and (11.52) describes a radial neural network. The unknown parameters (except the number of rules K) are estimated by means of a gradient method performing the steepest descent on a surface in the parameter space. Therefore the so-called learning set is necessary, i.e., a set of inputs for which the output values are known $\{\underline{x}_0(i), t_0(i)\}$; $i = 1, 2, ..., N$. The measure of the error of output value may be defined for a single pair from the training set:

$$E = \frac{1}{2} (t_0 - y_0)^2 , \tag{11.53}$$

where t_0 - the desired (target) value of output.

The minimization of error E is made iteratively (for parameter α):

$$(\alpha)_{new} = (\alpha)_{old} - \eta \frac{\partial E}{\partial \alpha}\bigg|_{\alpha=(\alpha)_{old}}, \qquad (11.54)$$

where η is the learning rate.

Now we derive the partial derivatives of error E with respect to the unknown parameters:

$$\frac{\partial E}{\partial c_j^{(k)}} = (y_0 - t_0) \frac{[y^{(k)}(\underline{x}_0) - y_0] R_k(\underline{x}_0)}{\sum\limits_{i=1}^{K} g\left[R_i(\underline{x}_0), w^{(i)}\right]} \frac{\partial g\left[R_k(\underline{x}_0), w^{(k)}\right]}{\partial R_k(\underline{x}_0)} \frac{x_{j0} - c_j^{(k)}}{\left(s_j^{(k)}\right)^2}, \quad (11.55)$$

$$\frac{\partial E}{\partial s_j^{(k)}} = (y_0 - t_0) \frac{[y^{(k)}(\underline{x}_0) - y_0] R_k(\underline{x}_0)}{\sum\limits_{i=1}^{K} g\left[R_i(\underline{x}_0), w^{(i)}\right]} \frac{\partial g\left[R_k(\underline{x}_0), w^{(k)}\right]}{\partial R_k(\underline{x}_0)} \frac{(x_{j0} - c_j^{(k)})^2}{\left(s_j^{(k)}\right)^3},$$

$$(11.56)$$

$$\underset{j \neq 0}{\forall} \quad \frac{\partial E}{\partial p_j^{(k)}} = (y_0 - t_0) \frac{g\left[R_k(\underline{x}_0), w^{(k)}\right]}{\sum\limits_{i=1}^{K} g\left[R_i(\underline{x}_0), w^{(i)}\right]} x_{j0}, \qquad (11.57)$$

$$\frac{\partial E}{\partial p_0^{(k)}} = (y_0 - t_0) \frac{g\left[R_k(\underline{x}_0), w^{(k)}\right]}{\sum\limits_{i=1}^{K} g\left[R_i(\underline{x}_0), w^{(i)}\right]}, \qquad (11.58)$$

$$\frac{\partial E}{\partial w^{(k)}} = (y_0 - t_0) \frac{y^{(k)}(\underline{x}_0) - y_0}{\sum\limits_{i=1}^{K} g\left[R_i(\underline{x}_0), w^{(i)}\right]} \frac{\partial g\left[R_k(\underline{x}_0), w^{(k)}\right]}{\partial w^{(k)}}. \qquad (11.59)$$

The respective derivatives are shown in Table 11.2.

The unknown parameters may be modified on the basis of (11.54) after the input of one data collection into the system or after the input of all data collections (cumulative method). Additionally, the following heuristic rules for changes of η parameter have been applied [15]. If in four sequential iterations the mean square error has diminished for the whole learning set, then the learning parameter is increased (multiplied by n_I). If in four sequential iterations the error has been increased and decreased commutatively then the learning parameter is decreased (multiplied by n_D).

Implication	$g\left(R,w\right)$ $\frac{\partial g(R,w)}{\partial R}$ $\frac{\partial g(R,w)}{\partial w}$
Lukasiewicz	$\frac{w}{2}\left(2R - R^2\right)$ $\frac{w}{2}\left(2 - 2R\right)$ $\frac{1}{2}\left(2R - R^2\right)$
Fodor	$\left\{\begin{array}{ll} \frac{w}{2}\left(1 - 2R + 2R^2\right), & \text{if } R > \frac{1}{2} \\ \frac{w}{2}\left(2R - 2R^2\right), & \text{if } R \le \frac{1}{2} \\ \frac{w}{2}\left(4R - 2\right), & \text{if } R > \frac{1}{2} \\ \frac{w}{2}\left(2 - 4R\right), & \text{if } R \le \frac{1}{2} \\ \frac{1}{2}\left(1 - 2R + 2R^2\right), & \text{if } R > \frac{1}{2} \\ \frac{1}{2}\left(2R - 2R^2\right), & \text{if } R \le \frac{1}{2} \end{array}\right.$
Reichenbach	$\frac{w}{2}R$ $\frac{w}{2}$ $\frac{1}{2}R$
Kleene-Dienes	$\frac{w}{2}R^2$ $\frac{w}{2}2R$ $\frac{1}{2}R^2$
Zadeh	$\left\{\begin{array}{ll} \frac{w}{2}\left(2R - 1\right), & \text{if } R \ge \frac{1}{2} \\ 0, & \text{if } R < \frac{1}{2} \\ \frac{w}{2}\left(2\right), & \text{if } R \ge \frac{1}{2} \\ 0, & \text{if } R < \frac{1}{2} \\ \frac{1}{2}\left(2R - 1\right), & \text{if } R \ge \frac{1}{2} \\ 0, & \text{if } R < \frac{1}{2} \end{array}\right.$

Table 11.2   Some needed derivatives for selected implications.

Another solution accelerating the convergence of the method is the estimation of parameters $\underline{p}^{(k)}; k = 1, ..., K$ by means of least squares method. The output value y_0 of the system in equation (11.52) may be considered to be a linear combination of unknown parameters $\underline{p}^{(k)}$. If we introduce the following notation:

$$S^{(k)}\left(\underline{x}_0\right) = \frac{g\left[R_k(\underline{x}_0), w^{(k)}\right]}{\sum\limits_{i=1}^{K} g\left[R_i(\underline{x}_0), w^{(i)}\right]}, \tag{11.60}$$

$$\underline{D}\left(\underline{x}_0\right) = \left[S^{(1)} \underline{x}_0'^T \vdots S^{(2)} \underline{x}_0'^T \vdots .... \vdots S^{(K)} \underline{x}_0'^T\right]^T, \tag{11.61}$$

$$\underline{P} = \left[\underline{p}^{(1)T} \vdots \underline{p}^{(2)T} \vdots .... \vdots \underline{p}^{(K)T}\right]^T \tag{11.62}$$

equation (11.52) may be written in the form:

$$y_0 = \underline{D}\,(\underline{x}_0)^T\,\underline{P}.$$ (11.63)

Hence parameters $\underline{P}$ may be estimated by means of the least squares method. To eliminate the matrix inverse we use the recurrent method. For k-th step, e.g., (k-th element from the learning set) we get [18]:

$$\underline{\hat{P}}\,(k) = \underline{\hat{P}}\,(k-1) + \underline{G}(k-1)\underline{D}[\underline{x}_0\,(k)]\left\{y_0(k) - \underline{D}[\underline{x}_0\,(k)]^T\underline{\hat{P}}\,(k-1)\right\},$$ (11.64)

$$\underline{G}\,(k) = \underline{G}\,(k-1) - \underline{G}(k-1)\underline{D}[\underline{x}_0\,(k)]\times$$
$$\times\left\{\underline{D}[\underline{x}_0\,(k)]^T\underline{G}(k-1)\underline{D}[\underline{x}_0\,(k)] + 1\right\}^{-1}\underline{D}[\underline{x}_0\,(k)]^T\underline{G}(k-1).$$ (11.65)

To initialize the computations we take:

$$\begin{cases}\underline{\hat{P}}\,(0) = \underline{0}, \\ \underline{G}\,(0) = \beta\mathbb{I},\end{cases}$$ (11.66)

where $\mathbb{I}$ is an identity matrix, β is a large positive constant (e.g., 10^6).

Finally in each iteration parameters $p^{(k)}$ are estimated on the basis of equations (11.64) and (11.65), whereas the other parameters are by means of a gradient method (11.54), (11.55), (11.56), (11.59).

Another problem is the estimation of the number m of if-then rules and initial values of membership functions for the premise part. This task is solved by means of preliminary clustering of the input part of training data using fuzzy c-means method [1], [23]. This method assigns each input vector $\underline{x}_0\,(k)\,;k = 1, 2, ..., N$ to clusters represented by prototypes $\underline{v}_i; i = 1, ..., K$ measured by grade of membership $u_{ik} \in [0, 1]$. The $K \times n$ dimensional partition matrix fulfills the following assumptions:

$$\begin{cases}\displaystyle\underset{k}{\forall}\quad\sum_{i=1}^{K} u_{ik} = 1, \\ \displaystyle\underset{i}{\forall}\quad\sum_{k=1}^{N} u_{ik} \in (0, N).\end{cases}$$ (11.67)

The c-means method minimizes the scalar index for parameter $r > 1$:

$$J_r = \sum_{k=1}^{N}\sum_{i=1}^{K} (u_{ik})^r\,\|\underline{x}_0\,(k) - \underline{v}_i\|^2\,.$$ (11.68)

Defining $D_{ik}^2 = \|\underline{x}_0\,(k) - \underline{v}_i\|^2$, where $\|\cdot\|$ is a vector norm (the most frequent Euclidean norm), we get an iterative method of commutative modification of partition matrix and prototypes [1]:

$$\forall_i \quad \underline{v}_i = \frac{\sum\limits_{k=1}^{N} (u_{ik})^r \; \underline{x}_0(k)}{\sum\limits_{k=1}^{N} (u_{ik})^r}, \tag{11.69}$$

$$\forall_{i,k} \quad u_{ik} = \left[\sum_{j=1}^{K} \left(\frac{D_{ik}}{D_{jk}} \right)^{\frac{2}{r-1}} \right]^{-1}. \tag{11.70}$$

According to the above written equations the obtained calculations are initialized using a random partition matrix $\underline{U}$ which fulfills conditions (11.67). Such a method leads to the local minimum for index (11.68). Therefore the most frequently used solution is multiple repeated calculations in accordance with equations (11.69), (11.70) for various random realizations of partition matrix initializations. The computations are stopped when the predefined number of iterations (in our case 500) are executed or when in two successive iterations the change of index value J_r is less than the set value (in our case 0.001).

As a result of preliminary clustering the following assumption for ANBLIR initialization can be made: $\underline{c}^{(j)} = \underline{v}_j; \; j = 1, 2, ..., K$ and:

$$s^{(j)} = \frac{\sum\limits_{k=1}^{N} (u_{ik})^r \, [\, \underline{x}_0(k) - \underline{v}_i]^2}{\sum\limits_{k=1}^{N} (u_{ik})^r}. \tag{11.71}$$

For calculations presented in the next section, the Reichenbach fuzzy implication and the following parameter values, $\eta = 0.01, n_I = 1.1, n_D = 0.9, \beta = 10^6, r = 2$, have been applied.

11.6 Application of ANBLIR to pattern recognition

In this section, we present an application of the fuzzy system described prior to a pattern recognition problem. If patterns from a learning set belong to classes ω_1 and ω_2 then we can build a fuzzy system whose output takes positive values for patterns from class ω_1 and negative or zero values for class ω_2. If we denote a fuzzy system as $y_0 = FNN(\underline{x}_0)$, we get:

$$y_0(k) = FNN_{12}\,[\underline{x}_0(k)] \begin{cases} > 0, & \text{if } \underline{x}_0(k) \in \omega_1, \\ \le 0, & \text{if } \underline{x}_0(k) \in \omega_2. \end{cases} \tag{11.72}$$

During the learning process of a classifier we take $t_0(k) = 1$ for pattern $\underline{x}_0(k)$ from class ω_1 and $t_0(k) = -1$ for pattern from class ω_2. For a bigger number of class $(\omega_1, \omega_2, ..., \omega_p, p > 2)$ an extension class-rest or class-class can be used [24], [25]. The latter was used in our method due to existence of common feature regions for which the classificator class-rest does not give the answer to which class the classified pattern belongs. The disadvantage of such a solution is the necessity of constructing a greater number of classifiers. Let us denote the classifier making decision whether a pattern belongs to the i-th or j-th class as:

$$y_0(k) = FNN_{ij}\left[\underline{x}_0(k)\right] \begin{cases} > 0, & \text{if } \underline{x}_0(k) \in \omega_i, \\ \leq 0, & \text{if } \underline{x}_0(k) \in \omega_j. \end{cases} \qquad (11.73)$$

Obviously we do not construct the classifier FNN_{ii}, and the information about membership to i-th and j-th classes can be obtained on the basis of FNN_{ij} or FNN_{ji} classifiers. Hence we construct $p(p-1)/2$ classifiers FNN_{ij} for $1 \leq i < p;\ j > i$. The classification condition for i-th class has the form:

$$\mathop{\forall}_{j \neq i} \quad FNN_{ij}\left[\underline{x}_0(k)\right] > 0 \Longrightarrow \underline{x}_0(k) \in \omega_i. \qquad (11.74)$$

The learning process goes as follows: for each pair of indices ij $(1 \leq i < p;\ j > i)$ we assume $t_0(k) = 1$ for pattern $\underline{x}_0(k)$ belonging to class ω_i and $t_0(k) = -1$ for pattern $\underline{x}_0(k)$ belonging to class ω_j (the patterns belonging to other classes are removed from the training set) and we conduct the learning process of the classifier. The final pattern classification is made on the basis of condition (11.74).

11.7   Numerical examples

All databases presented in this section were obtained from the UCI machine learning repository (http://www.ics.uci.edu/~mlearn/MLSummary.html). These standard databases are used typically for evaluating the performances of classifiers.

11.7.1   Application to forensic glass classification

The data come from forensic testing of glass collected by B. German on 214 fragments of glass. Each case has a measured refractive index and composition weight percent of oxides of Na, Al, Mg, Si, K, Ca, Fe and Ba. The fragments were classified into six types: window float (WinF - 70 cases), window non-float (WinNF - 76 cases), vehicle window (Veh - 17 cases), containers (Con - 13 cases), tableware (Tabl - 9 cases) and vehicle headlamps (Head - 29 cases). The above mentioned database has been tested exhaustively using standard methods of pattern recognition in [24]. The obtained error rates are as follows: linear classifier - 38%, logistic discrimination - 26.2 %, neural network (back-propagation with eight hidden units) - 24.8%, nearest neighbor method - 23.4%, learning vector quantization - 29.9% and tree-structured classifier - 32.2%. The method of classifier construction proposed in this chapter has been also applied to the above-described database. 500 iterations of learning have been executed for each classifier. The number of if-then rules varies from 2 to 5. Error rate equals: 18.22% (two rules), 12.62% (three rules), 10.75% (four rules) and 7.48% (five rules) with confusion matrix presented in Table 11.3.

K		WinF	WinNF	Veh	Con	Tabl	Head
	WinF	55	13	2	0	0	0
	WinNF	14	61	0	1	0	0
	Veh	4	2	11	0	0	0
2	Con	0	1	0	12	0	0
	Tabl	0	1	0	0	8	0
	Head	1	0	0	0	0	28
	WinF	58	10	2	0	0	0
	WinNF	6	69	1	0	0	0
	Veh	3	4	10	0	0	0
3	Con	0	0	0	13	0	0
	Tabl	0	0	0	0	9	0
	Head	1	0	0	0	0	28
	WinF	59	10	1	0	0	0
	WinNF	6	70	0	0	0	0
	Veh	2	4	11	0	0	0
4	Con	0	0	0	13	0	0
	Tabl	0	0	0	0	9	0
	Head	0	0	0	0	0	29
	WinF	66	3	1	0	0	0
	WinNF	8	68	0	0	0	0
	Veh	3	1	13	0	0	0
5	Con	0	0	0	13	0	0
	Tabl	0	0	0	0	9	0
	Head	0	0	0	0	0	29

Table 11.3 Simulation results for classification of the forensic glass

11.7.2 Application to the famous iris problem

The iris database is perhaps the best known database to be found in the pattern recognition literature. The data set contains 3 classes of 50 instances each, where each class refers to a type of iris plant. The vector of features consists of: sepal length in cm, sepal width in cm, petal length in cm, and petal width in cm. We consider three classes of patterns: Iris Setosa, Iris Versicolour and Iris Virginica. A confusion matrix for 500 learning iterations and two if-then rules has been shown in Table 11.4. Error rate is equal to 1.33%. The increase in the rule number did not cause the diminishing of the error rate.

	Iris Setosa	Iris Versicolour	Iris Virginica
Iris Setosa	50	0	0
Iris Versicolour	0	50	0
Iris Virginica	0	2	48

Table 11.4 Simulation results for classification of the iris database

11.7.3 Application to wine recognition data

These databases are the results of a chemical analysis of wines grown in the same region in Italy but derived from three different cultivars. The analysis determined the quantities of 13 constituents found in each of the three types of wines. The data were collected by M. Forina. The data were used with many others for comparing various classifiers. The classes are separable, though only radial discriminant analysis has achieved 100% correct classification (RDA: 100%, QDA: 99.4%, LDA: 98.9%, 1NN: 96.1%). 500 learning iterations have been executed for the classifier described in Section 6. A confusion matrix for two and three if-then rules is presented in Table 11.5. Correct classifications equal to 99.43% and 100% have been obtained for two and three rules, respectively.

11.7.4 Application to MONKS problems

The MONK's problem was the basis of the first international comparison of learning algorithms. The result of this comparison is summarized in [26]. One significant characteristic of this comparison is that it was performed by a collection of researchers, each of whom was an advocate of the technique they tested (often they were the authors of various methods).

K		Type I	Type II	Type III
	Type I	59	0	0
2	Type II	1	70	0
	Type III	0	0	48
	Type I	59	0	0
3	Type II	0	71	0
	Type III	0	0	48

Table 11.5 Simulation results for classification of the wine database

In this sense, the results are less biased than in comparison with results obtained by a single person advocating a specific learning method, and more accurately reflect the generalization behavior of the learning techniques as applied by knowledgeable users. There are three MONK's problems. The domains for all MONK's problems are the same. One of the MONK's problems has noise added. For each problem, the domain has been partitioned into a training and testing set. The vector of features for each pattern consists of 7 features which take the following values: first feature - 1,2,3, second one - 1,2,3, third - 1,2, fourth - 1,2,3, fifth - 1,2,3,4, sixth - 1,2. The patterns are classified into two classes. Taken from [26], the results of testing for various methods are collected in Table 11.6. It should be pointed out that methods, which gave the highest percentage of correct classification, have been selected. The testing results obtained by means of the method described in this chapter are presented in Table 11.6 as well. The number of if-then rules varied from 2 to 4 and the number of executed iterations varied from 25 to 6000 depending on the considered problem.

Method	MONKS-1	MONKS-2	MONKS-3
ANBLIR, K=2	97.9%	88.8%	92.9%
ANBLIR, K=3	100%	100%	97.6%
ANBLIR, K=4	100%	100%	95.5%
AQ-15 Genetic	100%	86.8%	100%
Assistant Professional	100%	81.3%	100%
NN with weight decay	100%	100%	97.2%
Cascade Correlation	100%	100%	97.2%
CN2	100%	69.0%	89.1%
ECOBWEB	71.8%	67.4%	68.2%
ID5R-hat	90.3%	65.7%	–
mFOIL	100%	69.2%	100%
PRISM	86.3%	72.7%	90.3%

Table 11.6 Simulation results for classification of the MONKS problems

11.8   Conclusions

The inference algorithms based on conjunctive operators in some cases seem to be faster, simpler and more exact than the fuzzy implication based inference system. Moreover, the interpretation of the fuzzy if-then rules based on fuzzy implications is sounder from the logical point of view.

In this chapter a new artificial neural network based on logical interpretation of if-then rules (ANBLIR) has been described. Such a system can be used for an automatic if-then rule generation. The innovations of that system in comparison with the well known from literature are the logical interpretation of fuzzy if-then rules and the moving fuzzy set in consequent. A combination of gradient and least squares methods of parameter optimization for ANBLIR has been used. For initialization of calculations preliminary fuzzy c-means clustering has been used. A promising application of the presented system to standard pattern recognition problems has been shown.

11.9 References

[1] Bezdek, J.C. (1981): *Pattern recognition with fuzzy objective function algorythms.* - New York: Plenum.

[2] Cao, Z. and Kandel, A. (1989): *Applicability of some fuzzy implication operators.* - Fuzzy Sets and Systems, Vol. 31, pp. 151-186.

[3] Cho, K.B. and Wang, B.H. (1996): *Radial basis function based adaptive fuzzy systems and their applications to system identification and prediction.* - Fuzzy Set and Systems, Vol. 83, pp.325-339.

[4] Cordon, O., Herrera, F., Peregrin, A. (1997): *Applicability of the fuzzy operators in the design of fuzzy logic controllers.* - Fuzzy Sets and Systems, Vol. 86, pp. 15-41.

[5] Czogała, E. and Lęski, J. (1998): *An equivalence of approximate reasoning under defuzzification.* - BUSEFAL, Vol. 74, pp. 83-92.

[6] Czogała, E. and Kowalczyk, R. (1996): *Investigation of selected fuzzy operations and implications in engineering.* - Fifth IEEE Int. Conf. on Fuzzy Systems, pp. 879-885.

[7] Dubois, D. and Prade, H. (1991): *Fuzzy sets in approximate reasoning*, Part 1: *Inference with possibility distributions.* - Fuzzy Sets and Systems, Vol. 40, pp. 143-202.

[8] Dubois, D. and Prade, H. (1996): *What are fuzzy rules and how to use them.* - Fuzzy Sets and Systems, Vol. 84, pp. 169-185.

[9] Fodor, J.C. (1991): *On fuzzy implication operators.* - Fuzzy Sets and Systems, Vol. 42, pp. 293-300.

[10] Fodor, J.C. (1995): *Contrapositive symmetry of fuzzy implications.* - Fuzzy Sets and Systems, Vol. 69, pp. 141-156.

[11] Fodor, J.C. and Roubens, M. (1994): *Fuzzy Preference Modelling and Multicriteria Decision Support.* - Dordrecht: Kluwer.

[12] Horikawa, S., Furuhashi, T., Uchikawa, Y. (1992): *On fuzzy modeling using fuzzy neural networks with the back-propagation algorithm.* - IEEE Trans. Neur. Net., Vol. 4, pp. 801-806.

[13] Jang, J.R. and Sun C. (1993): *Functional equivalence between radial basis function and fuzzy inference systems.* - IEEE Trans. Neur. Net., Vol. 4, pp. 156-159.

[14] Jang, J.R. and Sun, C. (1995): *Neuro-fuzzy modeling and control.* - Proc. IEEE, Vol.83, pp. 378-406.

[15] Jang, J.R., Sun, C., Mizutani, E. (1997): *Neuro-fuzzy and soft computing: a computational approach to learning and machine inteligence.* - Upper Saddle River: Prentice-Hall.

[16] Kerre, E. (1992): *A comparative study of the behavior of some popular fuzzy implication operators on the generalized modus ponens*, In: Fuzzy Logic for the Management of Uncertainty (L.Zadeh and J.Kacprzyk, Eds.). - New York: Wiley.

[17] Kosko, B. (1987): *Fuzzy associative memories*, In: Fuzzy Expert Systems (A.Kandel, Ed.) - Boca Raton: CRC Press.

[18] de Larminat, P. and Thomas, Y. (1977): *Automatique des systemes lineaires, 2. Identification.* - Paris: Flammarion Sciences.

[19] Lęski, J. and Czogała, E. (1997): *A new artifical neural network based fuzzy inference system with moving consequents in if-then rules.* - BUSEFAL, Vol. 71, pp. 72-81.

[20] Maeda, H. (1996): *An investigation on the spread of fuzziness in multifold multi-stage approximate reasoning by pictorial representation - under sup-min composition and triangular type membership function.* - Fuzzy Sets and Systems, Vol.80, pp.133-148.

[21] Mitra, S. and Pal, S.K. (1995): *Fuzzy multi-layer perceptron, inferencing and rule generation.* - IEEE Trans. Neur. Net., Vol. 6, pp. 51-63.

[22] Mizumoto, M. and Zimmermann, H.J. (1982): *Comparison of fuzzy reasoning methods.* - Fuzzy Sets and Systems, Vol.8, pp. 253-283.

[23] Pal, N.R. and Bezdek, J.C. (1995): *On cluster validity for the fuzzy c-means model.* - IEEE Trans. Fuzzy Systems, Vol. 3, pp. 370-379.

[24] Ripley, B.R. (1996): *Pattern Recognition and neural network.* - Cambridge: Cambridge University Press.

[25] Tou, J.T. and Gonzalez, R.C. (1974): *Pattern recognition principles.* - London: Addison-Wesley.

[26] Thrun, S.B. et al. (1991): *The MONK's problems. A performance comparision of different learning algorithms.* - Scientific CMU-CS-91-197, Carnegie Mellon University.

[27] Trillas, E. and Valverde, L. (1985): *On implication and indistinguishability in the setting of fuzzy logic,* In: Management Decision Support Systems using Fuzzy Sets and Possibility Theory (J.Kacprzyk and R.Yager, Eds.). - Köln: Verlag TÜV Rheinland.

[28] Weber, S. (1983): *A general concept of fuzzy connectives, negations and implications based on t-norms and t-conorms.* - Fuzzy Sets and Systems, Vol.11, pp. 115-134.

[29] Wang, L. and Mendel, J.M. (1992): *Generating fuzzy rules by learning from examples.* - IEEE Trans. Systems Man Cyber., Vol. 22, pp. 1414-1427.

[30] Yager, R.R. (1996): *On the interpretation of fuzzy if-then rules.* - Applied Intelligence, Vol. 6, pp. 141-151.

Index